Cubans in Angola

Africa and the Diaspora
History, Politics, Culture

Series Editors

Cubans in Angola

South-South Cooperation and Transfer of Knowledge, 1976–1991

Christine Hatzky

The University of Wisconsin Press

The translation of this work was funded by Geisteswissenschaften International, Translation Funding for Humanities and Social Sciences from Germany—a joint initiative of the Fritz Thyssen Foundation, the German Federal Foreign Office, the collecting society VG WORT, and the Börsenverein des Deutschen Buchhandels (German Publishers and Booksellers Association).

Publication of this volume has been made possible, in part, through support from the Anonymous Fund of the College of Letters and Science at the University of Wisconsin–Madison.

The University of Wisconsin Press
1930 Monroe Street, 3rd Floor
Madison, Wisconsin 53711-2059
uwpress.wisc.edu

3 Henrietta Street, Covent Garden
London WC2E 8LU, United Kingdom
eurospanbookstore.com

Originally published as *Kubaner in Angola: Süd-Süd-Kooperation und Bildungstransfer, 1976–1991*,

Printed in the United States of America

Library of Congress Cataloging-in-Publication Data

Hatzky, Christine, author.
[Kubaner in Angola. English]
Cubans in Angola: South-South cooperation and transfer of knowledge, 1976–1991 / Christine Hatzky.
pages cm. — (Africa and the diaspora: history, politics, culture)
Originally published as Kubaner in Angola: Sud-Sud-Kooperation und Bildungstransfer, 1976–1991, ©2012 by Oldenbourg Wissenschaftsverlag GmbH, Munich.
Includes bibliographical references and index.
ISBN 978-0-299-30104-0 (pbk.: alk. paper)
ISBN 978-0-299-30103-3 (e-book)
1. Angola—Relations—Cuba. 2. Cuba—Relations—Angola.
3. Education—Angola—International cooperation. 4. Literacy—Angola—International cooperation.
5. Teachers, Foreign—Angola. I. Title. II. Series: Africa and the diaspora.
DT1355.C9H3813 2015
303.48′26730729109048—dc23
2014013807

Photo on title page: Monument on Luanda's famous promenade, the "Marginal."
The monument was built by the Cubans themselves to commemorate their work in Angola.
(photo by Christine Hatzky)

Contents

Part III
Memories of Angola

Illustrations

Acknowledgments

This book is the English translation of my revised postdoctoral thesis submitted in November 2009 to the Faculty of Humanities at the University of Duisburg-Essen, Germany. It is the fruit of over five years (2004–2009) of work and research on three continents, which would not have been possible without the huge support I received from so many people wherever I went. Already as an undergraduate, I was fascinated by the relationship between Latin America and Africa and in the history of Latin America with all its global implications. Encouraged by Michael Zeuske, who was my professor at the University of Cologne in the 1990s, I became involved in the history of the Caribbean and Cuba. More than any other Latin American region, the Caribbean is a place where many different worlds and (world) histories coincide. It is also a region with particularly close links to Africa due to the transatlantic slave trade. The post-emancipation societies of the nineteenth and twentieth centuries, especially in Cuba, illustrate that the slave trade was not merely a unidirectional movement from Africa to America resulting from the forced migration of Africans. It was the start of a process of exchange and reciprocity.

In order to study these interrelationships, I had to look toward Africa, without neglecting my roots in the history of Latin America, and I regarded the dividing Atlantic as a bridge between the two continents. I received the final encouragement to embark on this transatlantic research project from Christoph Marx, professor of African history at the University of Duisburg-Essen, with whom I worked as an assistant professor from autumn 2002. His many suggestions, and his positive criticism and warm support made an invaluable contribution to the development of my postdoctoral project. I am particularly indebted to him. I could not have undertaken my research in Cuba, Angola, the United States, and Portugal without the two-and-a-half-year grant from the German Research Foundation. I therefore wish to take this opportunity to thank Guido Lammers, Angelika Stübig, and the foundation's panel of experts. I also wish to extend my gratitude to the Geschwister Boehringer Ingelheim Stiftung für Geisteswissenschaften, which helped fund the printing of the German edition by Oldenbourg Verlag Munich. I am honored to have been awarded the Geisteswissenschaften International Prize, which funded the translation of the book into English. My particular thanks go here to Cordula Hubert and Julia Schreiner of Oldenbourg Verlag for their support.

I also wish to express my appreciation to all the colleagues who helped me and my project throughout the years and over great distances: Angelina Rojas Blaquier (Havana), Nancy Jiménez Rodríguez (Havana), Rosa Cruz da Silva (Luanda), María da Conceição Neto (Luanda/London), Olga Portuondo (Santiago de Cuba), Orlando García Martínez (Cienfuegos, Cuba), Beatrix Heintze (Frankfurt/M.), Rainer Schultz (Boston/Cambridge/Cologne), and Michael Zeuske. David Birmingham (Canterbury), Franz-Wilhelm Heimer (Lisbon), Peter Meyns (Cologne/Duisburg), and Rita Schäfer (Essen) all read early versions and individual chapters of my work, and their constructive criticism kept me on the straight and narrow. Wilfried Loth (Essen) and Jost Dülffer (Cologne) were the examiners of my postdoctoral thesis and in cooperation with other editors included the work in their series of publications, Studien zur internationalen Geschichte (Studies in International History) with Oldenbourg Verlag. I sincerely thank them too. Gwen Walker of the University of Wisconsin Press prepared and oversaw the publication of the book with great care and professionalism. Daniel Giere showed great commitment and skill in formatting the manuscript. Mair Edmunds-Harrington produced a wonderful translation.

During the months I spent writing this book, I was supported by Sabine Vosskamp. Her critical reflections helped make the work go much more quickly and smoothly. I thank her warmly. I also wish to thank my husband, Jens Voelschow, for his untiring patience, his understanding, and his emotional and practical support, which gave me the calm I needed to complete this work.

I wish to thank the many people who supported my often very challenging day-to-day research, among them the librarians, archivists, and employees of the Ministries of Education in Cuba and Angola, along with the employees and colleagues of the Instituto de Historia de Cuba in Havana. I thank all those who, particularly under the difficult research conditions in Cuba, were prepared to answer my questions and helped to open doors, overcome hurdles, and provide practical support in my search for documents and interviewees. My very special thanks, however, go to all my interviewees from Cuba and Angola, including those living in exile, who were willing to share their stories with me. These Cubans and Angolans encountered each other as "internationalists," civil aid workers, pupils, students, teachers, and colleagues in Angola and on the Cuban Isla de la Juventud. Their memories and experiences are central to this story. Leading politicians in both countries may have been the ones who planned, established, and developed Cuban-Angolan cooperation, but without the personal commitment of Cuban *cooperantes* and their interaction with Angolan colleagues, and without the Angolan pupils and students who learned from them, cooperation could never have taken place. I dedicate this book to them.

Abbreviations

ATD	Associação Tchiweka de Documentação (Tchiweka Documentation Association)
BAB	Basler Afrika Bibliographien (Basler Africa Bibliographies, Switzerland)
CECE	Comité Estatal de Colaboración Económica (State Committee for Economic Cooperation, Cuba)
CIP	Centro de Investigação Pedagógica (Center of Pedagogical Research, Angola)
CIPIE	Centro de Investigação Pedagógica e Inspecção Escolar (Center of Pedagogical Research and School Inspection, Angola)
DNFQE	Direcção Nacional de Formação de Quadros de Ensino (National Directorate for Teacher Training, Angola)
DECD	Departamento de Educação, Cultura e Desportos do Comité Central do MPLA-Partido do Trabalho (Department for Education, Culture and Sport of the Central Committee of the MPLA-PT, Angola)
DISA	Direcção de Informação e Segurança de Angola (Directorate of Information and Security of Angola)
DNEFA	Direcção Nacional de Emigração e Fronteiras de Angola (National Directorate of Emigration and Borders of Angola)
DNEG	Direcção Nacional de Ensino Geral (National Directorate for General Education, Angola)
DPE	Delegações Provinciais de Educação (Provincial Delegates of Education, Angola)
DPI	Destacamento Pedagógico Internacionalista "Che Guevara" (Internationalist Teacher Brigade Che Guevara, Cuba)

EEC	European Economic Community
ESBEC	Escuela Secundaria Básica en el Campo (rural basic secondary boarding school, Cuba)
FAPLA	Forças Armadas Populares para a Libertação de Angola (The People's Armed Forces for the Liberation of Angola)
FAR	Fuerzas Armadas Revolucionarias (Revolutionary Armed Forces, Cuba)
FEEM	Federación de Estudiantes de Enseñanza Media (Federation of Secondary School Students, Cuba)
FEU	Federación Estudiantíl Universitaria (Federation of University Students, Cuba)
FLEC	Front de Libération de l'Enclave de Cabinda (Front for the Liberation of the Enclave of Cabinda, Angola)
FLN	Front de Libération Nationale (National Liberation Front, Algeria)
FMC	Federación de Mujeres Cubanas (Federation of Cuban Women)
FNLA	Frente Nacional para a Libertação de Angola (National Liberation Front of Angola)
FRELIMO	Frente da Libertação de Moçambique (The Mozambique Liberation Front)
GDR	German Democratic Republic
GICI/GII	Gabinete de Intercambio e Cooperação Internacional/Gabinete de Intercambio Internacional (Department of International Cooperation, Angola)
GRAE	Governo Revolucionário de Angola no Exilio (Revolutionary Government of Angola in Exile)
IHC	Instituto de Historia de Cuba (Cuban Historical Institute)
INABE	Instituto Nacional de Bolsas para Estudantes (National Scholarship Institute, Angola)
INDER	Instituto Nacional de Deportes, Educación Física y Recreación (National Institute of Sport, Physical Education and Recreation)
INIDE	Instituto Nacional de Investigação e Desenvolvimento da Educação (National Institute for Research and Development of Education, Angola)
ISCED	Instituto Superior de Ciências da Educação (Institute for Education Sciences, Angola)
ISP	Instituto Superior Pedagógico (teacher-training college, Cuba)
JMPLA	Juventude do MPLA (Youth of MPLA)
MED	Ministério da Educação (Ministry of Education, Angola)

MES	Ministerio de Educación Superior (Ministry of Higher Education, Cuba)
MFA	Movimento das Forças Armadas (Movement of the Armed Forces, Portugal)
MINED	Ministerio de Educación (Ministry of Education, Cuba)
MININT	Ministerio del Interior (Ministry of the Interior, Cuba)
MINSAP	Ministerio de Salud Pública (Ministry of Public Health, Cuba)
MINVEC	Ministerio para la Inversión Extranjera y la Colaboración Económica (Ministry of Foreign Investment and Economic Cooperation, Cuba)
MPLA	Movimento Popular de Libertação de Angola (People's Movement for the Liberation of Angola)
OAS	Organization of American States
OAU	Organization of African Unity
OMA	Organização das Mulheres de Angola (Women's Organization of Angola)
OPA	Organização dos Pioneiros de Angola (Angolan Pioneer Organization)
OSPAAL	Organización para la Solidaridad de los Pueblos de Asia, Africa e América Latina (Organization of Solidarity with the People of Asia, Africa and Latin America, Cuba)
PAIGC	Partido Africano da Independência da Guiné e Cabo Verde (African Party of the Independence of Guinea and Cape Verde)
PCA	Partido Comunista Angolano (Angolan Communist Party)
PCC	Partido Comunista de Cuba (Communist Party of Cuba)
PIC	Partido Independiente de Color (Independent Party of Color, Cuba)
PIDE	Polícia Internacional e de Defesa do Estado (International Police for the Defense of the State, Portugal)
PSP	Partido Socialista Popular (Popular Socialist Party, Cuba)
PUNIV	(Ensino) Pré-Universitário (pre-university education)
RPA	República Popular de Angola (People's Republic of Angola)
SADF	South African Defence Force
SWAPO	South West African People's Organisation
UAN	Universidade Agostinho Neto (Agostinho Neto University)
UJC	Unión de Jóvenes Comunistas (Young Communist League, Cuba)
UNDP	United Nations Development Program
UNEA	União Nacional dos Estudantes Angolanos em Cuba (National Union of Angolan Students in Cuba)

UNEAC	Unión de Escritores y Artistas de Cuba (National Union of Writers and Artists of Cuba)
UNITA	União Nacional para a Independência Total de Angola (National Union for the Total Independence of Angola)
UNTA	União Nacional dos Trabalhadores Angolanos (National Union of Angolan Workers)
UPA	União das Populações de Angola (Union of Angolan Peoples)
UPNA	União das Populações do Norte de Angola (Union of Peoples of Northern Angola)

Cubans in Angola

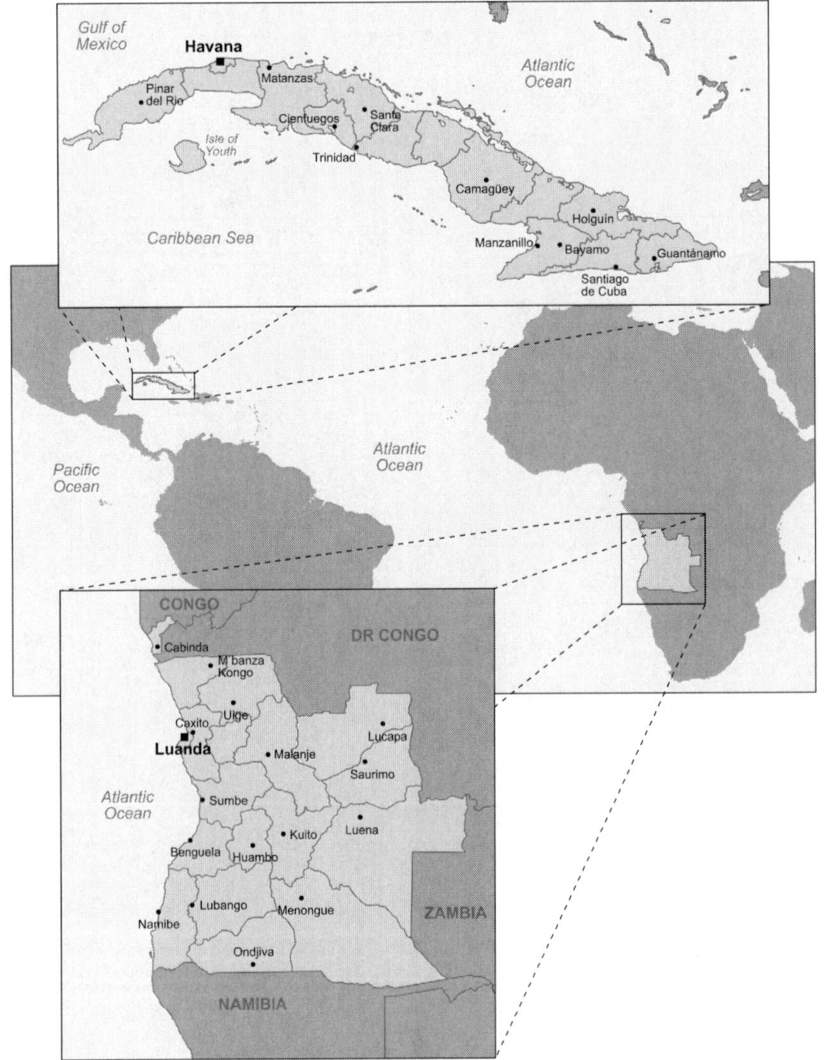

Map of Angola and Cuba (map by Daniel Giere)

Introduction

At the end of 1975, Angola became the focus of worldwide attention. In November that year, the Angolan liberation movement known as the Movimento Popular de Libertação de Angola (MPLA, People's Movement for the Liberation of Angola) had come to power in the former Portuguese colony after one of the longest and bloodiest colonial wars in African history. What interested the world, however, was not so much the fact that this process marked one of the final steps toward the decolonization of the African continent, but rather the political and military alliance between the MPLA, the Soviet Union, and Cuba. The Cuban government's involvement had extended to dispatching a large number of troops to Angola to support the MPLA. As early as December 1975, the United States Ambassador to the United Nations at that time, Daniel P. Moynihan, warned of the far-reaching consequences of a "Communist takeover" in Angola for the Western World.[1] This assertion anticipated the global political dynamics driven by the conflict between the US and Soviet superpowers, which would until 1991 lead to an escalation of the postcolonial conflict for Angola, a country rich in natural resources. As in many other regions of the Third World, the Cold War in Angola developed into a hot war.[2] Internally, the supremacy of the left-wing MPLA was challenged by the rival independence movements União Nacional para a Independência Total de Angola (UNITA, National Union for the Total Independence of Angola) and the Frente Nacional para a Libertação de Angola (FNLA, National Liberation Front of Angola). This power struggle received repeated support from

South African military intervention until the end of the 1980s. It was no secret that both the apartheid regime and UNITA received military and financial aid from the US government. UNITA in particular was armed systematically to create a bulwark of anti-Communism.

By the end of the Cold War, marked in Angola by the retreat of South African military forces and the withdrawal of Cuban troops in summer 1991, around 400,000 Cuban soldiers had been involved in the war of independence and the postcolonial conflict, while around 50,000 Cuban civilians,[3] the so-called internationalists, had provided civil aid to support the nation-building process of independent Angola.[4] The ideological premises of such extensive military and civil cooperation, carried out in the name of "internationalist solidarity,"[5] demand that it be interpreted within the context of the Cold War. Nevertheless, the postcolonial conflict in Angola was never purely a "proxy war": rather than come to an end in 1991, it lasted with unmitigated intensity until 2002, with war fronts running between local actors. The fixation on the superpowers, however, has to date obscured the considerable role that local, regional, and transatlantic structures and parameters also played in the development of an independent Angola. This emphasis on ideology has in particular led to a failure to recognize the amount of support the Cubans gave to the Angolan MPLA and the interaction that developed between the two governments. Till now the scope of this support and interaction in terms of both quantity and quality has remained largely ignored for what it really was—a unique example of transatlantic South-South cooperation of two formerly colonized countries. The huge number of Cuban soldiers and civilians who were actively involved in Angola between 1975 and 1991 is a clear indication of the historic significance of this South-South relationship.

This study therefore approaches the historical development of postcolonial Angola until 1991 from an Atlantic, Cuban-Angolan perspective, looking at the reciprocal interests of both parties and analyzing their influence upon each other. It looks into the interplay of both the Cuban and Angolan governments, who were acting on the periphery of a global power constellation, and it raises the question of to what extent they, as regional and local actors, were able to exploit the niches of the Cold War, each for its own benefit. The main emphasis, however, is not on the war of independence, Angola's postcolonial conflict, or the military engagement of Cuba, even though these processes did determine the conditions for Cuban-Angolan cooperation. The focus is far more on the significance of civil cooperation with Cuba and its impact on creating the nation-state of Angola and on stabilizing the power of the MPLA, which still governs Angola today. Taking up the idea of entangled or connected histories, this study examines the specific nature of this extraordinary South-South cooperation and the respective motivation behind it and analyzes its many facets, spheres of influence, and the resulting patterns of interaction.

Education serves here as a prime example of this cooperation. Although Cuba's civil aid extended to many other areas, including health, construction, technology, manufacturing, agriculture, administration, and the service industry, the education sector and the establishment of a new education system were among the most important and far-reaching remits of cooperation. New education models and (along with them) knowledge and power strategies were transferred from Cuba to Angola, where they were adapted, translated, and transformed to fit the Angolan context and requirements. Without a doubt, both governments were responsible for initiating cooperation in education, and their establishment of national and binational institutions was crucial for cooperation at all levels. Nevertheless, I give center stage to the historic role played by the many individuals, above all the approximately 10,000 Cuban teachers, students, education specialists, and advisors, without whose personal commitment as civil aid workers the nationwide introduction of the new education system in postcolonial Angola would not have been possible.

Cuban-Angolan cooperation involves so many different layers of meaning that it requires a multifaceted approach that considers not only the interaction between the Cuban and Angolan governments but also the many examples of sociocultural and political transfer. This study therefore moves the political and historical structures into the background in favor of a sociocultural focus, thus underlining the personal engagement of individuals and the challenges they faced. The aim is to analyze how cooperation worked at a grassroots level and to evaluate the various factors that shaped encounters between Cubans and Angolans—all in an attempt to understand the history of this transnational contact, as well as their everyday cultural practices. It therefore includes the attempt to create a "subversive micronarrative" to rewrite globalization more as vernacular and less as an expression of a political interaction of governments.[6]

Therefore in this study I compare the motivation and strategies of the various actors at the planning and implementation stage of education policy, and I reveal the resulting asymmetries and dissonances. I also deal with social interaction and intercultural encounters, giving expression to the personal memories and everyday experiences of Cuban civilians working in Angola and illustrating the way Cubans and Angolans regarded each other; the way they met each other as pupils, teachers, and colleagues; and the way they accepted each other or distanced themselves from one another. Beyond the binational administrative and institutional levels, the encounters between Angolans and Cubans during Cuban-Angolan cooperation opened up an interactive Atlantic, "Afro-Latin American" space of transnational dimensions.

State of Research

The postcolonial conflict and international involvement in Angola have been the subject of many studies, above all from a US and European research perspective. Although these studies take an explicitly academic approach, they are informed above all by a dichotomous perspective on East-West antagonism.[7] Publications prior to 1991 concentrate mainly on the military, political, and economic aspects of the supposed "threat" to the Western World from the Communist influence in Africa.[8] Moreover, these studies also share the common feature of arguing according to a hierarchic pattern determined by the superpowers of the Cold War. From this polarized stance, above all US academics and publicists have interpreted Cuba's support for the MPLA almost exclusively in terms of the global interests of the Soviet government, and in so doing have frequently underestimated the role of Cuba as an independent protagonist.[9] However, other historians and social scientists, such as Sergio Díaz-Briquets and Susan Eva Eckstein in the 1980s, did point to the dimensions and significance of Cuba's economic background and civil engagement in the Third World.[10] But, as occurred all too often during the Cold War, such alternative interpretations of Cuba's role fell on deaf ears. In this book, I pick up on the ground-breaking work of these scholars. I thereby come to an appraisal of Cuban-Angolan interaction that goes beyond the interpretation given by the many studies that emerged under the influence of the Cold War and that speak of Cuba's "intervention" in Angola within the Cold War framework. I work on the assumption that particularly in the civil sphere, Cuba's involvement in Angola was much more of a cooperation pact between the Cuban government and the MPLA as equal partners than an example of Cuban intervention.

At the end of the 1990s, greater access to information after the opening up of Soviet archives led to a reappraisal of the history of the Cold War. In view of the Soviet interest in anti-colonial movements, attention turned to the specific impact of the Cold War on the Third World. Postcolonial criticism and the resulting new global history also brought about a change in perspective, and the countries and regions of the Global South now became the focus of research interest. Scholars began to break away from the confines of the bipolar Cold War power constellation and to shed new light on the colonial and postcolonial conflicts following World War II. Particularly noteworthy are the recently published monographs and anthologies by the historians Odd Arne Westad and Melvyn Leffler (on the "global Cold War") and Bernd Greiner (who with others edited *Heiße Kriege im Kalten Krieg* [Hot Wars in the Cold War]).[11] In these works, the independence conflict in Angola is the subject of several excellent essays. However, new information from Soviet sources needs to be supplemented by local documents and studies specific to the region in question, because without them a new comprehensive interpretation of the Cold War within a global framework does not go far enough in recognizing the significance of local and regional protagonists.[12]

As far as the role of the Cuban government is concerned, evidence clearly shows that it engaged in the Angolan war of independence on its own initiative. Far from simply acting as a Soviet proxy, Cuba pursued power politics in its own interest. To date the Italian-born US diplomatic historian Piero Gleijeses, working primarily in international political and diplomatic history, has been the only one to provide proof of this, underlining in particular the global dimension of Cuba's foreign policy. But he also admitted that Cuban involvement in Angola over such a long period would not have been possible without the massive financial and military support of the Soviet Union. Even though in the 1980s there was already an awareness of Cuba as an independent, global political force, Gleijeses was undoubtedly the first to emerge from the shadow of Cold War polarity with his well-received analysis of Cuba's role in Africa.[13] He too, however, works on the assumption of a more or less one-sided and military initiative on the part of Cuba, and he pays little attention to the role of the Angolan MPLA as an independent protagonist. Only in his recently published book does he also refer to Cuba's civilian support for the MPLA in the process of postcolonial state and nation building.[14]

Angola's independence and the ensuing postcolonial conflict have also been the subject of a large number of solid political, historical, and sociological studies written from the point of view of Africa specialists in Europe and the United States. Many were motivated by their criticism of Portugal's colonial war, and their various approaches have contributed significantly to illuminate the background of Portuguese colonial rule, the colonial war, the struggle for independence, and the postcolonial conflict in and around Angola.[15] These studies also shed light on the nature of the national, regional, and international actors and their respective interests. Above all, recent sociological and political studies dealing with the postcolonial development of Angola concentrate on the causes and effects of the postcolonial conflict, which outlasted the Cold War and was bitterly fought out by the local protagonists, the MPLA government, and UNITA, until 2002.[16] The studies analyze the power structures within Angolan society shaped by the war and delve into the corrupt war economy—phenomena that go hand-in-hand with the consolidation of the MPLA as a ruling force. Though these studies focus on the development of Angola within a national framework and acknowledge regional influences, they reduce the international dimension of the postcolonial conflict largely to the world dominance of the United States, the Soviet Union, and their "proxies." Again

Cuban involvement is either completely ignored or limited to military involvement, and as such interpreted as an "intervention" within the Cold War framework. There are now several publications written from an Angolan perspective that deal with the postcolonial development of Angola and above all the history of the MPLA, but here again Cuba plays only a marginal role.[17]

In Cuba any attempt to historicize its engagement in Angola is hindered even today by the ideologically charged discourse that still portrays it as part of the official success story of the Cuban Revolution. The government and military remain the sole interpreters of the engagement in Angola and are free to categorize its protagonists (using the standard moral framework) as either "good" or "evil." The result is a strong narrative giving particular emphasis to Cuba's active role in Angola but generally confining that role to political and military engagement while reducing the Angolan partner's role to that of victim.[18] Angola, threatened by the "imperialists, neocolonialists, and racists" (meaning the United States, Western Europe, and South Africa), is saved by "Cuba's heroic solidarity with the people of Angola."[19] The "courage and selflessness of the Cuban internationalists" not only facilitated Angolan independence but also conquered apartheid and contributed to the cause of Namibian independence.[20] According to this official interpretation, "Cuban and Angolan blood mixed on the battlefields of Angola, and the pain felt for Angola's fallen heroes was transformed into an even greater love of and loyalty toward the *patria*," the Fatherland.[21] In brief, this is the only framework within which any sort of Cuban collective, public remembrance of engagement in Angola can take place. The references to the events of war, however, constantly divert attention to the actors who were directly involved in Angolan military engagement. The only people to receive recognition in the official politics of memory are high-ranking, loyal Angola veterans. By recognizing the memories of the civilians who provided development aid in Angola and by giving them a voice for the first time, this study therefore asks what traces this engagement left on Cuban society. This book therefore pays particular attention to Cuba's official silence on its engagement in Angola, which is still imposed today. Even though, for example, the 2013 theme of the renowned Havana Book Fair was Angola, neither were there any significantly different contributions, nor was there any attempt to initiate a broader public discussion on Angolan engagement. This is surprising, because in retrospect the intensity and quality of engagement in the civil sphere have proven to be particularly significant. Although the cooperation pact between the two countries ceased after 1991, it was recently revived. The relationship is flourishing, and today once again several thousand Cuban specialists are working in Angola. This situation would have been unthinkable without a history of previous cooperation.

Theory and Methods: The Cold War, Global History, Atlantic Perspectives, and Translocality

In keeping with the new "multipolar" interpretation of the Cold War demanded by Westad and Leffler, this study undertakes to overcome both the dominant perception of the superpowers as (almost) monolithic blocks and the resulting logic of ideological fronts within the East-West conflict.[22] My aim is to decenter the significance of the global powers. In focusing especially on South-South relations, I acknowledge current debates on new methods and new approaches to global history that analyze historical processes beyond Europe and beyond East and West, distancing themselves from most prevailing interpretations. The most fruitful approaches are the ones that break away from the dominance of hierarchic concepts, avoiding conceptual obstructions and giving prominence to the agency of social and political actors in formerly colonized countries.[23]

The example of cooperation between Cuba and Angola highlights the need for historic interpretation to overcome spatial boundaries: interpreting relations between (former) colonial powers and (former) colonies usually fails to go beyond familiar nation-state or continental frameworks or the North-South paradigm. In relativizing I do not intend, however, to obscure or deny either the existence of hierarchies or unequal development, or the national, regional, and international power constellations and networks that emerged and endured over the course of history. Nor do I intend to trivialize the postcolonial war, its drastic impact on the Angolan population (and on the Cuban soldiers and civilians), and the resulting structures of violence that still affect Angolan society today.[24] Indeed, civil cooperation was part of a mutually agreed-upon political and military grand strategy that also made a considerable contribution to determining the course of the postcolonial war. After all, the outcome of the independence struggle in favor of the MPLA is inseparable from the military engagement of Cuban troops. However, in order to shed light upon the motives and backgrounds behind this cooperation, it is not enough to consider the cooperative relationship of Angola and Cuba merely from the point of view of postcolonial conflict. To do so would be to ignore the significance of civil support—humanitarian, infrastructural, and administrative—which was to have a long-term impact on sociopolitical developments in Angola, and indeed in Cuba.

With reference to research into the impact of the Cold War on countries in the Southern Hemisphere, the historian Michael Latham advanced the theory that, much to the regret of their powerful (and not-so-powerful) supporters, the elites of the Third World countries were generally not just passive recipients of revolutionary or modernizing social models.[25] When Latham's theory is applied to cooperation between Cuba and Angola, parallels become apparent. First and foremost, shared political and ideological aims were indeed the basis of this cooperative relationship, and Cuba's socialism was initially regarded as a model for the postcolonial nation-state of Angola. However, considering only the ideological motives behind cooperation would mean ignoring the additional interests behind the (power) politics of the MPLA government. Just ten years after independence, the MPLA, which formed the elite of the new nation state, veered from its original socialist course and took a capitalist path. That did not, however, prevent the government from continuing to accept Cuba's military and civil aid. This suggests that the MPLA may to some extent have been using its past Marxist orientation to continue benefiting from cooperation with its Cuban partner.

This study is not founded on a teleological interpretation of history, which assumes either determinism in sociopolitical developments or an increasing intensification of relations, as some more recent reflections on global history seem to suggest. The processes and developments examined here were characterized more often by dissonance and discontinuity than by a clear trajectory, although at times they did lead to intense networking between both countries. Cuban-Angolan cooperation was closely tied to sociopolitical and wartime developments for a time, but after 1991 it dwindled to almost nothing for almost two decades.

The existence of the transatlantic South-South constellation of Africa and the Caribbean means that global-historic perspectives determined by the Cold War cannot provide a full, nuanced background to Cuban-Angolan cooperation and the resulting interactions. It makes much more sense to base analysis on the historical framework of the Atlantic region. However, the Atlantic in question must not be viewed as a space exclusively defined by European and Western civilization.[26] A much better methodological point of reference is the Atlantic region informed by the slave trade between Africa and America and the diasporas of millions of Africans to the Americas, along with the diverse social, economic, cultural, and ethnic repercussions, interactions, and aftermaths. It is the so-called Black Atlantic, which following the concept of the British-Guyanese cultural theorist Paul Gilroy has become the alternative paradigm to the White Atlantic of the Europeans and North Americans. Despite the justified criticism leveled at Gilroy's "Black Atlantic," the concept has served as a basis for new perspectives of the Atlantic that aim to highlight the influence of the African diasporas on North American and British cultures and the resulting agency of the Africans within the Atlantic space.[27] It has also contributed significantly to an understanding of the Atlantic as an intercultural and transnational space in which an Atlantic culture characterized by entanglements, fluidity, and change was able to develop. Today new studies have been able to counter the frequent criticism that the concept concentrates too much on North Atlantic and Anglo-American culture while neglecting the South Atlantic and the Caribbean.[28] A concept that is useful to express the complexity of social, cultural, and political relations and movements between people, ideas, and goods between regions of the South is "translocality." It is rooted in the considerations of cultural theorist Arjun Appadurai on multicultural spaces established by migratory flows beyond nation-states and refined by a team of researchers of the Berlin-based institute Zentrum Moderner Orient (ZMO).[29]

Nevertheless, Gilroy was not the first to point out the ethno-cultural links between Africa and the Americas or the first to counter the negative image of Africa and underscore the racism to which its inhabitants and descendants of the diasporas were exposed. Already at the beginning of the twentieth century, there were cultural and literary movements such as Négritude, political movements such as Pan-Africanism, and Back-to-Africa movements. All of these had a lasting impact on the twentieth century.[30] What they all had in common was a transatlantic perspective and an understanding of an Atlantic space formed by Africans and the descendants of the African diasporas, even if they did not yet express it in these terms. Inspired by the view of the Atlantic space as a bridge between Africa and the Americas, my study aims to make this link more solid by providing a concrete example from the twentieth century.

The Cuban head of state Fidel Castro offers an excellent starting point. He cited the historic links between Africa and America to justify Cuba's involvement in Angola. He alluded to the history of the transatlantic slave trade and the resulting common colonial history of Cuba and Angola, during which one million African slaves were shipped to Cuba. At the end of 1975, Castro created an interactive transatlantic space and went as far as defining Cuba as an "Afro-Latin American nation."[31] He therefore invented a tradition in the sense of Eric Hobsbawm, in establishing a continuity with a suitable historical past as well as symbolizing the membership of a real or artificial community, and, in spatial terms, a "Black Atlantic"—*avant la lettre*—at the same time.[32] In so doing, he was addressing the Cuban people and calling upon them to show solidarity and commit themselves en masse to military and civil engagement in Angola. In a kind of contemporary Back-to-Africa movement, the Cuban descendants of African slaves were encouraged to return to the continent of their ancestors in order to support their "relatives" in their struggle for independence and in the postcolonial establishment of the Angolan nation. He also indicated the considerable role that slaves and free slaves had played in Cuba's fight for independence against the Spanish colonial power between 1868 and

1898 and concluded that all Cubans had "blood ties" with Angola and therefore the historical duty to help the Angolans.

This study therefore also provides a new perspective on the varied significance of solidarity, because across the Atlantic world, manifestations of trans-border solidarity between geographically distant, different, or unequal groups and communities are phenomena of political life that accompanied the evolution of a transnational Left in the twentieth century. The idea of attaining justice in order to create a "fraternity" of humanity—a practical utopia of respect for liberty, equality, and social justice—became more important in the face of the imperialist designs of rival superpowers during the Cold War. Many of these expressions of solidarity were sparked by emerging anti-colonial movements (especially in Asia and Africa) that staked claim to power as a "Third Force," and by national liberation movements in Latin America. Especially the protagonists of the Cuban Revolution played a crucial role in developing a new concept of "internationalist solidarity" in the Global South.[33]

I also examine the extent to which the Cuban population took the appeal for solidarity to heart. I analyze the question of whether education and social mobility, introduced after the revolution to promote the social integration of people of African descent (who constituted over a third of the total population in the 1970s), explain the massive participation in Angola. Connected to this is the question of whether ethno-cultural background influenced the way Cubans and Angolans encountered each other and whether involvement in Angola led to a change in attitude toward a stronger transatlantic Cuban-Angolan identity. In combination with recent research on the influence of emotions on political activity at the macro level, this study assesses the emotional dimension and its long-term impact on memory at the micro level.[34]

An essential part of my fresh methodological approach to South-South solidarity is an analysis of all the different levels at which cooperation took place and a consideration of all the protagonists involved. My aim is to avoid reducing this common history to a purely political, diplomatic, or military narrative, and to provide a better understanding of the subject matter by looking at sociocultural and anthropological issues and redefining the areas in which interaction took place. In so doing, I aim to draw differentiated conclusions regarding the interactive mechanisms of interstate relations and the mutual interplay of transnational ties.

Outline

Based on the above approach, I have divided this study into three parts. Part I deals with the historical background and development of Angola and Cuba in the twentieth century, all of which set the stage for their transatlantic cooperation in 1975. This part looks at the colonial causes leading specifically to Angolan independence: the emergence of three competing anti-colonial movements, which fought separately against the Portuguese colonial power. Against the backdrop of international political constellations and motives, Part I discusses the relationship dating back to the 1960s between the members of the MPLA and the Cuban government. These ties influenced Cuba's decision to provide military backing for the MPLA shortly before Angolan independence. The Cuban Revolution is characterized not only by radical economic and social transformation but also by Cuba's desire to pursue independent foreign policies with its own interests and aims in mind, despite the constellation of the Cold War. At this time Cuba attempted to export revolution and to "internationalize" it, in active solidarity with friendly governments and anti-colonial and nationalist movements on the continents of Asia, Africa, and Latin America. The resulting "internationalist solidarity" became Cuba's new foreign political strategy, culminating in support for the MPLA.

Such zealous cooperation plans on the part of Cuba's and Angola's political decision makers could not have been realized without the massive personal commitment of the Cuban population, both soldiers and civilians. The ambitions of the Cuban government also had an internal effect. In the civil domain, thousands of doctors, teachers, construction workers, engineers, and other specialists were sent to Angola to work there without any particular material gain for one to two years. This raises a question: to what extent did such commitment owe itself to the propaganda and recruiting strategies of the Cuban government rather than individual motivations? On the basis of eyewitness interviews with people who were involved in this operation, I critically examine the influence of official propaganda on personal motivation, and whether the decision to become involved under prevailing political and social circumstances was purely voluntary.

At the end of the colonial era, the challenges Angola faced were similar to those of revolutionary Cuba: high levels of illiteracy and the lack of a trained workforce. Cuba's successes in modernizing its education system and the principle of educating "new men" pointed the way for Angola's postcolonial education policy. The Cuban-Angolan cooperative program in education was founded on common consensus. The "success story" of Cuba's education policy, which created sustainable literacy levels and involved the people in the national and revolutionary project, was to be transferred to Angola. As cooperation in education is central to this study, I analyze the extent to which the Cuban concept of education—its methods and ideology—was integrated into educational reform in Angola, and how it was adapted to suit the specific challenges of Angola's postcolonial transition.

Part II of the study is dedicated to the entanglements, dependencies, and dynamics of Cuban-Angolan cooperation in the civil sphere. By referring to concrete data as well as administrative structures and bilateral communication mechanisms, and by periodizing the various cooperative phases, I analyze how civil cooperation was initially negotiated and then established at an intergovernmental level. The considerable structural, administrative, and manpower deficits facing Angola during its rebuilding process meant that the government was dependent on Cuban aid. But was cooperation therefore based on an asymmetrical state of dependency, with the MPLA as the dependent? Documentary evidence regarding civil cooperation consistently suggests that there was a pattern of demand and supply between the cooperating partners. The starting point was always the needs and demands of the Angolans, which were then generally met by the Cubans. The pattern of interaction underlying the relationship is illustrated in the main focus of cooperation and in the many institutions and mechanisms created to coordinate and monitor its practical implementation.

This section also deals with the economic dimension of cooperation and asks whether civil involvement was motivated purely by political ideology and solidarity, or if Cuban engagement was to some extent financed by the Angolan government. I discuss whether Cuban-Angolan cooperation could not be better characterized as "internationalism with reciprocal benefits," as the Angolan Minister of Education put it during one of my interviews.[35] This assumption is backed here for the first time by Angolan documents from that period, including cooperative agreements and ministerial files.

Another point of interest is the extent to which asymmetries, dissonances, and conflicts of interest influenced the cooperative relationship. The focus here is on the structural and implementational levels. In addition to bilateral structures and communication mechanisms, as well as national institutions established in both countries, the Cuban government had at its disposal an autonomous, civil administrative body on Angolan soil. This section describes the aims and mechanics of the Cuban Civil Administration and takes a look at the issues within its dealings with Angolan institutions that specifically led to conflicts of interest. It also considers how asymmetries and dissonances resulted from the asynchronous development of the two countries and the Cuban head start in experience and knowledge.

Central to the cooperative program in education was the deployment of a professional workforce: advisors, education specialists, teachers, students, university professors, and lecturers. Based on their respective responsibilities and the challenges arising from cooperation in Angola, I critically examine the role these professionals played in the establishment of the Angolan education system. A second mainstay of the education cooperative program were the Angolan boarding schools on the Cuban Isla de la Juventud, the Isle of Youth. The study analyzes the link between cooperation in Angola and the establishment of these schools, along with the corresponding education policies and their immediate impact.

Part III concentrates on memories of engagement in Angola. These memories mainly stem from interviews I held with Cuban civilians who were involved in Angola, though a counterpoint to the Cuban perspective is offered by the memories and perceptions of Angolan eyewitnesses. The corresponding chapters are structured around basic experiences that affected the everyday lives of Cubans in Angola. The choice of issues is oriented toward the witnesses' memories, which played a central role in all the interviews I conducted. I have identified these issues as characteristic basic experiences that can be regarded as representative for Cubans in Angola. This microhistorical perspective offers a deep insight into how Cubans experienced and dealt with the challenges they faced in Angola, challenges that went beyond the intergovernmental agreements and overriding agendas.

These chapters also deal with the emotional dimension of cooperation and the positive or negative feelings this extreme situation provoked. The personal memories recorded here open up a perspective that focuses on subjective appropriations of this historical experience. They also give an insight into the scope of cultural transfer and social interaction that took place within the educational process. This subjective approach has the advantage of showing how encounters with "others" were individually perceived, understood, or misunderstood. Where possible, I back up these oral accounts with contemporary documents from Cuban administrative bodies and Angolan institutions, highlighting the extent to which individual experience diverges from or concurs with official claims.

The day-to-day life of the Cuban aid workers was in part shaped by their isolated existence in the "enclaves" specially created for them. These were not only enclosed areas but also sociocultural spaces defined by the prevailing social order in Cuba and affected by the many inclusion and exclusion mechanisms in place. The constant threat posed by the war also hung over the heads of the civilians. Here the link between civil aid and the overall political and military strategy is particularly apparent, and it highlights the consequences this had for civilians. I also give voice to the negative memories of these wartime experiences and the resulting trauma, along with the emotional strategies people developed to overcome difficult everyday situations.

This section also analyzes the challenges faced by Cuban teachers confronted with implementing educational reform in Angolan schools, and it attempts to define the characteristic features of social interaction between Cubans and

Angolans. I illustrate the processes of teaching and learning, along with the interplay of acceptance and resistance to which the teachers were subjected. I also examine the disruptions and ambivalences that corresponded to different viewpoints, contrasting and comparing the perceptions of the Cuban teachers, their Angolan colleagues, superiors, and pupils. The way Cubans and Angolans viewed each other and their mutual encounters was inextricably linked to self-perception. In exceptional cases, it was fascination that shaped people's perception of "the other," but more often it was based on cultural misunderstanding, which led to rejection. Otherness was regarded particularly by the Cubans as foreign and threatening, and as a result Cubans tended to denigrate the other while developing an exaggerated sense of self-importance.[36] Although the way Cubans and Angolans interacted with each other or dissociated themselves from one another runs through all chapters of Part III, this section closes with the question of identity and dissociation raised by several emblematic examples of how people perceived themselves and others.

Sources

In view of the lack of studies and publications on Cuban-Angolan cooperation, this book is primarily based on contemporary files and documents from Angolan, Cuban, and to some extent US and Portuguese archives. This written documentation is complemented by 127 interviews with 139 "ordinary" participants and experts. By experts I mean people who above all played an organizing or political role in civil (and military) cooperation from both Cuba and Angola. The method for conducting the interviews is described later in a separate section.

The most important location for my archival research was the Angolan Ministry of Education (MED) in Luanda. The difficulty, however, was that the ministry does not possess a regular archive with classified files (that is, files that are organized by archive numbers and letters, for example). It is more like a collection of documents from various ministerial departments, which are preserved in the cellar and in several other places in so-called dead archives.[37] Despite the obstacles to this archival research, the fact that I was able to look at non-classified documents gave me the distinct advantage of being allowed to view documents intended exclusively for internal purposes and marked accordingly. The most important sources, which form the basis for a large number of conclusions regarding the aims and mechanisms of Cuban-Angolan cooperation, originate from the Gabinete do Intercâmbio e Cooperação Internacional, or Gabinete do Intercâmbio Internacional (GICI/GII, Department of International Cooperation.) This department was responsible for organizing, coordinating, and administering all matters to do with the Cuban-Angolan cooperative program in education.

The documentation that I found for the period from 1976 to 1991 provides in-depth insights into the bilateral cooperation. It includes the cooperative agreement and contracts with Cuba, the minutes of meetings of the bilateral Cuban-Angolan commission, and written communication with the Cuban cooperative partners. Furthermore, the internal dealings are illustrated by all the notes and memos of the Department of International Cooperation, along with the correspondence within the ministry and with other ministries and Angolan institutions. The documents also include guidelines, directives, memos, accounts, reports, statistics, and analyses of the state of the education system. Additional documents include surveys regarding the number and distribution of Cuban aid workers in Angola and calculations of the resulting costs. Added to these were documents and papers from the office of the Minister of Education and from the planning and legal departments of the ministry. More documents pertinent to research on cooperation came from the (equally "dead") archive of the Agostinho Neto University in Luanda, the Angolan Planning Ministry, and the Foreign Ministry. Beyond the information on the aims and scope of cooperation with Cuba, these sources give a detailed insight into the structures and communication mechanisms underlying that cooperation and provide much evidence of hierarchies, asymmetries, and dissonances.

It proved much more difficult to gain access to written sources from the archives of Cuban state institutions and ministries responsible for organizing and coordinating civil engagement in Angola. During my research, I encountered the official silence resulting from the Cuban government's overriding monopoly on interpretation. I was permanently denied access to written documents by Cuban research institutes and ministries, often with the excuse that any such documents about Cuban engagement in Angola either no longer existed or never existed.[38] Nevertheless, thanks to the committed support of my Cuban colleagues, who were interested in the success of my research and helped me find these supposedly non-existent documents, I managed to locate written documentation about civil cooperation. Equally important in this respect were several of the eyewitnesses I interviewed who had been responsible for the organization of the cooperative program and who provided me with documents from their private archives.

A determined search through various ministries, archives, libraries, research and documentation centers, and museums uncovered further written sources, which to some extent complemented the Angolan documents. These documents deal mainly with cooperation in education and comprise files from various departments of the Cuban Ministry of Education, on the basis of which I was able to draw conclusions regarding the aims, planning, organization, and coordination of the engagement.

The documents, some of which came from private sources, and others (found in the cellar of Havana's Museum of Literacy thanks to a tip-off from an interviewee) include internal reports written by Cuban officials working in Angola.[39] They also include the so-called collective diaries of members of the student-teacher brigades, the Destacamento Pedagógico Internacionalista "Che Guevara," which they wrote during their stint in Angola and which provide an insight into internal organization.[40] Furthermore, in 2000 and 2002 the Angolan embassy in Cuba issued an award titled "Memories of Angola," which recognized the memoirs of people who had been involved in the cooperative program.[41] The submitted contributions include individual accounts of engagement in Angola and perceptions of Angola that complement the interviews I conducted.

My research in US-American and Portuguese archives and libraries concentrated above all on published sources from Cuba and Angola—newspapers, journals, magazines, and gray literature (that is, government reports and documents).

Methodology of Oral History: Biographical Interviews and Interviews with Experts

The subjective nature of the memories, recollections, and experiences recounted by Angolan and Cuban eyewitnesses provided crucial insights into the day-to-day implementation of the cooperative program. In Parts I and II of the study, the oral sources serve primarily to complement or contradict written sources, thereby highlighting the program's results, successes, and failures. This microhistorical approach forms an indispensable complement to a politico-historical approach and also provides the necessary counterpoint to the structural and sociohistorical foundation of cooperation. Addressing the subject from a microhistorical perspective demonstrates the extent to which civil cooperation was (and still is) dominated by an exceedingly complex interplay of politics, propaganda, symbolism, and power. Part III of the study brings subjective experience to the fore, with eyewitness accounts proffering a stark contrast to the official politics of memory. In addition, the analysis of the phenomena of perception, based on the interviewees' subjective statements, opens up a completely new angle on the significance and effects of cooperation.

During my various research visits to Cuba, Angola, the United States, and Portugal between 2004 and 2006, I held a total of 127 interviews with 139 Cuban and Angolan eyewitnesses.[42] The Cuban witnesses (106 individuals who spoke in 95 interviews) had mainly worked in the civil sphere in Angola, though some were also involved with the military. The Angolan eyewitnesses (33 individuals who spoke in 32 interviews) had worked with Cubans within the framework of civil cooperation or had been taught by them. The difference between the number of Cuban and Angolan interviewees is partly due to the focus of this study, which concentrates on Cubans working in Angola. It is also partly due to my difficulty in locating former Angolan pupils who had been taught by Cubans, whereas I was able to find and contact former Cuban civilians through Cuban government ministries and professional associations. Furthermore, while I was in Angola, I concentrated above all on studying the files on Cuban-Angolan cooperation contained in the archives of the Ministry of Education. Because I had been denied access to archival material on the topic in Cuba, this work in the Angolan archives was essential for obtaining the primary sources needed to analyze the cooperative relationship.

Ninety-nine of the interviews were biographical and geared toward understanding the experiences of "ordinary" participants during Cuban-Angolan cooperation. The remaining twenty-eight interviews were conducted with "experts," by which I mean organizers, planners, and Cubans and Angolans who held political responsibility for the cooperative program. These "experts" were also eyewitnesses, but owing to their positions of responsibility, they were able to shed light on the backgrounds, structures, and political intentions behind the cooperative arrangements. Furthermore, a characteristic feature of their memories was that they provided a higher level of abstraction. In many cases these "experts" helped me—whether intentionally or unintentionally—to place information from archival documents in their historical context, to make sense of bureaucratic processes, and to untangle personal networks. The interviews with the "experts" served above all to give me an overall view of cooperative structures and an understanding of concepts, backgrounds, and connections. The experts included journalists, historians, writers, film directors, and social scientists from Cuba and Angola. Some of the Cubans, including Cuban exiles, had been involved in constructing the official discourse surrounding engagement in Angola, for example through films, newspaper articles, and other publications. Others had investigated African and/or Angolan topics while conducting their own research. In my text, I examine the "expert" accounts separately from those of the "ordinary" participants.

The Experts

Among the Cuban "experts" were the politburo member Jorge Risquet Valdés, one of the key figures of Cuba's African policy; Rodolfo Puente Ferro, head of the African department of the Central Committee of the Communist Party of Cuba (PCC); and José Ramón Fernández, who at the time of interview was Deputy President of the Council of Ministers.[43] As former Cuban Minister of Education (1970–1990) Fernández was instrumental in organizing the education cooperative program with Angola. I also interviewed the then Cuban ambassador to Angola, Noemí Benitez de Mendoza, who from 1977 to 1984 as Deputy Minister for the Comité Estatal de Colaboración Económica (CECE, State Committee for Economic Cooperation) was responsible for civil cooperation with Angola.[44] Another interviewee was Zoila Franco Hidalgo, who between 1970 and 1990 held the post of Deputy Minister for Teacher Education in the Cuban Ministry of Education.[45] Among the Cuban exiles I interviewed as experts were the writer Norberto Fuentes, who in the 1980s was a high-ranking officer involved in military Angolan engagement, and Alcibíades Hidalgo, who was, until his escape into exile in 2002, one of the closest advisors in the then Ministry of the Interior and Chief of Staff to Raúl Castro.[46] He played a major role in the organization of military engagement in Angola. The Angolan "experts" included the former Deputy Minister of Education (1976–1982), the writer Artur Pestana (pen name: Pepetela), who was instrumental in planning and implementing the first education reform in postcolonial Angola; the first Prime Minister of independent Angola, Lopo do Nascimento (1975–1979), who helped plan and establish the cooperative program; António Burity da Silva, who was at the time of interview Minister of Education, and who in the 1970s and 1980s was responsible for selecting the scholars for the boarding schools on the Isle of Youth; the Deputy Minister of Education, Pinda Simão; and Manuel Teodoro Quarta, who at the time of interview was permanent secretary for the Angola National Commission for UNESCO.[47] The individuals from public life whom I interviewed as experts are named in the text and footnotes, whereas the "ordinary" interviewees are kept anonymous for their own protection.

The "Ordinary" Participants

I define "ordinary" participants as Cubans who were simply carrying out their duties as teachers, university professors, doctors, technicians, engineers, construction workers, and embassy staff during Cuba's engagement in Angola (ninety-one individuals of a total of eighty interviews). Among the Angolan "ordinary" interviewees were pupils who had been taught by Cubans, Angolans who had worked with Cubans in Angola, and Angolans who had been trained in Cuba (twenty individuals in nineteen interviews). The "ordinary" participants also include twelve members of the military, who were deployed in Angola either as soldiers and reservists or in a civilian and military capacity. Although the main focus of my research is on the circumstances surrounding civil cooperation and in particular cooperation in education, I frequently took the opportunity to record the recollections of military eyewitnesses in order to broaden my own understanding of the engagement.

Approximately half of the "ordinary" Cuban interviewees worked in Angola from 1978 to 1985, the years in which according to Cuban and Angolan statistics the highest number of civil aid workers was deployed. A quarter of the participants were there between 1975/76 and 1978; the remaining interviewees were deployed after 1985. Of the interviewees, fifty-one were male and forty female; forty-four were (visibly) of African descent and forty-seven were white. About half of them (forty-three) were involved in the education sector in Angola, some as advisors to the Ministry of Education, but most as teachers and university lecturers. Among the Angolan "ordinary" interviewees, eighteen were male and two female; six of them were (visibly) of Portuguese descent. At the time of interview, all the "ordinary" Angolan participants enjoyed a privileged position within Angolan society owing to their education under Cuban teachers or their school and university education in Cuba. They included teachers, university lecturers, scientists, civil servants, education specialists, priests, entrepreneurs, and engineers.

Before relating the method of my biographical interviews in detail, I would like to introduce a few theoretical comments regarding the way in which I deal with these subjective and personal recollections and how I explain and interpret them. Within the scope of this work, it is not possible to go into the numerous controversies and theoretical debates among historians with regard to such subjective sources. I therefore refer to historians including Lutz Niethammer, Alexander von Plato, Paul Thompson, and Jan Vansina, and their historical and anthropological research based on interviews, together with their differentiated, theoretical reflections on the methodology of oral history.[48] What I do wish to point out at this juncture is that some of the criticism surrounding the use of oral sources for representative statements also applies to written sources, as they too have been recorded by subjective individuals. Some of the points of criticism that are raised time and again are also based on the misconception that historic events can be reconstructed accurately on the basis of subjective memories.[49] To counter such criticism, I wish to emphasize that this study—and in particular Part III—is not an attempt to reconstruct historical reality; it is about personal memories that highlight the subjectivity existing in the history of Cuban-Angolan cooperation. Part III in particular deals with experiences based on concrete encounters between Cubans and Angolans and the way the participants perceived themselves and others. Precisely such insights into the subjective appropriation of historical processes offer a new scope for interpretation and open up a new angle on the plurality of history.

Part of the criticism regarding the use of subjective recollections as source material has to do with the unreliability of memory. Memory (it is argued) is constantly clouded and altered by later experience and by the way experiences are processed. The social and cultural paradigms of societies in which the eyewitnesses live further influence their memories.[50] Such reservations are indeed justified, and I took them into account when I conducted the interviews and evaluated the oral accounts. At this point, I wish to refer to the theses of "memory" and "collective memory" advanced by the French sociologist Maurice Halbwachs in the 1920s, according to which individual memories are influenced by the present and have a constructive character within a given social framework.[51] During the course of the last few decades numerous studies of memory and the processes of collective memory have picked up on Halbwachs's theories and developed and expanded them to a considerable degree.[52] Accordingly, in all societies individual memories are linked to processes of collective memory. Moreover, individual memories are constructed through interaction and communication with the social environment, from which the "social frameworks," the patterns of thought, derive. These social frameworks determine the content of the collective memory of the social group to which the interviewees belong. It follows that eyewitness memories are not objective reproductions of past experiences or a past reality; rather, they tend to be subjective reconstructions that depend on a given situation. When recalling memories from the past, the interviewee is actively collating data available in the present, and the memories must be understood as such.

In Cuban society today, the official historical interpretation of engagement in Angola as a success story defines the collective memory. This was confirmed above all in the interviews I conducted with the "experts"—the cooperation's organizers and planners living both in Cuba and in exile. In postrevolutionary Cuba, individual memories and recollections, including those of the exiled Cubans I interviewed, are particularly influenced by the hermetic, official discourse. The majority of "ordinary" interviewees have also appropriated this official version of events into their biographies. The prevailing "imperative of silence" and the lack of discussion within Cuban society about engagement in Angola have turned the "ordinary" participants into a subtle, unofficial, and private "memory collective," which only exists in the spoken word and which can only exchange subjective and individual memories of Angola in the private confines of family and close friends or with other former participants—a closed circle into which I was partially admitted during my research. The biographical approach I took when conducting the interviews revealed that although the Cuban people volunteered to participate in state cooperation initiatives, they were actually also pursuing personal motives and in so doing circumvented the official objectives and broke the state's monopoly on interpretation. Most of the interviews followed a similar pattern, frequently culminating in a catharsis during which the interviewees gave vent to their personal feelings and opinions.

In Cuba, I was generally free to choose my interviewees, and I was enthusiastically received by ordinary Cubans. However, state institutions and professional associations, upon which I relied to find interviewees, made frequent attempts to monitor me and influence my choice of interviewees.[53] Particularly at the beginning of my research, I met with considerable suspicion from state institutions, which at the beginning even tried to prevent me from carrying out my interviews. This was not surprising, however, since in autumn 2004 I was the first foreign historian to travel to Cuba to embark on an oral history project with former participants of the engagement in Angola. These difficult working conditions impacted the progress of my research project and required constant negotiation and compromise. For example, I had to accept the condition that a Cuban colleague be present at some of the interviews—though I was allowed to choose the colleague in question.[54]

Surprisingly, it was even more difficult to find suitable eyewitnesses among the exiled Cubans living in Miami. I could rely on the support of my colleagues, but some of the eyewitnesses they arranged were unwilling to be interviewed because they did not think I had distanced myself sufficiently from the Cuban government from the outset.[55] The Cuban community in Miami treated my research project with general distrust, obviously because they suspected me of acting on behalf of the Cuban government. Nevertheless, the interviews that I did carry out there were a valuable addition to those I conducted in Cuba, as the Cuban exiles spoke of aspects of the cooperation that were considered taboo in Cuba, and they were in general more critical of Cuba's engagement (and indeed their own) in Angola.

In Angola, the social framework was completely different. At the time of the interviews in 2006, the episode of Cuban-Angolan cooperation had long been consigned to history. After the withdrawal of Cuban troops and civilians in summer 1991, the civil war between the MPLA government and its opponents from UNITA had continued until 2002 with horrific brutality. In 2006, Angola was a society still recovering. The war had drastically affected the lives of the majority of Angolans, and it made the period during which the Cubans were present look comparatively peaceful. As many of my interviewees told me, the climate during the Cuban period had been, at least initially, one of social optimism following independence. Furthermore, the politico-ideological parameters in Angola had long since changed, unlike in Cuba. Already in the mid-1980s the Angolan government had departed from its original course of socialist nation building. After 1991 and particularly following the end of the civil war in 2002, the government introduced political reforms. In many ways,

Angola still cannot be considered a state with properly functioning democratic institutions, and a large section of its population remains excluded from active participation in political decision-making processes. But the government's shift in paradigm led to Cuban-Angolan cooperation being relegated to a past that no longer has any bearing on the current authority of the MPLA. Cuban-Angolan cooperation has therefore been freed from official historical interpretation, and this has had a direct effect on the information my interviewees were willing to provide. In general they proved considerably more open and self-critical regarding the Cuban-Angolan past than my Cuban interviewees had been.

In Portugal three of a total of five interviews with Angolans turned out to be a mixture of "ordinary" and "expert" interviews. I managed to find my eyewitnesses with the help of the Center of African Studies at the University of Lisbon.[56] An economist, an engineer, a journalist, and two historians, they had all had to deal to some extent with the postcolonial history of Angola and therefore qualified as experts as well as ordinary interviewees.

The UNITA perspective on Cuban-Angolan cooperation was not of central interest to my research since UNITA supporters not only did not work with the Cubans, but they actively fought against them. Nevertheless, on several occasions I tried in vain to speak to some UNITA supporters. Only on one occasion in Angola did I have the opportunity to interview a representative of UNITA (which in the meantime had transformed into the opposition party) about his recollections of Cuban cooperation. However, my interviewee had never had any contact with Cuban civilians or military and was only in a position to reiterate the party's general hostility toward Cuban-Angolan cooperation. According to this stance, Cuban civilians and military were perceived as enemies, and their presence was considered detrimental to the development of Angola. Even though the main tenor of this conversation was one of politically motivated prejudice, it nevertheless showed that the memory of Angola's independence continues to be split between the "winners" and the "losers" of the postcolonial conflict.

Conducting Biographic Interviews

In this section, I will limit my explanation of how I conducted my biographic interviews to the interviews with the "ordinary" participants from Cuba, partly because they represent the largest group of interviewees, and partly because the interview situation was particularly difficult because of the external factors described above. The central questions during all the interviews regarded the interviewees' own biographies, the impact their stay in Angola had on their own lives, and the significance of their encounters and work with Angolans. I rarely asked about (political) opinions or appraisals, or about concrete dates or events, but rather endeavored to unearth the way my interviewees saw themselves and perceived "the other." During the interviews with "ordinary" Cuban exiles in Miami, I also avoided asking them directly to give any political judgments: I wanted to discover as far as possible their "former" attitudes, before they were obfuscated by current assessments and political environments.

In the case of the Cuban interviewees, I asked open questions to encourage them to share what motivated them to go to Angola, what expectations and hopes they attached to their engagement, under what family circumstances they made their decision, and what their first impressions of Angola were. I also asked what preconceived ideas they had taken with them to Africa or Angola, and—depending on the color of their skin—I asked them about what they knew of their African forebears and whether the Afro-Latin American identity evoked by Castro had any particularly bearing on their decision to go to Angola. The only obviously "political" question I asked was whether their decision was entirely voluntary.

With regard to their stay in Angola, I asked the interviewees about their personal living conditions, day-to-day life (accommodations, food and drink, organization), and the type of work they were doing. I enquired about their feelings and which situations they found particularly difficult or particularly pleasant. I also asked them about personal impressions and perceptions of their surroundings and their contact with Angolan society, and following that, whether they felt accepted there and how they would assess their role as "internationalists" and civil aid workers in a foreign environment. I also tried to find out how they communicated and what personal and/or professional relationships they formed with Angolans, what their daily work entailed, with whom they worked or whom they taught, and how responsibilities were distributed at the workplace. Each interview ended with the question of how they had felt on returning to Cuba, and how their Angolan stay had changed them. By sticking closely to the biography of the eyewitnesses and by avoiding asking interviewees to express political judgments, this interview technique allowed my Cuban—and also my Angolan—interviewees to recount their personal impressions, recollections, feelings, and memories without feeling forced to legitimize their involvement.

Finally, the question of how representative these personal memories are needs to be addressed. How significant are these subjective recollections, and can one generalize from the conclusions drawn from them? The large number of biographical interviews I conducted allowed me to ascertain that certain experiences kept cropping up at various points in time and in various locations. In order to determine which of the interviewees' personal experiences might be representative for the experiences of Cuban aid workers and their Angolan partners in the education sector, I compared as far as was possible written and oral sources—Angolan, Cuban, and exiled-Cuban. This was partly an attempt to verify and confirm the personal memories of my interviewees with contemporaneous, written sources. Another way of checking how representative the personal memories were was offered by the "expert" interviews, in particular those I conducted with Angolan and exiled-Cuban eyewitnesses because they regarded cooperation more critically and with more distance than the Cuban "experts" and "ordinary" participants. The statements made by some of the Angolan and Cuban "experts" could be verified, because in their capacity as ministerial staff, for example, their names frequently appear in the files that I consulted, and in some cases they were actually the authors of the documents themselves. Nevertheless, it was impossible to find alternative sources to objectify all the personal memories. Nor could I check in every case how representative the accounts were. For this reason, I have taken a few memories that best contribute to an understanding of the cooperation situation, but were uttered by only a small number of the interviewees, and I have quoted them directly or attributed them to the speakers. Notwithstanding these difficulties with the methodological approach to sources obtained through oral history, I was able to ascertain that in the final analysis it was only thanks to the subjective memories of the "ordinary" participants and the explanations given by the "experts" that I was able to uncover so many details about Cuban-Angolan cooperation and the day-to-day circumstances surrounding it.

I would like to make one final comment here about my terminology. In the text, I use the term "Afro-Cuban" to refer to Cubans of African descent.[57] This term (which is analogous to "African American") is widely used above all in US research. Today, Cubans with African ancestry simply call themselves "Cuban," not "Afro-Cuban." I use the term as an alternative to "of African descent" when it is necessary to express the cultural and social differences between white Cubans and nonwhite Cubans.

In the Cuban context, the term "internationalism" is particularly loaded with a specific political ideology of "solidarity" and "internationalist solidarity." I use the term here to describe the associated phenomenon of foreign politics. A derivative of this is the term "internationalist," which even today is used to describe Cubans who are deployed abroad, also by the Cuban participants themselves. In view of the emotive nature of the term, I refer to the Cubans working in Angola as "civil aid workers" or "*cooperantes*" (to use a name given to them by the Angolan administration). As already mentioned, my use of the term "cooperation" reflects my assessment of the Cuban-Angolan relationship as one of cooperation between equal partners, and I thereby reject the idea of

Cuban "intervention." I also use the word "cooperation" to distance myself from the term "mission," which is frequently found in the Cuban context to refer to an engagement abroad. My choice of terms has not only to do with the fact that "mission" is ideologically tendentious. The word also has the paternalist connotation of one-sided activity on the part of Cuba, whereas I wish to emphasize that Cuban-Angolan cooperation was based on reciprocity. Therefore, on the few occasions that I do use "mission," it appears in quotation marks. My thoughts on the parallels between Cuban "missions" abroad and Christian missionizing are also given at an appropriate point in the text.

PART I

Angola and Cuba in the Twentieth Century

The Development of Transatlantic South-South Cooperation

1

Angola's Path toward Independence

The following chapters outline the historical development of Cuba and Angola during the twentieth century to provide a framework for the political, social, and cultural situations in the two countries that led to their governments entering into transatlantic South-South cooperation.

I begin by portraying the circumstances within Angolan colonial society that resulted in colonial war and the emergence of rivaling anti-colonial movements. I then outline the specific interests and reasons behind both the Cuban government's decision to provide military assistance to the MPLA and its readiness to pursue cooperation beyond Angola's independence in November 1975. Not only did cooperation continue until summer 1991, it was even extended to include a comprehensive civil aid program. Cuban-Angolan cooperation was founded on reciprocity, with both governments following—at least initially—the very similar sociopolitical aim of establishing a socialist society in postcolonial Angola. This was a project of alternative socialist modernization. Beyond the Atlantic, it was defined as a common, transnational, "Afro-Latin American" project of "internationalist solidarity." Each side took advantage of the interests of the other cooperation partner. However, it was the Angolan MPLA government that gained most of the long-term benefit. Following independence, the MPLA government needed Cuban support to assert its authority over the rivaling FNLA and, even more importantly, UNITA, and to stave off South African military attacks. The MPLA was able to appeal to the Cuban government's internationalist agenda of spreading Cuba's model of socialist revolution to the

African continent. The Cuban government, for its part, was therefore willing to overcome international political and military obstacles in order to supply enormous manpower to support the MPLA's goals. In so doing, Cuba was able to pursue its own political ambitions on the foreign stage.

Colonial Angola

Angola, Mozambique, Guinea-Bissau, Cape Verde, and São Tomé and Príncipe constituted the African territories that had been under Portuguese rule since the expansion of its empire in the late fifteenth and sixteenth centuries. The driving force behind Angolan and Portuguese relations during the sixteenth and eighteenth centuries was the slave trade. Angola and its bordering regions offered a pool of laborers who could be sent to the Portuguese plantation colonies of Brazil (for sugarcane production) and São Tomé (for sugar, coffee, and cocoa production).[1] Approximately two million slaves were shipped from Angolan ports across the Atlantic during this period. The fact that there had been a tradition of slavery in some pre-colonial societies of Central Africa, albeit in a different form, made it easier to round up slaves for the transatlantic market. The responsibility for procuring workers from Angola's hinterland was mainly in the hands of *mestiços*, Luso-African merchants and slave traders, who collaborated with European transatlantic slave traders while maintaining their own interests.[2] From the sixteenth century onward, the Luso-African merchant class became an essential component of a transatlantic economy that linked Africa, America, and Europe, and they shrewdly used the networks of the early modern Atlantic world.[3]

The region on the Atlantic coast of southern Central Africa, known to the Portuguese as Angola, was only officially integrated into the Portuguese Empire (along with Portugal's other overseas territories in America, Asia, and Africa) by the Portuguese Constitution of 1822. In that same year, Brazil had achieved independence. In economic terms, Brazil had been Portugal's most valuable possession, and it was only after its loss that the Portuguese turned their attention to the African territories, Angola in particular. During the nineteenth century, Portugal's attempts to subjugate and colonize the Angolan people proved a long, drawn-out process, during which African resistance was countered with extreme brutality. By the middle of the century, Portuguese authority extended little further than a narrow, sparsely populated coastal area with an average width of 80–130 km and fluid borders with the inland region. In addition to this area was a scattering of Portuguese strategic inland garrisons. The trade routes leading deep into the country's interior were controlled by the Luso-African merchants, who cooperated closely with the military, administrative, and ecclesiastical institutions of the Portuguese colonizers.[4]

Pressured by the European powers to conquer the African continent and exploit its raw materials, the Portuguese government finally determined to subjugate once and for all the territory of Angola, which it was granted under the terms of the Berlin Conference of 1885. Angola was now to become the "heart of the Portuguese Empire."[5] Alongside the Luso-Africans and a small number of Portuguese inhabitants, Angola had an extremely heterogeneous African population, which was split into different communities according to language, culture, and ethnicity. During the twentieth century, Angola's colonial society developed along three regional axes, depending on where the three main (but themselves in no way homogenous) population groups had settled. These three groups constituted approximately three-quarters of the Angolan population: the Ovimbundu, the mainly Umbundu-speaking people of the southern-central highlands; the Mbundu, who spoke mainly Kimbundu and who had settled in the northern-central region; and the Bakongo of the northwest, whose main language was Ki-Kongo. These areas had been divided up by missionaries and the colonial authorities.[6] The *mestiço* class of the "old" Luso-African elite emerged from the Mbundu, who lived in the hinterland of Luanda, the limited zone controlled before the end of the nineteenth century by the Portuguese. The Portuguese had also managed to assert their influence early on over sections of the Ovimbundu from the hinterland of today's Benguela. From the sixteenth century, the area had developed close trade and exchange links with Brazil. The centuries of relations and cultural links with the Portuguese meant that in the twentieth century members from both the Mbundu and the Ovimbundu—but primarily the Mbundu—had privileged access to education and better prospects within colonial society. Over the course of the twentieth century, such class structures and hierarchies would go on to create complex identities and conflicts among the nonwhite elite.[7]

In the nineteenth century, the Luso-African elite living in the coastal cities of Luanda and Benguela were the main group exercising political authority and military control over the hinterland population (albeit on behalf of the colonizers). In the twentieth century, however, Portugal imposed the principle of direct rule.[8] With the exception of the King of Kongo, Portugal did not recognize traditional African leaders, and they restricted the power of local chiefs (*sobas*) to enforcing colonial policies at the village level. Only those loyal to the colonial government were allowed to maintain their authority. Until the end of the colonial period, the chiefs served as a stabilizing factor within the system, for example by mediating between the colonizers and the rural population or by recruiting forced laborers.[9] Even Portuguese colonial officials at the very bottom of the administrative system were granted greater power than the highest traditional chiefs.[10] In some regions, two power systems coexisted until the end

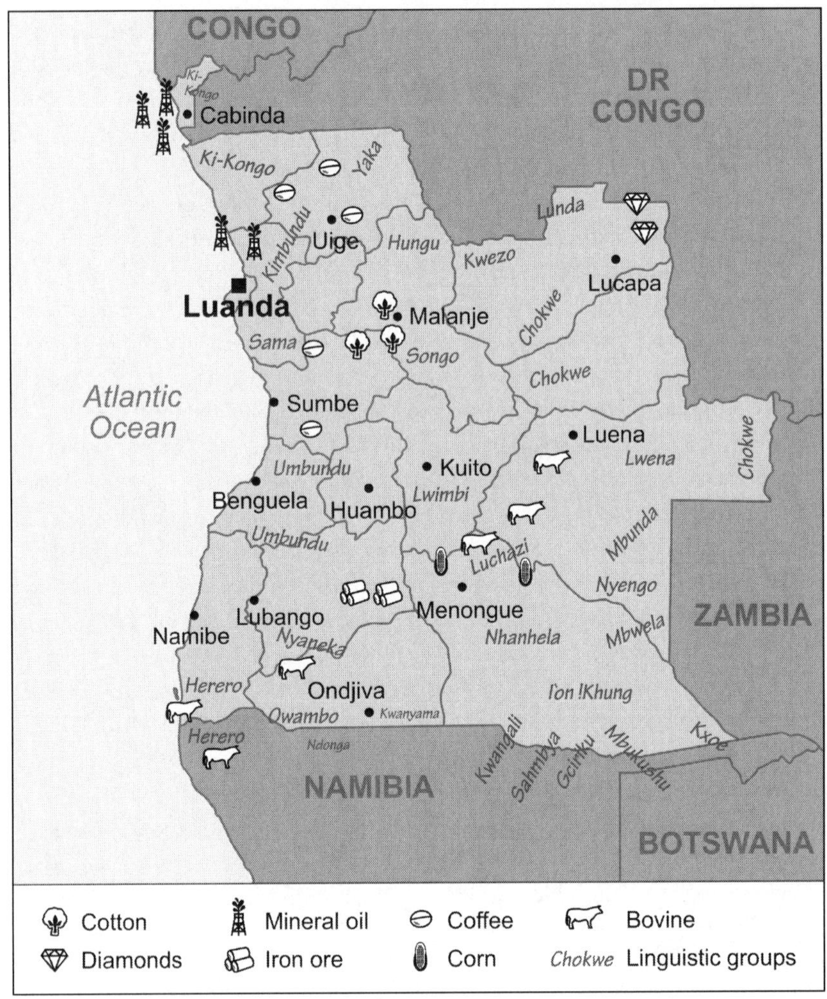

Angola in the twentieth century: linguistic groups, raw materials, and agricultural production (map by Daniel Giere)

of the colonial period, and the success of attempts to enforce effective colonial authority varied considerably depending on the region and locality.

Until 1910, when Portugal's constitutional monarchy was overthrown and replaced by the republic, fewer than 12,000 Portuguese lived in Angola. The majority of them were soldiers, merchants, missionaries, and convicts rather than settlers who farmed the land.[11] Systematic attempts by the new republican government to settle Angola met initially with little success. Those who did emigrate came almost exclusively from the uneducated, lower Portuguese classes. In general the Portuguese showed little initiative when it came to settling and working the land, and they left the hard physical labor to the Africans. This arrangement was reinforced by colonial legislation and measures introduced by the colonizers to coerce Africans into labor.[12] It was not until the 1930s that the authoritarian regime of António de Oliveira Salazar's Estado Novo established the political and administrative framework needed for systematic settlement and more efficient exploitation of Angola's resources. The Colonial Act of 1930 turned Portugal's "overseas possessions" into Portuguese provinces, thereby making them an integral part of the Portuguese nation.[13] The Colonial Act stated, "it is in keeping with the organic nature of the Portuguese nation to fulfill its historical function of possessing and colonizing overseas territories and civilizing the native populations thereof."[14] The colonization of African territories became synonymous with a cultural mission, a "crusade of religious and humanitarian nature" to spread "harmony" among the people. The almost spiritual vision of creating a universal, multiracial Portuguese people later became known as "Lusotropicalism." Backed by the Catholic church, the Portuguese government was able to use this quasi-religious mission to conceal the economic interest at the heart of its Africa policy.[15]

Following World War II, Angola developed economically into an extremely profitable colony, in which large natural resources such as diamonds, copper, and iron ore were discovered. Another profitable asset was its cash crops for the global market, primarily coffee, but also cotton, sugar, sisal, and tropical wood.[16] The economic upturn of Angola after World War II attracted many Portuguese settlers. In the 1950s and 1960s the settlement policy was therefore much more successful than before, particularly because it was state funded and accompanied by improvements in infrastructure. Angola became a white settlers' colony. There had, however, been little change in the type of settlers since the beginning of the century. They continued to be the poor farmers and members of the underclasses with very low levels of education. Although the colonial government introduced costly settlement programs in an attempt to motivate settlers to move to rural areas, they tended to gravitate to the larger coastal towns and cities of Benguela, Lobito, and above all Luanda, or to the moderate climatic zones of the highlands (for example Huambo or Lubango).[17] In rural areas, the Salazar government's policies to establish plantation farming and settlement nevertheless led to African farmers being driven from their fertile lands and to a drastic reduction in subsistence farming. Competition for land grew, and racialist criteria were used to determine ownership.[18]

The large numbers of white settlers who moved to Angola claiming power and property under Estado Novo's settlement policy fostered a growing racism against the African and *mestiço* population. As early as 1914, the then Angolan High Commissioner, José Norton de Matos, had initiated a "civilization policy" intended to create a multiracial society. He had therefore divided the population of Angola into a five-tiered hierarchy, which represented in principle a pragmatic compromise between racial segregation and assimilation.[19] The bottom tier comprised 99 percent of the African population, the so-called *indígenas*. They had virtually no rights and were generally at the mercy of the colonizers' coercive measures. The *indígena* status was retained after World War II, as was a repressive system of forced labor for paltry remuneration.

Only a small minority of blacks and *mestiços* had gained access to white Portuguese society through cultural assimilation. Prerequisites for achieving *assimilado* status were the ability to speak Portuguese, the wearing of European dress, "appropriate" social conduct, a place of permanent residence, and paid employment.[20] Together with the increased presence of white settlers, who had come to the colonies in search of a better life, the result of creating this indigenous Europeanized class was intense economic competition between blacks and whites: the so-called *assimilados* continued to be exposed to racial discrimination, and measures forcing *indígenas* into labor strengthened white control over the economy at all levels and protected white privilege. Blacks and *mestiços* who had achieved *assimilado* status and who had striven to find employment in the town or built up small urban businesses were forced to surrender their modest livelihoods to the whites, even if they were better qualified.[21] These were people who had struggled and succeeded in escaping the misery and forced labor of rural communities. Such racially motivated economic discrimination and exclusion provided the main reason for the emergence of an urban, anti-colonial resistance movement in the 1950s.

The *assimilado* class comprised no more than around 38,000 blacks and approximately 45,000 *mestiços*—only 1 percent of the Angolan population, which totaled approximately six million in the 1960s. This notwithstanding, both the African and *mestiço assimilados* were to play a crucial role in the development of Angola's urban anti-colonial movements.[22]

Around 1960, approximately 90 percent of Angola's black population still lived in rural areas. They either worked as laborers on the plantations and the Portuguese-owned farms, or they eked out a living in small villages by subsistence farming, herding livestock, and raising cattle. The remaining 10 percent lived partly in the provincial capitals such as Nova Lisboa (Huambo) and Benguela, but mainly in the Angolan capital (Luanda).[23] Shortly before independence, more than 300,000 Portuguese settlers were living in Angola, and approximately 50,000 soldiers were stationed there. Thus Angola had become the second largest settler colony in sub-Saharan Africa after South Africa.[24]

In the countryside, the settlers appropriated the most fertile land, and the colonial government enforced the expansion of monocultures for the export economy. In the 1950s, Angola's economic prosperity was based mainly on growing coffee for the world market. Again the settlers competed with African coffee growers. When the settlers did not run the coffee plantations themselves, they left the high-risk business of cultivation to the Africans and took over the more profitable task of marketing and transporting the beans. This led to racially loaded competition in rural areas, which gave rise to another strand of the anti-colonial movement.[25]

The Colonial War and Anti-Colonial Movements

A turning point in the political and economic future of the Portuguese settler colony was reached in 1961. That year numerous anti-colonial uprisings culminated in a colonial war. The anti-colonial struggle was triggered internally by a combination of factors: the settlers' constant pressure on the African population to submit to forced labor; economic exploitation by the Portuguese metropole; and racial, cultural, and economic discrimination against the African population. External factors were also at play, including the decolonization of most African colonies held by France, the United Kingdom, and Belgium between 1957 and 1960. The Angolan rebels were also spurred on by two other events: the hasty decolonization of the neighboring Belgian Congo after a spontaneous uprising in 1960, and the Sharpeville massacre in South Africa, when apartheid police shot and killed over sixty demonstrators.[26]

Angola's colonial war lasted from 1961 to 1974. Portugal's unwillingness to grant its African territories independence made it the longest colonial war across the continent. After Guinea-Bissau and Mozambique, Angola was the last Portuguese colony in Africa to gain independence. This was because the colonies that Portugal had declared "overseas provinces" in 1951 had experienced an economic boom after World War II. Angola in particular had developed into an essential part of the Portuguese economy, as its economy developed spectacularly during the colonial war. In order to stifle rebellion, the colonizers modernized the entire infrastructure of Angola and, in contrast to their earlier economic policy, brought greater foreign investment to the country to finance the war. This in turn quickened the pace of economic development. It was unsurprising that they were determined to retain their colonial territories at all costs.[27]

At the beginning of 1961 uprisings sprang up in various parts of Angola. On 4 February, rebels attacked a prison of the Portuguese Polícia Internacional e de Defesa do Estado (PIDE, International Police for the Defense of the State) in Luanda, and in March they launched an offensive against white coffee growers in the coffee plantations in the northwest provinces. The colonial authorities reacted with a brutality that cost the lives of tens of thousands of Africans, and the Angolan uprisings mutated into a persistent guerrilla war, whose momentum reached Guinea-Bissau and Mozambique. The national pride of both the Salazar regime and the white settlers took a further blow when in December 1961 the Portuguese colony of Goa was annexed by the Indian Union. This event led to even greater repression of the anti-colonial insurrections.

By the end of 1961, Portugal, one of the poorest countries in Europe at that time, was involved in a colonial war that was being played out on three different fronts in Africa: in Angola, Mozambique, and Guinea-Bissau. This war considerably weakened the governments of Salazar and his successor, Marcelo Caetano (1968–1974). On 25 April 1974, Caetano's government was finally toppled. The coup d'état was led by a small group of officers who had fought in the colonial wars and were convinced that a political rather than military solution was needed in Angola. On the very day of the coup, the officers, who had united to form the Movimento das Forças Armadas (MFA, Movement of the Armed Forces, Portugal), declared as one of their priorities decolonizing the "overseas provinces." In July, the provisional government of Portugal signed a ceasefire with the independence movements.[28]

The insurrections in Angola in 1961 were led by the urban, "modern" elite, many of whom where *assimilados*. As a result of their marginalization, they had formed cultural organizations in the towns and cities from which the anti-colonial resistance issued. Another movement in the anti-colonial struggle developed from the distress of workers in the coffee plantations of the northwest. Initially these workers demanded higher wages and better working conditions. Neither the urban nor the rural revolts, however, were planned long in advance, even though both the MPLA and FNLA later claimed to have been the instigators.[29] In particular, the so-called indigenous Angolans often lacked traditional chiefs who would have been able to develop alternatives to colonial policy. After 1961, three resistance movements emerged during the colonial war. Each of these three movements distanced itself from the other on a personal, socio-cultural and ideological level; each also had its own regional basis. The result was bitter fighting between the movements.

The relationships and distance between the Luso-African, African, and "assimilated" elites of Angola had an impact on tendencies within the anti-colonial movements. Initially, however, only two groups were responsible for the emergence of these movements: the Luso-African "Creoles" and the Bakongo elites.[30] The sociologist Christine Messiant included the "Creoles" among the "old" *assimilados*. They originated from Luso-African families with roots extending to the early colonial period of the seventeenth century. Through marriage and intermingling they had learned Portuguese and adopted the

Portuguese culture and Catholic faith.[31] Despite racial discrimination, they had achieved a solid status within white, urban society. They were joined by the "new" *assimilados*, who had gained their social standing only after World War II as a result of colonial assimilation policies, which allowed them to acquire education and professions, often through their affiliations with (Protestant) Christian denominations. These "new" *assimilados* regarded themselves as African and did not feel accepted by the "old" Creole elite. They therefore set themselves apart. This was a result of the Protestant missionary work in Angola of Baptists, Methodists, and Presbyterians, who were considerably more accommodating to African languages and culture than the Catholic Church.[32] To some extent, these three Protestant churches were in competition with each other, and each linked up with one of the three ethnic/linguistic groups (and thereby effectively joined with one of the three anti-colonial movements). As these churches were not established in Portugal but came from other European countries and the United States, they had little interest in "civilizing" in the manner that was common in Portugal and the Catholic Church. The MPLA was born of a combination of the urban elites of the "old" (Catholic) Luso-African *assimilados*, the "new" *assimilados*, the Mbundus from the hinterlands of Luanda, and the Methodist Church.

The second ethnic group to provide an anti-colonial movement with recruits was the Bakongo. Historically, they were indeed the first group to come into close contact with the Portuguese during the Christianization of the Kongo Kingdom in the sixteenth century. In 1960, however, the Bakongo of Angola's northwest had been marginalized in favor of the other two main African ethnic groups, the Mbundu and Ovimbundu. This was partly because thousands of them had been taken as slaves to work on the sugarcane and cocoa plantations of São Tomé during the nineteenth century. At the beginning of the twentieth century, this policy of forced labor had already led to an uprising, the quelling of which also targeted the Protestant missions in the area. The reprisals led to a mass exodus of the population into what was then the Belgian Congo. This in turn resulted in the neglect of the entire northwest region by the Portuguese colonizers.[33] The modern Bakongo elites emerged in Congolese exile and were therefore socialized in a completely different colonial society. Their cultural and economic center was not Luanda, but Léopoldville (today Kinshasa), where they were in part very successful members of the urban private economy. Their socialization in exile meant that they maintained their Bakongo and African identity, but they were still conscious of their Kongo Kingdom background and were influenced by Baptist missionizing.[34] Despite living in exile, they too were instrumental in the emergence of one of the anti-colonial movements, which later became the FNLA.

In the mid-1960s, UNITA was the third anti-colonial movement to surface from ethnic groups socialized under different cultural, social, and religious parameters within white colonial society. The political, cultural, and social areas of conflict that UNITA was able to draw upon differed from its counterparts, and it gained a regional base of political support among the Ovimbundu of the southern-central highlands.

Despite all their differences, all three movements had in common authoritarian, strong leadership and the formation of armed guerrilla organizations. Although the development of all three movements is outlined below, the emphasis is on the distinguishing political, social, and cultural features of the MPLA, since it was the MPLA who went on to govern Angola after independence and to enter into a transatlantic cooperative relationship with the Cuban revolutionary government.

Although there are many publications dealing with Angola's colonial war and the origins of the anti-colonial movements, knowledge of how they came into being is still relatively fragmented. One of the best and most comprehensive accounts remains the two-volume work of the US historian John Marcum, *The Angolan Revolution*, even though the author had little access to internal documents when he was composing it.[35] An annotated study by Ronald Chilcote containing early documents of the anti-colonial movements complements Marcum's analyses.[36] Franz-Wilhelm Heimer and Christine Messiant also published sociological studies analyzing the transition from colonial society to independence and the origins of anti-colonial resistance.[37] David Birmingham focused on the history of the colonial period and Angola's independence from a transregional perspective.[38] Further historical, sociological, and political studies appeared in the 1970s, many of which were politically motivated and, in the wake of Angola's independence, gave an MPLA-biased interpretation.

The story behind the origins of the MPLA remains a controversial topic even today, although the Congolese historian Jean-Michel Mabeko Tali has done much to clarify it through his research based on a wide range of internal documents and interviews. In his *Dissidências e poder de estado: O MPLA perante si próprio*, Mabeko Tali, the adopted son of one of the MPLA's most prominent politicians, Lúcio Lara, reached some very sobering conclusions regarding the organization's history.[39] In 1997, the Angolan historian and journalist Carlos Pacheco had already published a polemical work on the origins of the MPLA, which was also backed up by interviews with eyewitnesses and an evaluation of internal documents.[40] Two of Lúcio Lara's biological children, Paulo and Wanda, have also been studying the history of the MPLA for many years. Over the years, they have been preserving and archiving their father's documents, mainly letters, minutes of internal meetings, political manifestos, and photos.

The publication of the first volumes of Lúcio Lara's private collection of documents sheds considerable light on the early MPLA.[41]

There is no comparable research on the historical origins of UNITA or the FNLA. The most comprehensive publication on the history of UNITA remains the biography of Jonas Savimbi, which was written by the British journalist Fred Bridgland and is biased in favor of UNITA.[42] In the year 2000, the US historian Linda Heywood presented a detailed study on the cultural roots and identity of the Ovimbundu people in the nineteenth and twentieth centuries. It also mentions their links with UNITA.[43]

The Movimento Popular de Libertação de Angola (MPLA)

The MPLA shared its internationalist tendencies and radical African nationalism with the other two Marxist-orientated independence movements in Portugal's African colonies, Partido Africano da Independência da Guiné e Cabo Verde (PAIGC, African Party of the Independence of Guinea and Cape Verde) and Frente da Libertação de Moçambique (FRELIMO, The Mozambique Liberation Front), and it engaged closely with their leaders, Amílcar Cabral and Marcelino dos Santos. Although not yet fully substantiated, it is now thought that the MPLA was founded in 1960.[44] The MPLA itself maintains that it formed in Luanda as early as 1956 as an umbrella organization for various cultural, intellectual, and Marxist groups, including the Partido Comunista Angolano (PCA, Angolan Communist Party), which had been in existence since the 1940s. This insistence on the founding date is of symbolic importance because it affords the MPLA greater legitimacy as the "first" freedom movement before the FNLA and UNITA, which were founded in 1962 and 1966, respectively. Proof of the MPLA's early formation is provided in a political manifesto that in December 1956 called for a "Movimento Popular de Libertação de Angola," a broad front against Portuguese colonialism.[45] It is not within the scope of this work to discuss whether this manifesto really did represent the foundation of the MPLA.

The founding members of the MPLA were mostly intellectuals and students recruited from the ranks of the "old" and "new" elites of Africans (Agostinho Neto), Luso-Africans (Viriato da Cruz and Mario de Andrade were *mestiços*), and *assimilados*, along with several white members. Since the end of the 1940s, members of the Luso-African and African elites from the Portuguese overseas territories of Angola, Mozambique, Cape Verde, and Guinea-Bissau had had the opportunity of studying in the city of Lisbon. Many of these students were involved in activities against the Salazar government. They joined the Centro de Estudos Africanos, which was set up in 1951, and through the Casa dos

Estudantes do Império engaged in the struggle for liberation from Portuguese colonial rule. Under the repressive Portuguese regime, such activity was fraught with difficulty and led to frequent arrests and imprisonment. Nevertheless, the meetings and discussions between students, literary figures, and intellectuals were vital for the development of anti-colonial resistance. The main advocates included the Cape Verdean Amilcar Cabral; the Angolans Mario de Andrade, Viriato da Cruz, and Agostinho Neto; and Marcelino dos Santos from Mozambique.[46]

Some of them were influenced by the Négritude movement, which had developed in Francophone Africa and the Caribbean, and which since the 1930s had given expression to a predominantly literary vision of Africa as a proud, self-determining continent. They aligned themselves with writers such as Léopold Sedar Senghor from Senegal, Aimé Césaire from Guadeloupe, and the Afro-Cuban Nicolás Guillén. Guillén and Neto both defined themselves as "Afro-Latin" poets and thereby shared a common identity. The personal and artistic friendship that developed between them in the 1960s fostered ties between the Cuban government and the MPLA,[47] and it was possibly the intellectual source of the concept of an "Afro-Latin American nation," which the Cuban leader Fidel Castro invoked in 1975 to justify Cuban engagement in Angola and put it into a transatlantic context.

Prevailing global, African, and European influences provided ideological orientation to the anti-colonial movements in the Portuguese colonies. Politically, they aligned themselves with the pan-Africanism expounded among others by W. E. B. DuBois and propagated by numerous African politicians from very diverse independence movements.[48] European ideologies also proved highly attractive, particularly Marxism and anti-imperialism, but so did the ideals of Christian humanism. The various currents of African socialism and radical nationalism in the 1950s and 1960s also influenced the development of these movements. The determining factor for the MPLA's political ideology seemed, however, to have been its close links to the Communist Party of Portugal and the relationship thereby forged with the Soviet leadership.[49] But without a doubt it was the relentless position of the Portuguese government toward the anti-colonial movements and their exponents that had a particularly radicalizing effect.[50]

The background of the MPLA's founding members was partly reflected in their distinct antitribal and antiracist nationalist stance.[51] Their demands were "nationalist" in the sense that they appealed to the entire Angolan population and all inhabitants of the colonial territory, irrespective of their language, culture, and identity.[52] Their rhetoric was coined in Marxist and anti-imperialist terminology; their rudimentary analyses of Angolan colonial society, however, reflected the social categories of modern, secular Western and Eastern European societies rather than the social and cultural reality of Angola.

The MPLA's criticism targeted not only Portuguese colonial rule but also the social effects of capitalism and imperialism in general.[53] In an Angolan context, this Marxist social critique gave the MPLA the advantage of creating a united front by defining the population according to their productive roles rather than their ethnicity. According to the sociologist Franz-Wilhelm Heimer, the MPLA was always a more radical opponent of the capitalist social systems than were its rival groups.[54] The British historian David Birmingham commented critically in 1992 that the Angolan nationalism of the 1960s was essentially the concern of intellectuals living in exile, who had yet to find any real support among the Angolan people.[55]

Combined with the corresponding radical rhetoric, the MPLA's nationalist, antiracist, anti-imperialist, and internationally oriented program fulfilled all the ideological expectations of international, anti-colonial, and anti-imperialist movements and their supporters in European cities; such public declarations were part of the zeitgeist.[56] The MPLA developed at a time in which anti-colonial and national liberation movements throughout the three continents of Asia, Africa, and Latin America were commanding global attention through their radicalism and international networking. The revolution in Cuba was part of this process. In 1955, the Afro-Asian Conference in Bandung, Indonesia, brought together state leaders and representatives of anti-colonial movements who felt marginalized by Eastern and Western alliance systems. In 1957, government representatives and anti-colonial movements met in Cairo for the same reason. On both occasions, there was a demand for an end to colonialism and racism and for equality with the (former) colonial powers. It is therefore unsurprising that the MPLA attracted the attention of Cuban revolutionaries and came to be regarded as a potential ally of the Cuban revolutionary cause.

Within Angola it was only during the 1960s that the MPLA was able to establish a base of political support among both the urban population of Luanda and in the Mbundu region. These were the areas where the assimilation policy of the Portuguese colonial government had left its deepest marks and where over the centuries contact between Africans and Portuguese had been particularly intense. The Mbundu region corresponds approximately to the area that came under the influence of the Kingdom of Ndongo in the sixteenth century. From the arrival of the Portuguese in 1483 until its dissolution in 1630,[57] the Kingdom of Ndongo was the arena of intensive exchanges with conquerors, missionaries, colonizers, and slave traders. The rival anti-colonial movements therefore maintained that the MPLA was an organization of former collaborators with the colonizers. The MPLA, on the other hand, saw itself as acting within the tradition of the *ngola*, the ruler of the Kingdom of Ndongo, after whom Angola had been named, and it particularly played on the legendary Queen Njinga, whom it glorified as a "resistance fighter" against the Portuguese colonizers.[58] Njinga's resistance to the colonizers remains one of the creation myths of the MPLA today, which explains why it was very selective in its interpretation of historical events and careful in the construction of this tradition. The MPLA's narrative conveniently ignores that Njinga's undoubtedly self-confident political strategy against the Portuguese conquerors also led to her active participation in the slave trade and her conversion to Catholicism.[59]

The history of the MPLA in the 1960s is defined by its struggle for political survival against the FNLA and UNITA, and by its many internal factions and schisms. The physical distance between the exiled leadership and its supporters within Angola was another ongoing problem.[60] Rather than by democratic consensus, the frequent tensions between individual leaders and the various political wings of the organization were resolved by purges and expulsions. In 1962, after the expulsion of his internal rival Viriato da Cruz, Agostinho Neto (1927–1979), the son of a Methodist preacher, became the leader of the organization. He was both a writer and doctor, and his political activities and anticolonial poetry had already earned him international renown.[61] A further challenge for the MPLA was the constant search for a safe haven outside Angola, from which it could orchestrate its activities. For a while, its headquarters were in Congo-Brazzaville. From here the MPLA was able to launch military offensives in the Angolan enclave of Cabinda, which was surrounded by Congo-Brazzaville. But the lack of a common border with Angola was an obstacle to the activities of the fledgling guerrilla organization. Moreover, rival movements were operating in the same area, in particular the FNLA, which fought the MPLA from its base in Léopoldville (Kinshasa).

The MPLA had similar difficulties establishing a base in the neighboring country to the east, Zambia, which had attained independence in 1964. Again the location was far from the economic and political center of the colony. Furthermore, the government of Zambia had no wish to see the Benguela railway obstructed by military activity, as this was its only link to the Atlantic and the only way of guaranteeing shipments of Zambian refined copper.[62] The rivaling UNITA, founded in 1966, was also operating in this area and was not averse to collaborating with the Portuguese military in order to liquidate the MPLA. In the east of Angola it was also becoming evident that in practice the MPLA's policies deviated from their humanist claims: the most recent research by the anthropologist Inge Brinkmann shows that the MPLA leaders terrorized the civilian population of east Angola into cooperating, and they accused suspected "traitors" of "witchcraft" and executed them.[63] Previously, such accusations had only been leveled against UNITA. Although Brinkmann did not analyze whether these were isolated incidents or underlying strategies, her findings emphasize that the progressive rhetoric of the MPLA does not automatically indicate moral superiority over the other movements.

On the international stage, the MPLA representatives kept their distance from potential international allies and did not wish to adhere politically to either of the socialist superpowers, China or the Soviet Union. Among the Eastern-Bloc countries, Yugoslavia seems to have been the only constant companion to the MPLA in the early 1960s. The Yugoslav head of state, Josip Broz Tito, supported several African liberation movements and was at the forefront of the Non-Aligned Movement (NAM), founded in 1961. Owing to his policy of retaining sovereignty within the Soviet sphere of influence, Tito was particularly highly regarded by Neto as a political partner, since he too was renowned for his political independence.[64]

The desire to remain politically independent from the socialist superpowers also encouraged the mutual friendship between the Cuban leadership and the MPLA. After the 1959 revolution, contact between the Cubans and representatives of the MPLA in Portuguese exile had been rather sporadic. But in 1960, their relationship was formally recognized at the Cuban embassy in Conakry (Guinea). The Cuban government supported the MPLA between 1962 and 1964 by offering scholarships to Angolan students, who were also offered training in guerrilla warfare during their stay in Cuba.[65] From the mid-1960s, the political and military links were temporarily intensified by the presence of a Cuban expedition corps led by Ernesto "Che" Guevara, which trained the guerrilla units of the MPLA. Ten years later, this shared episode was to become the starting point for transatlantic political and military relations between Cuba and Angola. In spring 1975, only a few months before independence, Agostinho Neto requested financial, material, and military support from the Cuban government in order to combat the rival movements. In October 1975, the Cuban government reacted by dispatching a large contingent of troops, with whose help the MPLA was able to assert its authority over the other anti-colonial movements and lead Angola on its own into independence on 11 November.

The Frente Nacional para a Libertação de Angola (FNLA)

The second anti-colonial movement had its roots in the farming community and, as already mentioned, developed among the Bakongo elites in the northern highlands of Angola, the region of the old Kongo Kingdom.[66] This movement, which adopted the name FNLA in 1962, was the MPLA's largest and most powerful rival until Angolan independence. It started out in 1957 as the regional movement União das Populações do Norte de Angola (UPNA, Union of Peoples of Northern Angola). The political nationalism of what later became known as the FNLA was more moderate than the MPLA. The FNLA's insistence on an African identity distinct from the white population was, however, far more radical. The peasant revolts in northwest Angola were triggered in 1961 by the repression exercised by the Portuguese colonizers and the brutal confiscation of land in the coffee-growing regions of north Angola. The independence of Belgian Congo also played its part. Anti-colonial resistance was encouraged by the Baptist church and regional cross-border family networks. In comparison with the MPLA, the UPNA (after 1958, the União das Populações de Angola [UPA, Union of Angolan Peoples]) had the considerable advantage of being close to its base. This proximity allowed it to gather the support of both the Bakongo people, who had fled to Belgian Congo at the beginning of the twentieth century, and the approximately 300,000 refugees who had escaped the reprisals of the 1961 insurrection and gone to the now independent Republic of the Congo (Léopoldville), later to become Zaire.[67]

There were many fundamental differences between the FNLA and the MPLA, including their regional bases, the constitution of their supporters, and their ideologies. The FNLA aligned itself with the tradition of the Kongo Kingdom and resistance to the colonization of northwest Angola between 1913 and 1915. Its messianic religious roots were reflected in its language, its contacts, and a shared constructed (Bakongo) identity. Of equal importance were the many years its members and leaders had spent living in exile.[68] One of the core features of the Bakongo identity, which was instrumentalized by the FNLA in the anti-colonial struggle, was its disassociation from the Portuguese colonizers. Another core feature, however, was its distrust of the urban Luso-African elites, who had come together to form the MPLA.[69] The encounter between the MPLA and the UPA in Léopoldville after the suppression of the 1961 revolts seemed to be decisive in creating lasting division in the Angolan nationalist movement. In the eyes of the UPA leadership, the Creole and *mestiço* "pseudo-Marxists"—as they called the MPLA—were not authentic representatives of Africa. From the MPLA's point of view, the UPA's members were "tribalists" and "reactionary racists."[70] The political and ideological polarity of the Cold War period completed the division: unlike the MPLA, the UPA opted for capitalist, pro-West development, even though it was at this point in time receiving military and logistical support from the Chinese government, and did so for several years. Around the mid-1960s, its political stance earned it the covert support of the US government, channeled through the CIA.

By changing its name in 1962 to the FNLA, the movement signaled its claim to represent the entire Angolan nation. Initially, the FNLA was indeed far more successful in its endeavors than the MPLA. In 1962 it founded the Governo Revolucionário de Angola no Exilio (GRAE, Revolutionary Government of Angola in Exile) in Zaire and made Holden Roberto (1923–2007) its president and Jonas Savimbi (1934–2002) its foreign minister. GRAE was recognized by the Organization of African Unity (OAU) as the legitimate representative of Angola. The failure of the MPLA to become part of this government-in-exile seems to have had more to do with personal quarrels and Roberto's autocratic leadership style than the aforementioned political and cultural differences. The bitter political and military rivalry between the FNLA and MPLA continued unabated.[71] In 1964, the foreign minister, Jonas Savimbi, left the government-in-exile—likewise owing to personal differences with Roberto—to join a group of supporters from the FNLA and prepare the way for a separate independence movement, which later became known as UNITA.[72] Roberto and the FNLA also received the support of the president of Zaire, Joseph Mobuto, who came to power in 1966. This support, however, led to the organization becoming dependent on Mobutu's own, ambitious power politics, which involved turning Zaire into a regional hegemony. The fact that the FNLA was not able to formulate an independent, cohesive, sociopolitical alternative that could be applied to the whole of Angola goes a long way toward explaining why in 1968 the OAU withdrew its recognition of the FNLA-led government-in-exile as the legitimate representative of Angolan anti-colonialism.[73]

By the time the Portuguese government fell during the Carnation Revolution in April 1974, the FNLA was too weak to play any decisive role in the independence process. In autumn 1974, an FNLA military offensive had also led to the brutal forced return of 60,000 Ovimbundu coffee pickers to the southern-central highlands of Angola.[74] The incident led to a loss of support for the FNLA among the Angolan people and put further pressure on the already difficult relations between the independence movements. This was at a time when cooperation to ensure a peaceful transition to independence would have been imperative.

The União Nacional para a Independência Total de Angola (UNITA)

Five years after the outbreak of the colonial war, the third anti-colonial movement appeared on the scene. In opposition to the FNLA and MPLA, the former FNLA activist Jonas Savimbi, who had studied in Switzerland with the support of the Presbyterian church, founded UNITA in the east of Angola in March 1966. Initially UNITA strove for a pan-Angolan solution, a unification of all freedom fighters on the basis of anti-colonialism, anti-imperialism, and armed struggle. Following Maoist doctrine, UNITA later attempted to organize the peasants.[75] Under difficult conditions and with just a little help from the Chinese government, UNITA maintained military operations in east Angola and became a direct rival of the MPLA.

It was not until the beginning of the 1970s that UNITA began to concentrate on organizing the Ovimbundu people, from Savimbi's home region of the southern-central highlands. With around two million Umbundu speakers, they made up approximately 35 percent of the total Angolan population. The Ovimbundu did not constitute an "ethnic group" until the end of the nineteenth century, when their language was standardized by Protestant missionaries and colonial authorities.[76] The 1902 Mbailundu war, during which the southern highlands were finally conquered by the colonizers, destroyed the structures of around thirty small, independent kingdoms in the Angolan highlands. The construction of the Benguela railway took away the livelihoods of the traditional Ovimbundu caravan merchants and long-distance cargo carriers. Many had to go and work as coffee pickers in the northwest, leaving the Portuguese settlers to take over the fertile highlands.[77] A movement like UNITA, which promised to return lost lands, was therefore very welcome. Furthermore, after the outbreak of the colonial war, there was a strong military presence in the highlands to protect the white settlers. In order to repress revolt some of the African population had been forced to move to garrisoned villages, where they were coerced into joining special forces of the colonial government.[78] When UNITA moved its activities to these regions after the 1974 ceasefire and campaigned for support, it was welcomed with open arms. UNITA recruited the majority of its supporters from the villages and small towns and could thus call upon the support of Protestant networks.[79]

UNITA's carefully constructed identity as the legitimate representative of the rural, black, "authentic" Africa fell on fertile ground. Many Angolans saw independence as liberation from the white masters, and somehow they felt that the process was incomplete because it was led by the urban, Luso-African elites represented by the MPLA. The distrust between Africans, *assimilados*, and *mestiços* ran deep. In the hierarchy of Angolan colonial society, *assimilados* and *mestiços* had always occupied an intermediate position between the blacks and whites.[80] Although they were never of equal status, they often had privileged access to education and professions normally reserved for whites. They were therefore regarded by the black population with suspicion. When the Portuguese fell from power, many Africans feared that the Luso-Africans, *mestiços*, and *assimilados* would step into Portugal's shoes and take over in postcolonial society at the expense of the African population. As time would tell, this fear was not completely unfounded.

Notwithstanding its influence among the Ovimbundu, UNITA was a controversial organization, and for several reasons it lost its political legitimacy after a long, relentless struggle against the authority of the MPLA government in postcolonial Angola. One reason was Savimbi's dictatorial and self-obsessed leadership, maintained by a personality cult. His legitimacy further eroded because of his unscrupulous power machinations, which as early as 1972 led him into a pact with the Portuguese army to annihilate the MPLA in east Angola.[81] Following independence, UNITA entered a political and military alliance with the South African apartheid regime. And starting in the 1980s, it received crucial financial support and military equipment from Ronald Reagan's administration, which attempted to arm UNITA as a "bulwark of anti-communism" against the MPLA.

With the assistance of the South African regime, by the end of the 1970s UNITA had built up a powerful militia able to launch military offensives against the MPLA government and carry out acts of sabotage throughout the entire Angolan region. The destructive activities of UNITA did not spare the civilian population, and the attacks became a long-term obstacle to establishing an independent state and creating infrastructure. Not even Cuba's military support for the MPLA and the presence of thousands of civil aid workers could keep UNITA in check or prevent its culture of violence from permeating Angolan society. However, it is important to note that the MPLA government also gained an advantage from having UNITA as an opponent: the more UNITA pursued civil war and perpetrated acts of terror against civilians, the greater the government's excuse for expanding the army, buying weapons, and spending state funds on war. Savimbi's policies and the war UNITA waged against the MPLA increased the schism between the postcolonial state and its people, particularly the supporters of UNITA.[82]

Independence and the War for Supremacy in Angola (1975–1976)

A decisive event in the decolonization of Angola was the overthrow of the Portuguese government of Marcelo Caetano, Salazar's successor, in April 1974. The progressive military and left-wing politicians who combined to form the MFA and who took over power in Portugal after the Carnation Revolution were determined to bring the colonial wars to a quick end, and they demanded independence for the colonies Guinea-Bissau, Angola, and Mozambique. The West African Guinea-Bissau, the scene of the most dramatic defeats of Portuguese military forces during the colonial war, was granted independence as early as September 1974, under the leadership of the Marxist PAIGC. Mozambique was to follow under FRELIMO in June 1975. These regions had also experienced long and bitter colonial wars, but the rapid process of decolonization in Guinea-Bissau and Mozambique was facilitated by the dominance of only one liberation movement in each of these countries.

In Angola, however, the internal political crisis only came to a real head after the revolution in Portugal. Each leader of the three anti-colonial movements was convinced that only his movement had the legitimacy to lead Angola into independence. As the sociologist Franz-Wilhelm Heimer pointed out in his 1979 study of Angola's decolonization conflict, the social, economic, and structural visions for Angola's future could not have been more disparate: on the one hand there was the option of capitalist development, either involving or excluding the African people in political decision making; but on the other hand, there was the forthright rejection of a capitalist economy in favor of a socialist model of society.[83] Portugal's right wing and the Portuguese settlers were united in their anti-communism and therefore supported the FNLA and UNITA. The situation became even more complex through the polarized foreign support given to the three liberation movements within the context of the Cold War.

At the same time as having to deal with decolonization, Portugal was itself suffering from ideological struggles between various political camps and constantly changing government constellations. Portugal's domestic situation was precarious and rendered the new government incapable of exerting the pressure necessary for the Angolan independence movements to settle their differences. In addition, the leftist military and politicians in the MFA had their favorites and were initially unable to agree on supporting the MPLA. Hopes of consensus in the Angolan decolonization process were raised in Mombasa, in January 1975, when the three movements came under pressure from the OAU to reach a strategic agreement regarding decolonization negotiations. Shortly afterward, talks began in the coastal resort of Alvor on the Algarve with the Portuguese government. Although the three delegations participated as rivals, they managed to reach a detailed agreement on decolonization. One of the agreement's most important terms was the formation of a transitional government led by a "triumvirate," which was to include members of all three movements, Neto, Roberto, and Savimbi. Another term was that general elections were to be held before the end of October 1975 in order to elect a constitutional convention that would meet on the day of independence, fixed for 11 November 1975.[84]

In the meantime, each movement was to provide 8,000 soldiers who would form a united army. The Portuguese government undertook to provide this army with an additional 24,000 troops as an interim measure. During the transitional phase leading up to independence, the Portuguese government was represented in Angola by a high commissioner. This post was filled by Admiral Rosa Coutinho, a man who commanded considerable respect among the ranks of the new left-wing Portuguese government and who also had many years of military experience in Angola. But Coutinho, who belonged to the radical left wing of the MFA, was partisan and openly supported the MPLA, to the annoyance of the FNLA and UNITA.[85] According to David Birmingham's thesis, in the spring of 1975 the real power relationship in Angola between the three movements and the Portuguese settlers would have spoken for a coalition between the Bakongo elite in the north, the settlers, and the Protestants in the south of the country—a coalition that would have excluded the MPLA.[86] However, the prevailing power structures within the MFA after the Carnation Revolution favored the MPLA.

Shortly before the end of Portuguese colonial power, the MPLA found itself in a position that was precarious, both militarily and politically. Neto did his best to consolidate the organization under his control, but his authoritarian leadership style was controversial. In 1972, a grassroots attempt to democratize the MPLA's structures and politicize the members failed and led to the Eastern Revolt.[87] One consequence of this infighting was the formation of a splinter group (under the guerrilla commander Daniel Chipenda), which joined the FNLA. Several years later, another group within the MPLA criticized Neto's leadership style (the Active Revolt) and was discredited internally.[88] Neto emerged from these leadership battles even more powerful. Nevertheless, the MPLA had neither the political nor the military strength to win the power struggle in postcolonial Angola that ensued after the signing of the Alvor Agreement in January 1975.

The Alvor Agreement proved a disappointment: by March 1975 armed fighting between the three movements had already begun. The Portuguese government decided to remain neutral and instructed troops stationed in Angola not to become involved in the fighting. It was having its own difficulties dealing with domestic affairs in Portugal, and so it relied on the presence of its troops in Angola to provide sufficient stability.[89] In July 1975, the armed skirmishes between the movements developed into civil war. The MPLA had received consignments of arms from Yugoslavia and the Soviet Union, and in contravention of the Alvor Agreement, it expelled the FNLA from Luanda. Faced with escalating violence, the Portuguese settlers abandoned their homes, leaving in droves to return to Portugal, thus presenting the Portuguese government with another major problem. Soldiers from Zaire advanced from the northern Angolan border toward Luanda in order to support the FNLA, and the US government provided the FNLA with a multinational troop of mercenaries.[90]

Very few reports are able to give a satisfactory account of the complex and chaotic situation that informed events in Angola in the summer and autumn of 1975. The most impressive and vivid description of what happened during those months in Luanda was provided by the Polish journalist Ryszard Kapuscinski, one of the few foreign observers to remain there despite the fighting.[91]

In the polarized situation during the months leading up to independence, the Cuban military support for the MPLA from August onward played a decisive role in the MPLA's victory over the other two movements. The Cuban government had initially hesitated when approached by the MPLA. But eventually it consented to talks, during which the MPLA specified its needs: military training, weapons, transport, political advisors, and financial help.[92] The first Cuban military experts arrived in Luanda at the end of July 1975, under the command of General Raúl Díaz Argüelles. They were to assess the support Neto was requesting for the MPLA. After consulting with the Cuban government, Díaz Argüelles returned with military advisors to Angola to set up the first four military training camps at strategic positions in the country: in Saurimo (east Angola), in Ndalatando (in the hinterland of Luanda), in Benguela (on the Atlantic coast), and in the enclave Cabinda. The Cuban military was assisted by the Portuguese army.[93]

As Cuba was in no position, economically or militarily, to embark on a large-scale transatlantic engagement, the Cuban head of state, Castro, turned to the Soviet leader and Communist Party General Secretary, Leonid Brezhnev. He explained in person the aims of the Cuban intervention in Angola and lobbied Brezhnev for concrete military, financial, and logistical support. The Soviet leader's initial reaction was reluctance, and he turned down the Cuban request (even though the Portuguese colonies, and in particular Angola, did indeed fall within the Soviet's political and geostrategic orbit).[94] On the basis of archival documents from the KGB and the Soviet Ministry of Foreign Affairs, the Norwegian historian Odd Arne Westad argued in 2005 that in the 1970s the KGB in particular had been observing with suspicion the renewed alliance between the Nixon administration, the South African apartheid regime, and the Portuguese government. Moreover, according to Westad, the apparent military defeat of Portugal on three fronts during the African colonial wars had awakened Soviet interest in this region.[95] But at that point in time the Soviet Union was involved in nuclear disarmament negotiations and would not have wanted to jeopardize the hope of a détente in relations with the United States by becoming embroiled in Angola. Nevertheless, after some hesitation, it did supply the requested military equipment, though the reasons for its decision finally to support the Cuban military intervention remain a source of disagreement.[96] Whereas the US historian and political scientist Gleijeses regards the

Cuban government as an autonomous driving force, Westad emphasizes the crucial role of the Soviet Union. Westad's conclusions are, however, problematic in that he has only secondhand knowledge of the Cuban sources he uses to support his arguments. Gleijeses is to date the only foreign historian to have been granted access to the archives of the Cuban government, the Armed Forces, the Ministry of Foreign Affairs, and other institutions. He is also familiar with documents from the Soviet Union and the German Democratic Republic (GDR). On comparing these with Cuban files, he reached the conclusion that the Cuban government's decision to intervene in Angola was made independently of the Soviet Union, and that Cuba was indeed the driving force behind the whole operation.

Gleijeses's argument therefore seems more plausible than Westad's, and my own archival research on civil cooperation backs his conclusions. The Soviet Union may well have had a particular political and strategic interest in a friendly Angolan government and access to its raw materials and fishing grounds. And it did indeed wish to increase its influence in Africa. It also financed a large proportion of the military equipment required by Cuban forces for the operation. But it was definitely the Cubans who provided the personal commitment and the people on the ground. Moreover, the Cuban and Angolan governments agreed directly with each other to organize the civil (and probably the military) intervention. The Cuban government's decision to engage militarily in the Angolan independence war was also determined by developments in Portugal after the Carnation Revolution and the decolonization of Portuguese territories in Africa, which it followed with great interest and empathy. The Fuerzas Armadas Revolucionarias (FAR, Cuban Revolutionary Armed Forces) celebrated 1 May 1975 with a delegation of Portuguese soldiers.[97] At the end of July 1975, on the anniversary of the attack on the Moncada barracks, the Portuguese general Otelo Saraiva de Carvalho, founding member of the MFA and member of the Portuguese Revolutionary Council and the Junta of National Salvation, was received by Fidel and Raúl Castro with full military honors. Prior to this, the Cuban press had published several positive reports about Saraiva de Carvalho, who was very sympathetic to the Cuban socialist cause and who, together with other radical MFA members such as Admiral Coutinho, favored a socialist path toward the future of Portugal and Angola.[98] Because of the close contacts with the Portuguese military, the Cuban government was obviously well informed about the developments and power constellations in Angola in the spring and summer of 1975. It is probable that Saraiva de Carvalho took part in talks to ascertain the feasibility of large-scale military Cuban engagement in Angola.[99] It is also possible that his visit was the reason for Cuba finally agreeing to support Agostinho Neto and the MPLA after some initial hesitation.

It was, however, the military intervention of the South African Defence Force (SADF) that led to a critical escalation of fighting prior to the date that had been set for Angolan independence. The South African regime had initially provided UNITA with military support, giving it the capability to occupy the city of Huambo in the southern-central highlands. In October, the South African Zulu Force, an elite unit of white soldiers, marched directly into Angola, flanked by the FNLA. The South African regime felt its security acutely threatened by developments in Angola and feared the establishment of a left-wing government that would stoke resistance to apartheid. It wanted to see a "moderate," friendly government in Angola that, unlike the Marxist MPLA, would not support the armed struggle of the Namibian liberation front South West African People's Organisation (SWAPO). In the wake of the apartheid regime's direct military intervention, the prospect of Cuba's military engagement in Angola became acceptable, even to the many skeptics among African heads of state.[100]

The special units of the Cuban Ministerio del Interior (MININT, Ministry of the Interior) had been present in Angola since the beginning of September, but "Operación Carlota," involving the deployment of thousands of Cuban reservists, did not begin until early November.[101] Only the joint effort of Cuban troops and the military units of the MPLA and the Forças Armadas Populares para a Libertação de Angola (FAPLA, The People's Armed Forces for the Liberation of Angola) enabled the enclave Cabinda to stave off advancing troops from Zaire. This action prevented the South African force from reaching Luanda prior to 11 November 1975. The MPLA was thereby able to declare Angola's independence in the capital without the presence of other anti-colonial movements. The military details of these battles are not within the scope of this work. In their studies of diplomatic and military history, the historians Piero Gleijeses and Edward George provide detailed accounts and military analyses, based on material from Cuban and US archives.[102] Marina Rey Cabrera does the same from a Cuban perspective in her account of the military offensives.[103]

The result of the decolonization conflict in Angola can be summed up as follows: On 11 November, Angola was a divided country. Thanks to Cuban support, the MPLA seized control of the capital and was able to declare Angola's independence and found the socialist People's Republic of Angola. But its victory was anything but clear. It was faced with the dilemma of controlling little more than the capital on the day of independence, and it still had to conquer the rest of the country both militarily and politically. The war in which the MPLA defended its supremacy in postcolonial Angola ended provisionally on 27 March 1976, when the troops of the Zulu Force of the SADF were forced to retreat toward South Africa following the resistance of Cuban troops and the military units of the MPLA. The Cuban press created the terminology and framework of interpretation for the events unfolding in Angola: when the MPLA representative for international relations, Paulo Jorge Teixeira, visited Cuba, the Cuban press declared the "second war of liberation."[104] The Cuban military and the civil aid workers who went to Angola from 1976 onward filled the power vacuum left behind by the Portuguese colonizers when they left Angola immediately after independence. Nevertheless, the result of this "second war of liberation" proved to be a Pyrrhic victory, because what followed it was a political and military process of conquest, a war against UNITA and the South African army, which did not end after the final withdrawal of Cuban troops and civilians in the summer of 1991, but lasted until 2002.

2

Cuba, 1959–1975

Internationalism and the Angolan "Mission"

The Cuban Revolution was not only an experiment in radical economic and social transformation, but also an attempt to pursue a sovereign foreign policy within the internationally polarized Cold War constellation. At the heart of this foreign policy were Cuba's own interests and aims, which in the view of Cuba's revolutionaries were nothing less than exporting the revolution in order to internationalize it. They regarded their purpose as a revolutionary "mission." Although the revolutionaries were zealously anticlerical, their actions nevertheless paralleled those of Christian missionaries from bygone years. Like the missionaries before them, the Cuban revolutionaries laid claim to the universality of their cause, espousing their fundamental sociopolitical and moral beliefs with enormous conviction and involving the population in the process.[1] As part of this international political "mission," Angola was to become the lynchpin of Cuban foreign policy for one and a half decades from 1975 onward. This was the longest, most comprehensive and venturous foreign engagement in Cuban history. It was also an exceptional example of South-South cooperation between two formerly colonized countries. Between October 1975 and June 1991, almost half a million Cubans, soldiers and civilians alike, were stationed in Angola.

Although from a historical, geographic, and cultural perspective it was more obvious to export the revolution to Latin America, the Cuban government started to support anti-colonial and like-minded postcolonial governments in Africa from as early as the 1960s. But Cuba did not ignore the revolutionary movements in Latin America and even Asia, and its support for these causes complemented its vision of global politics. Its aim was to revolutionize Asia, Africa, and Latin America, the countries of the "Tricontinent," as they became known in the anti-imperialist jargon at that time, after the Havana Tricontinental Conference in 1966.

The following chapter sets out to explore the theory underlying these international political strategies and their practical implementation against the backdrop of the Cuban Revolution and its development between 1959 and 1975.

Internationalism as a Foreign Policy Strategy

The 1959 Cuban Revolution represented a watershed in Cuban foreign policy. Over the course of the 1960s and 1970s, the socialist island republic evolved into a global actor, whose international policy assumed dimensions not usually associated with such a small country. To put it in the words of the historian Jorge I. Domínguez in 1989, "Cuba is a small country, but it has the foreign policy of a big power."[2] After the end of Spanish colonization and the four years of US military occupation following official independence in 1902, Cuba had been largely dependent on the economic and political interests of successive US governments. Particularly in the first three decades of the twentieth century, the United States frequently interfered both politically and militarily with Cuba's domestic affairs and determined the imbalances in their economic exchange. After the 1933 revolution and the establishment of a new constitution, Cuba was able to free itself of US dominance. Nevertheless, until 1959 its economy remained largely dependent on the United States, Cuba's main market for its raw sugar and also a major outlet for its consumer and industrial goods. In matters of foreign policy, Cuba's agenda was also closely tied to the preferences of the northern hegemonic power. On 1 January 1959, the situation changed fundamentally when the Movimento 26 de Julio (M-26-7, the 26th of July Movement) defeated the authoritarian regime of Fulgencio Batista. Under the leadership of Fidel Castro Ruz (b. 1926), the revolutionaries were determined to free Cuba completely from the "imperialist stranglehold" of the United States. Immediately after the triumph of the revolution, Cuba embarked on its new foreign policy of "revolution export." From the outset, however, these ambitions on the foreign stage were severely restricted by the Cold War constellation and the antagonism between the two world superpowers, in whose crossfire revolutionary Cuba found itself. Cuba's revolutionary ideology was committed to supporting the liberation movements of the "Tricontinental" countries in their struggle against industrialized nations. Nevertheless, its main priority in making foreign policy was to secure the future of the Cuban Revolution in the face of overt US hostility.[3] After its dramatic break from the United

States in the early 1960s, Cuba began to approach the Soviet Union, though at a much slower pace and not always without conflict. This balancing act between the two superpowers determined the framework of Cuban foreign policy, in which the US government proved to be a ruthless enemy and the Soviet government an unreliable partner.[4]

With the pressure from the US government, Cuba's isolation extended across Latin America when it was excluded from the Organization of American States (OAS) in 1962. This effectively blocked off Cuba's immediate neighbors from its efforts to "internationalize" the revolution. With the exception of Mexico, all Latin American governments followed US policy, breaking off both diplomatic and trade relations with Cuba. The Cuban government, seemingly unimpressed, reacted by expanding economic relations with the Soviet Union and the countries of the Eastern bloc. Nevertheless, it continued to follow its own agenda in foreign policy, exploiting differences within the socialist camp between the Soviet Union and China on the one hand,[5] and supporting oppositional, nationalist, left-wing liberation movements in Latin America on the other. Cuba initially assisted guerrilla movements in Latin America (in Guatemala, Colombia, Peru, Venezuela, and Bolivia). This was seen also as a challenge to the Soviet Union, which regarded itself as the leader of the socialist camp and propagated a "peaceful path" toward socialism as part of its policy of peaceful coexistence with the United States.[6] When the US army intervened in Vietnam, Cuba sided with the South Vietnamese liberation front. It also planned to unite with North Korea in forming a common front within the socialist camp in order to encourage the Soviet Union to join the armed struggle of the Tricontinental countries.[7]

Revolutionary Cuba's bold and confident activity in the international arena owed much to the two charismatic revolutionary leaders Fidel Castro and Che Guevara (1928–1967), who enjoyed the strong backing of the people and the support of many admirers throughout the world following the triumph of the revolution.[8] Castro, the legendary charismatic leader of the revolution, and the popular Guevara, with his spectacular and provocative public appearances (for example, at the UN General Assembly in December 1964), were integral to Cuba's domestic and foreign policy. Whereas Guevara's writings and comments on internationalism were permeated with idealism, Castro took a more realistic and pragmatic approach. The Guevara-Castro combination of the personal and political, the utopian and the realistic, was initially highly successful: they managed (for a while) to transform Cuba into the "centre of global revolution," at least symbolically.[9]

It would, however, be facile to claim that such self-confidence in foreign affairs was due solely to the charisma of the two leaders or the support given by the socialist bloc. Indeed, as far back as the Spanish empire of the sixteenth century, Cuba's geographical location gave it key importance. Cuba was the springboard for the Spanish conquest of the American mainland; it was the arena of colonial experimentation; and it was a hub of ideas, information, and power strategies in the New World—a place in which knowledge from across the globe circulated. The port of Havana expanded to become the strategic outpost of Hispanic America, and for centuries it was the major marketplace for Mexican silver and (later) tobacco, coffee, and sugar. The Creole upper classes living in Havana quickly developed an awareness of their geostrategic importance.[10] Playing on the supposed weakness of being a small island, they went in search of powers and elites from whom they could benefit economically and politically. In the twentieth century, this mentality apparently lived on in those who, after the revolution, took up the challenge of profiting from Cuba's geographic position. In their turn, they sought out superpowers within the prevailing constellation of global politics and used them to their own advantage.[11]

In the day-to-day workings of the revolution, however, it was indeed the economic and political support of the Soviet Union that allowed Cuba to withstand the pressure of US foreign policy and to consolidate revolutionary change. The revolutionaries now faced the challenge of limiting the resulting increase in Soviet influence on domestic affairs and economic reforms. The organization responsible for implementing Soviet policy in Cuba was the Communist Party of Cuba.[12] But relations between the Cuban communists and the revolutionary government and Castro supporters (known as *fidelistas*) were strained owing to the Communist Party's failure to support the guerrilla war and the political aims of M-26-7 in the 1950s.[13]

In 1961, Castro merged the two parties and formed an integrated organization in which the old "Stalinists" lost all say and were replaced with Castro supporters. This move was emblematic of Cuba's refusal to build the new state according to the Soviet model. The revolutionary government favored the path of mass mobilization, in which Castro and his inner circle communicated their policies to the people through constant, public dialogue. This culture of staged "direct democracy," personified and represented by the Cuban leader, created a feeling of individual involvement in political processes. The aim was to establish stable mass support while simultaneously institutionalizing the state. The most important achievements of these years were in the cultural and social spheres. In 1961, a literacy campaign successfully eradicated illiteracy and resulted in the establishment of an extensive education system. Similar sustainable successes were made in medicine, hygiene, and nutrition. Far-reaching land reform was also introduced and changed the nature of land ownership radically. In the first few years after the triumph of the revolution, euphoria remained high, and the majority of Cubans held on to the "heroic illusion" that with a permanent international process of revolution they could change the world within a few years.[14] This optimism was shared by left-wing, progressive movements around the world.

In 1960, at around the time that Cuba began supporting Latin America's guerrilla movements, eighteen African countries achieved independence. This development brought high hopes, and Cuba set about establishing contacts with postcolonial African governments and offering practical assistance to anti-colonial movements. In its foreign policy toward Africa, Cuba may well have been taking a gamble that the United States would have little interest in Africa and therefore little incentive to retaliate against Cuba. Cuba's first contacts were with the government of Ghana, led by Kwame Nkrumah after Ghana gained independence in 1957, and the Algerian Front de Libération Nationale (FLN, National Liberation Front). The Cubans provided the FLN with military support in its struggle against the French colonizers. When Algeria became independent in 1963, it was also the first country to receive civil aid from the Cuban government in the form of a fifty-strong delegation of doctors and medical staff.[15] By supporting the FLN, the Cuban revolutionaries were sending a strong signal to Western European protest movements that condemned the French colonial war in Algeria.

The Tricontinental Conference, which took place in Havana in January 1966, was seminal in building relations between Cuba and countries of Asia, Africa, and Latin America. The conference was attended by eighty-two delegates representing their countries' governments and anti-colonial movements. Of Angola's three anti-colonial movements, only the MPLA was present, represented by Agostinho Neto. The aim of the conference was to spread the revolution throughout the Tricontinent. To this end the Organización para la Solidaridad de los Pueblos de Asia, Africa e América Latina (OSPAAL, Organization of Solidarity with the People of Asia, Africa and Latin America) was created with headquarters in Havana. Following the example of the Cuban Revolution, the hope was that a new political horizon would open up for the countries of Asia, Africa, and Latin America, and that the revolution would spread to this "fundamental field of imperialist exploitation."[16] Stripped of their revolutionary pathos, the political concepts presented at the Tricontinental Conference constituted a debate on an alternative, socialist modernism, which represented a response from the Global South to the development models of the Global North. The countries that had already liberated themselves were expected in turn to support liberation movements on the three continents; this was perceived as the true meaning of "internationalist solidarity."[17] According to plan, Cuba, Algeria, Central Africa, Vietnam, and Indonesia were to be the geopolitical centers, with Havana as the "capital" of the global revolution.[18] The Cuban revolutionaries were also convinced that they could empathize strongly with the Tricontinental countries and therefore had a special role to play: the Cuban people were not "white" but rather represented a mixture of ethnic, cultural, and psychological traits from Latin America, Africa, and indeed even Asia.

The Cuban government found like minds among the politicians and leaders of the Afro-Asian anti-colonial movements (who had already met at conferences in Bandung in 1955 and Cairo in 1957). At these conferences they discussed the status and influence of the participating countries within the international state system and concluded by calling for autonomy, recognition, equality, and fairer economic relations. The leaders of these countries had the intention to form a third power bloc facing both the United States and the Soviet Union, a "Third World," in analogy to the "Tiers État," the Third State of the French Revolution.[19] The Non-Aligned Movement (NAM), founded in 1961 by Yugoslavia's president Josip Broz Tito, also regarded itself as "Third World." Cuba was the only Latin American founding member of the NAM.[20] The Cuban government distilled the demands of the Afro-Asian leaders into its own political concept, that of "integrated coexistence." According to this idea, industrialized nations were admonished to follow a policy of peaceful coexistence not only with the Soviet Union but also with the governments emerging from the anti-colonial and liberation movements in the South. This is precisely what Guevara demanded in his New York address to the UN General Assembly in 1964.[21] It soon became obvious that the policy of independence from both superpowers was illusory when in 1968 the Soviet government put a violent end to Czechoslovakia's endeavors to become politically and economically independent. The Soviet Union received rhetorical support from Castro at a time when Cuba had been experiencing serious economic difficulties and was almost entirely dependent on the Soviet government for its crude oil supplies.[22]

At the end of the 1960s, the revolution entered its consolidation phase. The socialist experiment had met with little success on an economic level, and the strategy of catching up with development through industrialization and diversification in agriculture had failed. However, Cuba had managed to detach itself from the US economy, and the revolutionary government had managed to assert itself politically. There were, however, many Cubans who disagreed with the policies of the revolution, and, by the end of the 1960s, there were already half a million Cubans living in exile, above all in the United States, but also in Europe and Latin America. In 1968, the last wave of nationalization, which almost completely dismantled private property, caused another two hundred thousand Cubans to leave the island.[23]

After Guevara was killed in 1967 when trying to establish a revolutionary guerrilla movement in Bolivia, he was elevated in Cuba to the mythic status of revolutionary icon. In homage to his economic policies, one of the biggest voluntary economic experiments (and indeed the last) was carried out in true Guevara style: in 1970, the entire population was mobilized to bring in the "ten-million-ton sugar harvest," the biggest sugar cane harvest in Cuban history, to demonstrate the superiority of the Cuban socio-economic system. With the united effort of millions of Cubans, a historic harvest was indeed brought in, but it turned out to be only 8.5 million tons of sugar cane. This shortfall emphasized that the current economic policy was in need of restructuring and that mass mobilization programs would have to be replaced by organization and controls. Marifeli Pérez-Stable, one of the most eminent Cuban American historians, claims that the failure of the ten-million-ton sugar harvest marked a historic watershed: "the end of the revolution."[24]

The subsequent years saw a process of "Sovietization" in politics and economics. Three main measures were introduced in an attempt to consolidate the revolutionary government according to the Soviet model: the development of a centralized, planned economy based on the Soviet paradigm, according to which economic efficiency had priority and workers and employees were offered material incentives; the institutionalization of political authority by means of the party, trade unions, and mass organizations—under the leadership of the charismatic leader Fidel Castro; and the expansion of new international alliances, above all with the Soviet Union and Eastern bloc. In 1972, Cuba became the first country of the so-called Third World to join the Council for Mutual Economic Assistance (Comecon), the socialist economic community. This newfound pragmatism was incorporated in the figure of Raúl Castro (b. 1931), Fidel Castro's younger brother. As minister of the Revolutionary Armed Forces (FAR) and internal organizer, he seldom emerged from the shadow of his brother. Nevertheless, he was the one responsible for the day-to-day running of economic and military affairs, a task that he performed reliably and pragmatically from the wings, thus helping to consolidate the power of his elder sibling. From the 1970s onward, the Cuban economy became far more dependent on subsidies from the Soviet government and trade with the Comecon countries.[25]

Pragmatism also began to govern relations with the Tricontinental countries, though external developments were also in play here. The violent coup against the democratically elected, socialist government of Salvador Allende in Chile on 11 September 1973 put an end to revolutionary fervor in Latin America for the foreseeable future. Cuba responded by redefining the aims of its foreign policy and internationalism. In abandoning its policy of support for guerrilla and liberation movements and favoring diplomatic relations with progressive, internationally legitimized governments, the Cuban government was, however, not necessarily throwing its internationalist principles overboard.[26] On the contrary: internationalism became enshrined in the new constitution as the leitmotiv and political strategy of Cuba's future foreign policy. Proletarian internationalism and militant solidarity became the cornerstones of ideology; national wars of liberation and armed resistance against aggressors were considered legitimate; and the internationalist duty to help those under attack and those fighting for their liberty became the underlying principle of foreign policy.[27]

Internally, the process of institutionalization culminated in the First Congress of the Communist Party of Cuba in December 1975 and the signing of the new constitution in February 1976. The existing ministries had already undergone reorganization at the beginning of the 1970s, and new ministries had been established. Responsibilities had been distributed among the so-called state committees. The Council of Ministers, formed in 1972, had overall authority over the ministries. The first party congress passed a new system of economic planning, whose ultimate goal was efficiency and rationalization. This also involved the reorientation of the trade unions, which at the 1973 National Trade-Union Congress condemned the radical voluntary experiments of the past. The new task of the trade unions was to enforce working discipline and increase production standards.[28] The mass organizations (of women, youth, farmers, and the Committees for the Defense of the Revolution) were also expected to adopt the new political maxims.

The introduction of a new system of political organization, the *poder popular* (people's power), involved people in the political decision-making processes. There were, however, controls on this participation through decentralized elections at the local, regional, and national levels. The *poder popular* local and regional assemblies did indeed exercise authority and assume responsibility (for example, in the production and distribution of goods, public transportation, and regional justice) but they were excluded from national political decision making.[29] This period has since become known, even officially, as the "five gray years" (1971–1976) because it lacked the vitality of the "heroic" years of the revolution, and because of the intensely restrictive climate imposed by censorship and prohibitions.[30] On the other hand, during this phase, financial and economic support from the Soviet Union stabilized the economy, and large sections of the population were able to achieve a modest degree of wealth. The support also helped establish a comprehensive health and education system.[31] During this period, the material and institutional fabric was created for ambitious, enduring military and civil "missions," such as those that took place in Angola.

The military and civil engagement in Angola from 1975 to 1991 signified both the culmination and the turning point of Cuba's revolutionary internationalism. It represented the biggest foreign engagement in Cuban history in terms of duration, the number of people involved, and the quality of assistance provided. According to official figures released by the Cuban government, a total of 377,033 Cuban soldiers and "approximately 50,000" civilians were deployed during this period—a total of over 430,000 Cubans.[32] These figures leave no doubt as to the magnitude of the engagement, even though it is impossible to verify their accuracy; and indeed, the numbers vary from source to source. During his speech to mark the thirtieth anniversary of Angolan independence in December 2005, for example, Castro spoke of 300,000 members of the armed forces.[33] The official number of Cubans who lost their lives in Angola is 2,016.[34] The accuracy of this number has been contested and has not been verified to date, but no public attempt has been made to reappraise this event, so the recollection of an unbelievably high number of lives lost in Angola has lodged itself in the collective memory of the Cuban people. For many soldiers and aid workers, deployment in Angola has carried with it associations of considerable trauma. These feelings will be examined in Part III of this book.

The trauma linked to the Angolan war marks the turning point in Cuba's politically motivated internationalism. After 1990, Cuba no longer provided military support for friendly governments or liberation movements. With the collapse of the Soviet Union, economic, financial, and military aid dried up, and without the guarantee of cheap, subsidized support, Cuba was no longer able to engage abroad for purely political reasons. Furthermore, during its long engagement in Angola, the Cuban government had completely overstretched its budget, even despite the financial and military support provided by the Soviet Union and the payments made by the Angolan government.[35] The Cuban economy was suffering particularly from the absence of the many skilled workers deployed in Angola (as well as in other African, Asian, and Latin American countries). After 1991, when the last soldiers and civilians had returned from Angola, Cuba descended into the biggest economic crisis in its history, the effects of which are still being felt today. The Cuban government was left fighting for survival as the only socialist state in the Western Hemisphere.

The Angolan engagement also illustrated that "internationalist solidarity" entails not only political and military support. This was another turning point after 1975. In order to stabilize Angola during its transitional period, it was first necessary to provide a type of "socialist development aid" involving extensive, organized, and coordinated civil assistance. Angola was the first place where Cuban civil aid workers were deployed en mass. In the spirit of the early years of the Cuban Revolution, they are still called "internationalists" today. Whereas prior to 1975 civil aid workers—above all doctors—had been dispatched in small groups to friendly countries of the "Third World," thousands of skilled workers were now sent to Angola in large organized groups known as detachments. The types of skills they brought with them depended on the needs that had been assessed and finalized by bilateral commissions made up of Cuban and Angolan government representatives. Engagement in Angola demanded a broad process of professionalization, which, in accordance with the institutionalization phase, had an impact on the establishment of state organizations such as the CECE and specialized state enterprises such as Cubatécnica, which assumed responsibility for dispatching aid workers. The processes by which the international "mission" was professionalized and institutionalized are explained in detail in Part II of this book, using the example of Cuba's cooperation in education.

The following section deals with the ideologies, theoretical considerations, and historical and practical experience that formed the basis of Cuba's internationalist strategy.

The African Dream

Cuba's strategy of internationalism was an invention of Che Guevara and Fidel Castro. Their concept of "internationalism" and "internationalist solidarity" was a combination of all major revolutionary ideologies of the nineteenth and twentieth centuries, to which were added the Latin American and Cuban traditions of armed rebellion and a voluntaristic morality best summed up in Guevara's words "Be realistic; demand the impossible." From this perspective, internationalism was a political utopia on a global scale.

The Marxist theorists and practitioners of the nineteenth and twentieth centuries had a major influence on the development of the concept of internationalism. Karl Marx and Friedrich Engels's 1848 *Manifesto of the Communist Party* called for "proletarian internationalism," an appeal to the working classes to transcend national borders and unite in the class struggle across the globe. Even more important, however, was the theory of the Russian Revolution's most prominent politician, Vladimir Ilyich Lenin. He defined imperialism as the highest level of capitalism and demanded a world revolution to overthrow this system of domination. It was at Lenin's instigation that the Comintern was founded in 1919 with the aim of organizing and leading the world revolution. This was the first time that anti-colonial movements had ever been included in revolutionary strategy. According to Lenin's closest confidant, the theorist and revolutionary Leon Trotsky, the Russian Revolution only had a chance of long-term survival if it could develop permanently and succeed globally. Trotsky's concept had considerable impact on Cuba's vision of internationalism and "internationalist solidarity." From it Cuba derived its aspirations of a future on the world stage, which was to culminate in a revolution of the Tricontinental countries against the wealthy North. The solidarity in question not only originated from a common class situation but was also based on the assumption of united opposition to imperialist powers. A further source of inspiration, which gave ideological substance to this South-North perspective, was the Chinese Revolution led by Mao Zedong. Its large-scale, sociocultural experiments and emphasis on the leading role of peasants in the revolutionary process provided the model for social reorganization in the Tricontinental countries.[36] Other basic principles of internationalism and "internationalist solidarity" were, from the revolutionaries' point of view, firmly anchored in the political culture of Cuba: anti-imperialism and the moral sensibilities and frustration of a small island fighting the most powerful and technologically advanced country in the world.[37]

The most influential agent of Marxism and anti-imperialism in Cuba was the student leader and cofounder of the (first) Communist Party of Cuba, Julio Antonio Mella, who was assassinated in 1929 while living in exile in Mexico. Mella by no means restricted himself to European and Russian theories when he developed his ideas of radical nationalism and anti-imperialism, demanding a "revolution against the dollar" in 1927. On the contrary, he united his anti-imperialist and sociorevolutionary convictions with the tradition of armed rebellion during the Latin American independence revolutions of the nineteenth century. The political and military leaders of Latin American independence provided a source of inspiration, in particular Simón Bolivar (1783–1830), who wanted to transform the former Hispanic American colonial empire into the "heart of the world."[38] To the Cuban revolutionaries' understanding, "internationalism" and "internationalist solidarity" were therefore inextricably linked to armed struggle.

But even more than Bolivar, it was the polymath and visionary of Cuban independence, the "apostle," José Martí (1853–1895), who was the greatest source of inspiration to Mella—and to Castro, Guevara, and the generation of 1959 revolutionaries. Martí was the first to envisage an alternative society from the perspective of the South. His thought united nationalism with the vision of a nation that encompassed the whole of Latin America, in opposition to the imperialist ambitions of the United States, which Martí considered to be the greatest threat to Latin America.[39] His commitment to Cuban independence "with a pen and a machete" made him for future generations the embodiment of *Cuba libre*, a free and independent Cuba. Mella founded the political myth surrounding Martí by stylizing him as the archetypal Cuban revolutionary: intelligent and rhetorically gifted, with a willingness to transcend all national borders and fight for the rights of the downtrodden. The revolutionaries of 1959 consciously adopted this tradition and elevated Martí definitively to the status of national myth. Based on Martí's ideas, which were not founded on a Marxist analysis of society, all the "poor" and "colonized" were considered subjects of the revolution. The Cuban version of internationalism signified the struggle of the global village against the metropoles.

In accordance with Martí's thinking, Guevara declared in 1962 that the Cuban Revolution was of a humanistic nature and in solidarity with all the oppressed peoples of the world. Thus he declared the revolution to be part of a global struggle against colonialism, neocolonialism, and imperialism. In this struggle "every front was of vital importance."[40] Every country willing to take up the cause against imperialism would receive Cuba's support, Guevara declared. His "Message to the Peoples of the World" in April 1967 was a call to wage a "global war against imperialism" and an appeal for the creation of "a second or a third Vietnam of the world."[41] Guevara explained that the issue at stake was nothing less than the "sacred cause of redeeming humanity," and to die for this cause "would be equally glorious and desirable for an American, an Asian, an African, even a European."[42] From an early stage, biblical analogies were used to characterize the revolution: in 1963 a (former) Cuban revolutionary formulated the founding myth of the revolution, describing Cuba as a "Latin American David, who dared to break the geopolitical chains that seemed to bind him for eternity to the Goliath of the North."[43] The adoption of such obviously Christian topoi illustrates the missionary zeal of the revolution.

In the "Second Declaration of Havana" in 1962, which Guevara called the "communist manifesto of our continent and our time,"[44] Castro appealed to the people of Latin America to follow the Cuban example and organize a revolution. In his address, he emphasized that the only acceptable strategy for true revolutionaries was armed struggle in the form of guerrilla movements.[45] In 1960, Guevara had published his guerrilla handbook *La guerra de guerrillas* (*Guerrilla Warfare*), which contained the theories of armed struggle and defined the basic principles of the foco theory of insurgency. Based on the Cuban experience of (successful) guerrilla warfare, these principles can be summarized as follows: 1. Popular forces can win a war against a regular army; 2. The rebellious core of a guerrilla army can create the preconditions for revolution, even if those preconditions do not exist objectively; 3. In underdeveloped America, the armed struggle must be fought in rural areas.[46] These basic principles, which were also partly inspired by the Chinese Revolution, were to provide the model for the revolutionary struggle of the Global South against the Global North.

One attempt to apply these principles was the expedition led by Guevara to Africa in 1965, which aimed to lead the creation of a "revolutionary front against imperialism." Although the expedition was a failure, it paved the way for the military support that Cuba would give the MPLA in the final phase of the colonial war ten years later. From 1964 onward, Cuba had diplomatic representatives in the countries it considered to have the "most revolutionary" governments: Algeria, Egypt, Ghana, Guinea (Conakry), and Mali.[47] Latin America had witnessed the failure of several of its revolutionary movements (including those in Argentina, Peru, and Venezuela). This, combined with the political and economic isolation to which Cuba was being subjected, encouraged Guevara in 1964 to set out in search of new political networks across the globe. His Africa tour was intended partly to sound out opportunities for closer cooperation with revolutionary African liberation movements, and partly to consolidate already existing political relations between Cuba and friendly African states. His main concern, however, was to offer Cuban support in establishing revolutionary guerrilla movements in Africa, in accordance with his own foco theory. Altogether, the undertaking was a highly complex combination of interstate foreign policy, guerrilla warfare, and support for nongovernmental movements.

In 1964 Guevara left on a three-month tour that would take him to Algeria, Egypt, Mali, Ghana, Guinea (Conakry), Dahomey (Benin), Tanzania, and Congo-Brazzaville. Before beginning his journey, he gave an inflammatory speech against US imperialism at the UN General Assembly, in which he demanded revenge for the "crime committed in Congo," referring to the execution of the Congo Prime minister Patrice Lumumba. From the early 1960s, the Cuban government had already begun to establish foreign political relations with anti-colonial movements and postcolonial governments in Africa, when it provided military support and later civil aid to the Algerian Front de Libération Nationale (FLN, National Liberation Front). This happened against the backdrop of rapid decolonization in Africa in 1960, almost at the same time as the Cuban Revolution.[48]

A completely different reason why Guevara shifted his attention to Africa had to do with the political difficulties he was facing in Cuba. Guevara regarded himself as a revolutionary and not a proponent of realpolitik. As minister of industry he was responsible for the ailing economy, and he encountered growing criticism when his policies of nationalization and industrial centralization led to a drastic decline in production. Nationalization of agriculture had proven equally counterproductive, resulting in the rationing of basic foodstuffs from as early as 1962. The US trade embargo from 1961 onward exacerbated the situation dramatically.[49] Further problems arose when he aggravated the Soviet Union, Cuba's most important trading partner, by criticizing its foreign policy against the Tricontinental countries. During a speech held in February 1964 in

Algiers, Guevara went as far as to accuse the Soviet Union of economically exploiting underdeveloped countries.[50] Shortly before, however, Cuba had signed a new long-term agreement with the Soviet Union, which included an increase in the sugar quota and an expansion of trade with Cuba. The economic survival of the revolution was undoubtedly becoming more and more dependent on the contribution of the Soviet Union; for that reason Fidel and Raúl Castro pursued a very different policy and nurtured their contacts with the Soviet government and military. Here, the differences between the political natures and strategies of Guevara and Fidel Castro became obvious: although they both basically agreed to export the revolution beyond the Caribbean, Castro was more moderate and aware of his responsibilities as a statesman toward Cuba, whereas Guevara saw himself as a radical internationalist and unattached revolutionary.[51]

Another stop during Guevara's visit to Africa was Congo-Brazzaville, which along with the other territories of French West Africa and Equatorial Africa had gained its independence from France in 1960. Guevara's intention was to further relations with the government of President Alphonse Massamba-Débat, who had staged a military putsch against the conservative government in mid-1963 and was now fervently seeking support from socialist states. In 1964 he assumed diplomatic relations with Cuba, and he now asked Guevara for military aid.[52] But in January 1965, Guevara's main attention was on Congo-Brazzaville's neighbor, the former Belgian Congo, which likewise had gained independence in 1960. A year after independence, the first prime minister of the Democratic Republic of Congo, Patrice Lumumba, had been assassinated with the help of the Belgian government and the CIA. Lumumba's violent death made him a symbol of the anti-colonial struggle. It resulted in a long civil war, which was fought out in the many regions of the enormous state territory, including the eastern province of Kivu (bordering on Tanzania, Burundi, and Uganda). It was here that Guevara and around one hundred Cuban guerrillas tried, in vain, to establish armed units among the troops of the rebel leader Laurent Kabila.

A decisive step in the development of relations between Cuba and the MPLA was a meeting between Guevara and the leaders of the MPLA in the MPLA Brazzaville headquarters in January 1965.[53] Agostinho Neto, Lúcio Lara, and Luís de Acevedo from the MPLA took part in this first face-to-face meeting with a representative from the Cuban government. According to Lara, the conversation proved disappointing for the MPLA. Guevara apparently knew little about the MPLA and initially ignored their request for assistance in training guerrillas. Moreover, he demanded (according to Lara) that the MPLA join the offensives he was planning in former Belgian Congo, a demand that the MPLA refused.[54] At that point in time, the MPLA was militarily so weak that it only managed to survive through the support given by the Massamba-Débat government. Finally Guevara agreed to provide the MPLA with the help it requested and dispatched a second guerrilla unit, the Bataillon Patrice Lumumba, comprising around 250 Cubans. The armed unit, whose leaders included Jorge Risquet Valdés, arrived in Congo-Brazzaville in August 1965.[55] The unit was intended as a strategic reserve for Guevara's military operations, and it was also expected to give military backup to Massamba-Débat's government should the former Belgian Congo intervene as threatened. Its other task was to train MPLA guerrillas and assist them in their military offensives.[56]

Thus Guevara forged one of the closest alliances Cuba had ever had with Africa and unwittingly laid the foundations for Cuba's military engagement in Angola in October 1975. Cuba's first offer of direct military support for the MPLA lasted until the beginning of 1966, and retrospectively Risquet viewed it in a positive light.[57] But according to the Congolese historian Mabeko Tali, the MPLA's enthusiasm for the united military activity was muted. Mabeko Tali draws on accounts (given by Neto, among others) that tell of differences of opinion regarding military tactics.[58] The Cuban insistence on their experience with *foquismo* during the Cuban guerrilla war had left the MPLA feeling patronized. After 1966, relations between the Cuban government and the MPLA were, according to Mabeko Tali, considerably cooler.[59] Even Guevara gave a sober assessment of revolutionary progress in the Portuguese colonies of Angola and Mozambique during his message to the Tricontinental Conference in 1966: the struggle, he said, was being waged with "relative intensity" and "variable success."[60]

3

The "Afro-Latin American Nation"

Motives behind Cooperation

In this chapter, I will analyze the motives behind Angola and Cuba's joint decision not only to continue Cuba's military support for Angola beyond independence but also to intensify help considerably by introducing an extensive civil aid program. My starting point is the thesis that although both governments were acting within the confines of the prevailing Cold War constellation of global politics, they were nevertheless following their own domestic and foreign interests. Both governments were perfectly able to exploit the political situation in which they found themselves. While in the slipstream of the Soviet government, they had the opportunity to attune their interests and needs to develop a South-South cooperative relationship. Working in their favor was the Soviet government's policy of supporting and arming revolutionary groups in crisis regions of the Third World while simultaneously avoiding obvious direct intervention when it came to local and regional conflicts.[1] This was the opposite of Cuba's strategy of direct involvement, revolution export, and "internationalist solidarity." Neither the MPLA nor the Cuban government can therefore be regarded as a mere proxy of the Soviet Union. On the contrary, both actors were well able to make their own decisions, act on their own behalves, and pursue their own political strategies within the global political constellation. In the past few years, more recent studies have considered the Cold War on a global level, taking into account other regions of the world and historic contexts and paying particular attention to the "little" powers that seem totally dependent on superpowers. These studies reach a similar conclusion: that the agency of these minor powers has been considerably underestimated.

With regard to Cuba's engagement in Angola, all studies to date fail to take into account what motivated the Angolan liberation movement or subsequent MPLA government to enter the transatlantic relationship with Cuba. Instead they broach the subject from a US, European ("Western"), South African, or Cuban perspective. In so doing, they widely ignore the role of the Angolan government as a political actor pursuing its own political and strategic interests: in effect, they reduce Angola's role to a passive one within the context of a Cuban or Cuban-Soviet global strategy. According to my thesis, the historic perspective on Cuban-Angolan relations cannot be considered complete until the Angolan government is taken seriously as an autonomous agent. This essential change in perspective, however, has been made all the more difficult by the lack of systematic research and analysis based on internal government documents to provide an understanding of the MPLA's domestic and foreign political strategies and levels of activity before and after independence.

On the basis of my research into civil cooperation, I have meanwhile been able to ascertain that the MPLA did indeed employ the internationalist principles of the Cuban government. It thereby encouraged the expansion of their bilateral relationships in order to compensate its own deficits and follow its own power interests. The MPLA needed Cuba's support after independence to strengthen its power over internal and external antagonists. Moreover, in order to stabilize its dominance on a political and institutional level, it actively sought civil aid cooperation with Cuba to help it tackle the economic and administrative reconstruction of Angola and help it implement an extensive modernization and social welfare agenda. Within this framework, the MPLA tried to use all the resources at its disposal. For its purposes, the Cuban government represented the ideal partner because it was willing to offer the support requested by Angola, even though this exercise carried considerable risks in the foreign political arena and entailed enormous effort and expense, both logistically and in terms of the number of people needed.

In this chapter, I also want to demonstrate the strategic thought and motivation behind the Cuban government's decision to remain in Angola longer than originally planned, and I intend to show how Cuba justified this decision in public discourse within and beyond its borders.

Engagement in Angola provided an opportunity to demonstrate Cuba's independence from the Soviet Union and at the same time win political prestige among the countries of the Third World. By supporting a country rich in raw materials, such as Angola, Cuba also entertained hopes of solving the economic problems of the island republic in the long term. The political and ideological reasoning behind this transatlantic South-South alliance was the vision of the "Afro-Latin American nation" invented by the Cuban head of state, Fidel Castro, and shared, at least on the discursive level, by the MPLA government.

The Motives of the MPLA

The meeting in January 1965 between leaders of the MPLA and Che Guevara in Congo-Brazzaville, and the resulting military assistance, did not initially lead to close ties between the Cuban government and the MPLA. But it did illustrate that there were definite political and cultural affinities between them. The leaders, the majority of whom were intellectuals, were particularly conscious of these affinities, and this awareness eased communication considerably. Moreover, out of all the Central African political organizations and guerrilla movements with which the Cuban government had been in contact since the 1960s, the MPLA came closest to the Cuban vision of a revolutionary movement. The MPLA stood for the complete independence of Angola, the establishment of a homogeneous nation-state, and a socialist society with social equality for all Angolans regardless of skin color, gender, ethnicity, or cultural and class background. It also demanded agricultural reform, universal education, and universal medical care.[2] The MPLA's members comprised Africans, Luso-Africans, and whites; this composition, along with the organization's anti-tribal policy, undoubtedly appealed to the Cuban government. Even though Cuba's leaders were themselves almost exclusively white, they claimed to represent the whole of Cuban society, at least one-third of which was *mestiço*.

Politically and militarily weak, the MPLA turned to Cuba for support in spring 1975—above all for pragmatic reasons. The Congolese historian Mabeko Tali interviewed several MPLA politicians about why their search for military support in 1974/75 had led them to Cuba rather than to one of the Eastern bloc states. According to Mabeko Tali, his interviewees indicated that, at that time, they had considered Cuba to be the only state in the socialist camp prepared to launch itself into a project involving such great and unknown international risks.[3] They had also immediately seized on their positive experience with Cuban soldiers from the Bataillon Patrice Lumumba in Congo-Brazzaville when they trained MPLA troops in the mid-1960s. Moreover, they had taken the Cuban government's call for solidarity with African liberation movements seriously and reckoned with the internationalist ambitions of Cuban foreign policy (bearing in mind the political message given at the 1966 Tricontinental Conference in Havana: "Let us create not one but two, three, many Vietnams").[4] All these reasons had encouraged the MPLA leaders to seek Cuba's support after the overthrow of Marcelo Caetano's Portuguese government in April 1974.[5]

As already mentioned, without Cuba's military assistance, the MPLA would not have been able to assert its power over the FNLA and UNITA after independence. Together with the Angolan Forças Armadas Populares para a Libertação de Angola (FAPLA, The People's Armed Forces for the Liberation of Angola), a large Cuban military force had defended the capital of Luanda against domestic opponents and the advance of the South African Defence Force (SADF). At this point in time, the Cuban government was in no way prepared for long-term engagement in Angola, despite the military and financial aid provided by the Soviet Union, and it had intended to withdraw its forces immediately. The concrete occasion for this withdrawal was the end of the "second war of liberation" in spring 1976. With the help of the FAPLA, the Cuban forces of "Operación Carlota," comprising 36,000 soldiers fighting on Angolan soil, had managed to defeat the opposing FNLA supporters and force the South African military to retreat from Angolan territory. The MPLA had emerged as the political and military victor, and it seemed that it would quickly consolidate its power in Angola both internally and externally. The Organization of African Unity (OAU) had already officially recognized the MPLA government, and was followed by the governments of the European Economic Community (EEC) and the former colonial ruler, Portugal.[6]

The MPLA and the Cubans, however, seriously underestimated the military threat posed by armed rebels within Angola.[7] When the Angolan government recognized the serious danger emanating from internal and external opponents, Agostinho Neto, now president of independent Angola, turned again to the Cuban government. This time he requested not only continued military support but also additional civil aid to rebuild the nation and consolidate the power of the MPLA.[8] In order to retain and strengthen its hard-earned and precarious position of power in Angola, the MPLA government had to be quick in implementing a national reconstruction program. This program, which was to include social reforms and an education campaign, was to be the driving force of social modernization. The only ally who would supply such rapid, uncomplicated, and concrete support was the Cuban government. Moreover, Neto was an intellectual and the Cuban government's most influential partner within the Cuban-Angolan relationship. These factors partially explain why Neto's renewed plea for help was answered.

As had been the case a year earlier, when the MPLA asked for military assistance, this renewed request for Cuban support was based on pragmatism. Following the successes of their joint military offensives in November 1975 and spring 1976, the MPLA leaders had come to trust the organizational and military skills of their Cuban counterparts. In an interview I conducted with the former prime minister of the MPLA government (1975–1978), Lopo do Nascimento, he stated that the MPLA had been very impressed by the extent of support provided by the Cuban government during its military involvement after independence.[9]

Furthermore, according to Lopo do Nascimento, in comparison with the other allies from the socialist camp, the cultural and linguistic similarities between Angolans and Cubans were considerable; this commonality was essential if the civil reconstruction effort was to advance quickly and efficiently. The linguistic barrier between Spanish and Portuguese was relatively small, and Cuban advisors had few problems communicating with their Angolan counterparts. This was not the case with Soviet, Yugoslav, or East German aid workers, at least at the beginning of their cooperative relations. Cuba also had in common with Angola a colonial past and a long struggle for independence, all of which was still very much present in the collective memory of the Cuban people. The Cubans therefore felt solidarity with Angola.

But the most important factor in the MPLA's decision to approach Cuba was the political confidence that its leaders placed in their Cuban comrades.[10] While the new Angolan government under President Neto wished to develop in a socialist direction, it was not willing to orient itself toward the Soviet model, and it was definitely not prepared to accept the paternalism of the Soviet superpower and its Eastern European allies. Angola's new rulers, but above all Neto, were in search of an independent, socialist path. In the words of Franz-Wilhelm Heimer, the political and ideological mainstream of the MPLA government under Neto was "an undogmatic attempt inspired by Marxism to develop an autonomous, noncapitalist development model."[11] Accordingly, postcolonial Angola was to undergo a transition phase in which it would be transformed into a noncapitalist society. Upon gaining the broad approval of the population, Angola would then go on to develop step by step into a socialist society.[12] As already illustrated in Cuba's decision to provide military assistance in Angola, the Cuban government pursued a relatively independent foreign policy. The Neto government therefore had good reason to assume that Cuba would offer the necessary assistance without interfering too much in Angola's internal affairs.

In the 1970s Cuban socialism had drawn closer to the Soviet model with regard to its institutions and economy. Nevertheless, it retained an economic and social structure more in line with other postcolonial societies in developing countries of the Southern Hemisphere than with Eastern bloc countries. Cuba's alternative, socialist modernism therefore acted as an example to Angola. The relatively open nature of the Cuban experiment was also attractive. In the 1970s Cuba had not yet fully completed its transition to becoming a full-fledged socialist state and still largely followed the economic, political, and cultural dictates of the United States. It was therefore constantly trying out adjustments of policy to suit the existing situation. Such experimentation applied to Cuba's education policy. As I will illustrate later in more detail, Cuba had successfully introduced a literacy campaign, and it could now claim experience in establishing a catch-up education program. This policy seemed equally applicable to the situation in which Angola now found itself. The Cuban health system was also tuned to the specific needs of countries in the Southern Hemisphere. Cuban doctors were familiar with tropical diseases (e.g., malaria, yellow fever), and they had also proven themselves able to organize universal health care and broad preventative measures, despite an acute lack of medicine, equipment, and infrastructure. Then there was the Cuban construction industry. It specialized in building light, prefabricated buildings that, when adapted to the tropical climate, could provide fast and simple housing for a large number of people. Nationalization, collectivization, and the resulting planning failures meant that the Cuban agricultural industry was not running as efficiently as it should. Nevertheless, it was producing tropical crops such as cassava, sweet potatoes, rice, and export products such as coffee and sugar. The same crops were grown in Angola, which meant that Cuban agricultural experts could at least provide the necessary know-how.

An added bonus was the strict organization of Cuban society, which allowed the government to mobilize and dispatch its civilians quickly and efficiently. The Cuban population had been educated in the spirit of "internationalist solidarity" and would therefore be committed to their task. Cuban workers were used to being called upon for collective harvesting. They could therefore help pick coffee or provide other services that Angola so desperately needed, whether in public transport, in maintaining communications networks or advising diverse government ministries and administrative bodies, in agricultural and industrial management, or in the education and health systems. Moreover, Cubans were accustomed to difficult living conditions and were therefore expected to cope with the harsh living standards in Angola better than inhabitants of the so-called Second World (who despite material shortages had a comparatively high standard of living with respect to housing, food, hygiene, and cultural activities).[13]

Similarities in climate played a role in Cuban-Angolan cooperation that should not be underestimated. Cuba's climate was similar to the tropical zones of Angola, so it seemed likely that Cubans would be able to carry out physically demanding tasks without falling ill. The cultural characteristics that Cubans and Angolans shared also helped Cubans adapt to life in Angola. For example, beans, cassava, and rice were dietary staples for large sections of the population both in Cuba and Angola. Although the subject was not openly discussed, another cultural factor that must have made Cuban workers appear ideal from an Angolan point of view was their skin color. More than a third of the Cuban population was of mixed European and African descent. This meant that their appearance differed little from the Angolan *mestiços* from the urban areas that were the MPLA's original stronghold. Despite the prejudices of Africans toward *mestiços*, civil aid workers of *mestiço* origin would not be so easily mistaken for the former (white) "colonial masters," and the Angolans would accept them more readily than they would white Europeans. It was also generally felt that Cubans would harbor fewer racist sentiments toward Africans than Central or Eastern Europeans would have. After weighing all of these considerations, the MPLA government seems to have concluded that cooperation with Cuba would be ideal. It provided the prospect of assistance specifically tailored to Angolan needs, and there seemed to be no other country in the world that could offer such support. But there was one more advantage Cuban aid workers had over those of other nationalities that made them particularly attractive: the majority of them had military training, either as reservists or because the Cuban government provided them with basic military training before they left for Angola. In the case of a military attack, they would be able to defend themselves and possibly their Angolan colleagues, students, or patients. After 27 March 1976, the Cuban military remained stationed in Angola, and it made sense that the civil aid workers should take advantage of the military infrastructure and work in the vicinity of the military's strategic bases. The Cuban military's successful organization could also be applied to civil engagement, not only for military purposes but also as a way of meeting the aid workers' day-to-day needs. As they were to work in regions not completely controlled by the MPLA government, the civil aid workers would not only be able to defend themselves, but they would also have the military protection of their own troops.

The Cuban presence after the "second war of liberation" was therefore essential for the MPLA's survival in both military and civilian terms. Over the next fifteen years, Cuban professionals formed the largest contingency of international aid workers in Angola. Altogether, approximately 50,000 doctors, teachers, education specialists, students, university professors, construction workers, engineers and technicians, agricultural specialists, economists, financial advisors and administrators, journalists and artists went to Angola, and in so doing, they helped stabilize the power of the MPLA in the long term.

Faced with the task of mobilizing soldiers and aid workers to serve in Angola, the Cuban government had to justify its engagement to the people. On the Angolan side, the MPLA never publicly questioned the Cuban military and civilian presence. On the contrary, the central organ of the MPLA government, the *Jornal de Angola*, set about portraying the successes of the Cuban Revolution as exemplary; it emphasized that Cuban involvement was an act of solidarity from a friendly nation. From 1975, the *Jornal de Angola* regularly reported on

Cuban politics and cultural events, as well as on bilateral agreements and mutual state visits.[14] In the larger towns and cities of Angola (above all in Luanda), joint cultural and sporting events were organized around Cuban-Angolan cooperation, and there were numerous art and photography exhibitions; Cuban film festivals; and concert tours of Cuban music, dance, and theater groups—particularly in the first years of the Cuban presence. In return, Angolan artists were invited to Cuba.[15] There was, however, little public debate about the deployment of Cuban troops, or about the actual presence of aid workers. Owing to the polarized political situation in Angola following independence, the MPLA government was anxious to avoid criticism over the presence of foreign aid workers. The *Jornal de Angola* consequently played down the extent to which the Cubans were supporting the government.

Motives and Justifications of the Cuban Government

The Cuban government's major ambitions to set up a revolutionary South-South axis by supporting African governments and anti-colonial movements (thus removing them from the US sphere of influence) had basically already failed with the Congo expedition in 1965. Guevara recognized this, and in his 1967 *Message to the People of the World* he expressed doubts about spreading the revolution across Africa too quickly. (However, he gave no reason for those doubts.)[16] The concepts of a global, anti-imperialist struggle, which Guevara had propagated to his Congolese counterparts, generally emanated from the situation in Cuba. It might have been possible to apply such experiences to certain Latin American countries, but in this part of Africa and with these allies the concepts fell on infertile ground. The failure of Guevara's expedition was partly due to the Cuban revolutionaries' lack of knowledge about the economic, social, and cultural parameters in sub-Saharan Africa. Indeed, their fixation on ideology prevented them from developing an interest in such matters. Guevara's African counterparts had little understanding of the foco theory and Maoist strategies to organize and liberate the peasant classes. Even the MPLA, which came closest to the idea of an anti-colonial, anti-imperial movement, was unwilling to apply the Cuban model of guerrilla warfare and national liberation to its own situation.[17] The Cuban revolutionaries were by no means alone in their misjudgment: many Western supporters of African liberation movements also tried to project their own ideas of utopia onto the African continent; but they were actually more interested in armed struggle and socialist experiments than in African realities.[18]

Wherever the Cuban government had provided active political and/or military assistance to African governments and movements, there were serious setbacks after 1965. In 1966, Josef Mobutu, who supported the FNLA, seized power in the former Belgian Congo, and in that same year the President of Ghana, Kwame Nkrumah, an ally of the Cuban government, was overthrown. Mali's President, Modibo Keita, who had likewise nurtured relations with Cuba since the early 1960s, was also deposed in 1968. All that remained of Cuba's plans to "revolutionize Africa" was its support for African anti-colonial movements and guerrilla groups, primarily in the Portuguese colonies of Guinea-Bissau, Mozambique, and Angola. Apart from its relatively extensive military and civil support for the independence movement PAIGC in Guinea-Bissau in the war against Portugal, the role Cuba played in Africa from the mid-1960s to the beginning of the 1970s was small.[19]

Nevertheless, in the mid-1970s, there was a renaissance in Cuba's foreign relations in parts of Africa, culminating in its support for the MPLA. In the many political and historical studies that have appeared over the last twenty to thirty years on Cuba's Africa policies, there is no satisfactory explanation for this revival. Influenced by Cold War dichotomies and what the political scientist William LeoGrande called the "shock" that Cuba's military intervention in Angola produced in the United States,[20] scholars in the 1970s repeatedly conjectured that the Cuban government's decision to provide military assistance to Angola was dependent on the Soviet Union. As early as the 1980s, this thesis was rejected by LeoGrande and other eminent Cuba specialists in the United States, including Carmelo Mesa-Lago, Jorge Domínguez, Sergio Díaz-Briquets, Susan Eva Eckstein, and Nelson Valdés. Many of these scholars are Cuban exiles who have settled in the United States and are generally critical of Castro and the Cuban Revolution.[21] In 1988, the US political scientist William Pascoe realized that "far too much time has been spent in irrelevant debate over whether Cuba acts on its own . . . or whether it acts at the behest of its patrons in the Kremlin."[22] He then concluded that Cuba's involvement in Angola served the foreign political interests of Cuba and the Soviet Union likewise.[23] The sociologist and Cuba specialist Susan Eva Eckstein went even further and emphasized that Cuba's intervention was an act of sovereign foreign policy.[24]

Following the end of the Cold War, the Italian historian and political scientist Piero Gleijeses picked up on these assumptions. After 2002, his publications on Cuba's Africa policy emphasized the role of the Cuban government as a sovereign actor on a global scale. He backed his claims with evidence from US archives and, even more importantly, Cuban archives, and with eyewitness reports from Cuban politicians and former prominent Soviet politicians. He was thereby able to provide credible evidence for the conjectures of the 1980s: the Cuban government's decision to engage in Angola was a sovereign act made without the knowledge of the Soviet government, and indeed, it even conflicted with Soviet geostrategic interests. Gleijeses conceded, however, that engagement in Angola would not have been sustainable over such a long period had it not been for the considerable financial and military support of the Soviet Union.[25]

After 1977, the debate on the motives and reasons behind Cuba's involvement in Africa heated up after further Cuban military engagement there, this time in Ethiopia. Here, however, the situation was very different. According to Gleijeses, evidence from Russian, US, and Cuban archives shows that when the Cubans agreed to provide Ethiopia with military (and civil) assistance from 1977 to 1978 to help the head of state (Mengistu Haile Mariam) resist attacks from neighboring Somalia, it was not following the explicit orders of the Soviet government, but it had sought Soviet agreement and received its blessing.[26] Gleijeses thereby confirmed what US scholars had suspected more than a decade earlier.[27] It remains unclear what stance the Cuban government adopted when Mengistu's Ethiopian government emerged as a dictatorship and began waging war on the rebel province of Eritrea. But it is obvious that Cuba's military support for the Ethiopian government enabled it to engage in this war.[28] It is not within the scope of this study to discuss Cuba's intervention in Ethiopia in detail, but this example does illustrate that scholars must rethink assumptions they made about the different roles played by Cuba and the Soviet Union in Africa against the backdrop of the Cold War. This rethinking should entail taking into account the specific power interests of the Ethiopian government.

Gleijeses fails to take into account all of the reasons behind Cuba's involvement in Angola; in his view the greatest motivating factor was Castro's antiracist convictions in the face of the threat of South African intervention in Angola.[29] The argument that Cuba was responding to a sense of moral duty based on Castro's political principles is indeed justified. It is also correct to place Castro at the center of the political decision to engage in Angola. Nevertheless, this argument does not go far enough, particularly with regard to the aforementioned links between Cuban and Angolan interests. Furthermore, Gleijeses's conclusion seems to rely very much on the Cuban government's assessment of itself.[30]

Already in the late 1970s, the Cuban American sociologist Nelson Valdés forwarded a much more plausible explanation for Cuba's motives. He too based his argumentation on Castro's public declarations and concluded that Cuba's foreign policy remained "revolutionary" over the years, with internationalist principles trumping domestic developments in importance. According to Valdés, however, this was not only due to Castro's revolutionary convictions and principles. His government's foreign policies were far more attuned to prevailing global political constellations. In his observation that a revolutionary is "an opportunist with principles,"[31] Valdés summarized the reasons behind

Cuban foreign policy as follows: it was not only revolutionary idealism that determined foreign policy, but rather pragmatism; Castro combined the necessary with the desirable and the useful in order to reconcile revolutionary principles with the reality of (objective) political circumstance.[32] Susan Eva Eckstein, on the other hand, concluded that one of the main motives behind Cuba's foreign policy was the political duty to provide "internationalist solidarity" and the "commitment to proletarian internationalism and the combative solidarity of the peoples."[33]

It cannot be denied that the political principles and ambitions espoused by Castro played a decisive role in Cuba's involvement in Angola. Nevertheless, from the 1970s onward, even he, as the highest authority within the state, increasingly relied on support within the state apparatus and the Party when it came to implementing his ideas, particularly when making exceedingly risky decisions in foreign policy, such as engagement in Angola. But such far-reaching issues also provided Castro with an opportunity to manifest his rightful claim to absolute leadership within the state and to consolidate his role as an international leader of the Third World. Cuba's involvement in the Angolan war of independence and the fight against South Africa's apartheid regime provided it with the ideal opportunity to increase its prestige on the international stage, particularly among African countries. Such a project would also support Cuba's claim of independence from the Soviet Union in matters of foreign policy, regardless of Cuba's considerable reliance on the material assistance offered by the Comecon states. The decision was rather a manifestation of a political principle that had been established in the 1960s under the influence of the Non-Aligned Movement (NAM), namely the determination to pursue foreign policy without being pressured by either Washington or Moscow.

In December 1975, approximately 36,000 Cuban reservists, military advisors, and elite troops of the Ministry of the Interior were stationed on Angolan soil, and it became obvious that military engagement would last longer than planned. Castro therefore had to give credible explanations for this to state institutions and the Cuban people, particularly regarding a future extension of involvement. He chose the occasion of his final address at the First Congress of the Partido Comunista de Cuba (PCC, Communist Party of Cuba) in December 1975, consciously targeting the Party at a time when it was assuming a central role within the process of institutionalization and its power as political intermediary between Cuba and the Soviet Union in Cuba was increasing. Although Castro's authority (and with it the authority of the *fidelistas*, his supporters and advisors, i.e., anyone who kept their distance from the Communist Party) was not under challenge, he risked losing influence. He and the *fidelistas* had to defend, redefine, and renegotiate their positions as Party officials. The Angolan intervention represented a chance to strengthen Castro's personal authority in this process and demonstrate his claim for leadership within the Party and the Soviet Union.

Castro also had to secure the backing of the Cuban people for engagement in Angola. The majority of the Cubans who had supported the revolutionary change and were still living on the island in the mid-1970s backed the principle of "internationalist solidarity." Angola represented a return to Guevara's voluntarism during a time of increasing institutionalization and bureaucratization. The propaganda for engagement in Angola was similar to the mass campaigns during the first decade of the revolution. In the 1960s, hundreds of thousands of Cubans had been directly involved in "revolutionary campaigns," for example the literacy campaign, the Bay of Pigs invasion, and the ten-million-ton harvest. Once again, the charismatic authority of Fidel Castro and his patriarchal leadership style were decisive in encouraging Cubans to take up the Angolan cause and enthusiastically volunteer in large numbers.[34] At least in its initial phase, engagement in Angola showed the extent to which politicians could channel such popular revolutionary idealism in the 1970s with a view to realizing ambitious goals in foreign policy.

Revolutionary idealism, "internationalist solidarity," a sense of mission, and international political ambitions all provide credible motives for engagement in Angola. But the question remains: To what extent were completely pragmatic reasons behind the decision to offer long-term assistance to Angola? What role, for example, did the economic survival of Cuba and the hope of being able to benefit from Angola's rich natural resources at a future date play? With the exception of nickel, Cuba possessed no raw materials of its own. Already in the 1970s, one of the main economic problems the country faced was the supply of oil. It therefore seems likely that the prospect of improving supplies of petroleum and other raw materials in the medium term through a close alliance with the Angolan government was part of the political calculation and an additional motive for comprehensive engagement. This calculation was by no means reprehensible: it meant that Cuba was endeavoring to shake off its economic dependency on the Soviet Union. Moreover, Angola's agricultural resources and industrial capacity were considerable, and this made it an interesting trading partner and key market. Cuba's involvement in Angola can therefore not be traced to purely altruistic or ideological motives.

As will be explained in more detail later, the commitment to education was an example of activity for which Cuba received considerable financial compensation from the Angolan government.[35] Other examples of civil cooperation included numerous trade agreements (i.e., on exporting Cuban sugar to Angola) and commercial agreements in the construction sector. Together with the

Soviet fishing fleet, Cuba was able to share the rich fishing grounds in the Benguela Current off the Angolan Atlantic coast.[36] At the beginning of the 1980s, state-run import and export companies were even set up to manage trade.[37] Cuban troops were also responsible for protecting the facilities of Western oil companies that had been given licenses for petroleum production by the Angolan state oil company SONANGOL after independence. The income from petroleum secured the survival of the MPLA government by financing the war and guaranteeing funds to pay for Cuba's assistance.[38]

Officially Castro and the Cuban government addressed such financial concerns only indirectly, if at all. Any open admission of economic interest in Angola's rich resources would have been diametrically opposed to the revolutionary principles of "internationalist solidarity" and the altruistic support of friendly governments and liberation movements. Official channels either remained silent on the issue or merely hinted indirectly at material interests. In December 1975, during the First Congress of the Communist Party of Cuba, for example, Castro spoke of Angola's rich natural resources that had to be protected from the hands of the imperialists.[39]

In public, Castro developed another propaganda strategy to justify engagement in Angola. He "invented" a common tradition between Cuba and Angola, and without any ado he declared Cuba an "Afro-Latin American nation." He based his argumentation not only on Cuba's internationalist principles but also on the "blood ties" between Cubans and Africans, which had been formed through their shared colonial past. He concluded that every Cuban was thereby compelled by antiracist principles to help defend Angola's independence against attack from the South African apartheid regime. In the same breath, he managed to combine all this with a verbal attack on the US government:

> The imperialists want to prevent us from helping our Angolan Brothers. But we have to tell the Yankees that they should bear in mind that we are not only a Latin American nation, we are also an Afro-American nation. The blood of Africa runs deep in our veins. And it was from Africa, as slaves, that many of our ancestors came to this country. And these slaves fought hard; they fought hard in the liberation army of our fatherland! We are the brothers of Africans, and we are prepared to fight for the Africans! Once there was discrimination in our country. . . . How could we forget? How could we forget the discrimination that existed at universities, at the workplace, and in all other walks of life? And who are the representatives, the symbols of this abominable and inhuman discrimination? They are the fascists and racists of South Africa. And with no scruples whatsoever, the Yankee imperialists have sent the mercenary soldiers of South Africa to crush Angolan independence. That is why we have a duty to help

> Angola. That is why we have a duty to help Africa. We are duty-bound by our principles, our ideology, our convictions, and our own blood to defend Angola, to defend Africa.[40]

Fidel Castro was drawing on the historical fact that more than a third of the Cuban population descended from African slaves. Of the estimated ten million Africans who survived the Middle Passage across the Atlantic to America between the sixteenth and nineteenth centuries, about one million came to Cuba.[41] The island's wealth from sugarcane production for the world market in the nineteenth century was earned largely on the backs of slaves. Between 1868 and 1898, the majority of slaves and their descendants joined the struggle for independence against the Spanish colonial power, some of them as renowned military leaders.[42] They thereby managed to liberate themselves, and, by the same token, the war of independence made the abolition of slavery a real prospect, along with the integration of blacks into a society that until then had considered itself exclusively white. Slavery was indeed abolished in 1886, but the hoped-for integration was not achieved, although the wartime experience had led to alliances between blacks and whites.[43]

The major role played by African slaves and slaves of African descent in Cuba's war of independence and the implied "shared" experience in the struggle against imperialism provided Castro with another reason why all Cubans, regardless of skin color, were morally obliged to support Angola's war of independence. Castro's recourse to history was significant. Regardless of the disappointing results of independence (it failed to deliver full sovereignty or to integrate the former slaves), the cultural and national identity of all Cubans emerged from the war of independence, and it was firmly rooted in the collective memory of the Cuban people.

A further historic event substantiated this "invented tradition" by emphasizing Cuba's history of insurrection and slave rebellion. Cuba, like other societies across the Americas with a tradition of mass slavery, had constructed a popular myth around rebellion.[44] Part of this myth was the maroons, or *cimarrones*. These were slaves who had either escaped or were involved in uprisings. It was not, however, until after the revolution that the publication of the *Biografía de un cimarrón* (*Biography of a Runaway Slave*) in 1966 led to a recognition of the role the *cimarrones* had played.[45] One particular slave uprising in 1843 was especially significant to the Angolan cause. It was reputedly led by a female slave called Carlota, and was probably part of the largest attempted slave uprising (La Conspiración de la Escalera).[46] In 1975, the rebellious slave gave her name to Operation Carlota and became the "patron saint" of Cuban military engagement in Angola. The black and white Cuban soldiers who joined

Operation Carlota fought side by side with the troops of the MPLA and the FAPLA for a just and antiracist Angola against the South African apartheid regime. The Cuban government also used the story of the Carlota uprising to justify its military involvement in Angola to international sympathizers. In line with official Cuban propaganda, the Colombian writer Gabriel García Márquez published an essay in 1977 in the renowned international left-wing journal *New Left Review*. The essay was titled "Operación Carlota," and it backed Cuba's intervention in Angola.[47]

In terms of meaning and contextualization, the Afro-Latin American discourse to justify involvement in Angola went much further. By calling upon the people to help fight the racism of the apartheid regime, Castro implied that after 1959 Cuban society was free from the racial discrimination that had existed prior to the revolution. Following independence in 1902, Cuba's former slaves of African descent had not been integrated into society. Moreover, US influence on Cuba's postcolonial society had exacerbated racist sentiment, which outlasted the twentieth century. Together with social and economic reforms and the fight against corruption, one of the biggest challenges the 1959 revolution therefore faced was the integration of Afro-Cubans into an egalitarian Cuban nation. This is what José Martí had imagined a century earlier when he created the myth of *Cuba libre* as a nation "for all and with all," where no one would be excluded because of skin color, since being Cuban, according to Martí, amounted to being "more than black or white."[48]

In the postcolonial Republic of Cuba, power and opinion leadership (i.e., those societal power groups that lead public opinion) had remained in the hands of white Cubans. Martí's myth served as a discursive smoke screen to hide the inequalities. Because black and white Cubans were officially equal, discrimination could be tacitly accepted: white people could maintain their privileges, and the roadblocks to social advancement among the black population could continue.[49] The clearest expression of the Cuban state's indifference to discrimination within its borders was when the government banned the Partido Independiente de Color (PIC, Independent Party of Color), which had been founded by Afro-Cubans in 1908 to fight social, economic, and political discrimination. In protest against the Party's proscription, the PIC members called in 1912 for an armed rebellion, which was brutally oppressed by government forces.[50] In the 1940s and 1950s, the government of Fulgencio Batista, himself a Cuban of African (and Asian) descent, did offer Afro-Cubans the chance for social advancement in a few socially respected sectors, such as the police and military, but they nevertheless remained excluded from well-paid professions. As the Cuban American historian Alejandro de la Fuente illustrates in depth in his study on race and nation in postcolonial Cuba,[51] blacks continued to experience discrimination in hotels, restaurants, beaches, social clubs, schools, and in some towns even in public spaces in general.

After 1959, the revolutionary government did much to improve the social and economic status of Afro-Cubans by introducing anti-discrimination laws and a radical policy of wealth redistribution, but it showed little interest in pursuing an active policy of sociocultural integration. Racism was banned by decree after the revolution; the predominant opinion after 1961 was that it would automatically be overcome thanks to socialism and the demise of a class-based society.[52] The government systematically suppressed diverging opinions on this matter.[53] By reviving Martí's myth, it had accepted the postcolonial republic's "policy of silence" on racial discrimination. The Black Consciousness movement's demand in the 1960s for the "decolonization of minds" was never realized in Cuba.[54] Particularly in the private sector, stereotypical prejudices against nonwhite Cubans continue to exist even today, as recently illustrated in the extremely heated debate surrounding the hundredth anniversary of the defeated PIC rebellion.[55] Even in the higher echelons of political power, not to mention in government, Afro-Cubans remain underrepresented. "We are over-represented in sport and under-represented in the government,"[56] was how one Afro-Cuban described the situation. From the beginning, the revolutionary government was not interested in politicizing or mobilizing society along racial lines; instead it suppressed public manifestations of cultural difference (for example, Afro-Cuban cults and religions) in order to maintain national consensus.

The situation in Cuba's foreign policy was different. As Castro's words illustrate, on certain occasions race served political ends in public discourse. Several scholars, including de la Fuente and the social scientist Frank Taylor, advance the thesis that Cuba's image as an "Afro-Latin American nation" was the fulcrum of Cuban foreign policy, and that Cuba used the image on several occasions as a kind of "export identity" in order to demonstrate the extent to which the government identified with the liberation struggles of nonwhite peoples all over the world.[57] They cite the example of the Cuban government approaching the Black Power movement in the United States in the 1960s, inferring that its motive was to find another point from which to attack the US government. Stokely Carmichael, one of the exponents of the Black Power movement who was invited to Cuba at the end of the 1960s, seems to confirm this in his claim that after returning from his trip to Cuba, he realized that Castro's support for the black struggle was no more than "rhetorical."[58] When Taylor and de la Fuente's thesis is applied to Castro's 1975 speech, the "Afro-Latin American" identity he invokes can equally be understood as an "export identity." In this case, it did more than serve to mobilize the Cubans for the Angolan cause—it offered the people an identity, and, by giving recognition to their historical and cultural differences, it managed to sidestep the issue of the lack of integration of Afro-Cubans within Cuban society.

In a related point, Taylor also claims that at least until the end of the 1970s, Cuba's active foreign policy in Africa and its engagement in Angola not only increased the foreign prestige of Cuba (and Castro) in Africa and the non-aligned countries but also did indeed improve the acceptance of Afro-Cubans within Cuban society. According to him, even in the absence of affirmative integration policies, it became more acceptable to show cultural differences, for example through clothing, hairstyle, jewelry, religion, and music.[59]

Over the course of 1976, Castro repeatedly referred in public to the "Afro-Latin American" and the blood ties compelling Cuba to work with Angola. His address during the state visit of the Angolan President Agostinho Neto in 1976 was particularly effective and was the starting point for a recruitment campaign of thousands of Cuban civilians: "Because, who make up our nation? Who made up our people, but—in a very high proportion—Africans? And who struggled in our wars of independence of 1868 and in 1895—in a very high proportion—if not the African slaves of the past and their descendants? And among them, who knows how many descendants of Angolans?"[60]

At least initially, Castro's rhetoric managed to obscure the high risks inherent in engagement in Angola. Cuba was involving itself in a war against superior forces (South Africa) and unpredictable enemies (UNITA). It was a war that was escalating daily and whose global implications were unforeseeable. By becoming involved in Angola, Cuba was also risking the détente that had begun with the US government in 1974. On the other hand, the US policy of isolating Cuba had gradually lost momentum as more and more Latin American states began to resume diplomatic and economic relations with Cuba at the beginning of the 1970s. Moreover, the United States faced foreign debacles and domestic problems of its own as it began to withdraw its troops from Vietnam, and President Richard Nixon was forced to resign following the Watergate affair in 1974. All these factors relaxed tensions between the Cuban and US governments. During 1974, secret negotiations took place and there was a real prospect that some of the sanctions would be lifted.[61] This rapprochement ended abruptly in December 1975, when the US government discovered the extent of Cuba's military involvement in Angola.[62] It seemed that the Cuban government had expected this reaction. From its point of view the détente had given Cuba little, if anything at all, and they had nothing to lose by engaging in Angola. The improved relations with the US government had yet to bear fruit, and the relaxation of the trade embargo had not yet materialized. Involvement in Angola would—in the short term—increase Cuba's dependency on the economic and military support of the Soviet Union. Going it alone in foreign policy (by improving relations with the United States) would only run the risk of damaging Cuba's bilateral relations with the Soviet government.

Castro decided to take the bull by the horns. When the United States broke off negotiations, he launched a verbal attack in which he reverted to tried and true accusations that the US government was supporting the apartheid regime, and he affirmed Cuba's position as a small nation that would stand up to the most powerful nation in the world to denounce its racist practices. Such moralistic arguments and demonstrative self-confidence in foreign policy were part of Cuba's public image and symbolic politics, and the government drew a great deal of its domestic strength from its open conflict with the United States.[63]

Castro's anti-imperialist discourse and his verbal attacks on the United States met with great approval from the Cuban public. His condemnation of the superior enemy in the North solidified a national consensus, since most Cubans felt threatened by US policy toward Cuba. The economic shortages (which the Cuban government persistently blamed on trade embargos) had a direct and painful impact on the daily life of every Cuban. Moreover, ever since the end of the war of independence, the Cuban national consciousness had been based on antagonism toward the United States, which had become particularly pronounced since the revolution. Engagement in Angola therefore offered a welcome opportunity to avenge the "aggression of US imperialism." The chance to hit out at US imperialism by becoming involved in Angola (Castro likened engagement to the defeat of the United States in the Bay of Pigs[64]) would act as a valve allowing the Cuban people to direct their frustration at the lack of commodities and turn their anger into a collective fighting spirit.

Castro's public statements justifying engagement in Angola were confined to the early years of that policy, before the number of casualties had climbed so high that a swift military victory and troop withdrawal were impossible. After 1980, Castro mentioned Angola less and less in his public addresses. The issue did not fully disappear from the headlines, but in the end the people of Cuba were kept in the dark about the increasingly difficult political and military situation that developed from 1983 onward.

In 1989, when Cuban troops were beginning to withdraw from Angola, Jorge Díaz-Briquets, one of the leading Cuban American social scientists, ascertained that changes in the international power constellation (he named the withdrawal of Soviet troops from Afghanistan—he could not have anticipated the collapse of the Soviet Union at this time), along with the unforeseen length of engagement in Angola, had turned Castro's most visionary and at first highly successful project into a "foreign-policy nightmare."[65] Or, in the words of the social scientist Frank Taylor, "If initially the blood in Afro-Cuban veins had done much to lure Cuba to the African continent, by the late 1970s the blood spilled from the veins of Cubans on African soil now bound Cuba there, more deeply committed and involved in Africa than anywhere else on this planet."[66]

4

Recruiting for Engagement in Angola

Official Propaganda and Personal Motivation

According to official figures, more than 370,000 soldiers and approximately 50,000 civilians were stationed in Angola between 1975 and 1991.[1] This chapter analyzes the strategies the Cuban government deployed in 1976 to recruit volunteers for such a massive campaign. On the basis of interviews with former participants in Angola, I then intend to compare the official strategies with what truly motivated no less than 5 percent of the Cuban population, civilians and soldiers alike, to volunteer for a two-year period over the course of the next sixteen years.[2] This is the first study to deal with the importance of Cubans' personal commitment, without which the authorities could never have carried out their ambitious cooperation plans.

New Men, Internationalists, and Missionaries

Up until Cuba's engagement in Angola, there was little need for Cuban volunteers to take part in "missions" beyond their country's borders. This situation changed completely in 1976 when, within a very short space of time, the demand for large numbers of civil aid workers and soldiers increased dramatically. Just a few years later, the Cuban government sent out an appeal for several thousand more volunteers for large-scale civil and military campaigns in Ethiopia and Nicaragua. Initially the government was able to cover military personnel with reservists, special commando units, and elite troops of the Ministry of the Interior (MININT). But for the first time in 1976, it had to actively encourage civilians to engage extensively in Angola. The government needed committed people who could supply humanitarian aid in the name of the revolution. On this occasion the government specifically targeted women in order to reach the number of aid workers they required in the education and health sectors (and to some extent also in the military sector).[3]

The government's recruitment strategy aimed at mobilizing people to join the cause of their own free will. Consciously avoiding the use of force, it encouraged those who volunteered to do so in the spirit of solidarity and internationalist conviction. Thus the government declared engagement in Angola to be an "internationalist mission of solidarity" in pursuit of revolutionary ideals, and it therefore made no promise of material advantage—at least not explicitly.[4] The population had to be convinced that their involvement was a political necessity, and propaganda concentrated on making moral appeals to the revolutionary duty of every individual. The fact that the volunteers were to serve in a war zone was of secondary importance, and there was no mention of the dangers that this might entail. Instead the government emphasized the principles of "internationalist solidarity" and Che Guevara's vision of the "new man." The result was a political discourse that not only called upon the "duties of blood ties" but also drew on Christian humanistic values such as self-sacrifice and emphasized moral principles surrounding "guilt" and "redemption."

In order to realize the vision of a permanent, global revolution, the "subjects of the revolution" had to be included in the process of social transformation. It was crucial to teach the Cuban people to become "new men," whose duty it was not only to help revolutionize their own society but also to employ their revolutionary zeal globally. Guevara's ideal of the "new man" was someone who incorporated boundless self-sacrifice and revolutionary altruism and who was ever willing to serve the revolution. The Cuban government used this ideal as the moral high ground on which each individual should fulfill his duty by volunteering in Angola. The willingness to participate in such internationalist projects as a sign of solidarity and humanism now became the benchmark of individual revolutionary conviction. The *Übermensch* envisaged by Guevara was a mythological mixture of revolutionary heroism and sacrifice, in which Guevara linked elements of Martí's humanism to a Marxist-inspired image of man. Accordingly, self-liberation could only be achieved through a profound change of mentality.[5] The high moral demands that the revolutionary leaders had imposed upon themselves were thereby transferred to the entire Cuban population. Engagement in Angola opened a new chapter in the education of the "new man" at a time when the revolution had been consolidated at home. In 1975, Guevara's prophecies ten years earlier in his essay "El Socialismo y el hombre en Cuba" (Socialism and Man in Cuba)[6] seemed to have come true. In this essay, Guevara emphasized that the Cuban people had a particular duty to spread the revolution across the globe: in his eyes they formed the avant-garde who must show the masses in Latin America and throughout the world the way down "the ultimate path to freedom."[7] He saw the Cubans as a "chosen people" who had a special calling to revolutionize the world. The complement to this vision was José Martí's humanist idea that "the Fatherland is humanity," a statement that made the revolutionary call "Fatherland or Death" more pertinent and legitimate than ever.

Following his death, Guevara himself was elevated as the symbol of the "new man" and an example to all Cubans. Guevara's moral and political ideals were partly responsible for Castro's willingness to divert human resources from Cuba and deploy them on the MPLA's behalf in the struggle for power in Angola. Castro's message to the people during the July 1976 state visit of the Angolan president, Agostinho Neto, was unambiguous: "we expect from our people, our workers, and, especially, our youth, that in the same way in which hundreds of thousands were willing to go and fight in Angola there will now be tens of thousands willing to give Angola this civilian cooperation."[8]

In the spring of 1976, Neto had asked Cuba for considerable human resources to help them build independent Angola. That summer he came to Cuba as a petitioner, but he was also fully aware that his request corresponded with the Cuban government's claim of "internationalist solidarity." Castro put himself at the service of Neto and the MPLA and was prepared to provide the work force needed. He called upon the people to commit themselves to serving as "heroes of peace."[9] Owing to shared history and "blood ties,"[10] he claimed, every Cuban had a duty to sacrifice himself in order to repay Cuba's "debt to humanity."[11] The "collective guilt" to which Castro referred resulted from the nineteenth-century system of slavery and the fact that tens of thousands of slaves and former slaves had fought for Cuba's independence. There was no escaping the "blood ties" between Cuba and Angola and the resulting moral duty of all Cubans to engage in Angola as members of an "Afro-Latin American nation."

While in Cuba, Neto openly supported Castro's idea of a transatlantic "Afro-Latin American nation." His presence became central to the propaganda campaign, and his visit was carefully staged as a popular event. The Cuban government put on a resounding official reception for Neto. He and Castro traveled across the island, frequently appearing in Cuban media photos embracing like brothers.[12] During this visit, President Neto and the Angolans won a place in the hearts of the entire Cuban population. The presence of Neto's mother, Dona María da Silva, was particularly symbolic of the close "family ties" between the Cubans and Angolans. During the visit, Dona María adopted the Castro brothers into her own family, an event that received extensive photo coverage in the Cuban press.[13] The aim was to gain the trust of the Cuban people on an emotional level in order to make it easier to recruit volunteers in the near future. The visual and symbolic message of the visit portrayed Angola and Neto as the African counterparts of Cuba and its revolutionaries. The Cuban government even went so far as to compare Neto (himself a writer and poet) with the Cuban apostle, hailing him as the "African Martí."[14]

In order to guarantee continuity in major foreign engagement in the future, it was necessary for the government to involve the young generation that had grown up with the revolution. In the mid-1970s, the new generation's participation in Angola clearly illustrated that revolutionary consciousness had at this initial stage been passed on. One of the crucial factors was the sanctification of Che and his omnipresence as an icon and symbol of the ultimate "heroic *guerrillero*" to the young generation. It was not without reason that the motto of the children's organization, the Pioneers, was "*Seremos como el Che*," "We shall be like Che."

One of my interviewees, Belkis Vega Belmonte, who worked as a film director and was involved in the production of propaganda films about Angola in 1983 and 1994,[15] underlined the extent to which the revolution had influenced the generation who had grown up with it, and how it had awakened in them the desire to achieve something "heroic" themselves. As in her case, members of this generation even helped shape the role models of revolutionary archetypes and provide other icons: "I believe that many of my generation were influenced by Che Guevara and the Beatles. . . . I was an absolute fan of Guevara. . . . We were all too young to take part in the struggle against the Batista dictatorship. . . . We didn't experience either Girón or Moncada, and I wasn't involved in either the literacy campaign or the ten-million-ton harvest. We hadn't directly experienced any of these heroic actions. . . . That's what a lot of people thought, at least from my generation."[16]

The clearest link between the myth of Che and engagement in Angola were the brigades of student teachers, the Destacamento Pedagógico Internacionalista "Che Guevara" (DPI, Internationalist Teacher Brigade Che Guevara), founded in 1977. By 1986, these brigades had sent over two thousand students between the ages of seventeen and twenty-two to Angola to support the education campaign. The brigades were a prime example of how Castro's pragmatism tied in with political ideals. They were a social experiment, an attempt to produce a political and pedagogical elite troop of young cadres who were prepared to prove their revolutionary commitment by joining an internationalist mission abroad (and willing if necessary to replace their "pens with weapons").[17] The young Cubans were to be given a chance of "heroic" experience in Angola while strengthening their commitment to the revolutionary cause. As in all

Emblem of the Internationalist Student-Teacher Brigade "Che Guevara" (photo by Christine Hatzky)

other campaigns, this one was based on the principle that dedication to the revolution was not borne of theory but of practical experience.[18]

An "education mission" was perfectly well suited to the task of forging revolutionary cadres. War-torn, underdeveloped Angola would cast a spotlight on the successes of socialist Cuba. Particularly Cubans of African descent would become more aware of the benefits of an egalitarian society, which was, at least superficially, antiracist. Cuba's youth could experience firsthand the destructive impact of colonialism, capitalism, and imperialism in the Tricontinental countries.

"Every person on earth has the right to education and, in return, the duty to contribute to the education of others," was the motto of the student brigades.[19] The moral responsibility incorporated in this statement, however, had little to do with the historic guilt that Castro invoked, but rather referred to the fact that all Cubans, regardless of skin color and class, could benefit from the achievements of the revolution in the education sector and had the chance to learn a profession. Just as earlier it was taken for granted that Cuban youth would get an education, now they were expected to volunteer in Angola and contribute to education there. Making a commitment to helping in Angola was a way for the new generation to pay their debt to society.

Moral principles akin to the Christian concepts of guilt, redemption, and duty also seem to have been integral to the government's recruitment strategies. In his appeals to moral principle, revolutionary duty, self-sacrifice, and commitment to a just cause, Guevara's speeches were full of redemptive rhetoric and Christian imagery. Castro's words were likewise inspired by Christianity, but in contrast to Guevara, his analogies were less mythological and more practical and hands-on. In his recruitment campaign for Angola, Castro combined political propaganda with Christian values, consciously raising the question of historic, collective guilt, while offering the chance of redemption through practical assistance to "African brothers and sisters."[20]

In public, Castro very seldom admitted that his revolutionary ideals were partly informed by Christianity. His "nighttime talks" in May 1985 with the Brazilian Dominican friar Frei Betto on the subjects of Christianity, socialism, and liberation theology represent one of the few occasions when he did mention his inspiration from Christian sources. Referring to his Jesuit upbringing, Castro made several comments that complemented the revolutionary values defined by Guevara in the 1960s. Castro emphasized the Jesuit values of character, determination, personal courage, a sense of justice, strictness, and discipline. He even maintained that without the values instilled in him by the Jesuits, he may never have become a revolutionary, as Christian faith and revolutionary commitment were to his mind closely linked.[21] Such statements were all the more surprising in view of the fact that even in 1985 the Cuban government strictly distanced itself from the Catholic church and discriminated against followers of the Catholic religion and its syncretic offshoots. But Castro's comments have to be taken in context. The audience he was addressing was made up of followers of liberation theology, a strong movement within the Catholic church in Latin America, of which Betto is a leading representative. Nevertheless, Castro's claims are definitely credible, particularly with regard to the Christian influences on his life.

Of particular interest are the parallels that Castro drew during his talks with Betto between the Cuban internationalists and Christian missionaries. He emphasized the sacrifices that teachers and doctors in Africa and Latin America were willing to make: "We have [in place of missionaries] internationalists, thousands of Cubans who are fulfilling international missions [including] the example of our teachers who went to Nicaragua to live under dire circumstances with the families of peasants."[22] Castro summed up their contributions the following way: "the Cubans, who work as teachers, doctors, engineers, technicians and skilled workers in other countries (thousands are prepared to do so, even under the most difficult circumstances and sometimes at the cost of their own lives, which is proof of their dedication to their principles and high degree of solidarity) are an expression of the practical implementation of respect, reverence and love."[23]

The Motivation of the Cuban Population

To what extent was the official propaganda instrumental in motivating Cubans to volunteer to go to Angola? During my research in Cuba, the United States, and Angola, I asked former participants about their personal reasons for going to Angola. In this section their accounts and memories take center stage. During the interviews, one of my main questions was what actually moved them to travel six thousand miles to work in a war-torn region of Africa. When I evaluated their responses, I found that beyond the official discourse, there was a large variety of reasons for people volunteering. A sense of duty, humanist principles, the desire for travel and adventure, and the hope of career advancement or material gain all played a role alongside their commitment to the revolution. Although I analyze statements that illustrate discrepancies between personal motivation, subjective expectations, and the official government discourse, I also look at accounts indicating that government propaganda did indeed present individuals with a suitable framework within which they were able to incorporate revolutionary ideals into their own biographies. Finally, I ask to what degree this voluntarism was actually voluntary, and I comment on the extent to which social parameters allowed people to make their own decisions about taking part in it.

To date, there have been no studies on the personal motivations of Cubans (or any other nationals) for participating in military and/or civil engagement in Angola. With the exception of a few official statistics from Cuban ministries, no public information is available to date regarding the professional or sociocultural backgrounds of those who signed up. Cuban publications and films on the subject have served exclusively propagandistic purposes, giving the impression that all Cubans volunteered of their own free will and acted in the spirit of solidarity and revolutionary ideals. Almost all these films and publications glorify military engagement in Angola, emphasizing the courage of the soldiers and the effectiveness of Cuba's military strategy.

With only very few exceptions, a hierarchical structure governs the published accounts of engagement in Angola:[24] in general publications on the subject are limited to the autobiographical memoirs of high-ranking officials, and little is heard from the "common" soldier. The publications and films on Cuban engagement with Angola are a mixture of wartime adventure stories and edifying literature. Depending on their date of release, they served either to encourage even more soldiers to sign up for Angola or to justify the high number of casualties in retrospect.[25] The few publications that deal with civil engagement abroad (in Angola and other countries of the Third World) treat it as a given that the volunteers acted through altruistic and revolutionary ideals in the spirit of solidarity.[26] These works do include individual recollections, but they exclusively toe the line of official government propaganda.

Only very recently have gaps begun to appear in the hermetic discourse that has presented engagement in Angola as a glorified and idealized success story. In 2008, Limbania "Nancy" Jiménez Rodríguez, a Cuban social scientist and historian, published a study of Cuban women's involvement in international engagement worldwide. For the first time, she addressed gender aspects of the difficult family circumstances that women faced when they volunteered for "missions" abroad. She based her study on five hundred partly quantitative, partly biographic interviews with former civilian and military internationalist women. Jiménez, who herself held a position of responsibility in the military and civil education campaigns in Angola, was not so much concerned with providing a critical appraisal of Cuban foreign engagement. Her aim was to emphasize the crucial role played by women in internationalist projects and to give them their due recognition for their willingness to make sacrifices, such as leaving their children and families behind when they volunteered to go abroad.[27] Although Jiménez maintains the tenor of official government propaganda, she does ignore some of its prescriptions. For example, she portrays how important women were to the success of foreign engagement and puts them center stage, thereby breaking with the tradition of interpreting military and civil engagement from a purely male perspective. She also mentions individual motivations behind women's decisions whether or not to volunteer, and she describes the personal challenges they faced. She thereby shows that women volunteered for internationalist causes out of a wide variety of personal reasons, interests, and motives—not only out of revolutionary zeal. Her study illustrates clearly that the decision to volunteer was particularly difficult for women who had to leave children behind.[28]

Other interviewees who described their own personal and family circumstances also illustrated how difficult it had been to volunteer for Angola. When volunteers went to Angola, the government guaranteed their jobs in Cuba until their return and continued to pay their salaries to their families at home. The volunteers received no additional remuneration for their work in Angola, with the exception of a monthly allowance worth around ten US dollars. They also received free board and lodgings and did not have to pay travel expenses. In addition, each volunteer had the right to four weeks of annual home leave. These modest provisions were made with families in mind, but civil engagement in Angola nevertheless meant that families were separated for one to two years. Partners were generally left behind in Cuba, unless both had sought-after professions,[29] and even that was an exception that applied only to government officials and politically reliable Party members. If both partners were allowed to go to Angola together, children generally remained behind in Cuba to ensure that their parents would return after completing their stint. Even today, the Cuban government uses family separation as a means of preventing people from escaping when they are sent abroad. Again, exceptions were and still are made for high-ranking officials and Party members—persons known to be particularly trustworthy and loyal to the government.[30] However, all evidence suggests that citizens could, without fear of real social or professional repercussions, refuse to participate in the volunteer program on the grounds of family commitments.

Outside Cuba, doubts were being raised as to whether the Cuban people were serving in Angola voluntarily and out of true conviction. Most of these pointed remarks were politically motivated and belonged to critics of the Cuban government. The 1987 defection of the Cuban general in Angola, Rafael del Pino (who escaped to Miami and publicly criticized military engagement),[31] encouraged Cuban exiles to air their own suspicions. To date, only the exiled Cuban social scientist Juan M. del Aguila has made any attempt to provide empirical evidence for these aspersions in an essay he published in 1989, but he was unable to prove accusations of forced recruitment by the Cuban military. Following several interviews, during which del Aguila questioned exiled Cubans about their experiences of military engagement in Angola, he was only able to confirm the growing rejection of voluntary service in the Angolan war.[32] Despite the questionable reliability of his conclusions, del Aguila's account does reflect a tendency manifested also during my research. The Cuban people's initial enthusiasm for engagement in Angola gave way to increasing disenchantment, not least because of the rising death toll from the mid-1980s, which according to official figures was 2,016 after the end of Cuba's engagement in Angola in 1991.[33]

The eyewitness interviews I conducted also queried the significance of personal motivations and the extent to which the decision to go to Angola was voluntary. Even though my interviews in Cuba took place under difficult circumstances and were, as already mentioned, sometimes subject to restrictions, on the whole they afforded a surprisingly multifaceted view of the many and varied motives for volunteering. The interviews made me aware of the emotional impact on Cuban society of this engagement in Angola, but even more importantly, they gave me a better understanding of how individuals subjectively appropriate historic processes. This awareness arose not only from the technique of biographic interview, but also from the opportunity I had to compare the accounts and memories of eyewitnesses still living in Cuba with those of eyewitnesses now living in exile. Combined with this input, my analysis also incorporated written memoirs of former participants. The expert interviews

I held in Cuba, the United States, and Angola then allowed me to arrange individual memories and accounts into a wider sociopolitical context and to judge the extent to which my biographic interviews were representative. Biographic and expert interviews are not a quantitative survey with "measurable" statistical results. The memories that my interviewees shared about their involvement in Angola and their motivations for going there represent very subjective responses to and reflections on their own biographies and their personal and political motives. That is precisely why such memories give a unique insight into a discourse that can only be accessed in a personal interview because of restrictions on expression and the imperative of silence concerning engagement in Angola. It is particularly thanks to these memories that I was able to illustrate and highlight the gaps and discrepancies that exist between the official discourse and the motivation and decisions of individual people.

Revolutionary Duty, Historic Guilt, "Afro-Latin American" Identity?

Official discourse had a bearing on every interview I held and was reflected in the eyewitnesses' responses. The majority of interviewees living in Cuba emphasized their internationalist ideals and their sense of mission. "Che nostalgia" and the principle of "internationalist solidarity" were almost omnipresent. Many of the eyewitnesses recited—sometimes verbatim—the propaganda slogans disseminated by the government. Even though my interviewees may have acted out of true conviction, whenever engagement in Angola was mentioned, they responded with the same familiar slogans in a vehement, almost ritualistic manner. Moreover, my eyewitnesses were almost certainly affected by the interview situation, which required them to give personal accounts to a stranger who intended to evaluate their responses in a book. Perhaps their narratives were also influenced by the pressure to manifest their political determination to the outside world.

Upon further evaluation of the interviewees' statements, I came to realize that many of them referred to revolutionary duty rather than to their conviction, and that this was a way of distancing themselves from their decision to volunteer. The claim that they had done their duty seemed to express that individuals had acted out of a sense of social responsibility rather than deep-rooted conviction. In these instances the choice of words also appears to indicate a perfect awareness that engagement served the aims of government foreign policy.

But in what sense did Cubans feel they had a duty? According to the responses of my interviewees, Castro's propaganda about Cuba's historic "debt to humankind" that could be repaid by joining the Angolan cause was of crucial importance.[34] This sense of guilt and the opportunity for "redemption" through engagement in Angola had obviously become deeply anchored in the collective consciousness. But the awareness of being indebted and bound to repay the debt was not nearly as abstract as the official government discourse would have it. It was not Castro's definition of Cuba as an "Afro-Latin American nation" and the resulting collective historic guilt of Cuba toward Africa that made Cubans feel indebted; in most cases people felt they had a concrete and personal duty to share the education opportunities that the revolution had offered them.

The social reforms introduced after 1959, above all in education, provided an opportunity for many women, Afro-Cubans, and members of underprivileged classes to improve their status in society through school and through professional and university qualifications. The government's appeal for civilian volunteers to assist in Angola was understood as a call to pass on the benefits of a free education to their fellow mankind. More than half of my interviewees claimed that they had only been able to attain their professional and current social status through the education programs of the revolution, and they considered engagement in Angola as a chance to pay their dues for their own free education and social betterment. Government propaganda actively encouraged this attitude by holding up the "apostle" of Cuban independence, José Martí—with considerable impact: Cubans felt obliged to support Angola.[35] With regard to the "Afro-Latin American nation" invoked by the government, I asked my interviewees whether they had been motivated to go to Angola by this apparent transnational and transcultural identity. The responses to this question deviated considerably from the official discourse and could not have been more explicit. Irrespective of whether my interviewees had African ancestors or not, the majority rejected the idea that they felt a special affinity to Africa or Angola. This rejection was at times even more pronounced among Afro-Cubans. Nobody could or would identify with Africa and Angola. Some of my interviewees even made it quite clear that they regarded the propagation of the "Afro-Latin American nation" to be pure political fantasy and a clever government maneuver. Only three of my interviewees said that the search for their own roots on the African continent had been a motivating factor.[36]

My question regarding the "Afro-Latin American" identity was very revealing in another sense. The majority of my interviewees admitted that when they first heard the appeal to help in Angola they knew absolutely nothing of Africa. Before they went to Angola, Africa was a very remote and faraway place.[37] Judging from their answers, their knowledge of Africa was limited to a tiny number of stereotypical African images of "wilderness" and "people with a very low cultural level," of "jungles" and "wild animals" (lions, giraffes, snakes), and even "cannibals."[38] In many cases even "Tarzan" was cited as the immediate association with Africa.[39] According to the memories of many of my interviewees, the first time they sensed any real connection with Africa and Angola was during the state visit of Agostinho Neto to Cuba in July 1976.[40]

Nevertheless, the awareness of African roots in Cuban society was manifest throughout the interviews, if only indirectly. For example, some of my interviewees cited the popular words of wisdom referring to the high number of Cubans of mixed origin, "If you've got nothing of the Congolese, you've got something of the Carabali."[41] In cultural terms, this dictum indicates society's general acceptance that all Cubans, even those who appear "white," are very probably of African ancestry. But it also expresses the longing of people who are visibly of African descent to abolish discrimination and put an end to the social and cultural stigma attached to African ethnicity in Cuban society. On an even deeper sociopsychological level, however, the dictum signifies that it is enough just to acknowledge the African roots in Cuban society; there is no particular interest in discovering more about them.[42] This attitude accords with the government's political strategy of officially banning racial discrimination while remaining silent on the issues of race and cultural differences, and also avoiding public debate about slavery and racism in the assumption that sociopolitical measures would on their own lead to the integration of the black population. With reference to Angolan engagement, my interviewees seemed to consider that their personal involvement meant they had repaid their "historic and collective debt" to victims of slavery and racism. At least during the interviews, my interviewees never directly addressed in any detail the question of African roots in Cuban society and the resulting cultural differences, or the subtle discrimination that still exists among the population. Only one interviewee claimed that he had been motivated to volunteer because of racism and the apartheid regime of South Africa (citing one of the main official reasons for Cuban involvement in Angola).[43]

Humanists, "Chosen Ones," and Social Advancement

Based on my findings from eyewitness accounts, the government's appeal to values such as humanism and self-sacrifice was successful. Accordingly, one of the main motivations of volunteers was the opportunity to demonstrate their own humanism. At the same time, they could serve the moral and revolutionary ideals of the "new man" by selflessly contributing to the revolutionary and humanitarian cause and helping those they perceived as weaker than themselves. The volunteers placed great importance on practical actions that made them feel needed and therefore more "humane," as some of my interviewees expressed it. It would seem that Castro's appeal had created the ideal frame of reference within which people could construct connections with their individual biographies, whereby they also seemed to have strengthened their self-respect.

Some accounts indicate that the Cuban media effectively supported the propaganda encouraging self-sacrifice by portraying Africa as a continent blighted by hunger and underdevelopment. Images of poverty and malnourishment, which were on a par with reports on Africa in the Western media, evidently served to awaken compassion and the desire to help.[44] Two of my interviewees expressed these feelings with the following words: "The image I had [of Africa] before I left was based on what little I had seen on TV—a continent inhabited by blacks—poor countries, . . . because they kept repeating that Africa was the poorest continent in the world and that it had never been developed, even though it had rich resources."[45] The second interviewee confirmed this statement: "What . . . we saw on TV, . . . the thin, malnourished people . . . , all these terrible impressions that we weren't used to in Cuba. . . . All these thin people, lacking attention, without anything."[46]

This impression was confirmed by the Africa expert Juan Benemelis. In the 1960s he served as a Cuban diplomat in Africa before joining the Cuban Ministry of Foreign Affairs' expert committee of the Africa department and eventually going into exile in Miami, where he has been living since 1980. In the many publications he released in exile,[47] he has been highly polemical toward the Cuban government's foreign policy in the Third World. In the interview, he explained that the humanitarian vision was a crucial part of people's decisions to volunteer for the civil aid programs in Africa. In his opinion, the Cubans who worked in Africa were in many ways even "more revolutionary than the regime," and it was their huge personal commitment that made the success of the missions at all possible.[48] A similar opinion was expressed by the education specialist and historian Domingo Amuchástegui, who worked from 1985 to 1988 as an advisor to the Angolan Ministry of Education, and who has been living in exile in the United States since 1994.[49]

Benemelis and another Cuban exile I interviewed, Alcibíades Hidalgo, both believed that the engagement of thousands of Cubans in civil aid projects abroad considerably improved the foreign prestige of Cuba in the countries of the Third World and in Africa. However, both Benemelis and Hidalgo saw the participants as mere "tools" in the government's foreign policy agenda. Until his defection in 2002, Hidalgo was chief of staff and one of the closest advisors to the then minister of the interior and commander in chief of the armed forces, Raúl Castro, and as such he was instrumental in military engagement in Angola. It is worth noting that Rodolfo Puente Ferro, the former Cuban ambassador in Angola (1983–1986) and at the time of the interview Africa department head of the Central Committee of the Communist Party of Cuba (PCC), backed the Cuban exiles' assessment of the situation. During the interview he asserted that the quality of possessing know-how and sharing it with people in need, and the humanism and solidarity that this demonstrates, will always be positively received throughout the world, irrespective of the sociopolitical context in which the help was given.[50]

One particular attraction of volunteering for Angola was the chance for Cubans to improve their social prestige—both within their immediate social environments and within society as a whole—by setting themselves apart from others in a positive way and demonstrating moral leadership. Volunteers stood out as the "chosen ones," who had been awarded the privilege of fulfilling a mission of national and international importance in the name of the revolution. The "chosen" came particularly close to the prevailing social ideal of the "new man."[51] According to my interviewees, those who went to Angola were regarded as "heroes" in the eyes of the people.[52] Another interviewee summed up the image he had of himself in the following words: "I saw the situation that existed in Angola, but more from a distance in the sense that I had never considered getting a chance to visit this country or carry out a mission there. That's why I regarded myself as privileged, . . . chosen to carry out this mission."[53] Another interviewee remarked, "We were chosen; not everyone had the privilege of going there. We were lucky to be allowed to go."[54] One of the young members of the DPI expressed the feeling of having been "chosen" as follows in her written memoirs:

> I was 19 at the time. . . . I had never dreamt that I would ever have the chance to carry out a mission outside Cuba. My feelings at that moment were a mixture of concern, fear, enthusiasm, curiosity, solidarity, everything all mixed up . . . and the desire to be part of it! . . . I was third on the list, and my first thought was what my parents and brothers would say when I told them that their petted little girl was leaving Cuba for two years and going to a country at civil war![55]

The call for civilian volunteers in Angola inspired youthful optimism and provided a hitherto unknown opportunity for many young women to develop beyond parental control and break away from traditional role models. The formation of teacher brigades mainly comprising females gave young women for the first time the explicit opportunity to incorporate the heroic symbol of Che into their own female biographies.[56] But Angola also gave Cuban youth the chance to fulfill a need common to young people of both genders: the desire to leave the parental home. Most members of the student brigades were still minors when the chance to volunteer arose, and Angola provided them with the welcome opportunity to spread their wings and find self-fulfillment among their peers. For other young participants, many of whom were thirty and under, the journey to Angola was an initiation into adulthood, a test of maturity and courage. One interviewee described his experience in the military as follows: "I left as an adolescent and returned as a man."[57] It was no coincidence that the government's appeal targeted young people. Through the student brigades, the government was able to harness youthful desires (for knowledge, adventure, action, and self-realization) and channel them into its own political goals.

A stint in Angola also opened opportunities for a fast-track career among students, young professionals, and people with little work experience. The résumés of many of my interviewees confirm this and highlight the importance of career as a motivation for volunteering. An appointment as an advisor in Angolan government institutions such as the Ministry of Education, for instance, was considered equivalent to vocational training because it entailed responsibility for tasks of national importance within a foreign context. Some had only just completed their studies and had very little practical experience, and those who did have professional experience had till then only worked at a local or regional level.[58] Cuban teachers and education specialists helped to establish, among other things, the administration of Angolan education: they devised curricula and designed school books and teaching materials. Others helped conceive and implement the literacy campaign, worked in educational research, or specialized in fields such as teacher training. Those who went to work as teachers at the primary and secondary levels also hoped for better career opportunities upon their return. Often this hope was realized and the "simple" primary teacher was promoted to primary-school principal, as was the case with several of my interviewees.[59]

Engagement in Angola also offered individuals in other professional fields the chance to further their careers. It created an interest in scientific research and whetted the thirst for knowledge. Doctors, for instance, had the opportunity to practice in an unknown environment and expand their professional skills vastly. The doctors and professors of medicine whom I interviewed explained that during their stay in Angola they got to know and treat illnesses that they had only read about in textbooks.[60] Two of the doctors mentioned that they had worked for the first time with people who had never been exposed to pharmaceuticals such as antibiotics, and so the success of treatments was surprisingly high: "You could even treat malaria with Aspirin."[61] Angola also gave them the chance to learn from "all the medical schools of the world,"[62] as doctors had their first opportunity to discuss medical problems with colleagues from other countries and exchange treatment methods. The health sector was one area in which the Angolan government was able to rely on broad international cooperation, and the doctors therefore came from the Eastern bloc states, the Soviet Union, Vietnam and even the Western world.[63]

Cuban engagement in Angola offered the ten university professors whom I interviewed the welcome chance to expand their knowledge and skills, too.[64] Most of them worked in the natural and technical sciences as physicists, chemists, pharmacists, biologists, agricultural scientists, veterinary doctors, and engineers. As the majority of Portuguese lecturers and researchers at the University of Angola had fled the country, the Cuban scientists faced the exciting prospect of rebuilding and restructuring teaching and scientific activity. Angola allowed them to gain important administrative experience in setting up departments and even complete faculties. They were also able to profit from the fact that during the colonial period, university laboratories had been equipped with modern Western technology (laboratory tools, measuring equipment, etc.), which was, to a large extent, completely unknown in Cuba. Moreover, the Cuban scholars were able to familiarize themselves with results and methods of Western research, particularly in veterinary medicine, pharmacology, and biology.[65]

Travelers, Adventurers, and Dropouts

Another main personal motive for going to Angola was curiosity and the chance to travel and experience another country. At least that is what the spontaneous answers of most eyewitnesses seem to suggest. In Cuba of the 1970s and 1980s, the chance to travel was highly attractive, and it represented a status symbol. The prestige attached to travel resulted from the extremely stringent travel restrictions imposed by the government to curb the number of people emigrating. It was impossible for Cubans to visit non-Communist countries, except in an official capacity in government service (or where government interests were concerned). Cubans could undertake study and research trips to the Soviet Union and other friendly countries of the Eastern bloc, but only under certain conditions. In order to receive scholarships, candidates had to demonstrate either an exceptional academic record or exemplary political commitment. Trips to foreign socialist countries were also awarded for outstanding professional achievements and contributions to the Party, trade unions, military, and other social organizations.

Angola, on the contrary, presented Cubans with the chance to travel without having earned the privilege through academic, professional, or political merit. It also appears that Angola was considered a more attractive destination than the countries of the Eastern bloc—at least at the beginning, when the consequences of war were not yet visible—as Cubans did not consider it to be a socialist country (not to mention the fact that the Cubans harbored a dislike for the cold climate and mentality of Russia and Eastern Europe). The Cubans perceived Angola as a tropical and exotic place, and that made it all the more alluring. They projected all sorts of images onto it, most of which stemmed from prevailing stereotypes and their ignorance of the continent. Angola stirred exotic fantasies of wilderness in Africa; Angola promised adventure and all the things that people had only read about in books.[66] "I imagined Africa in the same way as I imagined it as a child. . . . Countries of indigenous tribes, lots of wild animals . . . and in a more touristy way, hunting and safaris. That was the picture I had. . . ."[67]

Many expected their journey to Angola to be an enriching experience that would expand their horizons. In this respect Cubans seem to have differed little from all other globe-trotters of this world.[68] And just like many other travelers in different contexts and throughout the centuries, many Cubans were simply looking for adventure.[69] For the majority, Angola was also a welcome opportunity to escape the routine of everyday life. This motivation was irrespective of whether the interviewees had been involved in the military or civil aid campaign, or in both. My Cuban exile interviewees also emphasized that a spirit of adventure and curiosity about Africa motivated many (young) Cubans to volunteer.[70] One of the interviewees, who had been involved in military engagement between 1986 and 1988, told of his great desire to get to know the country. As in many other cases, his curiosity about Angola had been roused by returnees' incredible stories: "I was incredibly curious. When they started to tell me about all the things that were there, I wanted to know for myself and I told myself that I had to go to Africa to see if it was all true. Because there are always these things that people tell you, . . . that there is a red mountain. . . . And you feel the need to go and see for yourself whether the mountain really is red. . . ."[71]

Others were tempted by the notion of boundless freedom in Angola and of an unchecked, free lifestyle, far from the monotony and responsibilities of everyday life. One of my interviewees, who initially served as a soldier in Angola in 1975 and returned for a second stint as a civil aid worker, recounted the excitement of his first stay, which inspired him to volunteer for a second time. "Hat, pistol, just like a cowboy—and a jeep. I was off on my own at the age of 19, 20—just a kid. And I did what I wanted; I was completely crazy. I went hunting at one o'clock at night. . . . When I went to Angola, my wife here in Cuba was pregnant."[72]

Quite apart from my eyewitnesses' associations of Wild West romanticism, volunteering for Angola was also apparently an escape hatch out of relationships and marriages.[73] It is not surprising that people saw it as a way out of family problems—at least for a while. In the 1970s family life in Cuba was characterized by early marriage and a high incidence of teenage pregnancies, combined with acute accommodation shortages, particularly in the towns and cities. Many young couples were not granted their own flat upon marrying and had to share cramped accommodations with their parents or in-laws, often for years. The acute lack of housing placed a strain on families, marriages, and relationships in general and prevented young people from breaking free of their parents: this is another reason why so many young Cubans found the prospect of volunteering for Angola attractive.

The possibility of going to Angola also raised hopes of material benefits. Even though the official discourse never openly broached the matter, the Cuban people associated a stay abroad with the chance of acquiring goods that were almost unavailable in Cuba in the 1970s and 1980s. Those who engaged in Angola expected to be able "to bring something back" with them. This "something" did not refer to great fortunes, but first and foremost to "Western" consumer goods and commodities.[74] Del Aguila, the aforementioned Cuban exile and social scientist, concluded from the statements of Cuban exiles he interviewed that in many cases people did not go to Angola out of revolutionary conviction, but in the hope of being able to secure material advantage.[75] The people whom I interviewed and who still lived in Cuba, however, were reticent on this matter. It seems that the connection between engagement in Angola and material benefits remains a taboo subject.[76] This reticence may in part be due to the fate of General Arnaldo Ochoa, who was operating in Angola and executed in 1989 following accusations of personal gain through illegal trade in diamonds and ivory. Nevertheless, several of my interviewees confirmed that, thanks to official government information and the stories told by returnees, everyone knew that Angola was a wealthy country and this had naturally roused people's interest.[77]

The information disseminated by the government contained ample and unmistakable references to Angola's rich natural resources. Although there was never any official debate about the Cuban economy being able to benefit from this wealth, Castro sometimes referred to the riches of Angola, which had to be defended by Cuban forces against "plundering imperialists."[78] The weekly periodical of the Fuerzas Armadas Revolucionarias (FAR, Revolutionary Armed Forces), *Verde Olivo*, also ran an article in November 1975 about the wealth of Angola, in which it described deposits of diamonds, oil, and ore and spoke of the ideal climatic conditions for coffee growing. The photo accompanying the article depicted a bowl filled with diamonds, together with the subheading "condemned to imperialist greed."[79] The overall article, the photo, and particularly the subheading illustrate the willingness to use the prospect of "war booty" in order to encourage people to sign up for military engagement. Taken in context, the article reads as an appeal to anticipate imperialist "greed," obviously not for personal gain, but for the benefit of the Cuban community.

The government was therefore aware that by referring to the wealth of Angola they might encourage individuals to volunteer. It would seem, however, that most participants had no abstract notion of "wealth" but were simply interested in the very modest prospect of obtaining Western consumer goods, which were rare in Cuba and therefore all the more desirable: transistor radios, cassette decks, electrical kitchen and household appliances, shoes, toys, stationery, or simply fashionable "Western" clothing. The government reacted very quickly to these demands, and from 1979 it arranged for the Cuban Civil Administration in Angola to open special shops stocking consumer goods for Cuban volunteers. These shops were given the somewhat pejorative nickname of "*as lojas de Risquet*," "Risquet's Stores," after the head of the Cuban Civil Administration in Angola and initiator of these shops, Jorge Risquet Valdés.[80] The idea behind this state initiative was to direct back into the treasury the money volunteers spent on private goods and to prevent people from buying things on the free market or on the huge black market, the *candonga*, which had already appeared in the late 1970s. Volunteers were forbidden to buy in private Angolan stores, and it was a punishable offence to visit the *candonga*. One of my Cuban interviewees described the mechanism of "permitted" and "forbidden" purchases by relating an actual quarrel he experienced on leaving Angola. An Angolan customs officer tried to confiscate all the consumer goods such as radios and fans that the Cubans had bought on the free market. Owing to the fact that the customs officer was Angolan, the Cubans directed their anger against "the Angolans" rather than against their own authorities in Cuba, who had forbidden the import of the goods into Cuba.[81]

Volunteers?

All my interviewees, whether living in Cuba, in Angola, or in exile in Miami, confirmed to me that their decision to go to Angola had been voluntary. Some, however, then went on to qualify their statements. They claimed that only those who did not belong to the PCC were able to ignore the official appeal to volunteer for Angola without suffering any considerable disadvantages. My Cuban interviewees and the Cuban exiles in Miami and Angola informed me that if Party members or university staff refused to answer the call to go to Angola, they ran the risk of sanctions, and their jobs were put at stake.[82]

In order to answer the question of to what degree Cubans had room to maneuver and exercise their freedom in making decisions, it is first necessary to take into account several other sociopolitical factors. One factor is the need to differentiate between military and civil engagement. Another is the date of engagement. Those who signed up between 1975 and 1980 were still riding on the initial euphoria and certainty of victory that the Cuban government had advertised, and they had joined voluntarily in large numbers.[83] From the early 1980s the armed conflict in Angola intensified, and confidence among the Cubans that engagement would lead to (rapid) victory began to wane. The death of Agostinho Neto in September 1979 represented a clear turning point in popular consciousness. Neto symbolized the political friendship and cultural ties between Cuba and Angola, and he enjoyed the confidence of the Cuban people. His leadership acted as a guarantee for the legitimacy of Cuba's military and civil involvement in Angola. His death gave rise to a general feeling of uncertainty about the future of the country, not only in Cuba.

Even in the absence of studies showing how the Cuban population's willingness to volunteer in Angola changed over the duration of the engagement, the escalating political and military situation in Angola is sufficient reason to assume that after 1980 the general willingness to join up declined considerably. Cuban civilians in Angola had become the target of assaults, and the number of military casualties was rising. In the end, not even the most politically committed Cubans wanted to go to a war-torn country whose conflict had little to do with their own reality, and where the danger of losing their lives was considerable. An important indication of this assumption is that in the mid-1980s the government seems only to have been able to maintain the number of soldiers needed for military engagement by passing a decree reducing obligatory military service (from three to two years) for those who volunteered for Angola.[84]

Cuba's civil engagement seems to have involved recruitment techniques designed to pressure individuals into volunteering, as I was told by one of my Cuban exiles who cited his own biography as an example. He had worked as an art critic and lecturer of philosophy at the University of Havana. He enjoyed a privileged position and had been allowed to undertake several business trips to Western countries. Suddenly he was refused permission to travel, and when he asked the reason, a university official for state security informed him that he was no longer entitled to a passport because the state feared that he would defect if he went abroad again. The official then made him the following "offer": if he spent a year as a volunteer providing civil aid in the Angolan city of Huambo, he would be able to regain the trust he had lost. My interviewee accepted the "offer," even though he was sent to Angola just shortly after the bombing of Cuban civilians in Angola in April 1984.[85]

It remains entirely unclear how many Cubans received such "offers" and were, as a result, persuaded to go to Angola. The extent of the Cuban state security's role in these decisions is also unknown. Having been a staff member to the then minster of the interior and commander in chief of the armed forces (Raúl Castro), the Cuban exile Alcibíades Hidalgo had inside knowledge of the recruitment practices of the time. During my interview with him he estimated that "thousands" of civilians may have been politically pressured into going to Angola.[86] He was unable to provide any proof, but his claims are similar to those of the exiled Angolan general Rafael del Pino, who claimed that military engagement in Angola served as a type of sanction, a "purgatory" used to punish politically suspect or unreliable officers, while providing them with the chance to "wash themselves clean."[87]

A clear sociopolitical sign of general dissatisfaction among the population was the exodus of 125,000 Cubans to the United States in the spring and summer of 1980. This exodus has to be understood within the context of international engagement. Cuba's intensive foreign involvement was exacerbating economic problems in Cuba itself—several tens of thousands of Cubans were simultaneously deployed in Ethiopia, Angola, and Nicaragua in civil and military campaigns. This gave rise to tensions within society, culminating in political crisis when the Peruvian embassy in Havana was occupied in April 1980, and several thousand Cubans vociferously and violently demanded permission to emigrate. The government reacted by opening the port of Mariel to the west of Havana and allowing Cuban exiles from the United States to collect their family members by boat. Many of the Cubans who seized the opportunity to escape were young men and women from urban areas, who had been raised in revolutionary Cuba and were candidates for engagement in Angola or had already participated. Among them were a large number of Afro-Cubans.[88] From the interviews he conducted, the social scientist del Aguila concluded that from the mid-1980s it had become evident that the war in Angola could not be won easily and that it was claiming the lives of many Cubans. Every time news of a fallen soldier arrived, it spread through Cuba like wildfire. And with every death, the people's rejection of Cuba's involvement in Angola grew.[89] For Cubans engaged in the civil aid campaign, the risk of becoming embroiled in military conflict was considerably smaller, which is why the decision for them to volunteer may have been easier. Nevertheless, from the mid-1980s at the latest, it also became obvious to potential civil aid volunteers that they too would be risking their lives. From 1983, Cubans became the target of military offensives and acts of sabotage perpetrated by UNITA and the South African army.

On analyzing the various sources of information I had at my disposal, I have been able to conclude the following. The Cuban government's public propaganda, with its subtle undertones, combined with sociopolitical circumstances to exert considerable influence on people's decisions to volunteer. The high pressure applied by society, the feeling of having to fulfill a "duty" and the desire simply to "be there" strongly influenced individual behavior. The ideological and moral tenor of governmental recruitment strategies extended to social institutions, political organizations, universities, schools, and work places, where individuals were explicitly approached regarding their willingness to volunteer, or where there was general peer pressure to conform. In particular the sociopolitical organizations, but also apparently the state-security apparatus, played a decisive role in attracting, selecting, and recruiting candidates. It is clear that only an authoritarian state would have been in a position to realize such a political project of mass mobilization. To counteract this social and political pressure, people developed their own discursive and practical strategies in order to reconcile public expectations with personal needs. Both political conviction and the feeling of fulfilling a social obligation combined with personal motivation, expectations, and desires that did not always correspond to the elevated ideological and moral cause cited by the government. Particularly the prospect of belonging to the ranks of the "chosen ones" by volunteering to go to Angola—and the feeling of living up to the ideal of the "heroic guerrilla," thus attaining greater respect within society—seems to have been extremely attractive to many Cubans. For others, Angola provided an opportunity to prove their own humanism by providing civil aid, for example in the health or education sector. Nevertheless, from the answers of my interviewees one cannot conclude that revolutionary, humanitarian, and altruistic ideals were the sole reasons for voluntary engagement. On the contrary, the call to join the Angolan cause offered people the chance to satisfy all sorts of individual needs. These included personal curiosity, wanderlust, the spirit of adventure, youthful enthusiasm, and also the hope of promoting professional and social status or acquiring material goods. Some saw engagement as a means of escape from difficult personal situations or the chance to win back lost political confidence. But against the sociopolitical backdrop of a rigidly organized, structured, and controlled society characterized by material deprivations, all these individual motives benefited the government's foreign policy aims—even though this has never been publicly addressed.

5

Education Policy in Cuba and Angola

It is impossible to grasp Cuban-Angolan cooperation in education without understanding the peculiarities of the Cuban education system and the MPLA's postcolonial educational objectives. I will therefore begin this chapter by looking at the salient features of the education reform initiated with the revolution and then go on to analyze the MPLA's educational aims and programs along with the many challenges these entailed. The central question revolves around the ideas behind education policy and the extent to which Cuban education concepts were applied and transferred to Angola and adapted to suit the specific circumstances of the country in its transition period. There is no doubt that Cuban education concepts served as a model for Angola. With its high level of illiteracy and acute shortage of skilled workers, postcolonial Angola faced many of the same challenges revolutionary Cuba did. The Cuban successes in modernizing its education system therefore pointed the way for planning and devising Angola's education reform. Cooperation also rested on a political consensus that Angola should adopt Cuban methods and their underlying ideology. Ten thousand Cuban education advisors, teachers, students, and lecturers, who had benefited from the educational opportunities of the revolution, were instrumental in establishing cooperation and helping to build Angola's education system between 1976 and 1991.

The Cuban Education System

One of the priorities of the 1959 revolution was to establish a modern education system. The overriding ideological principle was the formation of "new men" to be integrated into the new sociopolitical order. Through education, the Cuban people would become involved in the national and revolutionary project and in turn become the driving forces of social revolution. From that point on Cubans were to dedicate their skills selflessly to the common good rather than individual gain. Immediately after the triumph of the revolution, the new education system was set in motion. Over the years it was to undergo several reforms and adapt to new challenges. Alongside the establishment of universal health care, the Cuban education system is regarded as one of the success stories of the revolution. Within a very short space of time, the country made remarkable strides: by the mid-1960s, the Cuban government could boast education standards that were among the highest in the world.[1]

Access to education provided crucial impetus to social change in postrevolutionary society. Underprivileged classes, in particular Cubans of African origin, now had a real chance of social advancement. In the following pages, I will outline the educational offensive's salient features, which were partly embedded in far-reaching structural changes and in the ideological focus of a socialist education system. I will also look at the innovations in methodology and didactics that promoted the general acceptance of a project impacting all sectors of society. In the process I will highlight why Cuban education reform represented a suitable model for a new education system in postcolonial Angola and why some of the essential features of Cuba's education system transferred so easily.

Although the Cuban education system prior to the revolution was not the worst in Latin America, it nevertheless demonstrated many failings. In particular, there was great disparity between urban and rural regions. One year before the revolution, only half of the Cuban children required to attend school actually did so; only a quarter of adolescents over fifteen received a school education; and three-quarters of the rural population were illiterate or had failed to finish primary school.[2] As in the whole of Latin America, there was a tendency in Cuba to neglect state schools. Those who could afford it sent their children to private schools. The school system was therefore characterized by an extremely unfair distribution of educational opportunities, and pupils from wealthy urban families were at a distinct advantage. A World Bank report from 1951 confirmed the inefficiency of Cuba's educational structures. The report went on to condemn the system for teaching content that was divorced from the day-to-day reality of most Cuban children.[3] The new educational policies of the revolution managed to turn the situation around.

As early as 1959, the revolutionary government invested in education infrastructure and teacher training, encouraged the development of new curricula, and embarked upon a literacy campaign. It placed the entire education system under state control and in 1961 nationalized all private and confessional schools.[4] The Ministry of Education (MINED) and the Ministry of Higher Education

(MES), which was founded in the 1970s, were generally responsible for determining the content and structure of education. Between 1959 and 1961, hundreds of provisional schools were opened, particularly in rural areas, and a special teacher training program was introduced to train "folk teachers." Thousands of volunteers, pupils, and students were recruited to work at schools. Between 1959 and 1961 the number of pupils attending school had risen from 700,000 to 1.2 million.[5] Cuba's biggest military base, Campo Colombia (on the outskirts of Havana), was renamed the Ciudad Libertad (City of Liberty) and transformed into the largest teacher training institute in the country, which by 1961 was already accommodating 14,000 students.[6] It was here that the first university of pedagogy in Cuba was founded, the Instituto Superior Pedagógico "José Enrique Varona."

The most spectacular starting point for the government's new education policy was its literacy campaign, a domestic, national "education mission," which got underway in September 1960. The Cuban government called upon the principles of the nineteenth-century Cuban polymath José Martí, according to which every person had a right to education and a corresponding duty to contribute to the education of others,[7] and it appealed to the Cuban people's responsibility to join the campaign. More than 100,000 secondary pupils and students—half of whom were young women—answered the call at the beginning of 1961 and were drafted into the newly formed literacy brigades. Dressed in olive-green uniforms, each armed with a lantern, primer, and volume of Martí's poetry, the volunteers set out for the countryside, where they stayed for several months teaching the rural population to read and write. Another 150,000 volunteers remained in the towns and cities, where they dedicated their evenings to teaching people in deprived urban areas.[8]

The literacy campaign became the first successful large-scale sociopolitical experiment of mass mobilization, the objective of which was to popularize the aims of the revolution. It was not only a question of teaching the poorer classes to read and write and informing them of the purpose of the revolution; the young members of the urban middle classes were also to be politicized and sensitized to prevailing social injustice by being confronted with the desperate living standards of the rural population. The campaign's primary objectives were to incorporate the rural population in the revolutionary process and to promote an awareness of national unity in Cuba across the classes. To the Cuban population, the literacy campaign was the equivalent of a cultural revolution. The parents of young women from the middle and upper classes, fearing they were losing influence over their sheltered daughters' sexuality, protested against the campaign (a popular saying at the time was "One leaves, two return").[9] The rural community, for its part, was shocked at the behavior of the urban adolescents who joined the "Conrado Benitez" literacy brigades, because many of the young women wore trousers and smoked![10] Notwithstanding these protests and many other hurdles, including specific acts of sabotage by opponents of the revolution, the literacy campaign was a huge success. Within one year, 700,000 people learned to read and write, and in December 1961 the revolutionary government was able to proclaim Cuba a "nation free of illiteracy" and announce that the literacy rate among the Cuban population had reached 96 percent.[11]

After 1961, a comprehensive follow-up program and opportunities for continuing education sustained the successes of the literacy campaign. Thousands of people who had taught or been taught during the campaign were awarded scholarships in teacher training. Adult education programs also ran at evening schools and at the workplace. These again resembled political campaigns and were called in the revolutionary jargon of the day "Campaign for the 3rd Grade" or "Campaign for the 6th Grade." These initiatives proved very popular: half a million Cubans took part in the Campaign for the 3rd Grade. Hundreds of thousands of Cubans were able to benefit from elementary education, comprehensive professional training, and even university studies offered in the Worker-Peasant Faculties founded in 1963. More than 800,000 Cubans took part in educational initiatives for workers and peasants, 600,000 of whom achieved final qualifications.[12] The founding principles of the new Cuban education system were also echoed in the "Experimental World Literacy Programme" initiated by UNESCO in 1965.[13]

At the center of Cuba's educational initiatives was Martí's principle that study be linked to practical work in an effort to counteract people's unwillingness to perform physical labor, an attitude that had prevailed since slavery and the colonial period. Within the socialist economic and social system it became imperative to cultivate a new work ethic, since the incentive to work would no longer be regulated through financial gain but from the moral duty to contribute to the common good of society through individual effort. It was therefore easy to amalgamate Martí's principle with the same socialist and communist education objectives that could be found in the Chinese and Soviet education systems. In many respects, the Cuban education program resembled Mao Zedong's experiments to re-educate the masses, as they too aimed at connecting study to work.[14] Nevertheless, the main educational aims formulated at the beginning of the revolution were based on teaching reform concepts that had been developed in Cuba during the nineteenth and twentieth centuries. Even before the revolution, Fidel Castro, in his "History Will Absolve Me" defense speech of 1953, demanded far-reaching education reform and referred to Cuba's tradition of enlightenment by invoking the words of Martí: "An educated people will forever be strong and free."[15]

From the mid-1960s, however, this national tradition in education began to give way to the increasing influence of socialist pedagogy and psychology emanating from the Soviet Union (through the works of A. S. Makarenko, Anatoly Smirnov, and Sergei Rubinstein, among others) and the GDR (Lothar Klingberg).[16] Until the 1980s, the way forward was determined by socialist pedagogical elements (and their corresponding ideological orientation) from the Eastern bloc. It was not until the postsocialist era of the 1990s that there was a revival of Martí and other Cuban education specialists of the nineteenth and twentieth centuries,[17] but this revival was not accompanied by any fundamental changes to the inherent principles of stabilizing authority.

The dictum of "educating for work" and the link between study and work were applied at all levels of the education system. Preschool and primary school pupils tended school gardens, older pupils worked on farms or in industry, and in the summer students were regularly sent to the country for several weeks to help bring in the harvests.[18] From primary school onward, school children were systematically introduced to the working world and had to learn elementary technical skills and crafts. One important element of socialist work-promoting education that found its way into new teaching methods was the so-called orientation group, in which children were familiarized with working life. These orientation groups gave children the opportunity to find out about different professions, with the aim of awakening personal interests and encouraging children to use their abilities as early as possible. This approach was extended to extracurricular activities in Young Pioneer centers. Here working environments were built in miniature (for example a sugar factory, railway, hospital, or military base) in order to introduce children to their future professions through play.[19]

Due to the need for trained, skilled workers and employees, technical and scientific subjects received much greater priority than before the revolution. After leaving secondary school, pupils were able to attend specially established polytechnic schools in order to gain professional qualifications, for example in trade and economics; accounting; medical, agricultural, and veterinary technologies; and industry.[20] The regular school system that was established in the 1960s comprised six years of primary education (*primaria*), three to four years of basic secondary education (*secundaria básica*),[21] and three years of pre-university education (*preuniversitaria*).[22]

In order to increase pupil motivation, Cuban schools ran a type of socialist competition in the form of a "monitor system." The best pupils in each subject became "monitors" and were rewarded with the privilege of assisting their teachers. They were allowed to assume minor duties during lessons and were also responsible for helping weaker classmates. From the 1970s, monitor contests were organized at a national level. The authorities also applied modern, international education standards that were practiced by nonsocialist countries too, following the worldwide education reform movement of the 1960s. The authoritarian chalk-and-talk teaching style gave way to interactive models of teaching and new teaching methods aimed at encouraging students to participate actively in lessons. Encyclopedic learning was abolished from the classroom.[23]

The ideological aims of the revolution and socialist educational ideals became embedded in the new curricula. School books absorbed the official interpretation of the revolution as a success story and perpetuated the corresponding myths, raising up as moral examples the outstanding political and military leaders Fidel Castro, Che Guevara, and Camilo Cienfuegos.[24] The North American perspective on Cuban history that had prevailed before the revolution disappeared completely from the curricula and teaching materials. At the same time, literature contradicting the principles of the revolution was banned from school and public libraries, and lessons in Marxist theory became compulsory.

Teacher training also underwent a complete makeover and was adapted to meet the demands of the new education system. Prior to the revolution, teachers enjoyed little prestige and were poorly paid. Now, in the service of a socialist society, teachers were considered the "pedagogical vanguard" and expected to play a crucial role in the education system. The act of imparting knowledge was no longer their sole task; they were now responsible for the social and ethical cultivation of "new men," and they were to exert cognitive influence on their pupils' individual capabilities in order to raise them as members of a socialist society.[25] This restructuring of the school system (and extension of the duties of this "new type" of teacher to include shaping ideology) was intended to remove the traditional task of bringing up children from parents and families and transfer it to state-run institutions. The responsibilities of these institutions indeed went far beyond those of conventional public schools, for example in their active recruitment of children and adolescents for the newly formed political cadre and mass organizations, such as the children's organization the "Pioneers," the Unión de Jóvenes Comunistas (UJC, Young Communist League), and the national Federación Estudiantíl Universitaria (FEU, Federation of University Students).[26]

The "new type" of teacher was also encouraged to subordinate personal ambition to social responsibility. In 1962, intensive primary-school teaching courses were introduced to train teachers for deployment in rural areas. The first training institute of this type was named after the Soviet education specialist Anton S. Makarenko.[27] Students who took advantage of this intensive teacher-training program had to commit themselves to teaching in the countryside, at least temporarily. Those who had been teachers before the revolution had to undergo further training or face suspension. It was in protest against such measures, and specifically against the political and ideological aims of the new Cuban education policy, that more than 10,000 teachers left Cuba in 1961.[28]

The system of higher education also underwent fundamental changes, and university courses were redesigned. One of the first measures was the closure of all private and confessional universities, leaving only three universities in 1960: the University of Havana, the University of Santa Clara in central Cuba, and the University of Santiago de Cuba on the east of the island. As in schools, universities reoriented themselves toward the natural sciences and technical subjects. Humanities and law faculties made way for technical, medical, and agricultural faculties and teacher-training institutes, so that technicians, doctors, engineers, and teachers could be trained as quickly as possible.[29] Prior to the revolution, Cuba had been largely reliant on professionals from abroad. The majority of university students had studied humanities, social sciences, and law, which meant that the number of graduates in economics, engineering, and agricultural science could by no means meet national requirements.[30] This situation was seriously exacerbated after the revolution, when the majority of engineers, technicians, and doctors left the island.

But there were also ideological reasons behind the overall reorientation in education toward the natural sciences. In the future, young Cubans were expected to dedicate themselves to improving industry, agriculture, education, and health. Reflections about ethical, moral, constitutional, or philosophical problems, which were central to the humanities, were regarded as undesirable, as they might lead to a loss of loyalty to the aims of the revolution. The number of students who enrolled in scientific and agricultural courses after the revolution reflected the extensive restructuring of the national curriculum. From 1959 to 1967, a full 30 percent more students enrolled in these subjects. Among the students who graduated from the University of Havana in 1975, around 30 percent graduated in medicine; 17 percent in engineering; 10 percent in agricultural sciences; and only 12 percent in a field related to economics, social sciences, or the arts—while 7 percent had studied teaching and education science.[31]

The reform of the education system also led to the creation of completely new forms of schooling. In 1969, the first rural boarding schools for secondary pupils (Escuelas Secundarias Básicas en el Campo, ESBECs) opened their doors to provide pupils in rural areas with the opportunity of secondary education. Attendance at boarding school would also remove young people from the authority of their parents, making them easier to influence and raise in the spirit of the revolution. Boarding schools subjected their pupils to a strict regime of discipline in daily life and work. They were often located in the vicinity of agricultural or industrial centers, and, according to the principle of combining study and work, the students had to spend their free time working either in agriculture or in light industry. By working, they were also able to earn some of their room and board and became more self-reliant.[32] In the 1970s, a large number of polytechnic and teacher-training colleges were also set up as boarding schools in the countryside. In the 1990s, a total of 450 such boarding schools still remained. Despite the fact that these strict boarding schools were very unpopular, by the 1990s approximately one-third of all Cuban pupils and students had received their secondary and higher education there.[33]

At the start of the 1970s, the ambitious education system fell into crisis owing to the huge increase in student numbers, the impact of the baby boom that began in 1959, and the knock-on effects of the brain drain of teachers and professionals.[34] Particularly at the secondary level, there was an acute shortage of teachers because training programs and continuing education had still not been able to supply enough secondary-school teachers to cover the increased demand. Another difficulty was that despite the teaching profession enjoying greater prestige after the revolution, it was still not sufficiently attractive. A national survey in 1970 highlighted the precarious situation of the education system and the desperate need for action. Cuba's pupils were receiving poor grades and frequently quitting school. Among thirteen- to sixteen-year-olds, the number of students failing exams and therefore unable to advance was almost 90 percent in some areas. Over 60 percent of primary-school teachers did not have sufficient training in the subjects they taught or in pedagogy; in the secondary-school sector, this number rose to 75 percent.[35]

Faced with this situation, Cuban educational planners initiated a new offensive to counteract the failings of the new political and pedagogical measures. The "Congress for Education and Culture," held in Havana in April 1971, laid out the path to increased efficiency in education that followed the reforms adapting the Cuban economy to the economic standards of the Soviet Union.[36] The discussions that took place during the congress were overshadowed by a social climate of dogmatic intransigence and political intolerance—the beginning of the "five gray years." The principle of combining study and work in the spirit of Marxism-Leninism became a dogma. Determined action was to produce a "mentality of producers rather than consumers" among the new generation, and teacher training was to be instrumental in this.[37]

At the peak of the crisis, when thousands of children who had finished primary school could not attend secondary schools due to teacher shortages, the strengths of the new education system and its institutions manifested themselves in the flexibility they displayed in arriving at pragmatic solutions to the problem. In the 1972/73 academic year, MINED began a political campaign to recruit teachers and set up an emergency education and political initiative: a teacher brigade known as the Destacamento Pedagógico "Manuel Ascunce Domenech."[38] This project gave secondary-school pupils a fast-track opportunity to enter teacher training after only nine years of school rather than the obligatory twelve. What was particularly innovative and special about this experiment was that, following the principle of combining study with work, members of this brigade had to teach the lower grades at their own schools from their first year of study onward.[39]

Initial reactions to this emergency plan were, however, muted. It did not get fully underway until the head of state, Fidel Castro, committed the members of the UJC in April 1972 to participate in the campaign. In keeping with the curriculum, the emphasis was placed on training teachers in technical, scientific, and mathematical subjects. More than half of the candidates had to change their course of study to qualify for the program.[40] The first brigade (more than 4,000 strong) of fifteen- to seventeen-year-olds was sworn in by Castro personally, and he emphasized the national import of their task. The members of the brigade were at one and the same time students and teachers. For the next five years their working week comprised forty-four hours, twenty-four hours of which were dedicated to study, and twenty hours to teaching. Most of the young people were unable to cope with such high expectations, and over three-quarters failed to complete the course, with only 907 graduating in the summer of 1977.[41]

As part of the education offensive, Institutos Superiores Pedagógicos (ISPs, teacher-training colleges) rapidly expanded across the island alongside the introduction of the student brigades. By comparison with education sciences at the universities, the curricula at the ISPs concentrated on socialist educational objectives, and ISP graduates had the reputation of being ideologically reliable and loyal cadres. They were expected to volunteer to serve in the remote Cuban provinces to which no other teachers would normally go of their own accord.[42] The courses offered at the ISPs were generally tailored toward young people from the provinces who came from underprivileged sectors of society, among others Afro-Cubans, who, unlike young people from urban areas, had few opportunities to choose from. It was these ISP graduates who were later on to become the principle candidates for engagement in Angolan education.

At the end of the 1970s, the experiment with student-teacher brigades was extended to cooperation in Angolan education. Castro launched an appeal to go to Angola that was aimed at the sixth brigade of the Destacamento Pedagógico "Manuel Ascunce Domenech," who were ready to be sworn in after enrolling for the 1977/78 academic year. The student teachers were to gain their obligatory classroom experience not at school in Cuba but in Angola.

The reason behind this measure, which will be explained below in more detail, was the urgent request of President Neto for 1,000 teachers to teach at the secondary level, as the Angolan education system was unable to accommodate over one million pupils who were starting school. The Cuban government's response was pragmatic. Owing to the lack of teachers at the secondary level in Cuba, the call to help Angola went to the matriculating students of the student-teacher brigades.

Education Policy and National Reconstruction in Angola

Angola's reconstruction after the colonial period was severely hampered for several reasons. First, repeated intervention from the South African army posed a military threat. Second, armed opposition led to a prolonged decolonization conflict. And third, most of the Portuguese settlers, who had occupied all major positions in the colonial state and economy, left Angola. Since the beginning of the anti-colonial struggle in 1961, Angola's development had been determined by armed conflict and a repressive regime. The war against the colonial power had already divided Angola's population. And the postcolonial conflict between the ruling MPLA party and its rival UNITA gave rise to even more profound political, social, and cultural antagonism within Angolan society.

Nevertheless, in an attempt to create a feeling of national consciousness across all social and ethnic groups, the MPLA government embarked on a new education system and hoped that this would help establish a socialist society under its leadership. The pursuit of these objectives took place amid the upheaval of a historic change from colonialism to independence. The challenge was not only to overcome the legacy of colonialism during an armed decolonization struggle but also to "revolutionize" society and establish a new national culture. The new education system is an illustration of the break between Angola's colonial society and the dawn of independence in 1975 under the leadership of the MPLA. Unfortunately, the challenges of making a new political start and establishing a stable political and economic system under wartime conditions proved too great, and within just a few years all such efforts had been eroded by a rigid, centralized regime and widespread corruption. Education policy, on the other hand, did manage to maintain an element of emancipation. Despite the ideological premises underlying the education programs, the population was keen to take advantage of them. The newly created Ministry of Education (MED) was to engineer reforms in education, and to some extent it was successful in its role. It managed to sustain improvements despite obstacles placed in its way; it was willing to be self-critical when examining failings and unwanted developments; and it discussed and initiated new reform measures.

These conclusions are based on my intensive study of sources from files in the Angolan Ministry of Education, dated from 1976 to 1991.[43]

Following independence, education in Angola was in a catastrophic state. In 1975, around 85 percent of the estimated five to six million inhabitants were illiterate. In 1973 and 1974, there were around 600,000 pupils and students, of whom 500,000 were in primary school. Approximately 70,000 attended secondary school and 4,000 university.[44] From the secondary level, the majority were of Portuguese origin, and they left Angola with their families between 1975 and 1976. The educational situation frustrated any hopes that an African elite capable of undertaking the task of national reconstruction would soon emerge.

In order to gain an overview of the challenges faced in establishing the new education system within the overall social context of independent Angola, I will first outline the fundamental political, economic, and social structures along with the major political and ideological tendencies of the MPLA government.

The Challenges of Rebuilding Angola

On 11 November 1975, the MPLA founded the independent People's Republic of Angola and set about constructing a socialist society. The structure of Angolan society had abruptly changed after the departure of the Portuguese settlers, and it was proving difficult to maintain the modern, industrialized, and urban sectors that the Portuguese had dominated. The MPLA's intention was to retain the "modern" (albeit colonial) social structure as a basis for modernizing the state, economy, and society. The aim was to catch up in the long term with the industrial nations of the East and West. In order to gain hold of key positions in industry and administration, the MPLA government promoted its party members to middle and top positions in government and industry, regardless of whether they had the necessary skills to do the job. And as in many other postcolonial countries in Africa, such political patronage resulted in inefficient state infrastructure and a drastic fall in industrial productivity. It also promoted the economic and social interests of the old and new *assimilados*, the *mestiços*, and members of the Luso-African elites of former colonial society (the majority of whom supported the MPLA).[45] This preferential treatment offered them better career opportunities than the innumerable, uneducated people in search of jobs from Angola's rural regions.[46]

In February 1976, the government passed an act to nationalize and confiscate private property, following which banks, insurance companies, national and international trading companies, the public transport system, education, and health care all came under state ownership between 1976 and 1980. Large agricultural concerns producing coffee, sisal, cotton, bananas, and sugar for export were also nationalized, along with smaller, medium-sized businesses.[47] During these initial years, the MPLA government tried to apply its own vision in building a socialist state. It was not categorically averse to private economic undertakings; it tried instead to combine elements of a state-controlled economy with elements of a market economy. It should be remembered that the MPLA was a movement consisting of diverse social classes, including members of comparatively well-off urban segments of society, all of whom were pursuing different interests at the beginning of this new postcolonial era. Businesses belonging to foreign, non-Portuguese owners escaped privatization, as did very small subsistence-farming interests. In Angola's most important industrial sectors, diamond mining and petroleum production, the state retained a majority holding in the mining and exploration companies and granted licenses to US and European concerns.

Even before independence, agricultural output had not been able to cover national food requirements, above all in urban centers. Following Angola's independence, more and more people abandoned the countryside, and as a result food production declined drastically.[48] The nationalization of large-scale agricultural businesses could not compensate for the shortfall.[49] The problem of transporting goods between the countryside and cities was made even more difficult by the destruction of infrastructure, by the unraveling of the business network that had linked the provinces and urban centers in colonial times, and by ongoing acts of aggression. To make matters worse, there was a lack of skilled workers in agriculture, in processing, and in management. Although the MPLA government called upon the support of foreign advisors and specialist in all sectors of (agricultural) industry and administration, this could by no means stop the gap. Most of the foreign technicians, engineers, and administrators who worked in Angola from 1975 onward came from Cuba, though a number of them came from the Soviet Union, the GDR, Yugoslavia, Bulgaria, and Czechoslovakia.

Another production problem was the obvious drop in workforce productivity, which could not be improved, despite political campaigns to revalorize the social status of wage labor. Wage labor had been introduced to Angola by the colonial authorities, and it became largely synonymous with forced labor and exploitation, particularly in rural areas. Farm laborers and small holders therefore considered independence primarily as liberation from forced labor.[50] Industrial output did not begin in Angola until the early 1960s. Manual workers and employees therefore lacked a culture of employment and the political consciousness to go with it. The lack of work discipline among senior employees posed a particular problem. Their absenteeism and failure to accept responsibility negatively impacted the production process. Inefficient management structures and sluggish bureaucracy, inherited from the Portuguese colonial power, heightened the problem.[51] After independence, wages remained below subsistence level, which is why there was little incentive to increase productivity. The continuation of the decolonization conflict impeded state investment in production and infrastructure, and profits from petroleum went toward paying for imported foodstuffs and the war effort.[52] The scarcity of food and consumer goods already became apparent in the first years of independence, and this encouraged corruption and theft. Not only did party and government members endorse such behavior, but they became increasingly active in it. Scarce goods were exchanged or sold at the black market (*candonga*) at a considerable profit.[53]

Within the MPLA, the advocates of a socialist way into modernity initially managed to enforce their opinions. At its first party conference in December 1977, the MPLA called itself the Partido do Trabalho (MPLA-PT, Worker's Party) in an attempt to consolidate its socialist policies in the economy, politics, and society. Marxism-Leninism became the doctrine of the state. The party structure was centralized, and following the model of other socialist state parties, the MPLA-PT demonstrated its right to govern by establishing a single-party system in which it exerted complete control over the state.[54]

In 1977, Agostinho Neto was officially inaugurated as party chairman and state president. Just a few months earlier, his government had managed to overcome its worst domestic crisis since independence. In May of that year, Nito Alves, a leading cadre in the MPLA and highly successful military figure who had served as minister of the interior, led a military putsch that was brutally defeated within a few hours by the MPLA (with the support of Cuban armed forces). The group led by Alves included numerous leading MPLA cadres, members of the military, and prominent figures within the government. It was strongly critical of Neto's "pragmatic," socialist approach and pronounced Neto incapable of solving Angola's economic and political problems.[55] The members of Alves's group aligned themselves politically with the Soviet model and were possibly backed by Moscow. They used strong, radical left-wing rhetoric, drawing on resentment among Black Africans of whites and *mestiços*. The group had therefore grown popular with the inhabitants of the slums (*musseques*) in Luanda. Many of those inhabitants had drifted after independence from the countryside to the capital, only to find their hopes for better living conditions disappointed. Following the failed putsch, Neto announced his intention to rule from then on with a "firm hand." During the weeks and months that followed, the MPLA systematically repressed opposition and purged its ranks. Many of Alves's supporters were executed and sympathizers arrested or removed from their posts.[56]

Despite attempts to purge the party, factions with varying interests persisted. Repeated disagreements arose among party members, for instance regarding the extent to which Angolan economic policies should be determined by market forces.[57] The presence of Cuban soldiers and civil aid workers also seems to have caused internal divisions over the years, particularly in the 1980s, when the military conflict with UNITA sharpened. However, all disputes were fought out exclusively within the party's ranks, and signs of power struggles seldom leaked through to the public.[58]

In order to consolidate its authority throughout the state and society, the MPLA founded people's organizations and mass organizations, over which it exercised control. Among them was Organização das Mulheres de Angola (OMA, Women's Organization of Angola), União Nacional dos Trabalhadores Angolanos (UNTA, National Union of Angolan Workers), the children's organization Organização dos Pioneiros de Angola (OPA, Angolan Pioneer Organization), and the youth organization of the MPLA, the Juventude do MPLA (JMPLA, Youth of MPLA). Ostensibly, these organizations retained their non-party structure, with the exception of the JMPLA, which was eventually integrated into the party. Each organization nevertheless served the purpose of spreading the MPLA's political agenda, influencing public opinion and exerting control over the population, particularly after the Alves putsch. The MPLA government banned all organizations that did not align themselves politically with it, with the exception of churches.[59] Similarly, at the end of 1975, the state-security organ, Direcção de Informação e Segurança de Angola (DISA, Directorate of Information and Security of Angola), was set up for the purpose of pursuing political dissidents rigorously.

After the 1977 party congress, the MPLA government began to establish the institutions and structures of "people's power" (*poder popular*) in order to consolidate the single-party system and push ahead with nation building. Based on the Cuban system introduced in 1976, the organizations were intended to guarantee the decentralized and controlled participation of the people in political decision making, thereby integrating them into the state. But as in Cuba, the people's power to influence political direction through the institutions of the *poder popular* were very limited, because in Angola as in Cuba the legislative branch of the government was dominated by the executive. Just like the Communist Party of Cuba, the state authority of the MPLA was anchored in the constitution, and state organs and institutions had to follow party instructions. When President Neto died in Moscow on 10 September 1979, the MPLA had managed to consolidate its domestic position to such an extent that a transfer of power to his successor José Eduardo Dos Santos (b. 1942), the former Minister of Planning, met with no opposition.[60] Elections to the National Assembly, the highest body of the *poder popular* at local and regional level, were first held in 1980. The elected National Assembly then replaced the Revolutionary Council, which had been acting in a legislative capacity since independence.[61]

After 1977, the MPLA had secured a monopoly on all media outlets, including newspapers and radio and television stations. The Angolan mass media were responsible for informing, mobilizing, and educating the public in accordance with government views.[62] The new education system, to which the MPLA committed itself in a policy document during its 1977 conference, was regarded as a way of educating the people in accordance with government expectations.[63] The MPLA therefore considered it essential to its objectives.[64] Nevertheless, in comparison with the elitist and racist education system of colonial times, the goal of teaching people to read and write and provide a universal education system open to all Angolans was a decisive step forward.[65]

Education in Colonial Times

During the Portuguese colonial period, the education of the nonwhite, African population of Angola was almost completely neglected. The colonial education system was structured along racist, elitist lines and catered almost exclusively to the children of white settlers. Over the course of the twentieth century, however, the colonial education system in Angola did undergo reforms, and from the 1960s it opened its doors to the African population.[66]

Colonial schooling was based on a state education system introduced in the eighteenth century by Marquês de Pombal after the expulsion of the Jesuits from Angola in 1795.[67] Prior to this, education had been completely in the hands of Jesuit orders. It was not until the 1930s, after the consolidation of the *estado novo*, the authoritarian regime of Salazar, that confessional schools (Catholic and Protestant) were officially allowed to reopen.

Until the end of the 1950s, the Angolan population was subject to a 1914 law that divided it into "civilized" Portuguese and *mestiços* and "uncivilized" Africans. Among the Africans, further distinction was made between the *assimilados* and the *indígenas*, the latter group comprising 99 percent of the population. Right up to the start of the anti-colonial struggle in 1961, the colonial authorities showed little interest in the education of so-called indigenous Africans. In 1927, they had established a two-tiered education system, one tier for the "civilized" Europeans, settlers of Portuguese origin and *assimilados*, and the second tier for the so-called indigenous people. The curricula for the Portuguese and *assimilados* were intended to secure the "intellectual and moral unity of the Portuguese nation."[68] After Pombal's reforms, the curricula had been centralized throughout the Portuguese empire from the eighteenth century onward, and there was no difference between what was taught in Portugal and what was taught in its "overseas territories." In Angola, history and geography lessons concentrated on Portugal. Most pupils came from the urban centers, particularly from the cities of Luanda, Huambo (Nova Lisboa), Benguela, and Lubango (Sá da Bandeira), where the majority of Portuguese settlers lived.

Education of the "indigenous" people was adapted to the needs of the colonial power. The "indigenous" schools were set up to teach pupils to become "useful workers," who could serve the colonial economy in the mines or on plantations raising crops for export.[69] To this end, two types of school were set up: rural schools, which were usually confessional, and a few state schools. The confessional schools were often tied to missions; their main task was to "civilize the natives." The children were taught the basics in reading, writing, and arithmetic and received religious and moral instruction, along with lessons in health and hygiene. Although the education provided at these mission schools was basic, it nevertheless created a small, educated, African elite, whose members were later instrumental in organizing the anti-colonial movements.

While the mission schools did not always use Portuguese as their medium, the state schools founded from 1930 onward introduced Portuguese into the curriculum, and it became the official language of instruction. This was an attempt to curtail the influence of African languages and demonstrate the superiority of the Portuguese language and culture.[70] At state schools, the "indigenous" Africans likewise received religious and moral instruction. Girls and young women were trained in domestic service for rural households, while the young men were taught crop and livestock farming.[71] In 1950, a full 97 percent of the population was illiterate, and throughout the country only thirty-seven Africans completed secondary education that year. Following almost five hundred years of colonial rule, Portuguese had also become the lingua franca of Africans in rural areas, particularly due to the Luso-African traders and trading networks that stretched far inland.[72]

At the end of the 1950s, reform within the colonial system led to the abandonment of the racist classifications "civilized" and "uncivilized," and it was only then that education became standardized and improved for Angolans and Portuguese alike. Education reform in 1961, at the beginning of the anti-colonial struggle, contributed to integration. Particularly in the provinces, a network of state primary schools developed, benefiting all population groups alike. Secondary schools and vocational colleges opened, and in 1963 the University of Angola was founded. Although based in Luanda, it also maintained faculties in Huambo and Lubango. Prior to this, there had been no higher education institutes in Angola. Only a small, privileged section of Portuguese and *mestiços* and a handful of Luso-African families in the cities, some of whom belonged to the elite of the old *assimilados*, could afford to send their children to study in Portugal or another European country.[73]

In terms of modernizing colonial society and integrating the Africans and the *mestiço* population, the education system improved considerably in content and structure. Nevertheless, discrimination against the African people prevailed, as can be seen in the gap between school standards for whites and *mestiços* and for Africans. The primary schools in the provinces and deprived urban areas, which were mainly attended by Africans, were generally more poorly equipped and had few qualified teachers. Most of the new secondary schools and vocational colleges were located in the provincial capitals and aimed at the less wealthy sections of Portuguese settlers and at the *mestiços* and Africans living in the cities. Although the education reforms did have a positive impact on the development of an urban African middle class, it had little effect on cultural and socioeconomic progress among rural Africans.[74]

By the 1972/73 school year, the reforms had led to a quadrupling of the number of pupils and students, with a total of 607,064 pupils and students attending the various types of schools and higher-education institutions: 516,131 attended primary school, 75,667 were in secondary school, 3,336 were studying at the university, and 3,388 were at a polytechnic school.[75] Of the primary pupils enrolled in 1972/73, however, almost 40 percent were in nursery school, 29 percent were in their first year of primary school, and only 6.8 percent were in fourth grade. In rural and deprived urban areas, the proportion of pupils failing exams and dropping out of school was particularly high. There were approximately 25,000 primary-school teachers available, about half of whom had only four years of primary education themselves.[76]

In 1975, there were only five institutes for training primary-school teachers, and these were attended almost exclusively by whites and *mestiços*. About 30 percent of primary-school teachers had been trained there. The second category of teachers comprised the so-called *professores do posto*, teachers who had taught near the colonial administrative centers in the provinces. At best, they had four years of vocational training after their four years of primary schooling. The *professores do posto* represented about 20 percent of primary teachers. The majority of them came from the African population, as did the remaining 50 percent of primary-school teachers, who were either auxiliary teachers with no teacher training and little more than an elementary education, or so-called monitors, who by the end of colonialism made up almost 40 percent of all primary-school teachers.[77] Schools and teachers for secondary education were only available, if at all, in the provincial capitals, with the majority of secondary-school pupils in 1973 coming from the coastal city of Benguela and the capital of Luanda. Of the students matriculated in the University of Angola and the polytechnic schools, not even 10 percent were African or *mestiço*.[78]

Postcolonial Education Reform

In his declaration of independence on 11 November 1975, President Neto announced the objectives of the new education policy, giving particular priority to the elimination of illiteracy.[79] That same day the new constitution was announced. Articles 13 and 29 referred to the development of a new national culture and national education system; they declared that every Angolan citizen had the basic right to cultural development and access to education.[80] A new, emancipated education system would help overcome the legacy of colonialism, racism, discrimination, and paternalism in the consciousness of the Angolan population.

Following independence, the MPLA government was committed to two central phases of development: the creation of a modern nation-state that was culturally and politically homogenous, and the establishment of a socialist society. A new system of education was to be the main means of achieving these objectives. The MPLA's "Basic principles for the reform of the education system of the People's Republic of Angola" represented a radical break from education during colonialism. All Angolans, regardless of color, gender, ethnicity, religion, living circumstances, and place of residence, were to have free access to four years of basic education. From now on the state assumed central responsibility for education, and it nationalized all confessional and private education institutions in December 1975.[81]

The entire population was encouraged to become actively involved in the national education effort, and in 1976 compulsory education was introduced. Teaching content and new teaching materials and textbooks were adapted and adjusted across the country to reflect the new "reality of Angola." Any bias toward the former colonial power was completely eliminated from schoolbooks. The new history books dealt with the history of Angola prior to colonialism and took a critical look at the impact of colonialism.[82] By reforming and modernizing the curricula, the MPLA intended to catch up with international standards in science, technology, and culture. The educational institutions therefore underwent complete reorganization and centralization. In order to provide the promised universal access to education, the government prioritized the building of school infrastructure, particularly in the provinces and rural regions, in an attempt to close the gap between the urban and rural regions and to integrate rural communities into the new national project.[83]

The fundamental structure of the new education system remained in place until 1991, and it was only reformed and finally decentralized in the wake of Angola's political transformation into a multi-party system.[84] That same year, the Soviet Union collapsed and the countries of the Eastern bloc underwent radical political change. Also in 1991, the last of the Cuban troops and civil aid workers were withdrawn from Angola as agreed, and this was to have a crucial impact on the political and economic direction of Angola.

In the following pages, I describe the two developments at the heart of Angola's postcolonial education policy: the literacy campaign and the building of a national education system. The government faced a double challenge: while teaching the population to read and write, it also had to establish the foundations of the national education system and enable schools to open their doors for normal teaching. There were also some basic obstacles to the introduction of the new system of education, which I will analyze.

The Literacy Campaign

Even before the basic structure of postcolonial education had been finalized, President Neto gave a speech in the Luanda textile factory Textang on 22 November 1976, during which he announced a national literacy campaign. Under the motto "Learning is a revolutionary duty," the national "Fight for Literacy" campaign set out to combat the high rate of illiteracy.[85] The campaign was the first national political initiative with the aim of creating a united socialist nation. Not only did the MPLA intend to teach hundreds of thousands of Angolans to learn to read and write, but it also aimed to politicize and mold the population (including its many political opponents) according to its ideology and moral outlook and to encourage them to help build the new nation. In an attempt to promote cultural homogeneity, the literacy campaign taught solely in Portuguese. The MPLA also intended the campaign to increase its state authority throughout the Angolan territory. As one Cuban education specialist commented in retrospect, the Angolans were to develop a sense of patriotism and be mobilized for the MPLA cause.[86]

One glance at the primer used in the literacy campaign demonstrates its ideological nature. It bore the title "Victory is certain—the fight continues,"[87] and its choice of key words reflected the MPLA's intention to establish a new social and political order by constructing a reality determined by the MPLA's own agenda. The central topics of the book were explicitly attuned to the situation following independence, so as to anchor the MPLA's claim of authority across the Angolan territory in the consciousness of the population at large. Furthermore, the Angolans had to be prepared to take up arms to defend the MPLA's vision. The first words and phrases that the adults had to learn to read and write included political and military slogans. The primer was in fact an abridged version of the MPLA's manifesto.

> "Angola is our country" (Lesson 1)
> "The people are united" (Lesson 2)

"The united people fight" (Lesson 3)
"Long live the MPLA" and "Long live the people" (Lesson 4)
"The fight continues" (Lesson 5)
"February Fourth is a glorious date" (Lesson 7)[88]
"The people's struggle has a purpose"; "Power to the workers and peasants" (Lesson 8)
"Let us create new men" (Lesson 9)
"The FAPLA has arms to defend the people" (Lesson 14)
"The Angolan people are alert in the face of their enemies" (Lesson 15)

The primer ended with the lyrics of the new Angolan national anthem and a poem composed by Neto.[89] In the final exam of the literacy course, each candidate had to write a letter to the president.[90]

The teachers of the literacy classes were given a special handbook to prepare them for their task as "multiplying factors in the service of the revolution."[91] This handbook was specifically aimed at nonprofessionals—that is, volunteers who could read and write and had answered the government's appeal to join the campaign. Alongside the basics of didactics and pedagogy, it therefore included a detailed commentary on each lesson and instructions on how it should be taught.[92] It also provided additional background knowledge and corresponding political arguments, as well as geographic details of Angola's landscapes, vegetation, river systems, and natural resources. Furthermore, the handbook discussed the political events of independence and introduced the political and military leaders of the MPLA. The basics of a "civilized" society, such as hygiene, discipline at the workplace, punctuality, and cleanliness, were included in the handbook too, since only with such standards would the Angolan people be able to enter the modern, socialist world. In short, the handbook was a mixture of atlas, history book, and manual on conduct, aimed at popularizing the fundamental values of the new Angola. In principle, the primer and handbook incorporated the underlying methodology and content of the entire education reform project. They clearly show how the MPLA altered political and sociocultural paradigms. The handbook informed people's understanding of the geography of the Angolan nation-state within Africa (and throughout the world), as it did their perception of the history of independence, as seen from an MPLA perspective. For the first time, the handbook retold the history of independence as a national master narrative for the broad populace.

One of Angola's most influential contemporary writers, Artur Pestana ("Pepetela"), was one of the architects of the new education system in his capacity as deputy minister of education between 1977 and 1981.[93] Alongside the minister of education Ambrôsio Lukoki (1977–1981), he pushed through the new education policy across the country. In two interviews, Pepetela explained to me that the basic concepts of education had been drawn up before independence,

Adult primer, cover, "Victory is certain," Angola, 1976 (Ministério da Educação e Cultura, 1976b)

A VITÓRIA É CERTA
A LUTA CONTINUA

MANUAL DE ALFABETIZAÇÃO

EDIÇÃO DO MINISTÉRIO DA EDUCAÇÃO
DA REPÚBLICA POPULAR DE ANGOLA

1

Adult primer, title page, "Victory is certain—the fight continues," Angola, 1976 (Ministério da Educação e Cultura, 1976b)

and that a preliminary version of the primer and handbook had already been used for teaching literacy in the "liberated zones" of the MPLA. Angolan education specialists had combined the Cuban method of teaching to read and write with that of the Brazilian educator, philosopher, and leading advocate of critical pedagogy Paulo Freire.[94] Freire equated reading and writing with *concientização*, the development of a process of critical consciousness in which the oppressed individual takes an active part in his liberation. He was instrumental in designing the literacy campaign in the former Portuguese colony of Guinea-Bissau in West Africa, and he visited Angola on numerous occasions following independence in order to advise Angolan education specialists. Although Freire's method of teaching literacy rejected the use of ready-made primers, he did agree that it made sense to create a primer in Angola in view of the obvious dearth of people able to read and write. Pepetela assured me that Freire had advised him on all educational matters and had agreed on the combination of his method with the Cuban method. The final result, however, was an Angolan product, according to Pepetela.[95]

Although Freire had many followers in Angola, the most influential decision makers in education within the MPLA government came out firmly in favor of the "Cuban way." What were their reasons? Political trust and personal relationships had grown between the Cuban government and sections of the MPLA before liberation, and these prevailed during the first years of independence. The preference certain members of the MPLA government showed for the Cuban sociopolitical developmental model was an expression of this special relationship.[96] In particular, they considered that the ideal educational model for Angola was the Cuban education system, which had been successfully implemented after the revolution. The way the primer and handbook were conceived is indicative of the methods (and politics) that dictated the direction the new Angolan education system would take. The MPLA's education specialists chose the methodology that would help stabilize the government's rule by enforcing viewpoints, terminology, and interpretations that contributed to the MPLA's consolidation of power.

It is true that Freire's theory of pedagogy incorporated a Marxist approach to education and emphasized the interrelation between education and social change. But in contrast to the Cubans, Freire always pointed out the danger inherent in the contradiction between revolutionary intention, on the one hand, and the actual use of authoritarian methods to stabilize power on the other. He advocated that pedagogy should not be misused to enforce political dogmas, but should emancipate students and encourage a sense of awareness among them, so that they would be able to act as independent agents and free themselves from oppression.[97] This was the essential difference between his pedagogical approach and that of the Cubans. The Angolan education specialists had indeed consulted Freire, but they decided in favor of the methods and content of the Cuban model. Contrary to Freire's flexible method of teaching literacy using vocabulary drawn from the local environment, they designed the aforementioned primer. All that remained of Freire's method was the use of generative words that were then broken down into syllables, but these generative words were chosen arbitrarily rather than taken from the learners' immediate environment. The Angolans adopted from Cuba the symbols of political propaganda and of socialist propaganda in general. The cover of the primer depicted the main protagonists of the worker and peasant state: the worker, the peasant, and the soldier, all carrying their tools (shovel, hoe, and gun) and standing against the Angolan national colors, black and red, with the yellow cogwheel, sickle, and star from the national flag in the background. The photo of the president and Party chairman, Neto, on the book's back cover is a clear representation of the politics of hierarchy and personality.

The central topics of the primer revolved around the terms "people," "unity," "struggle," "victory," "defense," and "production." They were part of the vocabulary of revolutionary and socialist slogans, some of which had already been coined during the Russian and Chinese Revolutions. During the Cuban Revolution, the words had been taken and adapted to fit the situation in Latin America. The Cuban Revolution then spread these terms to many different countries and to many different sociocultural contexts, where they were applied universally. The terminology, representative images, political focus, and cultural value system were all adopted by the national freedom movements in Central America from the 1960s to the 1980s. After the victory of the Sandinista revolution in 1979, Nicaragua also embarked on a "literacy crusade" with very similar objectives.[98] Literacy in Nicaragua was also seen as a means of politicizing and mobilizing the people according to the revolutionary government's vision.[99] And once again, political and cultural transfer took place through the deployment of thousands of Cuban civilians who participated in the literacy campaign and helped to set up the education system.

Just as in Cuba and Nicaragua, literacy and education were to be the foundation stones upon which the "new men" of Angola would be created.[100] Despite the fact that the MPLA government based its reforms on the Cuban example, its vision was to educate the population first and foremost in the spirit of enlightenment, enabling them to reason and think rationally. It was expected that reason and rationality would overcome the racist legacy of the colonial era and also prevent the various population groups from focusing narrowly on their own cultural communities (i.e., engaging in what the MPLA vilified as "tribalism").

Within the Angolan context, the virtues of the "new men" oriented themselves toward the European values of occidental civilization. The new education system also seemed to serve as a way of redressing the failings of colonial Christianization and civilizing missions: the "new men" were to renounce selfish behavior, lack of discipline, laziness, lying, alcoholism, and prostitution, and they were to orient their behavior toward the selflessness of the MPLA guerrillas, who had sacrificed their lives in the struggle to free Angola from colonialism. In the teaching handbook, this idea was formulated as follows:

> The struggle of the Angolan people served not only to create an independent and developed country. . . . The people knew that we had to revolutionize our ideas, mentalities, and our approach to work. Our ideas are encumbered by old ways that we have to eliminate if we are to build a just society. . . . We have been taught that there are inferior and superior races and tribes. This is false prejudice; . . . in new Angolan society there is no place for either racism or tribalism, because they divide our people. . . . In our traditional culture, the people had little control over nature, and they interpreted many natural phenomena, for example disease, as witchcraft. . . . Free man will be free from such false ideas. We also inherited many vices from colonialism, which were detrimental to our struggle and our work. . . . These are all weaknesses typical of societies where workers have been extremely exploited and where there is poverty and suffering. In the new society of Angola, all this must disappear. . . . We have to fight against these evils, . . . and above all we have to educate our future generations so that they too will be free of such prejudices and false ideas, because they are the workers and leaders of the future. . . . During the MPLA's guerrilla campaign, the people already began to create new men. . . . Many of our heroes during the wars of liberation are examples of comrades who became new men and women by sacrificing themselves to our people—Deolinda, Hoji ya Henda, Jika, Valódia and many others.[101]

The literacy campaign was preceded by months of preparation, in which Cuban experts were actively involved. The first twelve Cuban education specialists arrived in Angola in mid-February 1976. On behalf of the MPLA and under the protection of Cuban troops, they led a pilot project for a national literacy campaign in the enclave of Cabinda. The MPLA was likewise able to call upon its experience in literacy projects, which it had gathered during the anti-colonial struggle in the 1960s when it had introduced reading and writing programs in the "liberated zones" and established a network of schools.[102]

When it came to the practical implementation of the literacy campaign, however, it soon became evident that neither the cultural patterns nor the experience of the 1960/61 Cuban campaign could easily be transferred to the

Angolan context. Having already attained independence in 1902, Cuba had introduced an education system that provided enough literate people in 1959 to realize a successful literacy campaign among the entire population within just one year. As in Angola, the Cuban campaign also aimed to strengthen national unity and was based on the conception that unity meant linguistic homogeneity. But the preconditions in Cuba were much more conducive to realizing the campaign's goals: during the colonial period, Spanish had already become the lingua franca and the main day-to-day language of the population.

In Angola the situation was entirely different. The illiteracy rate was considerably higher and the number of literate people able to assist in the campaign was considerably lower than in Cuba.[103] This problem became evident at the launch of the campaign in the Textang factory in Luanda. Only 141 of the 1,100 factory employees could take part in the first literacy course, as there were only twelve teachers available.[104] Moreover, Angola's territory was about ten times bigger than Cuba, and its infrastructure was comparatively poor, having been developed only sporadically by the Portuguese colonizers either to meet the needs of the white settlers or to help fight insurrection during the colonial war. By contrast, the Cuban Revolution had happened without civil war and without large-scale structural damage. Another problem in Angola was that although large sections of the Angolan rural population had some knowledge of Portuguese, they mainly spoke African languages. Those who were able to read and write in Portuguese, however, frequently spoke no African languages. A further difficulty was presented by the fact that until independence, most African languages existed only in spoken form, and orthographic standards and grammar were set down only gradually. And finally, continuing internal conflict and the resulting division of the people into MPLA supporters and UNITA supporters hindered the introduction of a literacy campaign on a national level.

In view of prevailing circumstances, the MPLA government decided to deviate from the Cuban model and carry out the campaign in consecutive stages of five months each. When organizing these stages, the government gave preference to the groups who backed it, so that once its supporters had learned to read and write, it could appoint them as teachers. Top priority was given to the military (FAPLA), to workers and peasants who had organized themselves into cooperatives, and to the women's, children's, and trade-union organizations that were affiliated with the MPLA.[105] The members of the women's organization (OMA) proved to be very active supporters of the campaign,[106] as was the JMPLA youth organization, which modeled its "Hoji ya Henda" brigade on the Cuban literacy brigades.[107]

The literacy campaign continued until the end of 1997, and the difficulties it faced are highlighted in a report published by the Angolan Ministry of

Education in 2005. According to the report, a total of 2,417,094 school-aged children and adults had learned to read and write over the period of twenty-one years. Considerably more than half of them were women (1,336,514).[108] The study also shows that the success of the literacy project varied considerably from region to region. As in colonial times, the inhabitants of urban areas profited most, particularly in the cities of Luanda, Huambo, and Benguela. The different stages of the campaign also met with varying success, which was largely dependent on political and military developments. According to official figures, by 1982, six years after the start of the campaign, the number of Angolans who had acquired literacy skills was 505,045.[109] This number represents one-fifth of the total number of people registered as literate in 1997. Both official and unofficial statistics on the success of the campaign show that, from the beginning of the 1980s, the campaign was extensively hampered by the escalating conflict due to heavy military aggression, supported by UNITA and directed at the MPLA government, from South Africa.[110]

The Education System

Parallel to running the literacy campaign, the MPLA government began setting up a new education system from 1977 onward. It too was regarded by the MPLA as having an explicit political function. The education system was to bear responsibility for educating the Angolan population to become good patriots and soldiers. It was to teach them to follow the aims of "internationalist solidarity" and encourage them to develop into physically and mentally healthy, conscientious workers, ready to dedicate themselves to the collective tasks of defending and rebuilding the nation.[111] The education system was to promote the national unity of Angola throughout all regions and to spread the new symbols of nationhood by means of ritual greetings. As a direct result of the influence of Cuban teachers and education specialists, each school day in Angola started with an obligatory flag-raising ceremony, during which the pupils recited the slogan "From Cabinda to Cunene—one people, one nation."[112]

The teachers themselves were given a central role, and according to the new teacher-training guidelines and the Cuban model, future teachers were regarded as the vanguard of the revolutionary process. The "new type" of teacher would not only teach pupils reading, writing, and arithmetic but also perform the task of "political cadres." The new teachers were expected to be moral examples in every respect and to influence the cognitive interests of the pupils in order to form "new," socialist men.[113] In Angola, as in Cuba, the teachers' sphere of influence was not restricted to the classroom, but extended to the family and neighborhood. Pupils' families were expected to increase the acceptance of educational reform by becoming actively involved in the process of forming revolutionary consciousness.[114]

The enforcement of Portuguese as the national language was of central importance to the creation of a nation-state. Portuguese was seen as the language of official representation both at home and abroad. The policy paper for the new education system made mention of Angola's linguistic and cultural diversity only with reference to the backwardness of the country.[115] National education policy did not acknowledge Angola's ethnic groups (commonly divided into the Bakongo, the Mbundu, the Ovimbundu, the Lunda-Kioko, the Nhaneka, the Ambó, the Ngangela, and the Herero, each of which features its own local and regional variations of Bantu and Khosian languages). Well aware of this cultural and linguistic diversity, the MPLA government did not exclude the future possibility of multilingual lessons. The problem was, however, that there was no single language that the entire population could understand. The only language alongside Portuguese that had spread to any extent during the colonial period was Kimbundu, owing to trading networks stretching far inland.[116]

By recognizing Portuguese as the official language, the government hoped to maximize its chances of being accepted into the international community. As did most postcolonial African states, the MPLA government chose to adopt the language of the former colonizer. It aimed to create a modern nation-state that was united both politically and culturally, and it therefore expected that Portuguese would progress from being the official language of public life to the language of everyday interaction between the various linguistic groups. This hope was expressed in 1978 by the then minister of education, Ambrôsio Lukoki, during the opening ceremony of the Institute of Angolan National Languages.[117] In the mid-1980s, a comprehensive study of Angola's linguistic and ethnological status was conducted in cooperation with Cuban historians, anthropologists, sociologists, and linguists, the results of which were never published.[118] It was not until after 1997 that multilingual lessons and the teaching of literacy in several African languages began.[119]

Completely pragmatic considerations were also prominent alongside political and ideological aims. The new education policy faced the challenge of producing managers and skilled workers of all types as quickly as possible. To counteract the enormous lack of professionals, specialists, and technicians, who were desperately needed to rebuild the nation, vocational training institutes opened up, and new training courses and curricula were introduced.[120] Once again, the influence of Cuba was apparent in the priority given to technical and scientific subjects in Angola. In the early years, adult education received a particular boost, in an attempt to make up for the huge deficit in education among adults.[121]

One of the biggest challenges was providing follow-up education once people had learned to read and write. Those who acquired literacy skills had to have the opportunity to continue their education so that they would not lose their new abilities. In order to provide such continuing education programs, a three-phase school structure (again based on the Cuban model) was set up in 1977. The three phases comprised primary, secondary, and higher education, with the first two stages affording adults the chance of a fast-track education. The new system also intended to close the gap between manual and intellectual work and to encourage the combination of study and work.[122] In February 1976, the first minister of education in independent Angola, the writer António Jacinto (1975–1976), therefore assigned university students to manual labor so that they would learn about living conditions in the countryside.[123] The JMPLA and the OMA joined Cuban aid workers to organize voluntary work projects for students, pupils, parents, and neighborhoods on a regular basis.

Primary education within the new national education system was divided into two streams: the regular eight-year stream, and a six-year stream for adults. Stage one comprised four years of elementary education, stage two comprised the fifth and sixth years, and stage three the seventh and eighth years. Normally children started school at the age of six and completed primary school at 14.[124] The six-year option was aimed at adolescents and adults who had been unable to attend school in childhood. The level at which adults entered the system was flexible, depending on their reading and writing skills. In order to begin training as a skilled worker in agriculture and industry, it was necessary to have successfully completed primary education.[125]

The secondary education phase focused on vocational training at colleges and polytechnic institutes. It aimed at supplying much-needed technicians and specialists (mechanics, electricians, primary-school teachers, agricultural specialists, oil and mining technicians, skilled construction workers, health workers, administration employees, etc.).[126] To provide new teachers, teacher-training colleges were set up.[127] This middle phase comprised classes nine to twelve, and upon graduation from the twelfth class, students were able to attend university. There were also pre-university schools specializing in the natural sciences or humanities (Ensino Pré-Universitário, PUNIV), which enabled their students to acquire the necessary qualifications to attend university within a shorter time span.[128] These provisions, along with professional development training, aimed at providing the managerial staff needed in administration and industry as quickly as possible.

Higher education was offered at the University of Angola, which had formerly been called the University of Luanda and is today the Agostinho Neto University. The University of Angola also had branches in Lubango and

Huambo. In 1977, there were faculties of agricultural science, medicine, engineering and natural sciences, humanities, and economic science.[129] The law faculty, which had opened in 1976, was closed for political reasons in May 1977 after the Alves putsch and did not reopen until 1979.[130] In the initial years after independence, university activity was considerably hindered by the lack of professional staff, and teaching was strongly dependent on the support of foreign professors, most of whom were Cuban, though there were also German and Russian professors. Scholarship programs were set up to allow school graduates with excellent academic records and members of the MPLA or organizations affiliated with the party to attend a university abroad—in the Soviet Union, the GDR, and Cuba in particular.

The Angolan Ministry of Education (MED) was the central body and engine of the education reform program. As a result of the reforms, the government reorganized the ministry in order to reinforce state and party authority over the education system. The ministry did, however, retain its centralized character, which went right back to the colonial era. In accordance with the MPLA's 1978 guidelines, the MED was organized vertically. The minister of education had the highest authority over the departments and branches of the ministry in the provinces.[131] He was supported by two deputy ministers, who reported to the minister of education, and whose task it was to supervise the departments under their responsibility. The minister of education was directly in charge of the legal, financial, and planning departments, and of the Gabinete de Intercambio e Cooperação Internacional/Gabinete de Intercambio Internacional (GICI/GII, Department of International Cooperation), which was responsible for coordinating and supervising cooperation with foreign countries.[132] The provincial directorates of the MED's regional offices, which had been set up in each of the eighteen Angolan provinces, also answered directly to the minister of education. The provincial directorates in turn controlled the education institutions of the municipalities and local districts. Although the MED underwent frequent reorganization, it retained its vertical structure until 1991.[133]

The structures of the Ministry of Education reflected the MPLA government's intention not only to unite Angola both politically and culturally but also to dominate the whole territory through institutions such as the provincial directorates and a network of education establishments. But this intention first had to be achieved in the ministry itself. The staff who worked there had to develop an awareness of how significant in practical terms the creation of a national education system was. Thanks partly to the support offered by Cuban advisors, the Luanda-based ministry was able to take an active part in planning and implementing education reform in the capital and territories under MPLA control as early as 1976. But in the newly established provincial directorates coordination and communication proved slow and cumbersome. It was, however, essential that there be effective exchange with the provincial branches if reforms were to be successfully introduced across the country, and if the foreign aid workers were to be properly coordinated and controlled at a national level. The responsibilities of the GICI/GII indicate that the deployment of foreign (above all Cuban) aid workers accelerated the process of national consolidation within the MED and encouraged the establishment of regular communication between the ministry in Luanda and its provincial departments.

Basic Problems in Education Reform

Even in its early stages it became apparent that the postcolonial education reform program faced enormous problems regarding existing structures and planning. In this section, I will therefore take a look at the extent to which the program's ambitious educational objectives could actually be realized. The main problems in implementing the plans to reform education lay in the lack of school infrastructure and the scarcity of teachers. These problems were made worse by a dearth of planning data, the unwieldy organization of the Ministry of Education, and the inability of the MPLA government to provide proper support for the reforms it had initiated. My analysis is based on internal, unpublished documents from the Angolan Ministry of Education in Luanda. Most of the files originate from the GICI.[134] The documents from 1975 to 1991 to which I had access clearly illustrate the problems and challenges of establishing an education system. The information contained in these memoranda, internal analyses, and accounts is illuminating because it provides critical reflection on the education situation and the reform process. Moreover, I was able to compare these documents with external studies drawn up by international aid organizations, such as UNICEF. A further source of comparison was provided by individual reports from Cuba written by key figures in educational cooperation with Angola. The numbers and statistics contained in the documents are, however, incomplete and often do not tally or even contradict each other. This means that all the data cited here can only be regarded as approximations. Above all, documents from a conference on education reform organized by the MED in July 1991 critically assess the implementation of postcolonial education reform. The results of this conference marked the beginning of a new education reform program.[135] This new reform process reflected the Angolan system's change in direction to a market economy and pluralistic political system, which led to the education system turning its back on ideologically charged objectives and adopting more democratic forms of learning and working.

But in 1975, such developments were not yet foreseeable. The announcement of a new education policy, which offered the opportunity of a school education, raised expectations among the Angolan population of a brighter future, and the resonance across the country was very positive. The opening of schools and free access to education led to an explosion in the number of pupils during the first years of independence. In 1979/80, over two million pupils and students were enrolled, four times more than in 1973.[136] Angola's educational institutions were, however, by no means prepared for this rush. The school infrastructure was severely deficient, and even increased efforts proved inadequate. One of the reasons for this was that the MED lacked basic planning data. For example, the number of schools and number of pupils, as well as fundamental demographic data, had not been properly recorded, especially in the provinces. The planning department of the MED was aware of this problem from the beginning of the 1980s, but was nevertheless unable to rectify the situation over the next decade.[137] Even in the 1980s, there was no systematic survey of the education situation, although the Cuban government submitted a comprehensive offer to conduct one in 1982.[138]

One of the documents to which I had access was a report written in 1978 by one of the Cubans responsible for cooperation in education. The report criticizes the lack of crucial data on the education situation, and it points out other structural and administrative weaknesses. According to the document, the MED was hardly capable of planning, organizing, and implementing the education reform program at the national level, never mind keeping an audit of the results of the process. Owing to communication problems with the provincial directorates, those responsible in the provinces had not been fully advised of the reform's objectives as formulated in 1977. The school principals and teachers therefore had little in-depth knowledge of the contents of the reform program. The Cuban report strongly recommended drastic improvements in teaching methodology, curricula, and teaching materials.[139] An internal MED report from 1982 repeated the criticism. This report quotes statistics from the United Nations on the Angolan education system. According to these figures, the eight-year elementary education system had a mere 8.3 percent success rate, one of the lowest in the world. These results were based on delays in school entry, the school dropout rate, and the number of pupils who had to retake the year.[140] The situation changed little during the 1980s. A UNICEF study from 1987 still shows failings in Angolan schools, teaching materials, and administration.[141]

According to the UNICEF study, the number of schools in the mid-1980s was 6,733, compared to the MED's figure of 7,241 in the 1981/82 academic year.[142] The institutions listed in the UNICEF report were by no means all schools in the conventional sense: some rural schools were little more than a tree providing shade during lessons.[143] Although the MED was endeavoring to improve school infrastructure, it was failing because of the apparent absence of backing from the government. In 1982, it reported that the construction of schools was being delayed by a lack of building materials, and the Ministry of Construction was failing to react to its requests.[144] Another problem was the unequal distribution of schools, teachers, and pupils throughout the country. Internal ministerial documents indicate that even after independence, the urban centers of Luanda, Huambo, and Benguela were considerably better equipped with schools and teachers than the provinces and rural regions in general.[145] The marginal provinces were particularly poorly provided for, as was the case in Angola's most northerly province, Zaire, and Kunene in the far south. Since independence, Kunene had suffered especially from the constant interventions of South African forces and was almost permanently under a state of emergency.[146] Also in the provinces of Huambo, Malanje, Bié, Kwanza Sul, and Benguela, hundreds of schools had to close due to the precarious political and military situation.[147] UNITA had intensified military attacks and acts of sabotage in these areas, and it was increasingly targeting civilian infrastructure.

The main problem in establishing the postcolonial education system, however, was the scarcity of trained and experienced teachers. All the documents I consulted from between 1976 and 1991 agreed on this point. During colonialism, the majority of teachers were of Portuguese origin, and they had left Angola when it attained independence. Although the Ministry of Education prioritized teacher training, as did international cooperation agreements, the new teacher-training institutes did not have enough capacity to cover the demand for teachers, which rose considerably after 1976. One MED document indicates that in 1984, nine years after independence, Angola had approximately 50,000 teachers, of whom 35,000 were only able to teach the first four years of primary school.[148] In comparison with the 25,000 teachers recorded prior to independence, of whom a large number left the country, these figures were indeed an absolute success. But they bore no relation to the enormous increase in the number of pupils. And of these teachers, 80 percent did not meet the pedagogical standards and subject knowledge required in their professions; many were also not proficient in the Portuguese language.[149]

There were several reasons for the lack of teachers. Teacher training standards were low, and teacher training in general could only be maintained with the help of foreign, above all Cuban, teaching professionals. This was partly due to the lack of candidates with sufficient education to embark on teacher training in the first place. Many teaching students were stretched beyond their limits because they themselves had not mastered the basics of education.[150] Another problem was that there was little incentive to become a teacher. Despite the ambitious education targets set by the MPLA government, Angolan teachers continued to receive a low salary after independence. The poor school infrastructure and classroom numbers that went way beyond the capacity of existing teachers were further disincentives. In 1981, primary teachers had to cope with an average of forty-one pupils.[151] For many Angolans the prospect of teaching in the provinces, possibly even in a war zone, was highly unattractive. Following independence, the majority of Angolans sought to improve their living and working conditions, and in view of the precarious supply situation, this could only be achieved in urban areas, regardless of whether a province was affected by war or not. To remain in the provinces, or, even worse, to return to the provinces, was regarded as a regressive step in all respects.

For teachers who had been trained during colonialism, the changes in the system were an enormous challenge. The adoption of new curricula and content meant an increase in their workload. Moreover, the new educational concepts demanded that existing teachers radically rethink pupil-teacher relationships. Whereas in the colonial education system teachers exercised absolute authority over their students and had little pedagogical training, they were now expected to abolish hierarchies and treat pupils almost as friends. The old teachers had to come to terms with new didactic concepts and motivate their pupils to take an active part in lessons. From 1981 to 1988, mainly for the reasons just enumerated, 12,707 teachers left their jobs for employment in more attractive and lucrative sectors.[152]

After the 1980/81 academic year, the lack of teachers and the closure of schools due to the ongoing conflict led to a dramatic fall in the number of pupils. The number remained low until the mid-1980s, when it began to recover slightly, but it never returned to earlier levels.

Approximately one-third of primary pupils dropped out of school in the 1981/82 academic year.[153] The year 1984/85 represented a low point in the development of the education system. In that academic year only 36.7 percent of primary pupils met classroom targets, and the dropout rate was 31.8 percent.[154] Another problem that accelerated the fall in the number of pupils and teachers was military conscription, which affected male teachers and pupils alike. The MED criticized the frequent practice of recruiting for the government's FAPLA forces in the middle of the school year.[155]

In 1991, the Ministry of Education issued a report on postcolonial education policy in which it blamed negative developments on the lack of organization and administration at the national level. The "excessive centralism of the Ministry of Education,"[156] the deficient network of schools and training institutes across the country, poorly educated pupils, and a dissatisfying pupil-to-teacher ratio came in for particular criticism.[157] One aspect that none of the internal ministerial reports deals with in any detail, however, is the social and psychological well-being of the school pupils. Many of the children and adolescents of school age suffered from malnutrition and the absence of medical care. The ongoing war led to a drastic increase in the number of refugees within the country, and many children had lost their parents and were suffering from neglect. Others were not able to attend school on a regular basis or had to leave school to help their parents work on the farms. Pupils living in remote regions far from the nearest provincial town were generally unable to attend school after the first four years of primary education because there was almost no available public transport. Although the new education policy aimed to break with the traditional moral values, prejudices, and sociocultural inequality of the colonial past, it was precisely in the rural regions that these aims were often undermined by traditions and social reality. The children and adolescents living in the countryside were generally tied to the subsistence farming of their families, and owing to the lack of school infrastructure, they could not begin school at the normal age of matriculation. Moreover, the centralized education system did not allow for any coordination between the academic calendar and the harvest calendar. As a result, pupils missed out on schooling during harvest time.[158] Particularly within rural village communities, the distrust of state institutions outlived colonialism, and parents were therefore reluctant to send their children to school. Patriarchal traditions and gender-specific roles also played their part in preventing girls and young women from receiving an education.[159]

The Ministry of Education was aware of the problems and set up boarding schools in the provinces. These provisional schools were intended to benefit adolescents who had been unable to attend school until fourteen to eighteen years of age. Many of these provisional schools were just extensions of the rural schools during colonialism. Even after independence, their main purpose alongside giving adolescents a rudimentary education was to provide them with the practical skills needed for agricultural production. Because of their boarding-school character, they were almost exclusively attended by male adolescents. Girls and young women, therefore, remained excluded from this chance to receive an education and were expected to help in their parental households. These provisional schools generally had to cope with a large number of students, and they suffered from an extreme lack of teaching staff and equipment, as critically recorded in an internal Angolan Ministry of Education study from 1983.[160] Although the provisional schools had initially been intended as an interim measure,[161] they continued to exist far into the 1980s.

What conclusions can be drawn from this analysis of the Angolan education system, in which Cuban professional assistance played a pivotal role at both the planning and implementation stages? Although the Angolan planners did stamp their own mark on postcolonial education reform, the influence of the Cuban education system is prominent. The fundamental planning elements and, even more importantly, the contents of the socialist educational approach developed in Cuba (together with the accompanying symbols and rhetoric) were transferred to Angola. In reforming education, the MPLA government did indeed manage to break clearly from the elitist and racist tradition of colonial education. Furthermore, during the first fifteen years of independence, it laid the foundations for a national, uniform education system and the establishment of a nationwide network of education establishments. Nevertheless, the reports and statistics detailed here provide clear evidence that in 1991, the education program failed to reach the ambitious targets that had been set initially. The complex economic, political, and social realities after independence were not all that prevented the reforms from being implemented, and neither was the ongoing postcolonial conflict. The reforms fell short also in large part because centralized structures within government institutions proved incapable of properly coordinating requirements and planning among the various ministries.

In the final analysis, the first attempt to reform education after independence also failed on account of the demands it placed upon itself, suffering as it did from an overload of visionary objectives, ranging from the building of a socialist society with "new men" to the homogenization of national culture. Its fundamental ideology and the application of a top-down method turned the education reform program into an instrument of maintaining power whereby the original aims of improving education standards among large sections of the population took a back seat. The education reform program finally ended up supporting authoritarian tendencies within the state and government machinery.

Part II

Cuban-Angolan Cooperation in Education

6

Scope of Action

Structures, Institutions, and Communication

A look at the organization and operation of this extraordinary South-South cooperation is crucial to an understanding of its nature, with all its hierarchies, dissonances, and negotiation processes. Clarification about the relationship's structure is essential since the tendency to view Cuban-Angolan cooperation from the Cold War perspective presents a distorted view of its history. I therefore intend to analyze how Cuban-Angolan cooperation in the civil sphere was actually implemented at different levels. To do so, I draw on statistics; describe the relevant structures, institutions, and communication mechanisms; and provide a chronological outline. My analysis is founded primarily on records from the Angolan Ministry of Education that were previously inaccessible; I was given the opportunity to scrutinize and evaluate them for this study. Access to these records presented me with a new and unexpected angle on the Cuban-Angolan relationship. Both sides set up bilateral institutions and committees to negotiate, implement, and monitor cooperation, and they established a number of communication and control mechanisms for this purpose. Insights based on these materials provide a clearer picture of binational and bilateral levels of cooperation, and they give a better understanding of how emerging bureaucracies initiated the processes of organization and institutionalization at national levels, in both Angola and Cuba.

The internal information illustrates that the Angolan government's reliance on Cuban support did not automatically mean that cooperation constituted an asymmetrical relationship of dependency, with the MPLA at a disadvantage.

Cooperative agreements resulted from the demands of the Angolans, to which the Cubans generally responded positively. For this reason, I define the mechanism determining the dynamics of this relationship as one of "supply" and "demand." This mechanism suggests that this specific pattern of interaction also applies to other areas of cooperation in the civil, political, and possibly even military sectors. Cooperation was also of a reciprocal nature, as the Cuban government drew profit from it. Not only did the Angolan government pay for the support Cuba provided but the cooperative agreements were also linked to trade agreements that benefited the Cuban economy. However, it is important to note that without such financial and material compensation from the Angolan government, Cuba would probably not have been in a position to offer such extensive civil support.

My findings, which are documented in the bilateral agreements and corroborated by the existence of institutions and their communication mechanisms, open up a completely new perspective on this transatlantic relationship. In contrast to the public statements of both governments describing cooperation purely in terms of political motivation and solidarity, it was in fact neither an altruistic undertaking nor a unidirectional relationship of dependency. It is an example of "internationalism with reciprocal benefits," as the Angolan Minister of Education defined it during my interview with him.[1] There is much evidence to suggest that the Angolan government profited most from these "benefits." Namely, civil cooperation was part of an overall political and military strategy, which in the long term served to consolidate the MPLA's authority. The MPLA government expected Cuba to provide quick and efficient help as Angola rebuilt, and that aid was to be adapted to the country's specific requirements.[2] The civil aid program was essential to the government's survival: the presence of specialists and civil aid workers—or *cooperantes*, as they were called in Angolan administrative jargon—strengthened state institutions, guaranteed social services, and secured the government's popularity. The MPLA government therefore had a vital interest in sustaining the civil aid program through binational contracts and bilateral communication structures, but it also aimed at expanding cooperation. Furthermore, the government bore the financial brunt of this cooperation and therefore had an interest in establishing the needed institutions and control mechanisms to ensure that the agreed-upon services were provided.

The institutionalization of cooperation led in both countries to the creation of structures for organizing the mass deployment of Cuban civil aid workers and implementing the programs. For Cuba this proved to be the starting point for many civil aid projects abroad, which even today earn international prestige and are an important source of income for the state. Alongside the national and bilateral structures, the Cuban government also established its own organization and civil administration framework on Angolan territory, which largely acted autonomously of the Angolans. It bore responsibility for the Cuban civilians working in Angola and operated along similar lines to the Cuban Military Administration. The organization had considerable influence on how cooperation was applied. Although the bilateral cooperation negotiations were generally conducted on an equal footing, the resulting parallel structures were a frequent source of conflict between Angolans and Cubans. As the example of cooperation in education illustrates, asymmetries, conflicts of interest, and dissonances emerged at this intersection.

The Cuban government was indeed prepared to provide prolonged civil aid to the MPLA in order to lend credibility to Cuban foreign policy and internationalist aims. But unlike the MPLA, it initially intended to limit cooperation to "help for self-help" so as to keep the number of people involved to a minimum. However, as economic pragmatism played a role in the cooperation, and the MPLA was paying for the aid, the Cubans continued to respond to the MPLA's demands until the mid-1980s. The basis of civil cooperation evolved into the large-scale deployment of Cuban aid workers to Angola, and, to a lesser extent, into a scholarship program to allow Angolan pupils and students to study in Cuba. The MPLA government also had cooperative agreements with other socialist countries, such as the Soviet Union, Yugoslavia, Bulgaria, and the GDR, but in every respect the civil aid provided by Cuba was by far the most significant.

Dates, Numbers, Statistics: The Scope of Cooperation

The previous chapters have already mentioned the number of Cuban aid workers who were involved in civil cooperation in Angola. I now want to offer an overview of the complete scope of civil engagement by providing numbers and statistics from published and unpublished Cuban and Angolan sources. Although the overview concerns the entire cooperation venture, the focus is on education. From the numbers, it is clear that, alongside the deployment of health workers and civil engineers, cooperation in education was by far the most comprehensive project.[3] Cuba also provided skilled workers and advisors for almost all productive and technical sectors of agriculture and industry, as well as for the administrative, communication, finance, and service sectors. The available information emphasizes that Cuban-Angolan cooperation was until 1991 the largest example of civil aid engagement abroad in the history of Cuba. It remains difficult, however, to provide exact data, because the Cuban authorities generally refuse public access to detailed records, and the numbers that I had at my disposal did not always coincide. Nevertheless, the information I was able to obtain from both Cuba and Angola was sufficient to allow me to draw relatively reliable conclusions.

According to official government figures, approximately 400,000 Cuban soldiers and 50,000 civilians were engaged in Angola.[4] The records I consulted backed these figures, at least for civil engagement. The numbers and statistics contained in these records are solely quantitative, and they reflect little of the local and social origins of the volunteers, or of their gender, age, skin color, qualifications, or training. According to an internal set of statistics from the Cuban Ministerio para la Inversión Extranjera y la Colaboración Económica (MINVEC, Ministry of Foreign Investment and Economic Cooperation)—which grew out of the CECE in 1976 to take responsibility for civil cooperation—a total of 44,206 aid workers, many of them specialists in their professions, were deployed in Angola between 1975 and 1991.[5] Although this figure deviates from official government figures by several thousand, it nevertheless confirms the overall scale of engagement.

I was able to compare this MINVEC statistic with an unpublished study from the archive of the Instituto de Historia de Cuba (IHC, Cuban Historical Institute).[6] This study was compiled in the early 1990s by the historian Angel R. García Pérez-Castañeda,[7] and it mainly comprises statistics and basic information concerning the countries across the globe receiving civil aid from Cuba between 1963 and 1990. The information contained in the study stems from documents gathered by García Pérez-Castañeda from the archives of Cuban ministries that provided aid workers for overseas. In the appendix of the study, García Pérez-Castañeda quotes a figure of 45,197 aid workers for all sectors of civil engagement in Angola between 1975 and 1990.[8] How he arrives at this figure, however, is not completely clear. The sum of the aid workers listed under the particular cooperation sectors (health, education, construction, etc.) is 48,957.[9] Even though both figures differ from the number given by MINVEC, they too come reasonably close to the official number of fifty thousand volunteers.

From the information available, I was unable to explain fully why the figures do not coincide. One feasible explanation, however, is that different criteria were used for collecting data. It is possible that some ministries counted not the number of persons involved but the number of years they served.[10] Since the majority of aid workers went to Angola for two years, the resulting figures were inflated. There is, however, no proper indication of how the statistical data was recorded. The data therefore have to be taken as given, but they do serve the purpose of highlighting the extraordinarily high number of people engaged in Angola.

Another problem with accurately determining the total number of civil aid workers results from some of them making a smooth transition from the military to the civilian sector in spring 1976. This is dealt with in greater detail in chapter 6. The persons in question were approximately one thousand reservists who had come to Angola as soldiers in 1975/76, and whose professions in civil life meant that they could stay and support the reconstruction of Angola. These reservists were not registered in any ministry as civil aid workers, as they were subordinated to the Cuban military authorities in Angola.

Having compared Cuba's civil aid operations throughout the world, García Pérez-Castañeda reached the conclusion that in purely quantitative terms, civil engagement in Angola represented "Cuba's largest example of internationalist cooperation."[11] In his rankings of African countries receiving civil aid from Cuba, Angola is far out in front, followed by Ethiopia with 6,179 aid workers. In third place is Mozambique (4,026 aid workers), followed by Guinea-Conakry (1,258), Guinea-Bissau (1,135), and Tanzania, to which Cuba sent 1,012 aid workers and specialists.[12] According to García Pérez-Castañeda's figures, the only civil aid project that approached anywhere near the size and scope of Angola was Nicaragua. After the success of the Sandinista revolution in 1979, which had been supported by the Cuban government in political, military, and civil terms, 16,787 civil aid workers were sent to Nicaragua between 1979 and 1990, the majority of whom supported the education sector.[13]

For the period between 1976 and 1988, García Pérez-Castañeda quotes a figure of 10,661 civil aid workers cooperating in education in Nicaragua, though he does not specify the areas and school types in which they were deployed.[14] The figures given by García Pérez-Castañeda are largely confirmed in Nancy Jiménez's publication on the involvement of women in Cuba's international military and civil aid projects. On the basis of statistics from the Cuban MINED, she cites a figure of 11,105 teachers and education specialists at the primary- and secondary-school levels between 1976 and 1991.[15] She also quotes another statistic from the archive of the Cuban Ministry of Higher Education (MES) that puts the number of university lecturers and professors at 475 between 1977 and 1992.[16]

I was able to compare these Cuban statistics with figures contained in the MED archive pertaining to the scope of Cuban cooperation. The Angolan sources do not provide an overall figure for the Cuban aid workers during the relevant period; instead they refer to specific years or regions in which the workforce was deployed. The Angolan figures for individual years, particularly during the 1978–1984 phase, when Cuban-Angolan cooperation was at its height, coincide with the Cuban figures quoted by MINVEC, García Pérez-Castañeda, and Jiménez.[17]

Another important area of cooperation in education involved the Angolan boarding schools on the Cuban Isla de la Juventud, the Isle of Youth, which opened their doors in autumn 1977. Again there is no detailed information available concerning the number of Angolan pupils and students who completed their schooling or studies in Cuba between 1977 and 1991. One unpublished study from the Cuban MINVEC on the international boarding schools, which was compiled in 2004, quotes a figure of 13,858 Angolan school graduates for the period of 1977 to 2003.[18] According to this figure, 8,558 Angolan children and adolescents completed basic secondary education (tenth grade), 2,063 youths managed to complete their pre-university education, and 3,237 young adults received a university degree. Jiménez, on the other hand, quotes a figure of 8,083 school graduates from 1977 to 2005, and 2,612 university graduates.[19] These figures are inherently vague and in both cases deal only with the number of successful graduates, without taking into account how many Angolan children and adolescents actually attended boarding schools and universities in Cuba (including those who did not graduate).

Documents and statistics from the MED regarding the scholarship program in Cuba likewise do not give any details on the total number of pupils and students involved. They do, however, underline the magnitude of this cooperation project: in autumn 1977, the first eight hundred Angolan children embarked on their voyage to Cuba.[20] During the 1980s, there were constantly between two thousand and three thousand Angolan children and adolescents attending the boarding schools of the Isle of Youth.[21] Unlike all other areas of cooperation in education, the scholarship program was maintained even after 1991 and still exists today.[22]

All available statistical information on civil cooperation underlines how extensive this transatlantic endeavor was in terms of the number of persons involved. The fact that the records originate from the education ministries in Cuba and Angola and from MINVEC emphasizes the professional nature of cooperation and the extent to which it was institutionalized. The statistics also provide an insight into the different phases of cooperation. By comparing them with García Pérez-Castañeda's study, one can deduce that the various phases that determined cooperation in education to some extent are also relevant to the other cooperation sectors. This is another reason why the findings that apply here to the education sector are also pertinent to other areas. To provide a comparison of the entire civil cooperation program, however, would be too extensive for the scope of this study, and the lack of available data would make such a comparison even more difficult.

The Dynamics and Characteristics of Cooperation from 1976 to 1991

I will now attempt to outline the various phases of Cuban-Angolan cooperation from a diachronic perspective. I have divided the periods according to the number of Cuban civil aid workers and specialists deployed in Angola between 1976 and 1991. The extent of their presence is indicative of cooperative developments and phases. I have also taken into account political and military circumstances that had a significant influence on civil cooperation. Alongside the external and internal political situation of the first fifteen years of Angolan independence and the dynamics of the military conflict, the intensity of the cooperation relationship was affected by the personal and political relationships between the governments and their leaders. With these factors in mind, I have divided cooperation into three phases using developments in the education program to illustrate them.

The first phase covers the years 1976 to 1977/78, which marked the beginning of civil cooperation. The beginning of this period was a test phase to determine the future shape of cooperation. The initial intention was to offer "help for self-help," which is why the project at first concentrated on sending advisors and providing Angolans with specialized training. From mid-1976, the Angolan government's request for more and more extensive support for national reconstruction led to the signing of various bilateral agreements, which fixed civil cooperation at a binational level. These cooperative agreements determined the framework and established bilateral control mechanisms and institutions, which rapidly led to cooperation becoming institutionalized on both sides of the Atlantic. Although the Cuban government initially intended to limit strictly the number of people it deployed, the contractual agreements signaled an acceptance of the MPLA's wish to prolong and expand the civil aid program.

The second phase covers the years from 1978 to 1983/84. This was the most intense period of cooperation, during which the size of the civilian workforce was at its height. It was also during this phase that comprehensive bilateral cooperation projects came into being, and the boarding schools on the Isle of Youth opened their doors. The focus of cooperation had already changed by the beginning of this period. The Angolan government no longer considered teacher training for Angolans a priority and instead compensated for the lack of Angolan teachers with Cuban teachers. The third and final phase began between 1983 and 1984 and ended with the withdrawal of Cuban troops and civilians in the summer of 1991. This period was characterized by an escalation of the civil war. The reasons for this escalation can be traced in part to the global Cold War power constellation, which led to the antagonistic superpowers, the United States and the Soviet Union, fighting a type of "proxy war" on Angolan soil. Backed by the United States and military offensives of the South African army, the UNITA rebels advanced from the southeast to the areas controlled by the MPLA government. The Soviet Union in turn supported the Angolan and Cuban troops, exacerbating the war and bringing the reconstruction efforts in many parts of the country to a standstill. During these developments, the number of Cuban civil aid workers declined considerably. On the international stage, the United States initiated a so-called peace process. The negotiations culminated in the New York Accords between Cuba, Angola, and South Africa in December 1988. The accords set the timetable for the withdrawal of all Cubans from Angola.

Phase I: 1976 to 1977/78

The beginning of cooperation in education was part of a political and military strategy that had been planned by the Cuban government and the MPLA to consolidate the MPLA's power after independence. Initially, a pilot education project was introduced in February 1976 in the enclave of Cabinda. This civil aid project also included a team of Cuban doctors, and it ran alongside Cuban military operations with the intention of stabilizing the economically important enclave. Next to Luanda, the province of Cabinda was crucial to the MPLA in terms of economy, geography, and military strategy, and the MPLA's extension of power depended on it securing the region.

Cabinda was rich in petroleum and under constant military threat from Zaire, which worked closely with the FNLA and threatened to annex Cabinda. The guerrilla Front de Libération de l'Enclave de Cabinda (FLEC, Front for the Liberation of the Enclave of Cabinda), supported by Zaire, also launched military offensives in the area. Cuban military units were stationed in Cabinda as early as autumn 1975 and helped the MPLA troops, FAPLA, defend themselves against the rebels. Their other task was to provide military protection for petroleum production in order to secure the revenues for the MPLA government. In February 1976, Cabinda and Luanda were the only territories that were completely under MPLA control and therefore the only regions in which public institutions were able to function and the schools were open. In all other Angolan provinces, the continuous fighting had forced schools to close.[23]

A group of twelve education specialists, who were under the Cuban military's authority, arrived in Cabinda to assess the education situation in Angola and test the waters for a national literacy campaign and teacher-training program. They were to communicate their findings to the recently established MED in Luanda with the aim of transferring the pilot project to the rest of Angola. Working on the basis of the Cuban education system, the Cuban education specialists were to join their Angolan counterparts to work out the topography of the new education policy and educational facilities throughout the country.[24]

The Cabinda pilot project embodied the political and military strategy with which the Cuban government intended to support the MPLA in the future.

This strategy involved defending the territory while simultaneously deploying small groups of civil specialists to support the construction of a network of state-run social services, for example in health and education.[25] This would strengthen the confidence of the population in the new MPLA government. The strategy drew on the focus strategy of the Cuban guerrilla movement, and with it the Cuban government expected to keep the deployment of civilians to a minimum.

The education specialists who were sent to Cabinda were a group of hand-picked cadres regarded as politically reliable and all belonging to the Communist Party of Cuba. They also had teaching qualifications and/or had gained experience during the Cuban education campaigns. The choice of persons and the preparation they received before being sent to Angola were kept strictly secret. Shortly before they were dispatched, the then minister of education, José Ramón Fernández, explained to them that they were members of an elite unit destined to carry out a task of "national import" in Angola on behalf of both governments.[26] Before going to Angola, each member completed basic military training, but they traveled as civilians and worked under the authority of the Cuban military. The composition of the group reflected the priority the Cubans gave to the natural sciences. It comprised two geography teachers, two biology teachers, two chemistry teachers, and two mathematics teachers. A literacy campaign specialist, who had helped create the workers' and peasants' faculties in Cuba, was also part of the group, along with three experts in school organization.[27]

In April 1976, a request from the Angolan President, Agostinho Neto, frustrated the Cuban government's plans to limit civil aid to such small, specialized cadre units. Neto asked the Cuban government to increase the number of specialists in order to accelerate the reconstruction process. The Cuban government found a quick and pragmatic answer to the problem. It invited the reservists stationed in Angola to remain and employ their civilian professional skills to support reconstruction. Approximately one thousand reservists responded to this call.[28]

This de facto civil cooperation pact was finally legalized in a binational framework agreement during Neto's first state visit to Cuba in July 1976. The agreement officially sealed the friendship and political partnership between Cuba and Angola that Neto's state visit symbolized. It also effectively extended cooperation considerably, increasing bilateral obligations primarily for the benefit of the Angolan government. The military support Cuba had given the MPLA in 1975, which was originally intended to be limited and short-term, thus finally evolved into a long-term transatlantic relationship encompassing cooperation on political, economic, cultural, and military levels.

During Neto's state visit to Cuba, the "Economic, Scientific and Technical Cooperation Framework Agreement" was signed on 29 July 1976, in Havana.[29] In the following months, the agreement served as a basis for sectoral agreements specific to the various areas of cooperation, which in the case of the education sector included a payment agreement for services provided.

As already illustrated, the organization of the state visit and its media coverage reflected the respective interests of both governments and the importance they attached to their cooperative relationship. By staging the visit and surrounding it with propaganda, the Cuban government hoped to win over the people's trust for this new partnership with Angola. It also wanted the world, both East and West, to take note of the new transatlantic axis between Cuba and Angola and to see that Cuba was not tied to the foreign policies of the two superpowers. The other intention (above all of Castro) was to cast Cuba among the ranks of the nonaligned states as the leader of the Tricontinental countries. The Angolan government, for its part, supported this propaganda strategy because it hoped it would lead to comprehensive and sustained military and civil support from Cuba. But it was also anxious to demonstrate its political sovereignty to the Angolan population, to those within its own ranks who were skeptical about its cooperation with Cuba, and indeed to the Cuban government. Although the MPLA government was well aware of its reliance on foreign aid, it was at pains to avoid any relationship of dependency that could be interpreted as neocolonialism.

Neto emphasized how important the new cooperative relationship with Cuba was by traveling with a delegation of forty high-ranking government politicians and members of the MPLA politburo.[30] The Angolan President was received in Cuba with the highest diplomatic and military honors, including the Playa Girón military medal for "outstanding services in the fight against imperialism."[31] The visit culminated in celebrations (held on 26 July, Cuba's most important national holiday) commemorating the Castro-led attack on the Moncada barracks in Santiago de Cuba in 1953. In his speech, Castro emphasized the common legacy of colonialism and underlined his definition of an "Afro-Latin American" Cuban-Angolan nation. Neto reiterated their shared experience and depicted the solidarity between Cuba and Angola as an "effective instrument against imperialism"[32] He praised the advances of the Cuban Revolution in the sectors of the economy, education, and health, and he underlined that he hoped Angola could follow a path of socialist development similar to Cuba's.[33] The official final declaration, which was reported in the media in both countries, demonstrated the Cuban government's willingness to meet Neto's request to support the military and to push ahead with civil reconstruction in Angola.[34] At that time, Angola's main daily newspaper and the MPLA's mouthpiece was the *Jornal de Angola*. Its coverage of the Cuban state visit clearly illustrates an attempt to persuade the Angolan people. Its reports on Cuba, the Cuban way of life, and Cuban politics, and details of Cuba's socialist development were intended to preempt any possible objections to the large presence of the Cuban military and Cuban civilians on Angolan soil.[35] The news coverage concentrated on the enthusiasm with which the Cubans welcomed Neto, thus emphasizing the friendship between Cuba and Angola and the solidarity between the two countries.[36] The newspaper printed excerpts from speeches in which Neto insisted on the reciprocal nature of the relationship: "We believe that this visit has been of great use to our lives here in Angola—of great use in political terms, because we have strengthened the ties of friendship and solidarity, and we will cooperate with each other in the future even more closely than today, . . . and all this serves the progress of both our nations."[37]

The *Jornal de Angola*, however, also emphasized Angola's political sovereignty. While Neto was in Cuba, his deputy, Prime Minister Lopo do Nascimento, went to Yugoslavia, where he negotiated an extension of military and civil aid with the head of state Josip Broz Tito. At the same time that it reported on Neto's state visit to Cuba, the front page of the *Jornal* ran a piece on Lopo do Nascimento's state visit to Yugoslavia, signaling that the MPLA had no intention of becoming dependent on Cuba, but was counting on the support of another socialist state that likewise was determined to remain independent of the Soviet Union.[38] Lopo do Nascimento emphasized this point in the interview I conducted with him. According to his statement, the MPLA always made sure that it secured support from many different parties. But the relationship with Cuba had always been easier because Cuba and Angola were both "Third World" countries, and this status had contributed considerably to their mutual understanding. Moreover, according to Lopo do Nascimento, the language barrier and differences in mentality between Cubans and Angolans had been much less significant than with Yugoslav or Soviet citizens.[39]

Of crucial importance to the relationship between the MPLA and the Cuban government during the first phase of cooperation was the political confidence that existed between them, in particular between the heads of government, Neto and Castro. On the Cuban side, this confidence was based on the conviction that the Angolan government wished to follow a socialist path of development that resembled Cuba's and was independent of the Soviet Union. President Neto was the guarantor of this position on the Angolan side. Several examples from 1977 reflect the extent of Angola's confidence in Cuba, and they illustrate how this trust—combined with political and diplomatic skill—managed to secure Cuba's willingness to provide comprehensive military and civil support to fill the gap in Angolan know-how. In 1977, for example, the

Angolan government gave Cuban experts full responsibility for organizing and introducing the new national currency, kwanza, which was to replace the Portuguese escudo.[40]

In March 1977, the Cuban-Angolan friendship was reinforced by Castro's visit to Angola. The state visit was part of a larger tour through Africa that took Castro to Algeria, Libya, Yemen, Ethiopia, Somalia, Tanzania, Mozambique, and Angola. One of the aims was to position him as spokesman for the countries of the "Tricontinent."[41] The support Cuba gave the MPLA government in maintaining its sovereignty against an onslaught from the South African apartheid regime proved to be particularly significant. Through it, Castro was able to secure the approval of the African states normally hostile to socialism. During Castro's visit to Angola, Neto was able to use Castro's political ambitions by emphasizing that the South African military, UNITA, and even the FNLA still posed a real threat. A complete withdrawal of Cuban troops would, he maintained, seriously undermine the consolidation of his government. A comparison of the two leaders speaking together in public illustrates the different interests that they were pursuing, despite their mutual friendship and confidence. Castro assured Neto that Cuba would continue to support him, but he also indicated that Angola's development was dependent on the efforts of the Angolans themselves. Neto responded that Cuba and Angola shared the long road ahead of them.[42] While the government of Cuba wished to limit its involvement, Neto opted for an extension of cooperation.

Two months later, Cuba's willingness to engage on behalf of the MPLA was put to the test when Neto's government came under serious threat from a military putsch, led by an internal opponent, Nito Alves, on 27 May 1977. All research to date shows that the quick end to the putsch was largely due to Neto's apparent success in convincing Castro to provide him with Cuban troops to help fight the rebels.[43] Following the putsch, the MPLA was dependent more than ever on Cuban support. As early as September, Neto presented Castro with further requests to help consolidate his government. Referring to the cooperation agreement for education that had been signed at the end of 1976, he requested one thousand Cuban teachers to be sent to Angola as a matter of urgency.[44] Angola's education initiatives had been welcomed by the Angolan population, and, by mid-1977, the new education system was buckling under the strain of over one million new pupils. Neto and the MPLA thought that by providing sufficient classes to satisfy the increased demands for education they would be able to regain the popular support they had lost after their violent suppression of the putsch. Again, Neto's new requests illustrate that cooperation as it stood did not go far enough to ensure the success of reforms or to guarantee the long-term stability of the MPLA government.

Cuba's response was once again affirmative, and it arranged for a brigade of over seven hundred Cuban student teachers to be sent to Angola starting in spring 1978 to work in primary and secondary schools. Moreover, during a visit by Minister of Education Fernández to Angola in October 1977, the cooperation agreements in education were extended, made more specific, and adapted to meet the huge need for teachers. At the same time, the Angolan boarding schools on the Isle of Youth received their first eight hundred pupils.

Phase II: 1978 to 1983/84

The deployment of the student brigades in Angola marked a turning point for cooperation in education and the beginning of the second phase. From 1978 (and eventually to 1991), the focus was on sending Cuban teachers to Angola and educating Angolan children and adolescents on the Isle of Youth. The cooperation program's original intention of "help for self-help" took a back seat. No longer was the emphasis on specific education and training programs; cooperation now revolved around making up for the lack of Angolan teachers by sending Cuban teachers instead. Internal discussions within the MED show that the original sustainable approach had apparently also been favored by Angolan education specialists and their advisors, but this approach now had to give way to the Angolan government's political priority of increasing the size of the workforce.[45] The large-scale deployment of civil aid workers that then began led on both sides to professionalization and institutionalization, and to the establishment of bureaucratic structures and communication mechanisms to organize and control the project.

Military attacks, such as the massacre of Kassinga perpetrated by the South African air force in May 1978,[46] did not interrupt the mass mobilization of Cuban civilians. On the contrary, the South African attack on Kassinga provoked worldwide protests against the apartheid regime, and the extensive coverage it received in the Cuban press encouraged even more volunteers to sign up.[47] Until the 1982/83 academic year, the number of Cuban teachers at Angolan schools rose continuously. By mid-1982, it reached its peak of over two thousand. In that year, Cuban teachers accounted for almost 80 percent of the total number of foreign staff working in education; the remaining 20 percent comprised mainly Portuguese but also Soviet, Bulgarian, East German, and Vietnamese teachers and lecturers.[48] The majority of Cubans were deployed in primary schools and secondary education.[49] By 1982/83, the Angolan Ministry of Education had obviously resigned itself to covering the need for teachers with Cubans in the longer term. Because of the Cuban government's successful recruitment campaign, Cuban teachers were readily available, and in comparison with other foreign workers they were a convenient, low-cost solution: they could be deployed flexibly and were relatively low-maintenance because they arrived in large organized groups and were taken care of by the Cuban Civil Administration.

In 1979, the death of President Neto represented a turning point in this phase. Neto was not only the Cuban government's most important ally within the MPLA; after his state visit in 1976, he was also regarded by the Cuban public as a symbol of the just political and moral cause of Cuban-Angolan cooperation. Neto died in Moscow, where he was being treated by Soviet doctors, despite having previously been under the care of Cuban doctors. This is an indication of the extent to which the Cuban-Angolan relationship had apparently cooled off on the governmental level. It seems also to be indicative of the diverging interests of the Cuban and Soviet governments in Angola. The cooling of relations was never openly discussed, but it is clearly hinted at in the Cuban government's deviation from protocol on the death of a friendly head of state by not publishing its letter of condolences until three days after the announcement of Neto's death in the *Jornal de Angola*.[50] Civil cooperation remained unaffected. It was sustained by existing cooperative agreements and had by now developed its own dynamics, as the increase in the size of the Cuban workforce in Angola demonstrates.

Within the MPLA government, the political balance of power remained stable, and just a few days after Neto's death, José Eduardo dos Santos of the MPLA was named his successor.[51] Dos Santos continued the bilateral partnership and cooperation with the Cuban government. Under his presidency, the government initially continued to extend both military and civil support. Nevertheless, political relations between Dos Santos's government and the Cuban government were more detached and less amicable than they had been while Neto was alive. But Dos Santos's government was aware that it still needed Cuba's assistance, and it therefore endeavored to maintain good relations.[52]

Another pivotal event during this phase of cooperation had much more far-reaching and immediate political and military consequences than Neto's death: in January 1981, Ronald Regan was inaugurated president of the United States. Reagan's administration supported the "total strategy" initiated by the South African prime minister, P. W. Botha. This was a policy of open aggression against the Angolan government and the Namibian national liberation front, SWAPO. The governments of Botha and Reagan were united in their fight against "world communism." The US government therefore actively supported the apartheid regime's open aggression toward the MPLA and SWAPO and toward their foreign supporters, the Cuban and Soviet governments.[53] It financed weapons for UNITA, which from 1981 began to coordinate its military activities in Angola with the SADF.

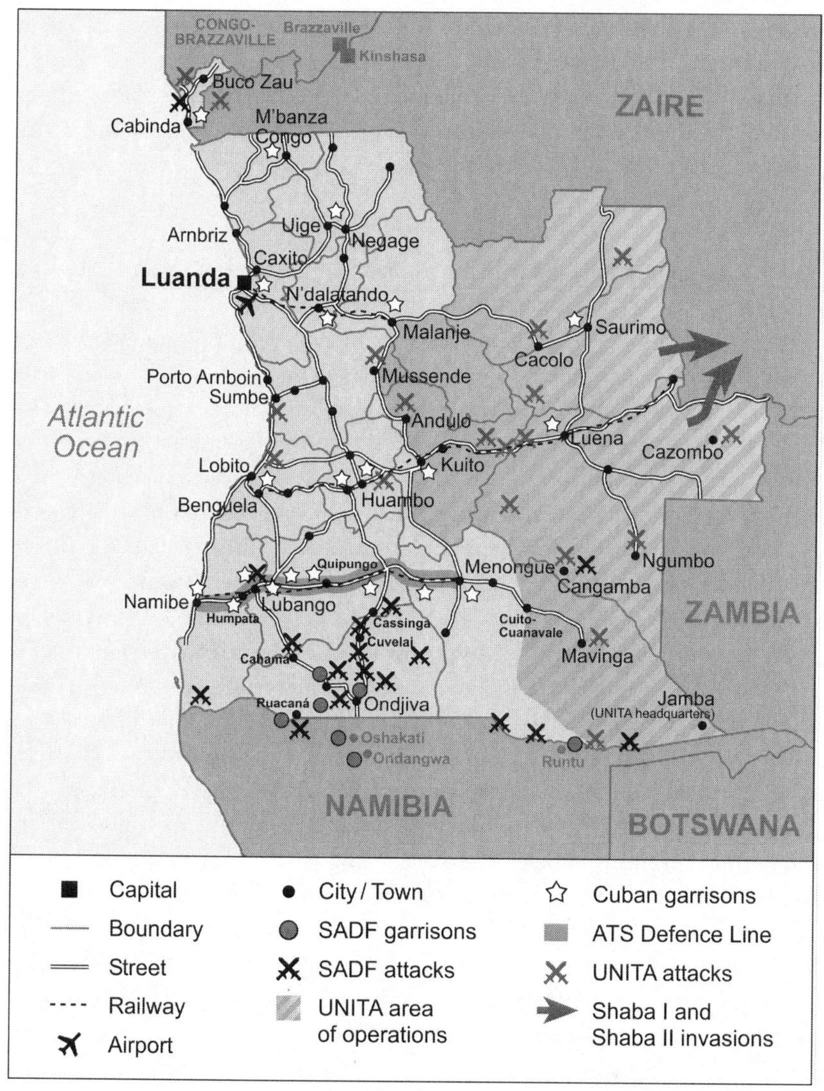

The development of the conflict until 1984 (map by Daniel Giere)

One immediate consequence of the new offensive strategy was "Operation Protea," which culminated in South African troops occupying Kunene, the most southern province of Angola. This marked the beginning of a long period of instability and escalating military conflict.[54] Through its indirect engagement in Angola, the Reagan administration was able to challenge the Cuban government on several fronts and on both sides of the Atlantic. At the same time, the US government's direct intervention in Grenada in 1983 and its support for the anti-Sandinista Contras in Nicaragua were attempts to undermine the political influence Cuba exercised in the Caribbean and Central America.

Phase III: 1983/84 to 1991

The offensive strategy pursued by the Reagan administration and South Africa had a clear impact on Cuban-Angolan cooperation and finally resulted in its gradual reduction in size. From the summer of 1983, UNITA, supported by the South African military, increasingly carried out targeted attacks and acts of sabotage with the aim of destroying civilian infrastructure. It also directly assaulted Cuban-Angolan garrisons.[55] From their base in the province of Kuando Kubango in the far southeast of the country, the UNITA militia advanced in a northwesterly direction, moving ever further into the central highlands with the intention of destabilizing the regions controlled by the MPLA and bringing them under their own control. The UNITA offensive represented a real threat to the MPLA government, and the response was a considerable increase in MPLA armament. The Soviet Union now intensified its involvement in Angola and boosted its financial and material support to the Cuban and Angolan military. Cuban troops stationed in Angola also intensified joint military activity with the MPLA forces (FAPLA) and concentrated on training them to become a regular army able to defend itself against internal and foreign attacks. The first climax of UNITA's destabilizing tactics was its siege of Cangamba in the remote eastern province of Moxico in the summer and autumn of 1983. In the ensuing battle, two thousand soldiers from both sides lost their lives.[56] UNITA's advance through Cangamba was unstoppable, even though the defending FAPLA received ground and air support from Cuba. From 1984, UNITA intensified its attacks on economic targets and infrastructure, and the Angolan civilian population, caught between two fronts, was drawn increasingly into the conflict. In spring 1984, UNITA launched a direct attack on Cuban civilians for the first time in Sumbe and Huambo.

Parallel to these military offensives, the governments of South Africa, Angola, and Cuba were called around the negotiating table in 1981 at the US government's instigation. These talks formed part of the offensive tactics to weaken Cuba and destabilize the MPLA government. The aim was again to force the withdrawal of Cuban troops from Angola, this time through diplomatic means. The negotiation strategy not only demanded the withdrawal of Cuban troops as a precondition for the withdrawal of South African troops from Angola; it also linked withdrawal to the independence of Namibia, which was at that time a South African protectorate. Furthermore, the talks called for decommissioning SWAPO, which was fighting against the South African government and maintained bases in the south of Angola. Since 1976, South Africa had been using SWAPO as its official justification for intervening in Angola. This diplomatic strategy of "linkage" called upon the 1978 Resolution 435 of the UN Security Council, which demanded Namibia's independence from South Africa and the recognition of SWAPO as the legitimate representative of the Namibian people. The linked condition of a Cuban withdrawal, however, was completely new and could be traced back to the offensive tactics of the United States and South Africa.[57]

The negotiations did lead to several interim agreements—for example, the Lusaka Accords of 1984, in which the MPLA government promised South Africa to close SWAPO bases in south Angola. But the war nevertheless continued to escalate. The role of Angola's President Dos Santos during the peace negotiations was very ambiguous with regard to the Cuban government. On the one hand, his government negotiated with the United States and South Africa without consulting Cuba. On the other, it actively pursued military and civil cooperation with Cuba because it was unable to consolidate its power without Cuban support. Cuban politicians and military leaders were obviously well aware of this double dealing, and during the 1980s, it led to frequent disagreements and a marked deterioration of the once friendly atmosphere.[58]

The escalation of the political and military situation in Angola was accompanied by a deep financial crisis, whose drastic impact on state finances could no longer be balanced by petroleum revenues. The trade deficit, which had been increasing since 1978, was worsened by falling oil prices on the international market. From 1982, approximately 50 percent of Angola's state revenues flowed into the defense budget; 30 percent was spent on importing food and consumer goods; and the remaining 20 percent was dedicated to servicing debts.[59] The MPLA reacted by setting up a national crisis plan to impose rigid austerity measures on the ministries and administration and to encourage better efficiency in all branches of the state-controlled economy.[60] Starting in 1983, spending in education was thus effectively controlled for the first time. Internal accounts from the Ministry of Education show that the financing of foreign specialists represented an enormous cost factor, and that financing the Cuban teachers and experts was the biggest cost item.[61] Although the Ministry of Education still regarded Cuban support as necessary to maintain the education system, beginning in the 1980s it had difficulties paying the Cuban government for services rendered under the cooperative agreement.

From 1985, the Angolan government abandoned its planned economy. It introduced market-economy reforms and accepted the structural adjustment programs imposed by the International Monetary Fund and the World Bank with the aim of reducing inflation and the budget deficit.[62] Despite this new economic policy, the centralized and undemocratic structures of the socialist era remained in place, offering fertile ground for corruption within the state apparatus.[63] The Cuban government may not have approved the economic reforms or corrupt practices, but it remains unclear whether it actually criticized the Angolan government for its new economic policies or whether it was aware of the extent of state corruption. It is a fact, however, that on Cuba's initiative civil cooperation in education and particularly in the deployment of teachers was considerably reduced by the end of 1983. The Cuban government used the pretext of military escalation and, more concretely, the attacks on Cuban civilians to reduce drastically the amount of support it was providing for education. It would seem, however, that this reduction mainly had to do with disagreement between the two governments and the MPLA government's inability to pay.

Already during the 1984/85 academic year, the number of Cuban teachers had halved in comparison with 1982. Internal records from the Angolan Ministry of Education cite a mere 957 teachers for this period.[64] The lack of safety was first used as an excuse to withdraw teachers from the municipalities and provinces where clashes with UNITA were flaring up. Frequently, the Cuban Civil Administration withdrew the teachers on its own initiative, without first consulting the Angolan Ministry of Education.[65] In March 1984, there were no longer any Cuban teachers working in the provinces of Kuando Kubango, Lunda Norte, and Lunda Sul, nor in Zaire. Their withdrawal had a massive impact on schooling, as more and more schools had to close because of a shortage of teachers. From the mid-1980s, Cuban cooperation concentrated mainly on secondary and higher education, which ensured that teachers and lecturers would be deployed primarily in urban centers.[66] In 1986, Cuba stopped sending its student brigades, leaving only 549 Cuban teachers in Angola.[67] In January 1988, the number of Cuban teachers fell further to 414.[68] In accordance with the agreements reached in the New York Accords, all teachers and troops were finally withdrawn in 1989 from the southern province of Namibe and from the south-central highland provinces of Huila and Bié.

Starting in 1989, the withdrawal of Cuban teachers and the austerity measures imposed by the government caused the Angolan MED to become increasingly critical of its reliance on Cuban cooperation. Members of the MED became convinced that the massive deployment of foreign teachers had been unable to address the fundamental problems of the Angolan education system (a shortage of teachers and schools, a high rate of illiteracy and failure, the poor quality of teaching). On the contrary, the project had done much to hamper Angolan initiative. At the same time, the MED endeavored to compensate for the loss of Cuban teachers with teachers provided through international development organizations, such as the United Nations Development Program (UNDP). However, this only covered a small portion of the teachers needed.[69] Even during this phase, the MED could not entirely renounce Cuban aid. The Cuban government agreed not to bring the education cooperation to an abrupt end, but it insisted that if it were to continue cooperating, the teachers would have to be paid for in accordance with conditions on the international market.[70]

Institutionalization: Structures, Communication, and Control

In both Cuba and Angola, the deployment of Cuban specialists led to the institutionalization and professionalization of cooperation. After the first cooperative agreements were signed, the numbers of Cubans involved called for comprehensive and detailed organization in order to coordinate the cooperative programs properly and deploy the workforce as efficiently as possible. At the binational level, this process of institutionalization entailed setting up negotiation and control commissions and establishing bilateral communication mechanisms. On the basis of the agreements, the bilateral commissions determined the content and structure of cooperation, working out specific conditions and trying to reach a consensus.

Apart from these commissions, both Cuba and Angola established their own state bodies for planning, managing, and implementing the cooperation program. The ministries opened new departments to administer, care for, and monitor the civil aid workers for whom they were responsible. In addition, the Cubans set up the Civil Administration in Angola, which was independent of Angolan institutions. Its task was to mentor and monitor the Cubans working in Angola and to help the Angolan authorities coordinate them.

In this day-to-day teamwork, the asymmetries in the cooperative relationship became particularly apparent. Whenever Angolan infrastructure and administration proved insufficient to guarantee the well-being of the workforce, the Cubans had to manage their own affairs. Cuba's many years of experience in organizing state bodies meant that their administrative structures in Angola were considerably more advanced than those of the Angolans. In addition, their apparently highly efficient information network allowed them to react more quickly to political and military challenges. In Angola, the institutionalization process of cooperation was sluggish by comparison. Nevertheless, it did make a fundamental contribution to strengthening state administrative structures throughout the country, which had remained underdeveloped after independence. Government bodies were able to exploit foreign cooperation by extending their coordinating and controlling powers into the provinces, thereby creating an integral area of dominance.

For Cuba, organizing civil cooperation with Angola was pivotal for two reasons. The sheer size of the workforce now meant that its deployment had to be centrally organized and professionalized. Through this process, it became quicker and easier to dispatch large numbers of aid workers to Angola and other countries. Second, the civil aid contained in the cooperation agreement with Angola was linked to economic benefit for the first time.

The Framework Agreement

On 29 July 1976, both governments signed the "Economic, Scientific, and Technical Cooperation Framework Agreement" in Havana, marking the beginning of the cooperation pact's bilateral legalization and institutionalization.[71] The agreement was based on reciprocity and encompassed the framework agreements governing Cuba's undertaking to provide aid in health, education, industry, and agriculture, and to help improve infrastructure. It also included a number of agreements on economic cooperation that benefited Cuba's economy (for example, quotas for Cuban sugar imports into Angola and a fisheries agreement). The two signatories further agreed that Cuba would receive financial compensation for the civil aid it would provide in the future and had already provided. In connection with the Framework Agreement, political and administrative cooperation between the two governing parties, the PCC and the MPLA, was also agreed upon.[72]

In the months to come, the Framework Agreement led to other sectoral agreements setting out the details of cooperation—both existing and planned—between the ministries. At the beginning of December 1976, educational cooperation was finalized in Havana in the presence of the Angolan and Cuban ministers of education and their deputy ministers. There were two specific cooperation agreements, the first covering primary and secondary education, and the second covering higher education. Under these agreements, the cooperation program came under the responsibility of the Angolan MED and the Cuban MINED and MES.[73] On behalf of Angola, the agreements were signed by the first minister of education and culture following independence, the poet António Jacinto, and his recently appointed deputy minister, the writer Pepetela.[74]

The agreements gave priority to training Angolan teachers, specialists in education, technicians, and administrative staff.[75] Further provisions were made for Cuban advisors to help the various departments within the Angolan Ministry of Education implement the new education policies. These advisors were to provide assistance in all organizational and administrative matters of the new national education system. The agreements also included the following measures aimed at creating a substantial basis for cooperation. Advisors from both Cuban education ministries were to work with their Angolan counterparts at national and provincial levels to carry out a survey of the overall education situation. On the basis of this data, they were then to devise concrete cooperative programs and determine how many teachers and education specialists would be required. Alongside this, a small number of Cuban teachers and education specialists were to design teacher-training programs for Angolans, which they would implement on-site in Angola. The Cuban Ministry of Education also provided short-term scholarships to train Angolan education specialists in Cuba, and it offered a number of university places to Angolan students to enable them to complete their studies in teaching or in technical and administrative subjects.[76]

Initially, it was only in higher and university education that the direct deployment of Cubans was to play a major role. Cuban professors and lecturers were sent to Angola to help reconstruct the university. During the colonial period, university teaching and research in Angola had been conducted solely by academics of Portuguese origin who returned to Portugal after independence. The majority of students followed suit, leaving a gaping hole in young academic talent. The university therefore had to be reconstructed almost entirely by foreign, in particular Cuban, professors and lecturers. The Cuban MES undertook to deploy for the short term thirty university professors of natural science, engineering, and agriculture. The ministry also offered one hundred scholarships at Cuban universities and polytechnic institutes, where students could gain the necessary qualifications to attend university. The ministries further agreed to exchange four experts of higher education each, whose task it would be to analyze specific requirements and evaluate the impact of cooperation in order to plan how to proceed with it.[77]

The cooperative agreements stipulated the timeframe within which the Angolans had to submit their demands in order to guarantee the Cuban ministries enough time to provide the required specialists. Each agreement was valid for one year and was flexible in nature, which meant that agreements could be modified, extended, or canceled if both sides consented. Matters regarding the deployment of civil aid workers, the establishment of bilateral commissions, control mechanisms, and payment terms were not determined at the Ministry of Education level, but were settled in separate agreements drawn up between the two governments.[78]

Cooperation in education was complemented by two further cooperative agreements in sports and culture. The sports agreement was drawn up by the Cuban National Institute of Sport, Physical Education and Recreation (INDER) and the Angolan National Council of Physical Education and Sport. The initial agreement provided only for the deployment of Cuban advisors in various disciplines.[79] In the years that followed, however, the agreement changed to allow for the deployment of Cuban physical education teachers at Angolan schools. In the cultural sector, the agreements aimed at promoting "friendly relations between the people of Cuba and Angola in the spirit of solidarity and united struggle."[80] Provisions were made for cultural exchanges involving groups of artists, musicians and dancers, folklore groups, art and photography exhibitions, concerts, book readings, and film showings. In the library, archive, and museum sectors, an agreement was made on the exchange of knowledge and know-how. This agreement extended to cultural events and congresses in Cuba and Angola, to which delegates from the partner country were to be invited. Cultural exchange also envisaged the dissemination of national symbols and the observance of memorial days and holidays celebrated in the partner country.[81]

Only one year later, it became apparent that the agreed-upon measures could by no means balance the huge deficits of the Angolan education system. The Angolan government was also interested in considerably increasing the number of people working in the civil cooperation program so as to guarantee the success of education reform. In August 1977, the Angolan government addressed these two concerns in its request to Cuba for more teachers. Even before the 1976 agreements had elapsed, they were modified at the beginning of October 1977 and widely extended at Angola's request. Instead of "help for self-help," Cuba now agreed to send Cuban teachers directly to Angolan schools to make up for the lack of teaching staff.[82]

The first such measure involved the deployment of over seven hundred student teachers and primary- and secondary-school teachers. At the same time, the newly opened Angolan boarding schools on the Isle of Youth received their first pupils.

Bilateral Commissions

The supreme bilateral authority in charge of cooperation was the Comissão Mista Intergovernamental (Joint Intergovernmental Commission). Together with the bilateral Control Commission, it represented the most important communication structure between the two countries. It was here that regular exchanges between both governments and their ministries took place. The Joint Commission was responsible for all sectors of civil cooperation as set out in the 1976 Framework Agreement. It met to negotiate the conditions of cooperation, concentrating above all on the quantity and quality of the projects and the terms of payment. It was also here that decisions were made regarding the extension and modification of the cooperative agreements. The Joint Commission also had authority regarding agreements on economic and trade relations, which included forestry and agriculture, food production, fisheries, and the construction industry. It also determined the responsibilities of the various state-controlled companies that were established as part of the cooperation program on both sides between 1976 and 1991. The Joint Commission and the Control Commission were made up of high-ranking officials from both governments, the two parties, and all the ministries involved. Representatives of the Cuban Civil Administration in Angola took part in the meetings too, sometimes substituting Cuban government officials. The Joint Commission met every one to two years either in Luanda or Havana. Its first meeting took place in Luanda in November 1977, and the last of a total of eight meetings was held in Havana in 1990.[83]

Using the data provided by the respective Angolan ministries, the Joint Commission determined the scope of the cooperation programs, generally deciding in favor of Angolan requests. The commission was also responsible for regulating the deployment of the workforce, which involved frequent negotiations regarding payment for the assistance provided. It established the criteria that categorized the workers according to the quality of their work, and it fixed payments accordingly. It negotiated the conditions and terms governing payment exchanges between the two states; that is, the Angolan government paid the Cuban government directly.[84] Negotiations also dealt with transportation costs to and within Angola, food and accommodation, medical care, work and safety regulations, and accident insurance. Even though over the years specific points of cooperation were altered, the overall 1977 Framework Agreement remained in force, as did the stipulation that the Angolan government should bear all costs incurred through cooperation. From the outset, the Cuban government counted on complete compensation for its assistance. In return, it undertook to care for Angolans who received scholarships in Cuba, paying for their food and accommodation.

The Comissão Bilateral de Controlo (Bilateral Control Commission) was closely tied to the Joint Intergovernmental Commission in terms of members and organization and represented the highest control organ of the cooperative program. It also worked on the governmental and party levels. It convened every year to evaluate the results of cooperation and take stock of how the cooperation programs fixed by the Joint Commission were being implemented in all sectors.[85] The Control Commission checked the efficiency of cooperation, and it was responsible for overseeing payments. It also monitored the economic and trade relations and financial transactions between the two countries. Some of its responsibilities overlapped with those of the Joint Commission since at its meetings there were constant negotiations regarding conditions and changes in the cooperation program.[86] Just how efficiently the two commissions—with their overlapping membership and responsibilities—monitored cooperation is demonstrated in the minutes of meetings. They show that the commissions' work was results oriented. Whenever there were any difficulties in applying cooperation or a service had not been rendered, either side would lodge a complaint and they would discuss the matter and seek a joint solution.

The institutionalization of cooperation in both countries led to the creation of two state-run bodies permanently responsible for managing, coordinating, and monitoring cooperation between the meetings of the bilateral commissions. In Angola the Secretaria de Estado da Cooperação (State Secretariat for Cooperation) was set up in June 1978 and was placed under the authority of the Ministério das Relações Exteriores (Ministry of Foreign Affairs).[87] In Cuba, the responsible body was the Comité Estatal de Coloboración Económica (CECE, State Committee for Economic Cooperation), which had already been created in December 1976 and fell under the authority of the Council of Ministers. The activities of both bodies were defined by the bilateral cooperation agreements. On this basis, both institutions coordinated with the respective ministries to provide fundamental planning data and continually check and document the services and terms of cooperation.

The Angolan State Secretariat for Cooperation was responsible for communicating with all foreign governments, international organizations, and companies who had signed economic, technical, or scientific cooperation agreements with Angola, or who were interested in establishing cooperation. All ministries benefiting from foreign aid programs and foreign specialists had to coordinate their requirements with the State Secretariat and justify their requests on economic and technical bases to receive approval. On the basis of the data supplied by the ministries, the State Secretariat made an assessment of the overall need, which it then submitted to the binational negotiations of the Joint Commission and Bilateral Control Commission. The decisions reached at these meetings were then forwarded by the State Secretariat to the responsible ministries. Departments of International Cooperation had been set up in each ministry seeking international assistance. They acted as the interface between the ministries and the State Secretariat.

The CECE was founded during the institutionalization and centralization phase of the Cuban state apparatus during the 1970s. It was part of the reform package to centralize administration and increase efficiency in the planned economy. State committees were founded in an effort to revamp political organization, administration, public services, and above all the economy and finance, and to bring them under the overall authority of the Council of Ministers. The CECE's task was to manage, coordinate, and monitor all binational economic activities.[88] It was responsible for coordinating all economic exchange programs both with donor and recipient countries and organizations. This included the financial and material support that Cuba received from the Soviet Union and other states belonging to Comecon. The committee was also responsible for economic cooperation with foreign enterprises, both state-run and private.[89]

The formation of the CECE was therefore not a direct result of the Economic, Scientific and Technical Cooperation Framework Agreement, but cooperation with Angola did lead to an extension of its responsibilities because this was the first time that Cuba had provided development aid on such a large scale. In coordination with the respective ministries, the CECE was in charge of providing the workforce and specialists to send abroad, drawing up cooperation offers and preparing the meetings of the Joint Commission and the Control Commission. The CECE officials responsible for cooperation with Angola were also members of both commissions.[90] Under the CECE was the state-controlled company Cubatécnica. Founded in 1977, it was charged with putting the cooperative projects into practice and handling the corresponding logistics. The work of Cubatécnica encompassed all aspects regarding the deployment of civil aid workers, from providing temporary accommodation, arranging medical examinations, and carrying out emigration formalities to making special arrangements for the workforce abroad to communicate with families at home.[91] The Angolan counterpart of Cubatécnica was the state-run company Logitécnica, which fell under the authority of the State Secretariat for Cooperation. Logitécnia bore responsibility for providing the Cuban workforce (and all other aid workers) in Angola with food, accommodation, and transport, in accordance with the binational cooperation agreements.[92]

The Departments of International Cooperation

In Angola, departments were specially created within the ministries to deal with the implementation and monitoring of foreign cooperation. To illustrate how these departments were organized and how they operated, I will use the example of the Department of International Cooperation, the GICI/GII, which was created in the MED in 1977.[93] This department was of major strategic importance within the ministry because the Angolan education sector was particularly dependent on foreign aid. The GICI/GII answered directly to the minister of education and was responsible for coordinating all cooperation matters within the ministry.

The department was also responsible for all contacts abroad, such as international developmental aid organizations like UNESCO and UNICEF, which supported the education system through projects or by providing teachers and experts. Further tasks of the GICI/GII included acting as an interface between the ministry and the State Secretariat for Cooperation, and coordinating with the Cuban Civil Administration.[94]

As regards the actual application of cooperation, the GICI/GII had the following duties. It was charged with the coordination, management, and monitoring of the foreign workers, who until 1991 came mainly from Cuba.[95] To this end, it documented, analyzed, and archived all information and experiences regarding the foreign workforce. Furthermore, at the request of the State Secretariat for Cooperation, the department was expected to create a national database for the education sector, through which it would be possible to determine the need for foreign teachers and experts, in order to negotiate with the donor countries.[96] Prior to such negotiations, the GICI/GII had to establish the size of the workforce that was actually required. To do so, it coordinated with the two Ministry of Education departments, which were divided according to school form, and the respective Provincial Directorates of the Ministry.[97] The head of the GICI/GII attended the commission meetings himself.[98]

The GICI/GII also had the task of selecting and looking after the Angolan pupils and students who from 1977 were sent abroad to attend school or university or participate in professional training programs. They were financed by numerous scholarship programs, most of which came from Cuba and the Soviet Union. On the initiative of the GICI/GII, the Cuban Instituto Nacional de Bolsas para Estudantes (INABE, National Scholarship Institute) was founded to provide further funding for pupils and students studying abroad.[99] Another task of the department was to select and care for the Angolan teachers who taught at the boarding schools on the Cuban Isle of Youth. Within just a few years, the GICI/GII developed into a centralized organization and control body that proved itself surprisingly capable of managing the foreign workforce, particularly considering the prevailing structural problems in Angola and the department's own lack of qualified staff. Its competence is illustrated in the statistics and surveys that the GICI/GII produced regarding the scope and quality of cooperation.

The fact that the results are not always completely consistent stems from the difficult terrain in which the department operated as it tried to reconcile its monitoring duties with the lack of qualified personnel in its own department. Its task was made even more difficult by deficient administration and gaps in communication structures. Various statistics from the GICI/GII show that from 1977 to 1985 mainly Cubans were employed in the education sector. They were joined by citizens of Portugal, the Soviet Union, Bulgaria, the GDR, Vietnam, Romania, Italy, France, Spain, and Brazil—along with a small number of Africans from Cape Verde, the Congo, São Tomé and Príncipe, and Guinea. Between 1980 and 1985, the twenty to thirty-strong team of the GICI/GII had to coordinate and supervise approximately two thousand foreign workers every year.[100]

The department was responsible for all teachers and specialists in the education sector to whom the Angolan government had accorded the legal status of *cooperantes extrangeiros* (foreign cooperators). This status defined the foreign workforce as "foreign citizens who have been contracted by the People's Republic of Angola to perform a service."[101] All non-Angolan workers fell under this definition. The largest group comprised all those working in Angola under binational agreements, including Cubans and workers from socialist countries. The second main group comprised workers from Western countries who had either signed individual contracts with the Ministry of Education or been sent there by international development organizations and NGOs. The third group comprised all foreign residents of Angola, some of whom had already been employed by the state prior to independence. These were mainly Portuguese nationals who had remained in Angola and continued to teach after 1975.[102]

The main difference between the first and the other two groups was their remuneration. Members of the second and third group received their individual salaries from the Ministry of Education. By contrast, the salaries of the first group of *cooperantes* from socialist countries were paid by the Angolan government directly to the respective cooperating government. The *cooperantes* themselves only received a small allowance that, in the case of the Cubans, was also paid by the Angolan government. From the Ministry of Education's point of view, the Cubans were therefore welcome because they did not burden the ministry's budget. Furthermore, the amount of work they created for the ministry was comparatively little as they arrived and left in large organized contingents and had their own, locally based administrative body to take care of them.[103]

The GICI/GII worked together with the logistics organization Logitécnica to prepare for the arrival of *cooperantes* and to arrange their food, accommodation, and transportation. If the *cooperantes* were from Cuba, it also coordinated with the Cuban Civil Administration. The logistics of organizing the Cuban *cooperantes* were considerable, as they arrived and departed in large groups, sometimes several hundred people at a time. When they arrived in Angola, the GICI/GII registered them and filed their details.[104] Together with the Cuban

Civil Administration, it then decided on the basis of requirement analyses where to send each *cooperante.* Each individual received from the GICI/GII a *salvatorium,* a safe-conduct pass verifying that person's status as a foreign *cooperante.* The safe-conduct pass (a necessity for the journey to work) authorized the *cooperante*'s passage through the military checkpoints that had been set up throughout the country. It also allowed arrival, departure, and movements within Angola to be monitored.[105]

The work of the GICI/GII illustrates the contradictions inherent in the large-scale deployment of a foreign workforce. For the Angolans, cooperation meant a lot of bureaucracy and high costs, while the long-term benefits proved modest. An internal GICI/GII memorandum assessing the withdrawal of Cuban teachers and education specialists from the mid-1980s clearly indicates that the Cuban involvement had hindered development in the Angolan education system rather than improved it.[106]

The Cuban Civil Administration in Angola

Alongside the aforementioned institutions that were established on bilateral and national levels to implement cooperation, the Cuban Civil Administration was set up on Angolan territory as a parallel administrative organ, operating independently of the Angolan authorities and answering directly to the Cuban government as a "state within a state." In the first few years of civil cooperation, this Cuban structure was neither clearly defined nor institutionalized. It had close links with the Cuban Military Administration, mainly in terms of staff, but also with regard to its organization and structure. It operated at a national, regional, and local level and, in keeping with Cuba's governmental structures, it was hierarchical. The intention behind this independent administrative body, however, was not to establish any kind of neocolonial or imperial position of dominance in Angola, but rather to supervise and manage independently the large number of Cuban civilians working there.

Unlike Cuban troops, who were stationed at barracks and garrisons, the civilians were deployed in many different working and living environments. They therefore automatically came into close contact with Angolans. The Cuban government believed there was a hidden danger of their citizens falling under the influence of "harmful" ideologies, which it tried to prevent by introducing strict control measures and by banning Cubans from fostering contact with foreigners from nonsocialist countries, as it also did in Cuba during the 1970s and 1980s. Similarly, the Cuban government was anxious to establish a "Cuban space" to separate the civil aid workers during their engagement from Angolans and other foreigners and to draw boundaries between them in terms of organization, communication, and social and cultural interaction. These boundaries were to be reinforced by the constant monitoring, disciplining, and permanent surveillance of all Cuban civilians in Angola—an enormous logistical task. I will discuss in greater detail the actual effects of this spatial and cultural separation from the viewpoint of the Cuban civil aid workers at a later point in this book.

The Civil Administration was able to compensate for deficits in Angolan administration, particularly with regard to the communication, transportation, and supply bottlenecks that made the lives of the *cooperantes* even more difficult and hindered the recruitment of new volunteers. The officials of the Civil Administration coordinated the deployment of the *cooperantes* with the responsible Angolan institutions. In education, their main contact partner was the Department of International Cooperation (GICI/GII). The Civil Administration also offered the civilians protection against military attack because the control it exercised was based on an internal communication and information network, which provided information not only about the Cuban workforce but also about military and nonmilitary activity that had a bearing on engagement.

To date, the Cuban authorities have generally refused access to written documents that could clarify the organization and structure of the Cuban Civil Administration in Angola. Nevertheless, combined with the few documents I had at my disposal,[107] the eyewitness interviews I conducted with several persons in charge during civil engagement have provided enough information to enable me to outline how this administrative body operated.[108]

Between 1976 and 1979, Cuban civil engagement was headed by Jorge Risquet Valdés (b. 1930), a high ranking party and government official who had since the 1960s been instrumental in the development of Cuban Africa policy. In 1965, he had led the Bataillon Patrice Lumumba in Congo-Brazzaville, a military unit that was dispatched by the Cuban government to support Che Guevara's Congo expedition. In independent Angola, Risquet Valdés acted as the direct emissary of Fidel Castro.[109] In this capacity, he resided in Luanda before being called back to Havana in mid-1979, where he continued to be responsible for civil engagement. Following his relocation to Havana, the Civil Administration that he had set up was nominally placed under the economic section of the Cuban embassy in Luanda.[110]

After becoming part of the Cuban embassy, the Civil Administration was organized as follows. The main cooperation sectors such as health, education, and civil engineering were allocated their own Luanda-based "contingent leaders" (*jefes de contingente*). They were responsible for all the civil aid workers deployed within their professional sector in Angola. The contingent leaders were politically reliable at every level; in other words, they were Party members or members of the Young Communist League. They were the direct contact persons for the Angolan government and ministries while simultaneously representing the interests of the Cuban *cooperantes* to the Angolan institutions. On the basis of the bilateral agreements, they coordinated the cooperation program's implementation with the Angolan partners. In the education sector, they were in constant dialogue with the Department of International Cooperation of the MED. Together with the Angolan representatives of the CECE, they were the direct contact persons during the periods between the meetings of the commissions.[111] The contingent leaders also maintained close contact with the Cuban Ministry of Education (MINED), from whom they received instructions regarding the content and pedagogical focus of cooperation. They worked particularly closely with MINED to arrange and coordinate the deployment of the student-teacher brigades. As the student teachers were to continue their studies while teaching at Angolan schools, it had to be ensured that they could follow the Cuban syllabus for teacher training during their stay.[112]

The contingent leaders were assisted in their task of managing and coordinating cooperation at the national level by their subordinate provincial representatives. They were located in the provinces and had to report back to their superiors either in writing or orally. They were responsible for the civil aid workers who worked in their province in their particular professional sector, and they were charged with supervising them at work and in their daily lives. The provincial representatives were in turn supported by local representatives who led the groups of *cooperantes* on-site, organized their day-to-day life, and maintained internal discipline. They too were accountable to their direct superiors. Each report documented and commented on all internal and external matters to do with the *cooperantes*. These included cooperation with Angolan colleagues, superiors, and local authorities; the general political and military situation in the area; the working environment; and the development of political and cultural activities within the Cuban community.[113] The local representatives were also responsible for communicating with the Cuban military, since the civilians were often deployed in the vicinity of Cuban garrisons. Furthermore, they had to report to their direct superiors if there were any unusual events such as serious illness, accidents, crime, politically incorrect behavior, the violation of rules, or attempts to escape. They also had to report any political or military activity from government opponents. To a certain extent, the local and provincial representatives had the right to sanction the "ordinary" *cooperantes* if they violated internal rules.[114]

The Cuban organizational and party structures that existed at national, provincial, and local levels played an essential role in this internal management process, as they supported the representatives in their executive functions of organizing and supervising the *cooperantes*. The Party members among them were under particular obligation to the Cuban government and were expected to monitor and register the political and social behavior of each individual and forward their findings to the next higher authority. The internal Cuban information network was dependent on the oral and written reports between the national, regional, and local representatives and party representatives. The local Party representatives were also responsible for upholding discipline and morale within the group. They organized the internal political, cultural, and sporting events (e.g., national celebrations, commemoration days, or traditional Cuban evenings).

The Angolan state administration was in many respects inferior to the organization and communication network that the Cuban Civil Administration established. The Cubans had at their disposal civil and military information and data from all sectors and regions of the country where Cubans were deployed, and this represented a power factor. They did not always pass this information on to their Angolan counterparts: they also used it to operate independently without consulting them. This was the case, for example, from the mid-1980s, when the Cuban Civil Administration decided on its own initiative, without first consulting the Angolan Ministry of Education, to withdraw Cuban teachers working in areas threatened by UNITA military attacks.

The available information regarding the interaction between the Cuban administrative bodies and Angolan institutions indicates that the Angolan government was very sensitive to this loss of control (whether imagined or real) and acted to limit the influence of the Cubans in Angola over their core business of military support and civil development aid. One example of the Angolans trying to counteract Cuban influence and insisting on the institutionalization of bilateral relations seems to be the withdrawal in 1979 of the head of civil engagement, Risquet Valdés, who at that time was located in Angola. According to eyewitnesses, the Cuban government recalled him to Havana following differences with the Angolan government.[115] The Angolans were anxious to defend their recent independence from Portuguese colonial rule and were therefore determined not to enter into a new relationship of dependency with another foreign power. The resulting asymmetries, conflicts of interest, and power conflicts are described in a later chapter.

Internationalism with "Reciprocal Benefits": Payment for Cooperation

The deployment of Cuban advisors, teachers, and lecturers in Angola was not a policy solely founded on the commonly cited ideals of "internationalist solidarity." Although even today the Cuban government insists that it took nothing from Angola "but the dead,"[116] documents from the various departments of the Angolan Ministry of Education tell a different story. They clearly show that the Cuban workforce was paid for, and that the amount was graded according to qualifications. This fact sheds a completely different light on the Cuban-Angolan relationship, emphasizing its economic pragmatism. Cuban-Angolan cooperation was in part a commercial relationship, in which the Cuban government met the MPLA's requests for support to rebuild Angola and thus improved its state revenues by "hiring out" skilled workers.

Cuba was by no means an exception among the socialist countries cooperating with Angola. Payment for skilled workers was commonplace in all bilateral cooperation agreements made between the Angolan government and socialist countries, and such payment was carried out at an intergovernmental level. The Angolan government paid the Cuban government contractually agreed-upon monthly salaries for civil aid workers, and at least half of the amount was paid in hard currency (i.e., in US dollars).[117] The Angolans even undertook to adjust payments according to currency fluctuations of the US dollar.[118] The *cooperantes* themselves did not receive a salary, but their transportation, food, and accommodations were provided, as was an allowance of approximately ten US dollars a month, paid to them in Angolan kwanza by the Angolan government through Logitécnica (and later directly by the Ministry of Education).[119] The only proper compensation offered to Cuban aid workers was the guarantee of their jobs in Cuba and continued salary payments to support family members remaining in Cuba.[120] In the 1970s and 1980s, this type of compensation was of actual value since the Cuban currency still had real purchasing power (thanks to its exchange rate among the socialist economies). With the exception of these expenses, engagement carried no other cost for the Cuban government. No civil aid workers sent to Angola were aware that their work was being remunerated at the intergovernmental level, and people were left in the belief that they were providing altruistic, "internationalist" support in the spirit of solidarity.

According to all evidence to date, the Angolan government began paying Cuba for its aid in education in 1977 at the latest, and it carried on doing so until the Cuban withdrawal in 1991.[121] This study was unable to ascertain whether such payments had been made in other spheres of cooperation, but it seems illogical that they would have been limited to the education sector. What is more, the Cuban workforce was not offered at the cheap rates that might have been expected, given the Cuban government's insistence on the obligations of internationalism. A comparison with payments made by the Angolan government for specialists from Western countries and other socialist countries clearly shows that Cuban support was only marginally cheaper. The advantage of the Cubans over other foreign workforces, however, was that their stay was partly organized by the Cuban Civil Administration, and that they were flexible regarding where they were deployed. Also, their accommodation requirements were modest.

The fact that the Cuban government accepted payment from the Angolans in return for skilled labor is by no means reprehensible. After all, the Cuban government itself faced constant economic and financial constraints that would have prevented it from providing such comprehensive support free of charge. On the contrary, it would have been surprising had the Cubans not demanded recompense for their assistance. It is true that cooperation in the education sector (and in all other civil sectors) primarily involved workers, specialists, and know-how rather than goods or materials, which cost the Cuban State nominally nothing. Nevertheless there were indirect costs involved, as over a period of more than fifteen years the Cuban national economy was drained of thousands of young, well-educated professionals. However, double standards seem to have been at work in the practice of remunerating according to qualifications. In the state-controlled Cuban economy, workers were paid a uniform salary regardless of their qualifications and could only supplement their pay with performance-related bonuses. The socialist principles of the planned economy obviously did not apply to cooperation abroad. After all, this was not a question of private gain but of profits for the sole good of the state.

Internal accounts drawn up in 1983 by the Ministry of Education's Department of International Cooperation detail the salaries of foreign workers. The recorded monthly expenditures—excluding the cost of accommodation, food, and transport—for the salaries of Cubans working in education alone came to a total of 1,354,876 US dollars with an average monthly salary of 743.80 US dollars per person for the total of 1,823 employees at that time.[122] The accounts also show that payment was incremental according to qualifications or the area of education in which the *cooperantes* were employed. The items marked "DPI" refer to student teachers who came to Angola from 1978 with the DPI brigades. According to the calculations, no salaries were paid for the students in 1983, which means that the Angolans only paid for food, accommodations, and transportation. Other documents show that the work of the students was at first remunerated but then provided free of charge, apparently at the request of the Angolan government. Nevertheless the deployment of the DPI continued to incur costs even after 1983. Since the students were doing their obligatory teaching practice in Angola and studying at the same time, they were accompanied by their Cuban lecturers. Even though these lecturers were not teaching

Function	School level	Number	Salary scale	Monthly costs ($ USD)	Annual costs ($ USD)
DPI	III (Primary)	359	Not given	Not given	Not given
Teacher	II (Primary)	650	V	860	559,000
Teacher	III (Primary)	478	IV	960	458,000
Teacher	Sport	90	IV	960	86,400
Pedagocial advisor (curricula, teaching material)	INE (teacher training institute)	92	IV	960	91,200
Lecturer	PUNIV (pre-university)	44	IV	960	42,240
Lecturer	IMT (polytechnic school)	9	IV	960	8,640
Lecturer	Pedagogical instructor for DPI	25	IV	960	24,000
Advisor	Ministry of Education	3	IV	960	2,800
Advisor	Ministry of Education	13	III	1,092	14,196
Professor	University	60	II	1,140	68,400
Total		**1,823**	**Average salary: $743.80** (incl. DPI) **$926.10** (excl. DPI)	**9,812**	**1,354,876**

The payment of Cuban teachers and advisors (table by Daniel Giere)

in the Angolan education system, the Angolan government had to pay their salaries, which fell into category IV and amounted to 960 US dollars per person per month.

The salaries of the majority of Cuban teachers fell into the lowest category. These were teachers who taught from the sixth year of primary school right up to an advanced level in technical colleges and teacher training institutions. Others worked in the Angolan MED assisting with the creation of school curricula and teaching materials. Advisors working in the MED and university professors held the highest paid positions (categories III and II, from 1,092 to

1,140 US dollars). The salary scale followed the standard principles of market economies, as shown by a comparison with the salary scale of Brazilian and Portuguese teachers.

There was a considerable difference in the salaries of top Brazilian and Portuguese professionals compared to those of their Cuban counterparts—apart from the fact that the former were actually paid their wages. Portuguese and Brazilians employed in top positions received almost twice as much as Cuban professionals with the same qualifications. Brazilian and Portuguese university professors in the GICI/GII were paid according to category I on the salary scale (a category that did not even exist for Cubans), receiving up to the sum of 2,400 US dollars a month. The difference in the lower salary brackets between Cuban teachers and teachers from countries in the West was less pronounced. Portuguese and Brazilian teachers in category V received 1,000 US dollars, and teachers in category IV between 1,000 and 1,250 US dollars. In the lowest categories, however, professionals from the West were at a disadvantage: on average primary-school teachers received only 500 US dollars a month—half as much as Cuban teachers with the same qualifications.[123]

In the higher categories, the monthly salaries of workers from other socialist countries such as Bulgaria, the Soviet Union, and the GDR were approximately commensurate with those paid for Cubans; at the lower end of the scale, however, they were considerably higher. According to GICI/GII records, a Bulgarian teacher in category IV deployed from the eighth class onward would receive a salary of 1,050 US dollars and a GDR teacher 1,010 US dollars, while a lecturer from the Soviet Union teaching at a teacher-training college was paid 876 US dollars a month, which was less than their Cuban colleagues. Vietnamese teachers and lecturers who were employed in Angolan classrooms particularly from the mid-1980s were paid according to the same scale as the Cubans.[124] Primary- and secondary-school teachers from other African countries, for example Cape Verde and Congo-Brazzaville, were also paid on average the same salary as Cubans with similar qualifications.[125]

What is clear, however, is that Cuban *cooperantes* represented the highest cost factor because they constituted by far the highest proportion of foreign aid workers in Angola. According to the above GICI/GII records for March 1983, there were 1,823 Cuban teachers, lecturers, advisors, education specialists, and university professors, followed by 99 Bulgarians, 85 Portuguese; 53 East Germans, 34 specialists from Cape Verde, 31 from Congo-Brazzaville, 23 from the Soviet Union, and 17 from Vietnam. An additional 205 teachers and lecturers were working under individual contracts. These were mainly Portuguese residing in Angola and a handful of teachers and education specialists from the Western world, such as the Brazilians mentioned above. According to the GICI/GII accounts, the total monthly cost of all foreign *cooperantes* was 1,903,802 US dollars, 1,354,876 US dollars of which was paid out for Cubans.[126]

What is not clear is whether and to what extent these payment conditions changed over the years—with the exception of those for student teachers, as already mentioned. The GICI/GII's 1983 calculations for foreign *cooperantes* can be traced back to government austerity measures introduced to counteract the economic crisis. Notwithstanding this, the payment agreements with Cuba seem on the whole to have remained in place until 1991. But though payment agreements remained in force, the Ministry of Education's files include payment demands from Cubatécnica, which appeared with increasing frequency from 1987 onward.[127] It was not possible to ascertain whether these open invoices were ever paid. According to my Cuban exile interviewee Alcibíades Hidalgo, some of the outstanding payments were not made. Hidalgo claims that this failure was due in part to corruption that had become so rampant in Angola from the mid-1980s that the Angolan government had no longer been able—or willing—to pay its bills.[128]

Some of my Cuban interviewees had held high administrative positions in Angola and should therefore have been able to clarify the subject of payments. They proved reluctant to provide information. Instead of giving explanations, they merely reiterated the official government line, even when confronted during the interview with the cost calculations from the Angolan Ministry of Education. José Ramón Fernández, who was minister of education from 1970 to 1990, maintained that he knew absolutely nothing of any payments made for cooperation in education.[129] Another of my interviewees was Noemí Benitez de Mendoza, the Cuban ambassador in Angola in 2006, who in her capacity as vice president of Cuba's CECE had been actively involved in the negotiations of the bilateral commissions. She summed up the matter of payment in diplomatic terms by explaining that any aid provided during Cuban-Angolan cooperation was "disinterested."[130] The Angolan Minster of Education in 2006, António Burity da Silva, was responsible for selecting Angolan students for scholarships at boarding schools on the Cuban Isle of Youth in the 1970s and 1980s. He also couched his answer to my question regarding payments in diplomatic terms, although his statement does reflect much more clearly the essence of Cuban-Angolan cooperation. According to him, there was no such thing as disinterested aid, and cooperation with Cuba was an example of "internationalism with reciprocal benefits."[131]

The Cubans I interviewed who had been involved as "ordinary" *cooperantes* in Angola also adhered to the official government line when confronted with the subject of payments. In general, they even defended the government's stance and emphasized the united, "disinterested" and internationalist character of their engagement. This is understandable from their perspective; after all, they themselves received almost no remuneration for their work, in keeping with the altruistic ideals propagated by the government. The majority of them were completely unaware of payments exchanged between the two states. When I carefully suggested that such payments had been made, they expressed disbelief, were visibly upset, or simply fell silent. Only one of my Cuban interviewees, who was living in Angola, seemed to have any idea of the extent of the financial exchange, but he did not wish to go into details. He merely indicated that the topic of "finances" was never discussed in Cuba or among the Cubans working in Angola, at least not among the "ordinary" *cooperantes*.[132]

The Cuban government's silence regarding payments from Angola served (and still seems to serve) to maintain the myth it constructed around its engagement in Angola. According to this, Cuba provided assistance to the "Angolan brotherland" purely under the banner of "internationalist solidarity." The fact that this engagement was remunerated shatters the myth of the only nation in the world acting out of true solidarity and in the interest of helping to overthrow colonialism and neocolonialism. Unlike Western countries, Cuba ostensibly had no interest in exploiting Africa. As the recollections of my interviewees suggest, this myth promoted a sense of identity, not only for those directly involved in Angola but for society as a whole. Many of those I interviewed emphasized the positive impact their work in Angola had on their self-confidence because it increased their social prestige within Cuban society.

Against this background, the realization that the Cuban government profited from the commitment of its citizens would prove painful for those who had served in Angola. The confusion of my interviewees when I suggested that civil cooperation had been paid for indicates that any deconstruction of this myth would be extremely compromising for the Cuban government. It would be an admission to the people of Cuba that their supposed voluntary humanitarian aid was in reality a commodity. It would prove particularly demoralizing if the public began to regard those who had been involved in Angola as unwitting "mercenaries" hired out by their own government and sent to a distant country and a foreign war. A few years ago, Piero Gleijeses indicated that payment might also have been exchanged for Cuban military operations, but he did not present evidence to back this claim.[133] He confirmed nevertheless in his most recent book the payment for civil cooperation.[134] Any talk of the deployment of "mercenaries" would be fatal for the Cuban government, which in the 1970s and 1980s so vociferously criticized the supposed use of mercenaries in the South African army. Its portrayal of the evil, white mercenaries in the service of both the South African apartheid regime and imperialism provided the Cuban government with a convenient contrast to its own noble endeavors in the name of a free Angola.[135] Regarded in this light, the myth continues to consolidate the regime's power even today. The obstacles I faced during my research further illustrate just how much the Cuban government relies on its exclusive right to interpret engagement in Angola in order to perpetuate this myth.

Asymmetries and Dissonances

At a governmental level, the Cuban-Angolan relationship was based on mutual respect and reciprocity. To a large extent, it oriented itself toward the requirements of the Angolans, not least because of the payment that Cuba received. This respect and reciprocity are reflected in the aforementioned content of the bilateral agreements on civil cooperation and the bilateral structures and institutions set up to preserve a mutual balance of interest. Nevertheless, the relationship was not free of asymmetries and dissonances, above all at the planning and implementation levels. Here the Angolans were at a distinct disadvantage.

The asymmetries were in part caused by the different levels of development in the two countries. Angola's underdevelopment was manifest in its lack of functioning governmental institutions, infrastructure, and communication networks and through its structural, organizational, and administrative deficits. Within the cooperative framework, the Cubans tried to compensate for these deficiencies by establishing their own administration. The result was an even bigger gap, widened by the information and communication network accompanying Cuba's civil administration, and the resulting tendency among the Cubans to implement the cooperative program autonomously and independently of the Angolans. This tendency in turn led to the Angolans losing sovereignty and control. In the following analysis, several examples taken from the everyday operation of the cooperative program illustrate these asymmetries and conflicts of interest and authority.

Unlike the Angolan government, in the mid-1970s the Cuban government was able to rely on a well-functioning administration. Despite centralization, the state institutions proved flexible enough to create the institutional and organizational parameters with which they could quickly implement cooperation with Angola. This was partly thanks to the principle of learning by doing, which applied to almost all sociopolitical experiments in Cuba. New challenges were weighed against existing experience in order to find a flexible response both on the level of individual officials and on the institutional level.[136]

In view of the prevailing conflict in Angola and the structural and organizational deficits the country faced after independence, the Cuban government considered it essential to set up its own specially adapted body to ensure the maintenance and management of civil cooperation. In order to solve infrastructure problems, Cuba was able to fall back on its own military structures that already existed in Angola. Another advantage was that having stationed troops in various regions throughout Angola, the Cubans had already gathered knowledge about the political and military situations and social and cultural backgrounds there. They were able to use this knowledge to introduce civil development aid even outside the areas controlled by the MPLA. The aforementioned military and civilian pilot project in Cabinda, which began at the beginning of 1976, was part of this flexible deployment strategy.

The Cuban government also enjoyed sufficient social prestige among its own population, along with an effective propaganda apparatus and closely knit network of social control and discipline mechanisms. It was able to call upon all these to recruit the workforce needed for Angola. The CECE and Cubatécnica were therefore faster and more efficient than the Angolan counterpart organizations, which were all founded at a later date. These structural parameters, combined with the Cubans' political experience and flexible strategy, put them at an advantage over their Angolan partners with regard to information, knowledge, and organizational skills. At the structural level of the cooperation program, this advantage led to asymmetry between the Cuban and Angolan structures, or in other words, to a power imbalance that became apparent during the practical application of cooperation.

The Angolan government was forced by necessity to call on foreign specialists to help them reconstruct the nation. The cooperation agreements and the Cuban Civil Administration meant that it too had to establish a similarly efficient administrative system in order to coordinate and monitor the operations of foreign aid workers. This was an almost insurmountable task, as state administration was only in the early stages of development, and in the first few years of independence it did not extend much beyond the capital. Other problems stemmed from the lack of basic planning data and a dearth of managers capable of taking on board the job of coordinating the cooperative program nationally. In addition, postcolonial Angola was yet to develop a proper sense of national identity after the experience of colonialism. Even the cadres in the Angolan Ministry of Education first had to develop an awareness of how imperative it was to establish the new education system in the provinces as well. In comparison with the Angolans' focus on urban centers, the Cuban structures operated across large areas of the country.

The meticulous detail involved in the bottom-up reporting system that was characteristic of the Cuban administration meant that those in charge had informed status reports and problem analyses from all over the country at their disposal. This again put the Cubans at an advantage in terms of communication and information, and this advantage in turn represented a crucial power factor in the relationship with their Angolan counterparts and provoked permanent conflicts of interest and authority.[137] The Angolan Ministry of Education's GICI/GII was persistent in its attempts to rebalance the situation. But communication between the Ministry in Luanda and the Provincial Directorates, for example, could not be established until the end of the 1970s, which meant that the GICI/GII had difficulties in compiling planning data and coordinating the deployment of teachers and advisors. This in turn increased dependency on the Cuban administration.

One constant conflict of interest that resulted from this situation was the Angolans' loss of sovereignty and control to the Cubans. The Angolans felt this keenly and believed that the Cuban Civil Administration frequently acted independently, for example, when it removed teachers from certain areas without first consulting the GICI/GII or the Provincial Directorates of the Ministry of Education.[138] Another constant bone of contention was the Cubans' four weeks of annual leave that was set down in the cooperation agreements. Every summer, all Cuban teachers left Angola in large groups. This presented enormous logistical problems, as they first had to be brought to Luanda from all over the country. In view of the poor transportation system and the destruction the war had caused to rural infrastructure, this task was only possible with the help of the Cuban military. The Cuban Civil Administration therefore organized the collective departure of the teachers internally, often without coordinating with the local school authorities or the GICI/GII. Yet another associated problem was posed by the dates of the Cuban holidays, which frequently did not coincide with the end of the Angolan academic year. The Angolans addressed both matters time and again during the meetings of the bilateral commissions and even proposed a ban on leaving the country before the end of the school year. Nevertheless, the Cubans insisted on keeping to their holiday period, arguing that the teachers had a right to spend their annual leave at home with their families during the Cuban school and work holidays.[139]

But it was also the Angolan institutions' inability to coordinate the *cooperantes* properly that often led the Cuban Civil Administration to act independently in order to guard its interests. Frequently, the lack of planning data and communication between national and provincial authorities rendered the GICI/GII incapable of guaranteeing that the Cuban teachers would be sent where they were needed.[140] Lists stating the numbers of teachers required had to be submitted a year in advance for certain school grades and subjects, and they often did not correspond (or no longer corresponded) to actual requirements. Such discrepancies often did not come to light until the Cuban teachers had arrived in Angola, and they then had to teach either subjects or grades for which they were not qualified.[141] The Cuban Civil Administration often corrected the inappropriate deployment of teachers, either by sending the teachers back to Cuba or by using its own information network to find out where the teachers were needed and then transferring them without consulting the GICI/GII.

Internal records from the GICI/GII and the minutes of the bilateral commission meetings indicate that the number of such "autonomous" relocations increased after 1983.[142] This was mainly due to the worsening political and military situation at the beginning of the 1980s. Areas that had previously been deemed safe for Cuban teachers were now increasingly subjected to military attacks and acts of sabotage by UNITA. The Cuban Civil Administration therefore began to relocate teachers from these areas, often without first consulting the GICI/GII.[143] It is, however, understandable that it was in the Cubans' interest to deploy the workforce they were providing effectively and properly. Furthermore, the Cuban Civil Administration was responsible for protecting Cuban civilians, and it had to be prepared to react quickly if it had evidence of impending enemy attacks.

It was not, however, the practice of relocating teachers for security reasons that the GICI/GII criticized. What riled them was the lack of communication between the Cuban and Angolan institutions. The Cubans generally failed to respond to Angolan demands for better communication and coordination, to the point that the Angolans accused the Cubans of "unilateralism" during the meetings of the bilateral commissions.[144] The GICI/GII internal reports indicate a definite self-critical stance toward these problems. They make frequent mention of homegrown organizational and structural deficits, which in turn encouraged the Cubans to act "unilaterally."[145] Nevertheless, the autonomous activities of the Cuban Civil Administration were still regarded as an infringement of sovereignty: they cast doubt on the GICI/GII's capabilities as the central coordination and control body of the educational cooperation.[146]

Another constant conflict of interest between the partners concerned the selection and qualifications of the teachers, education specialists, and advisors. Both in the cooperative agreements and in the bilateral negotiations, the Cubans had indeed undertaken to respect the employment profiles drawn up by the Angolans. It had been agreed that the Cubans would present the *cooperantes'* résumés and qualifications to the Angolans *before* dispatching them, so that the Angolans could select the people they needed according to their criteria.[147] This did not happen in practice. Instead, the Cubans sent the teachers who were available and only made sure that the subjects the teachers taught corresponded to Angolan requirements. In view of the lack of teaching staff that also existed in Cuba, it was understandable that the Cubans tended to send less-qualified personnel to Angola. Quantity did indeed take priority over quality: a quarter of the teachers sent to Angola from the mid-1980s were student teachers doing their in-class training in Angolan schools. Many of them had neither the necessary subject knowledge nor teaching experience. The Angolan Ministry of Education, and in particular the GICI/GII, had no real say in the selection process and often had to make do with underqualified teachers, even though the Angolan government was paying for each teacher provided. These conflicting interests could not be resolved and were discussed time and again during the meetings of the bilateral commissions.[148]

The GICI/GII therefore faced several dilemmas. Its own internal planning, coordination, and control mechanisms were inefficient in comparison with Cuba's. For their part, the Cubans were failing to offer the agreed-upon transparency with regard to the quality of the teachers they were sending and the locations they were sending them to.[149] Because of their own inefficiency, however, the Angolans had difficulty imposing their demands on the Cubans. Discussions within the Angolan Ministry of Education show that the Angolans were aware of this imbalanced dependency.[150] From the early 1980s onward, they therefore increasingly sought alternatives by trying to extend cooperation to other countries, such as Vietnam, the Soviet Union, Bulgaria, Cape Verde, and Congo-Brazzaville.[151]

The discord and conflicting interests outlined here were rarely aired openly because the Angolan government had few alternatives to accepting Cuban support. Even internal records frequently document this state of dependency, and the corresponding comments indicate that, despite the problems, the Angolans were—at least in general terms—grateful for Cuban support. The few occasions on which criticism was openly voiced, however, illustrate just how sensitively the Cubans reacted to any criticism of the services they were providing and just how fragile the Cuban-Angolan relationship actually was. One such occasion was an article printed in the *Jornal de Angola* in November 1982 about Agostinho Neto University in Luanda.[152] The article expresses two instances of restrained criticism regarding the (supposedly) insufficient qualifications of the Cuban lecturers working there. This very objectively written article was part of an internal study commissioned by the Ministry of Education about reform in higher education. In response, the Cuban embassy in Luanda penned a letter to the then Angolan minister of education, Augusto Lopes Teixeira, in which it accused the article of being an "attack on the brotherly relations between Cuba and Angola."[153] Shortly afterward, the Cuban deputy minister for higher education met to "exchange thoughts" with the Angolan minister of education. Just a few weeks later, the Cubans took "unilateral" action and considerably reduced the scope of the cooperative agreements that had already been negotiated for the 1983/84 academic year. This event also shows how ready Cuba was from the mid-1980s to use any excuse it could to withdraw from cooperation with Angola.[154]

7

Cooperantes and Cooperation Programs

Civil Aid Workers—The *Cooperantes*

The deployment of a specialized workforce was central to Cuban-Angolan cooperation in education. In this chapter I therefore concentrate on characterizing the various types of civil aid workers: advisors, education specialists, university professors and lecturers, teachers, and student teachers. I discuss the various challenges that these aid workers faced, depending on their areas of responsibility and specialization, and assess their role in establishing the Angolan education system. I then move on to the second focus of cooperation in education—the Angolan boarding schools on the Isle of Youth—and analyze the direct impact of these schools and the aims of the education policy accompanying their opening. The information underlying this chapter again comes from internal records and files from the Angolan Ministry of Education, along with a number of project and accountability reports from the Cuban Civil Administration. I complemented this written documentation with the personal views of my Cuban and Angolan interviewees.

The different types of Cuban *cooperantes* who went to Angola depended very much on the different phases of cooperation. During the first phase from 1976 to 1977/78, mainly education specialists were sent as advisors, the majority of whom assisted in the Angolan Ministry of Education or were responsible for teacher training.[1] This "help for self-help" was accompanied by the deployment of university professors charged with the reconstruction of university teaching and research in Angola.[2] The second cooperative phase featured the arrival of huge numbers of teachers and student teachers, who went into the classrooms of primary and secondary schools to make up for the lack of Angolan teachers. During this second phase, the importance of the advisors began to dwindle, although university professors continued to be deployed right until the end of cooperation. As already mentioned, 1977/78 marked a turning point when the focus changed from the selective support of advisors and education specialists to the mass deployment of teachers. Linked to this was the opening of the boarding schools on the Isle of Youth, which gave Angolan children and adolescents the chance to receive a school or university education on scholarship.

Before turning to the responsibilities of the various types of civil aid workers, I will first discuss which social classes the specialists were recruited from and what criteria were used to select them. Generally it is very difficult to acquire statistics, figures, or census information of any kind in Cuba, and because of this lack of data and information the conclusions I can draw are quite limited. Particularly with regard to Cuban involvement abroad, the only available material is the official and correspondingly sparse documentation that I have already referred to on several occasions in this book. My conclusions here regarding the background of the aid workers are therefore based partly on my findings from the interviews I conducted and partly on information I gleaned from several dozen files on Cuban personnel that were kept in the Angolan Ministry of Education. These afforded me a considerably better insight into the sociocultural and professional backgrounds of the civil aid workers. According to this information, the average primary- and secondary-school teacher who went to Angola was between twenty and thirty years of age and just beginning a career in teaching and education. The members of the student brigades of the DPI were an exception: most of them were between the ages of seventeen and twenty-two. They had completed at best one to two semesters of their teaching studies. With regard to gender, the female ratio of the DPI brigades was relatively high at almost 60 percent.[3] This indicates that the percentage of women among the fully qualified teachers was probably similarly high, particularly because in the 1970s and 1980s the majority of teachers (especially at primary schools and in the lower secondary-school grades) were women.[4] As was the case with the DPI student brigades, the majority of teachers probably came from the Cuban provinces, where career opportunities and professional prospects were limited. This explains why a stint in Angola was more attractive to them than to the inhabitants of Havana.

The university professors and lecturers who worked in Angola were also frequently just beginning their careers. Because of their longer education, they were slightly older (generally between twenty-five and forty years of age).

According to my interviewees, the majority of them were male. Angola mainly needed lecturers in the natural sciences, technical subjects, and engineering, and in Cuba of the 1970s and 1980s, these were usually male domains. The locations of the Cuban universities in Havana, Santa Clara, and Santiago de Cuba meant that the professors and lecturers came from those cities. The education specialists, many of whom were deployed as advisors, were also mainly male and aged between twenty-five and forty. Before going to Angola, most of them worked as lecturers at polytechnic schools or in various educational or technical and administrative areas of the Cuban education system. They therefore mainly came from Havana or the provincial capitals of Cuba.[5]

The absence of records and studies on the subject means that I can draw only very tentative conclusions about racial and social background, based on my own observations or on the observations of my interviewees. The biographic interviews indicate that many of my interviewees of proletarian or peasant origin had seized the education opportunities offered after the revolution to improve their social status by training to become a teacher or by studying. One can only make assumptions regarding the proportion of Afro-Cubans among the civil aid workers. Half of my Cuban interviewees were Afro-Cubans. But as I had only a limited say about whom I would interview, it does not automatically follow that half of those participating in the overall civil aid program or in the education cooperation program in particular were Cubans of African origin. Nevertheless, it is probable that a high percentage of the *cooperantes* in education were Afro-Cuban women, particularly among the primary- and secondary-school teachers. After the revolution, the education sector offered job security and social advancement, and a stint in Angola was a good way of improving future career prospects.[6] Castro's invention of the "Afro-Latin American nation" was probably in part a political and strategic device to encourage Afro-Cubans in particular to sign up for Angola. As I have already mentioned, however, the information I received during my interviews did nothing to indicate that identification with Africa was a major reason for people deciding to go to Angola.

There is much evidence to suggest that political conviction was one of the main criteria in the selection of teachers and education specialists. Accordingly, candidates were favored if they were politically or socially engaged, belonged to the Communist Party, or had completed their studies at one of the ISPs that had been established in the 1970s. After all, as the "new type" of teacher, they were role models, and alongside their teaching responsibilities they had a political mission to fulfill in Angola. The importance of political conviction is confirmed by documents from the MINED that provide information about the selection criteria for the student brigades. They also show, however, that it was not compulsory to be a member of a political organization.[7] A selection committee comprising officials from the Ministry of Education and members of the UJC and the student organization (the FEU) showed a particular concern for the candidates' irreproachable conduct, reliability, morality, and politically sound family background. The final decision regarding political "suitability" rested, however, with the Cuban MININT.[8] In the final analysis, almost half of the "chosen ones" did in fact belong to the Young Communist League.[9]

The statements of my interviewees indicate that the same or similar criteria applied to all other aid workers. Party membership was not a prerequisite, but political integrity, revolutionary consciousness (proven through active political and social commitment to the revolution) and irreproachable social conduct were. Those wishing to assume a position of responsibility in the Civil Administration in Angola, on the other hand, had to be Party members. Graduates of the teacher-training colleges seemed to have been regarded as more politically reliable than the education science graduates from the universities. In the 1970s many teacher-training colleges had opened in the provinces. They were organized according to the same principles as the boarding schools. The courses they offered were subjected to much more rigid political and ideological regulation than was the case at conventional universities.[10] However, the main selection criterion for these teachers, lecturers, and professors was whether the subjects they taught corresponded to what the Angolans needed. Cuban *cooperantes* were mainly employed in the natural sciences (particularly biology, chemistry, and physics), in mathematics, and also in geography and history. At the universities there was also a need for doctors, veterinarians, economists, philosophers, and all types of engineers.[11]

Advisors

The first phase of cooperation primarily focused on providing the Angolan MED with advice and support from Cuban education specialists, technicians, and administrators. As in all sectors in Angola, education suffered from a lack of know-how and qualified staff, and as a result Angola depended upon help from abroad to rebuild its education system. In principle, every single Angolan ministry and nationalized enterprise likewise relied on external assistance following independence, and advisors were deployed in all sectors. The majority were Cuban, though some also came from Portugal, Brazil, the Soviet Union, the GDR, and other Eastern-bloc countries.[12]

The main task of the Cuban advisors was to support their Angolan colleagues but not to replace them. Advisors were not to assume managerial tasks but to follow the instructions of their Angolan superiors. All findings to date indicate that in general the Cubans and Angolans formally adhered to this basic hierarchy. However, owing to the huge deficit of qualified staff, it was not always possible for the foreign advisors to remain in a backseat advisory capacity. It would seem that they frequently had to take charge of areas where there was no qualified Angolan counterpart available. This was particularly true of teacher training, and for this reason Cuban education specialists were specifically charged with developing and implementing training programs. Their work as advisors extended from gathering planning data and organizing the new education system to core areas of education policy, such as the development of curricula and teaching materials. When giving advice on the direction the education system should take in terms of teaching methods, administration, technical matters, and education policy, the advisors generally recommended that the Angolans adopt the structures and contents of the Cuban and GDR education systems.[13]

When the cooperation agreement was renewed in autumn 1977, the number of advisors initially increased and their spheres of responsibility became more specific. The various school departments—organized according to school form—of the Ministry of Education were each to receive one Cuban advisor. Furthermore, the MED's department of educational research was to be provided with a Cuban specialist for each school subject, with the exception of Portuguese.[14] Another advisor was to be sent to each of the Ministry's Provincial Directorates in the sixteen provinces at that time.[15] Even the Minister of Education and his deputy received a personal advisor.[16]

Although Cuban advisors were active at all cardinal points in the early days of the new Angolan education system, it is in retrospect difficult to ascertain the extent to which they actually influenced the strategic direction of Angolan education policy. Contemporary records from the Angolan Ministry of Education and Cuban Civil Administration, and the memories of Angolan and Cuban eyewitnesses, all indicate frequent conflicts of interest and authority. These conflicts concerned both the advisors' spheres of responsibility and the specific priorities of education policy. Moreover, the de facto lead that the Cuban advisors had over the Angolans in terms of expert knowledge and experience created an asymmetrical relationship, which also led to disagreement regarding who was responsible for what. As early as 1978, just shortly after the cooperation agreement had extended the deployment of advisors, the Angolan education planners insisted that the number of advisors be reduced and that they be limited to purely technical and administrative functions. Subsequently, only the advisors in the MED's Provincial Directorates appear to have exercised any major influence.[17] In order to provide insights into how the Cuban advisors and their Angolan colleagues worked together and to understand the dissonances that arose as a consequence, the following section provides some examples of how both sides perceived and evaluated the situation.

During an interview, Lopo do Nascimento, who served as Angolan prime minister between 1975 and 1979, expressed the opinion that the work of the Cuban advisors had been essential in the first years of independence and that the Cubans had in many ways replaced the Portuguese. But the difference, he continued, was that the Cubans were not colonial masters, but technicians who made no attempt to impose their political agenda.[18] The memories of two other eyewitnesses, however, indicate that the presence of Cuban advisors was indeed perceived as "patronizing." This feeling is expressed in the recollections of a former deputy minister of education (1976–1981), Artur Pestana (the writer "Pepetela"), and the long-serving head of the Angolan Instituto Nacional de Investigação e Desenvolvimento da Educação (INIDE, National Institute for Research and Development of Education),[19] the education specialist Pedro Domingos Peterson. According to Pepetela, neither he nor the then minister of education, Ambrôsio Lukoki, greatly appreciated the presence of the many advisors in their ministry. As reported by Pepetela, they had immediately demoted their personal advisor to a technical level because they were determined to take the political decisions regarding education reform themselves. Both Pepetela and Peterson emphasized that at that time they had considered the Cuban education system to be much too rigid and too influenced by the Soviet system. Also at the departmental level and in the technical and administrative sectors, the support offered by the Cuban advisors apparently did not meet with universal approval. According to Pepetela, most of the advisors were not qualified to advise at a national level and were merely capable of following instructions.[20] Peterson shared this view and added that he had assigned the advisors in his department to the corresponding working groups, where they carried out their task of planning teaching material and syllabuses together with their Angolan colleagues.[21]

One of Domingos Peterson's former Cuban advisors, who worked in the INIDE in teacher training, confirms the Angolan reports of disagreement over hierarchies and responsibilities. According to him, Peterson checked all his proposals thoroughly and always reserved the right to reject them. This had led to the advisors in his department mainly concerning themselves with organizational and administrative tasks and the pedagogical side of developing teaching programs, whereas the Angolan colleagues and superiors had determined the direction the content of education should take. Between 1976 and 1979, this advisor's main responsibility had been to train primary-school teachers in pedagogy and school subjects at the national level, so that they could return to their home provinces and create a ripple effect by passing on what they had learned. Peterson had always done a "sentence for sentence" check of the teaching materials developed in Cuba for this purpose. When the advisor I interviewed had returned to Cuba in 1979, Peterson did not want any advisors at all.[22] A 1978 report by the first Cuban advisors in education about their work in the Ministry of Education corroborates that there were many disagreements with the Angolans. From the advisors' perspective, however, the disagreements arose not from their own shortcomings, but rather from their Angolan colleagues' failure to implement the Cuban advisors' proposals.[23] After 1978, the importance of advisors in the Ministry of Education diminished. They were still employed in the various departments of the Provincial Directorates, but in much smaller numbers. One reason for their loss of importance was that deploying them had failed to overcome the enormous deficits in Angolan education, and in particular it had fallen short of the promise to address the teacher shortage.[24] But the conflicting subjective assessments of the cooperative program also show that the decisive change in focus had to do with Angolan education planners attempting to guard their sovereignty by consciously limiting the influence of the advisors.

Despite their criticism of the Cuban advisors, my Angolan interviewees did admit that they had nevertheless made an essential contribution to establishing the education system and its pedagogical basis. Moreover, they admitted that the Cubans had produced a stabilizing effect on the technical and administrative areas of the education system.[25]

University Professors and Lecturers

Between 1977 and 1982, Cuban university professors and lecturers played a major role in re-establishing teaching and research at the University of Angola.[26] They were responsible for developing syllabuses, for the resumption of teaching, and for all the technical and administrative tasks involved in reconstructing the faculties. They also reorganized scientific research and rebuilt laboratories and research stations.[27] In many respects, the professors enjoyed a privileged position in comparison to the primary- and secondary-school teachers. They were able to work in the city; their stay in Angola lasted on average only one year; and their professional status afforded them greater individual freedom.

Cuban professors were active in the university's three campuses in Luanda, Huambo, and Lubango. In Luanda they were mainly responsible for natural sciences, engineering sciences, economy, philosophy, and Marxism-Leninism. There they worked together with professors from the Eastern bloc, mainly from the GDR and the Soviet Union, but again the Cubans formed the majority.[28] In Huambo the faculties' focus called mainly for Cuban biologists, doctors of medicine, veterinary doctors, and agricultural scientists. Here, the Cuban scientists were particularly able to benefit from their stay in Angola because the modern research stations (for example for cattle breeding) and laboratories left behind by the Portuguese matched Western standards. This gave the Cuban scientists the opportunity to further their own professional skills considerably.[29] A smaller number of professors and lecturers worked in Lubango, the capital of the southern province Huila, where the university maintained a faculty of education science, which was supported by Cuban teachers and education specialists. After 1982, Cuban professors continued to play a crucial role in university teaching and the training of young Angolan scientists.[30] Their work was accompanied by a scientific exchange program that allowed Angolan students and young scientists to take their degrees at Cuban universities. From the Angolan viewpoint, the deployment of Cuban academics was indeed effective, but the fifteen years in which they worked at the universities were not enough to nurture a new generation of Angolan scientists in every subject.[31]

Teachers

Between 1978 and 1991 (and especially between 1979 and 1983), the cooperation focused on employing Cuban teachers at Angolan schools. They worked there for one to two years from the sixth grade of primary school, at secondary schools, and at polytechnic schools. Owing to the difference between Spanish and Portuguese, the Angolan MED determined that the Cuban teachers should not teach below the sixth grade level. In general, the Cuban teachers were only able to speak *portuñol*, a cross between Spanish and Portuguese. Although it was thought that they would have few problems communicating with adolescents and adults, the Angolan education planners rightly considered the language barrier detrimental to the teaching of literacy to primary-school children, many of whom did not even speak Portuguese because their mother tongue was an African language. The language difference also meant that with few exceptions the Cuban teachers were permitted to teach only natural sciences (mathematics, biology, chemistry, and physics) as well as history, geography, and the obligatory "Marxism-Leninism" because in these subjects their language deficit was considered less serious. Portuguese (and Brazilian) teachers were called in to teach language-related classes at the elementary level and Portuguese in the higher grades.[32]

The Cuban teachers subsequently played a major role in the Angolan school system. According to an internal MED report from 1982, around 80 percent of middle and higher education was covered by foreign teachers, the majority of whom were Cubans.[33] In mid-1982, the number of Cuban teachers reached its absolute height. Of a total of 2,309 foreign teachers, 1,779 came from Cuba.[34] The statistics from the MED's Department of International Cooperation show that just under 10 percent of foreign teachers were Portuguese, while the rest came mainly from Bulgaria, the GDR, the Soviet Union, and Vietnam. Because of the much greater language barrier that these teachers faced, they worked almost exclusively in higher education or as advisors. A small number of teachers were recruited from other African countries or other countries in the West.[35]

From 1978, the number of Cuban teachers increased steadily. In 1979 approximately one thousand Cubans worked in Angola's education system. By November 1980, this figure had already increased to 1,168. Almost one thousand of them worked at the primary level, while the rest were employed in the basic-secondary and pre-university levels and at the polytechnic schools. This number also included the seventy-nine professors and lecturers at the University of Angola and the faculty of educational sciences at the Lubango campus and in teacher-training colleges, along with the fourteen advisors working in the Ministry of Education.[36] At the end of 1980, Cuban teachers accounted for 69.2 percent of foreign workers in education, followed by 338 Portuguese, Bulgarians, Soviets, and East Germans. Angola's urban areas profited most from their presence because the majority of the teachers worked in Luanda (540), followed by Huambo (160) and Benguela (144). Unlike their Portuguese or Eastern-bloc colleagues, Cuban teachers also taught in sixteen of the eighteen Angolan provinces. The unequal distribution of teachers was particularly noticeable in the remotest parts of the country. In 1980, only six Cuban primary teachers were working in the southeastern province of Kuando Kubango, twenty-two were teaching in the northeastern province of Lunda Norte, and thirty-three in the northwestern province of Zaire.[37] Because of frequent military attacks from South African forces, the province of Kunene was considered a war zone, and no foreign teachers at all were sent there. As already mentioned, between 1983/84 and 1991, the teachers were gradually withdrawn from Angola, at first mainly from the embattled provinces. Starting in 1985, they taught almost exclusively in the towns and cities mainly at the secondary level, at polytechnic schools, and at the university. The withdrawal of teachers seriously undermined the schools' operation.[38]

The Cuban teachers were not only there to impart knowledge. They also played key educational and political roles in enforcing the nationwide education reforms of the MPLA government. As the Cuban teachers had already undergone their own "revolutionary" education process, the MPLA and Cuban government considered them to be politically and ideologically more steadfast than their Angolan colleagues. Their duties therefore included using education to integrate the population into the new political, social, and national cause. Despite the reservations of Angolan education planners, the curricula, teaching methods, and education aims developed by the MED essentially adhered to the Cuban principles of education. Cuban teachers were therefore the ideal vehicles for carrying out this "mission" in education policy. In order to achieve this, the Cuban teachers enthusiastically introduced modern, interactive teaching and learning methods that had been developed and tested in Cuba. On the one hand, the new approach did away with the authoritarian "chalk-and-talk" teaching style of colonial times. But these unarguably better teaching methods were also intended to increase public acceptance of the new political project.[39]

Because of their ideological imprint, Cuban teachers were also sent to teach political economy, history, and Marxism-Leninism at the school for cadres, which the MPLA founded in 1977 in Luanda.[40]

Student Teachers

Approximately one-quarter of the teachers were student teachers who had been mobilized for the student brigades of the Destacamento Pedagógico Internacionalista "Che Guevara," established in 1977. The Cuban government encouraged the creation of these brigades in response to President Neto's request for one thousand teachers. As Cuba itself was suffering from a lack of teaching staff at the time, it could ill afford to meet Neto's demands. And so Castro reacted by setting up this educational experiment in the hope of serving the interests of both governments. He called upon the aspiring student teachers who had signed up for the emergency education teacher-training program, the Destacamento Pedagógico "Manuel Ascunce Domenech," to join the Angolan cause. The young people were to do part of their obligatory in-class training in Angolan schools and simultaneously make a contribution to building the Angolan education system. The government made it clear that the task awaiting them was of national importance. In the tradition of Che Guevara they were to prove their worth as model revolutionaries by carrying out an "internationalist mission" and by representing the sociopolitical aims of the Cuban Revolution in Angola.[41] They had neither teaching qualifications nor classroom experience, but unlike the majority of qualified teachers who went to Angola, the student teachers received instruction to prepare them for their stay. Special boarding schools were set up in which they spent a four-month preparatory semester, during which they received Portuguese lessons, training in their subjects, and instruction in political ideology.[42] Apart from teaching subject matter, the training program was mainly geared toward consolidating the adolescents' ideology and encouraging discipline and work ethic in order to prepare them for the task ahead. In Angola, the students continued their studies under the supervision and instruction of Cuban lecturers while doing their in-class training. Between 1978 and 1986, a total of 2,026 student teachers were sent to Angolan primary and secondary schools.[43]

From the very outset, the Angolan education planners, from the former deputy minister of education to Angolan education specialists at every level, regarded the deployment of student teachers with skepticism. Almost all my interviewees agreed that these young people were often completely out of their depth in Angola. Their instruction in Cuba had made little mention of the conflict in Angola for fear of frightening them off. They were therefore unprepared for the war situation. Moreover, they had neither the subject knowledge nor the teaching experience to make any real contribution to the education of Angolan pupils.[44] A comment at that time from one of the Provincial Directorates of the Angolan Ministry of Education in 1978 demonstrates this negative assessment: "The teachers of the DPI have no idea of the reality of Angola. Their teaching skills and scientific knowledge are very rudimentary."[45] The Angolans subsequently demanded the reinstatement of experienced teachers because they had the impression that the Cuban student teachers had learned more from their Angolan pupils than they had been able to teach them.[46] All findings to date indicate that the deployment of student teachers seemed primarily designed to train pedagogical and political cadres who could return to Cuba and dedicate themselves to spreading the political and ideological aims of the Cuban social system.

The Impact of Teachers and Education Specialists on Angolan Education Reform

The impact Cuban teachers and education specialists ultimately had on Angola's education reform is ambiguous. The ambitious reform program would not have been possible without the extensive cooperation agreements between Cuba and Angola. On the other hand, it was already apparent in the early 1980s that the large-scale deployment of Cuban teachers had pushed the training of Angolan teachers into the background and that the original principle of "help for self-help" had failed. Both conclusions indicate that the MPLA government's education reform program—supported by Cuba—seems finally to have served its own power interests.

It is true that part of the Angolan population was indeed able to profit from education reform, but the ultimate result of Cuban engagement in the education sector—for example in establishing public education structures—was to stabilize the authority of the MPLA in the long term. The same applies to other civil and military sectors. Regardless of political and military escalation and all the asymmetries and dissonances that cooperation brought about, the MPLA managed to continue extending its power throughout the country even after 1991.

In the early phase of education reform, the support given by Cuban advisors and education specialists to the Angolan Ministry of Education was without a doubt needed to establish the new education system. During the second phase of cooperation, the Cuban teachers and lecturers who worked at ground level filling in for Angolan teachers also played a vital role in introducing education reform across the country. The advantage Cubans had over Angolan teachers and teachers from other countries was their extreme flexibility. The Cubans who volunteered to go to Angola had no say whatsoever in where they would be deployed. They could be sent wherever they were needed, including to the provinces, where no Angolans would go of their own accord and where no other foreign civil aid workers could be deployed.[47]

The civil and military administration and infrastructure that had been set up for Cuban troops stationed in Angola were crucial to this flexibility. It had been agreed that Cuban teachers would only be deployed in regions that were not immediately threatened by war. Nevertheless, unlike *cooperantes* from other countries, the Cubans were able to work in more remote regions of the country thanks to the presence of Cuban troops in many areas and the resulting military infrastructure that existed there. Cuban civilians were therefore often sent to work close to Cuban garrisons, where they could be protected by their own soldiers and could benefit from their transportation system, medical care, food supplies, etc. The Angolan government was unable to guarantee such basic facilities in very remote rural areas, irrespective of whether they were war zones or not. And so the Cuban teachers were particularly welcome as "stopgaps" in the education system. What is more, all Cuban civilians had received basic military training and in an emergency would be able to defend themselves and their pupils.[48]

Armed with their ideology and sense of political mission, the Cuban teachers working on behalf of the Angolan government became the "civilian outposts" of the state and the MPLA. They were sent to work in regions and provinces where, following independence, the concept of an Angolan state had yet to emerge and the MPLA's opponents had considerable political influence. In many cases, the commitment of the Cuban teachers in the classroom meant that they did more than just maintain a presence on behalf of the political system: they represented the new government's promise of a progressive education policy. The teachers' work, combined with the medical care provided by Cuban doctors, often in the same locations, served as an advertisement for the MPLA governmental program by propagandizing the government's ability to bring about social change and care for the welfare of its citizens. The teachers served to spread the MPLA's political agenda and new national project among the population, supporting the introduction of Portuguese as the language of instruction across the country and thereby aligning themselves with the MPLA's assimilation policy through linguistic homogeneity (even though the Cuban teachers themselves by and large had little knowledge of Portuguese). The Cuban teachers willingly acted as vehicles of political, social, and cultural change because their educational mandate represented the objectives of the MPLA both in content and symbolically. As government "representatives," they supported the administration and control of the territories claimed by the MPLA. They themselves had been socialized in a state with functioning infrastructure and a nationwide social-service network and administration. Against this background, their education mandate also included supporting the nation-building process in Angola and the consolidation of the MPLA's power. They were the representatives of the new social order and new political system.

Despite the Cuban teachers' agenda and their massive presence, sobering accounts paint a picture of an Angolan education system in the midst of an inexorable backward slide. Alongside the escalation of the military situation in the southern and central provinces, which had a dramatic impact on education from 1981/82 onward, the acute lack of qualified teachers became steadily worse. Between 1981 and 1984, a full 23.6 percent of teachers abandoned their profession because of poor pay and career prospects. This had a knock-on effect on the pupils. The number of school-aged children and adolescents who attended school consequently fell from 63.7 percent in 1980 to 37 percent in 1984. The provinces of Huambo, Malanje, Bié, Kwanza Sul, Benguela and Zaire were particularly badly hit.[49]

The gradual withdrawal of Cuban teachers from 1983/84 revealed that their deployment and "universality" were partly responsible for the stagnation of teacher training in Angola. In an internal memo in 1990, the Angolan Ministry of Education was self-critical in its appraisal of the situation. The sobering conclusion of internal meetings was that the constant, cheap availability of Cuban teachers had made the Angolans too "comfortable" and had led them to neglect completely the training of their own teachers.[50] Not only had the original principle of providing "help for self-help" retreated into the background; the presence of Cuban teachers had hindered de facto the development of a feeling of responsibility. The wartime conditions, the destruction of infrastructure, and the lack of communication structures were not the only causes of this decline in the ability to educate Angola's citizens: homegrown problems within the ministry also played their part. Angolan teachers continued to receive a paltry salary, and the lack of guidelines, coordination, and suitable curricula hindered attempts to improve teacher training, as can already be seen from an internal MED report from 1982.[51]

At the end of the 1980s, the Cuban government's intention of helping the MPLA to build a socialist state by offering its assistance in education (and all other civil sectors) failed once and for all. The MPLA had reformed its economy according to market-economy principles while retaining the centralized and undemocratic state structures of the socialist era. This provided fertile ground for governmental corruption. In the education sector, this development expressed itself in the "excessive centralization of the Ministry of Education," which was held responsible for the inefficiency of the school system, as an internal problem analysis from the Ministry in 1991 illustrates.[52] A report commissioned in 1989 by the United Nations Development Program (UNDP) stated that the catastrophic situation of the Angolan education system resulted from the devastating impact of the war inside and outside Angola, which had destroyed the foundations of the Angolan economy and infrastructure. The criticism, however, also extended to the content and implementation of education policy, which had been based on a completely false assessment of the economic and financial situation of the country: "The education system, which has been in place since 1978, was introduced without proper knowledge of the amount of financial resources, materials and human resources available to ensure its normal progress. Over the years, the original principles and objectives have therefore been compromised."[53]

Although the help Cuba provided in building the postcolonial education system in Angola laid the foundation stone for universal national education and a national network of educational institutions, after 1992, all educational activity was severely hampered by the ongoing struggle between the MPLA and UNITA for power and for material and moral objectives. This battle, which they waged with unabated intensity after Cuban withdrawal, continued until 2002. The civil war forced millions of Angolans to flee and cost the lives of several hundred thousand, doing much to destroy the little progress that the cooperation program had achieved. Furthermore, education through Cuban support had become an instrument of maintaining power because the transfer of central elements of the Cuban education system backed the authoritarian and centralized tendencies within the Angolan government apparatus. The Cuban teachers and educators therefore played a particularly ambiguous role. They were the transcultural vehicles of innovative teaching and learning methods. But they were also the agents of a system transfer, which helped to consolidate indefinitely the power of the MPLA government well beyond the socialist era.

The Angolan Boarding Schools on the Isla de la Juventud

The Angolan boarding schools on the Cuban Isla de la Juventud (Isle of Youth) formed the second main component of education cooperation.[54] The beginning of cooperation with Angola and the corresponding high expectations placed on the Cuban government sparked the Cuban government's idea of creating an international school center on the island. Not only Angolan children and adolescents would be able to receive an education there, but also young people from other friendly states in Asia, Africa, and Latin America. Education could be used to turn these young people into revolutionary cadres and "new men," who could then carry the ideas of the revolution back to their home countries. The boarding schools were also an expression of the government's internationalist ambitions in foreign policy and its desire to present itself as the avant-garde of the Tricontinental countries. They proved to be an extremely effective tool in Cuba's cultural diplomacy. At its height, the large-scale social experiment on the Isle of Youth comprised thirty-four national education centers for over ten thousand students and pupils from across the globe.[55] It was a political gesture par excellence, proving that Cuba took "internationalist solidarity" seriously and demonstrating the superiority of Cuba's social model at an international level. Unlike Cuba's educational involvement in Angola itself, the scholarship program continued after 1991 and still exists today. According to data from the Cuban Ministry of Higher Education, forty thousand pupils and students had graduated from schools and universities on the Isle of Youth by 2004. Almost thirty thousand of these pupils and students came from Sub-Saharan Africa, eight thousand of whom were from Angola.[56]

My main aim here is to illustrate how the boarding schools operated and to outline the educational objectives behind them within the framework of the cooperation program in education. It is not possible within the scope of this study to draw conclusions about the long-term impact of the education of thousands of Angolan children and adolescents in Cuba because fundamental data and documents were not available. Nevertheless, the information I obtained from the archives of the Angolan Ministry of Education and the few documents from Cuban educational institutions, combined with my eyewitness interviews, have provided me with enough material to be able to discuss the main characteristics of this ambitious education experiment.

In spring 1977, the Cuban and Angolan governments agreed to set up boarding schools for Angolan pupils on the basis of the cooperation agreement on education that had been signed in December 1976. In addition, it was decided that scholarships be awarded for Cuban universities and polytechnic schools.[57] In this agreement, Cuba undertook to build and equip schools, to supply Cuban teaching staff, and to provide food, accommodation, and medical care for the pupils and students. The boarding schools were to run along the lines of the Cuban rural boarding schools (the ESBEC), which had existed since the early 1970s and which followed the pedagogic and political principle of combining study and work.[58] Like the ESBEC, the boarding schools were co-educational with an emphasis on strict discipline both in work and daily life. The pupils were subjected to comprehensive physical and mental education and discipline. Participation in work assignments and all sport, cultural, and recreation activities was obligatory, as was the wearing of school uniforms.[59]

The project was launched with the opening of four schools in October 1977, two for children and adolescents from Angola, and two for those from Mozambique. One month later, the first group of eight hundred Angolan pupils arrived. They were between ten and sixteen years of age and had completed the fourth grade. Each of the first Angolan boarding schools, the "Agostinho Neto" and the "Saidy Vieira Dias Mingas," had space for six hundred pupils.[60] By the mid-1980s a further three schools were opened, and from then on over three thousand Angolan children and adolescents were on the island.[61] The boarding-school pupils were initially expected to complete lower-secondary education up to ninth grade over a period of six years. Depending on their average grades and the school and training places available in Cuba, they were then offered the chance to complete their pre-university education and go on to study in Cuba. The option of studying at the university, however, was reserved for those who had an exceptional academic record, were politically reliable, or were members of a political organization (for example, the JMPLA). Moreover, they were not free to study whatever they wanted; the degree courses they could take depended on Angolan requirements at a given time and were adjusted during consultations between the Cuban and Angolan Ministries of Education.[62]

The Angolan government welcomed the opportunity to educate children and adolescents in Cuba, and it rewarded deserving cadres and former guerrillas by offering their children the chance to attend the boarding schools. When selecting children, it also gave preference to war orphans from the Angolan provinces.[63] The Angolan Ministry of Education supported the education project by providing and financing Angolan teachers and a scholarship program.[64] It was not only the solid, revolutionary nature of Cuban education that was so attractive to the Angolan government. Unlike those educated in "Western" foreign countries, Angolans who completed their education in Cuba would under guarantee return to their home country and be available to help with reconstruction. In general, the Cuban authorities did not grant foreign pupils and students residence permits after they completed their education. Furthermore, Cuba's social and economic system was not attractive enough to persuade graduates to settle there permanently: they considered the system much too rigid, and it offered no money-earning prospects whatsoever.[65]

For Angolan parents who decided to send their children to boarding school in Cuba, the chance of an education abroad, let alone a university education, was very attractive since this was a privilege that had during colonial times been reserved for the Portuguese or members of the Luso-African elites. Boys and young men benefited most from the education program in Cuba. The Cuban and Angolan eyewitnesses whom I interviewed were unanimous that this was because of the traditional views of the parents. The honor of a

Angolan pupils on the Isla de la Juventud, ca. late 1970s or early 1980s (from the private archive of the author)

scholarship was more likely to fall to the male members of the family—the future bread-winners—than to the females. The parents also feared for the sexual integrity of their daughters and hesitated to send them abroad for several years.[66] The result was that on the Isle of Youth an average of 70 percent of the pupils and students were male and only 30 percent were female.[67]

All the boarding schools were arranged according to nationality. Each "nation" had its own school building with living and working quarters, school gardens, recreation rooms, and its own teachers for lessons specific to the country in question.[68] The only exceptions were the teacher-training institute, the Instituto Superior Pedagógico "José Enrique Varona," and the General de Brigadas Raúl Díaz Argüelles military academy, where students of every nationality studied together. The reason for organizing education according to nationality was to promote a feeling of national identity among pupils from the same country. This was considered particularly important for Angola, in view of the division within Angolan society. All ethnocultural, regional, or linguistic peculiarities and differences were consciously ignored because they were seen as detrimental to the national unity of Angola and as beneficial to the MPLA's opponents. In keeping with the MPLA's sociopolitical agenda, the Angolan pupils and students were to be educated as "new men" and as members of a socialist society and culturally homogenous nation. The boarding schools brought together children and adolescents from the different regions and cultural contexts of Angola. Often the sole bonds they shared were the Portuguese language and Angolan citizenship. In many cases, they only developed an awareness of a common national identity during their schooling in Cuba.

The education they received was also designed to prevent them from becoming socially and culturally alienated, since on their return they would have to be able to integrate back into Angolan society and support the nation-building process. To this end, Angolan teachers were engaged to teach Portuguese, geography, and history. Their job was to ensure that pupils did not forget their Portuguese "mother tongue" and to familiarize them with their "national traditions."[69] These "national traditions" were determined and redefined in consultation with the Angolan boarding-school teachers in keeping with the MPLA government's endeavors to create ethnocultural homogeneity. The educative measures to promote this new sense of national identity included regularly singing the national anthem, observing national days of celebration, and reflecting upon the art and literature of the country of origin. Regular cultural and folklore festivals brought the pupils of all nationalities together to present their different traditions in folklore, dance, art, and music contests. During these contests, only culture that was officially recognized as having a nationally unifying character was presented. These occasions were also associated with an array of culinary "national" specialties from the various countries. Importance was placed upon allowing the pupils to use all their senses to discover and learn about their far-off home countries.[70] Despite the importance of the home countries, Spanish was the language of instruction at all boarding schools, and Cuban teachers taught all lessons with the exception of the aforementioned subjects.

The example of the Angolan boarding schools illustrates some of the challenges and conflicts of interest that lay beneath the surface of Cuban-Angolan cooperation in education. By setting up the schools, the Cubans hoped in part to be able to limit the number of teachers they had to send to

Angola. Furthermore, besides offering pupils the chance of an education far from the conflict raging in Angola, the Cuban authorities saw the enclaves on the Isle of Youth as a chance to remove children and adolescents from external influences and turn them into revolutionary cadres by teaching them exclusively according to Marxist educational principles. The island off the south coast of Cuba had served as a prison until 1959, and its location was considered ideal because it allowed the children and youths from abroad to live in almost total isolation from the rest of Cuban society. This in turn meant that the feared contact between Cubans and foreigners from nonsocialist countries could be controlled and to a large extent avoided.

At all schools, discipline was strictly observed. Any serious misdemeanors—escape, violence, drug abuse, illegal marketeering, and also pregnancy—resulted in expulsion from the school and Cuba.[71] Despite the serious consequences, rules were frequently breached, and there were often disciplinary problems. Boarding schools throughout Cuba had a high underage pregnancy rate (partly for reasons of inadequate sexual education), and the Isle of Youth schools were no exception. Here, as in the rest of Cuba, the usual disciplinary procedure was to try to persuade the pregnant girl to agree to an abortion. Should she refuse, she was "dishonorably" suspended from school and sent back to her home country with no qualifications.[72] Another common problem was high levels of aggression between male adolescents, who were in the majority. Cuba's usual policy of physical discipline, for example in the form of sport, proved unable to keep this aggression in check. Feuds and fighting often broke out between the schools (and different nationalities), frequently over girls and young woman.[73]

Another recurring problem was caused by pupils leaving school grounds without permission. Pupils managed to escape the confines of the Isle of Youth and hide out in Havana. These temporary escapes were usually linked to black-market activities. Many of the pupils received money in foreign currency from their parents, which they could legally spend on much-sought-after Western goods from Cuba's foreign-currency stores. They then resold the goods on the black market to Cubans, who were not entitled to use these stores (which were reserved exclusively for foreigners). In 1983 one such case of black marketeering involving twenty-two Angolan pupils went as high as the bilateral commission and led to the expulsion of a large number of pupils. The Cuban government reacted to such events with great anger because they represented an infringement of the fundamental rules of socialist society.[74] An attempt by Cuban school principals to stop parents from sending money failed after massive protests among the students, culminating in strike action.[75] The school strikes ended only after the visit of a high-ranking enquiry committee from the Angolan Ministry of Education.[76]

The strict discipline administered at the boarding schools was another reason for many protests and strikes. These actions often came to a head when pupils returned to the Cuban boarding schools from their vacations at home in Angola, after which they felt the absence of family and friends and the sting of the school's tough discipline and rigorous workload more acutely than before.[77] Much of the dissatisfaction was caused by the pupils' long separation from their parental homes and the lack of care and attention provided by Angolan (educational) institutions. Internal reports and correspondence between the ministries make frequent mention of this fundamental problem. They show that the authorities from the Angolan Ministry of Education placed their trust in the educative skills of the Cubans and all too often relinquished responsibility for the education of the children and adolescents to the boarding schools. There was hardly any form of continuous, official contact between the pupils, the Angolan Embassy in Havana, and the Ministry of Education in Luanda. Delegations only visited when the pupils made their voices heard through protest actions.

And this is where the limits of this experiment become apparent. By all accounts, the boarding schools were too far from the pupils' countries of origin. Even if there had been continual correspondence, it is unlikely that their feelings of neglect or alienation could have been completely avoided. In Angola there was vociferous criticism of this project because many feared that the children and adolescents would have difficulty reintegrating into Angolan society on their return. Another criticism was leveled at the practice of having pupils help bring in the citrus harvest.[78] The combined program of study and work was contrary to many Angolans' image of privileged education abroad.[79] The opponents of the MPLA—particularly UNITA—were quick to draw on this dissatisfaction for propaganda purposes by claiming that Angolan children were being "kidnapped" and sent to Cuba as "slaves."[80]

After 1991, the sociopolitical paradigms in Angola shifted. From then on, education in Cuba became regarded as "inferior" to school and university educations obtained in Western countries. Nevertheless, Angolans continued to take advantage of Cuba's offer and still do today. Even now an education obtained in Cuba has the potential to further an individual's career. Many of those who benefited from a socialist education in Cuba now occupy positions in politics, government administration, and the military. Many are even successful in business.[81] One of my Angolan interviewees commented on this phenomenon with a hint of irony by quoting words he attributed to the first president of Côte d'Ivoire, Félix Houphouët-Boigny (1960–1993): "If you want your children to become communists, send them to be educated in the West. But if you want them to become capitalists, then send them to be educated in a socialist country."[82]

Part III

Memories of Angola

8

Memories of Everyday Life

This chapter deals with the memories of Cubans regarding their day-to-day lives and work in Angola during civil cooperation; the next chapter looks at the way Cubans and Angolans perceived each other, and how they experienced identity and otherness during civil cooperation. Detailed descriptions of daily living conditions show what Cuban-Angolan cooperation entailed on the ground, far from intergovernmental agreements and political propaganda. My aim is to demonstrate how Cubans and Angolans encountered each other: people from different cultural contexts who, thrown together because of cooperation between their countries, had to interact. The following chapters therefore also deal with the emotional dimension of this cooperation. Another guiding thread running through this section traces the circumstances under which the encounters took place and assesses their impact. The purpose of this microhistorical analysis is to establish whether the official aims of cooperation were realized and where asymmetries, dissonances, and breaks occurred.

Again the focus is on education, although I do mention other areas in which the Cuban aid workers were generally confronted with common experiences and circumstances. All chapters are based primarily on oral recollections and the few available written records of Cubans describing their work in Angola, the way they perceived themselves, and how they perceived others. As a counterpoint to the Cuban perspective, Angolan eyewitnesses also give voice to their memories and perceptions. Such recollections provide an insight into how individuals perceived, understood, and misunderstood situations in Angola.

Whenever possible, I reinforce the oral eyewitness accounts with contemporaneous documents from Cuban administrative authorities and Angolan (education) institutions in order to highlight whether these subjective memories converge with or diverge from the prevailing viewpoint at that time.

Central to this analysis are experiences with which Cuban aid workers in Angola had to come to terms. I have divided these experiences into five separate sections, chosen according to the answers my interviewees gave to my open questions regarding their most potent memories of Angola. The five sections cover what I interpret as characteristic basic experiences. The first recurring topic is how Cubans were separated from the Angolan population in their Cuban enclaves. These were not just geographically defined spaces but sociocultural spaces defined by the prevailing sociopolitical order in Cuba. The related inclusion and exclusion mechanisms defined not only the status of the Cuban *cooperantes* within Angolan society but also the way they perceived Angolan society and the Angolans themselves. The second section focuses on another dominant theme in the Cuban civilians' everyday recollections: the omnipresence of war. The accounts are marked by the fear and trauma caused by rejection of their presence in Angola, violence, and death. This section illustrates how closely civil cooperation was linked to the overall political and military strategy and the extent to which Cuban civilians became involved in the war.

Section three deals with the great challenges confronting the (former) teachers I interviewed about their endeavors to introduce educational reform in schools throughout Angola. Because of the physical separation of Cubans and Angolans, the schools became an interspace where the only legitimate contact between them could take place. Here the encounters between teachers and pupils were defined by the status of the Cubans, who as the vanguard of education policy at the service of the MPLA government were responsible not only for teaching new curricula and modernizing the school system but also for propagating new values and codes of conduct. At this concrete level of activity numerous ambivalences in this "mission" become particularly apparent, and the complexity of acceptance and resistance animated by this teaching and learning process emerged.

The fourth section deals with the emotional strategies Cubans developed to cope with their difficult daily lives. According to the recollections of my interviewees, temporary romantic and sexual relationships between Cubans working in Angola were not uncommon—a phenomenon referred to as the "Angolan marriage." And although the Cuban authorities imposed curfews and segregation measures, "cross-border" relationships between Cubans and Angolans did happen. Marriages allowing Cubans to remain in Angola gave some the chance to realize their own individual aims in life.

The fifth section deals with the many negative memories evoked by violence, trauma, and the shock of encountering a culture that was completely alien. These are memories that still have no place in the official Cuban interpretation of the Angolan operation. During my interviews, Cubans were for the first time able to break away from the official version of events and express their own impressions of their work in Angola. Some experiences, however, were obviously so traumatic that they could not be expressed in words but only conveyed in the emotion that was palpable during the interviews.[1] The witnesses' negative memories contradict the official success story. These accounts break both taboos and the official silence surrounding Angola, opening up a new angle from which the Cuban intervention in Angola could be regarded as a failure.

During engagement in Angola and the encounters between Cubans and Angolans, the way people perceived "the other" was inextricably linked to the way they perceived themselves. These perceptions were at times shaped by a sense of fascination, but more often by rejection and repulsion. The second chapter deals with confrontations with "the other." The Cubans in particular tended to denigrate anything they found strange and threatening, while simultaneously reevaluating their own self-importance. This is an example of one of the essential aspects of reflexivity, which is a characteristic feature of intercultural communication processes that has been corroborated in numerous studies based on cultural encounters from other epochs and cultural contexts.[2] Although all the chapters look at the way Cubans and Angolans interacted with each other or excluded one another, the final chapter analyzes why both sides remained to a large extent alien to the other and why the Angolan experience generally caused Cubans to re-identify themselves with Cuban culture and society.

Space

The space that the Cuban *cooperantes* inhabited during their stay in Angola was central to their understanding of daily life and to the way Cubans and Angolans encountered and perceived each other. Civilian life was organized along military lines and was largely played out in controlled spaces reserved exclusively for the Cubans. These spaces were protective zones and safe havens, but they also served as areas of ideological control and social discipline.[3] The spaces were "islands," self-contained enclaves in which accommodation had been built for the sole use of the Cubans. They lived in them separated from the Angolan population, only leaving to go to work. These spaces, however, were not only physically separated territories. They were spaces in the sense of Bordieu's social space, where the organization and structure were defined by the prevailing social order and political rules in Cuba.[4] The internal regulation and external control mechanisms were in the hands of the Cuban Civil Administration and the political organizations. These spaces and the accompanying regulation mechanisms determined the status of Cuban aid workers within Angolan society. They were also an integral part of the internal information and communication network that the Cuban Civil Administration established in Angola.

Apart from providing protection from external threats—whether posed by war, "wrong" ideologies, or contact with Angolans and foreigners in general—the Cuban spaces helped to construct and maintain the *cooperantes*' collective identity as Cubans and revolutionary internationalists. Reminding Cuban civilians working in Angola of their "homeland" was intended to help them retain their Cuban identity and feel connected to Cuba and the revolution during their one to two years of absence.[5] The enclaves in which these workers lived were intended to replicate Cuban society in terms of culture and social and political organization.[6] Life within these enclaves was crucial to how Cubans perceived and later remembered Angola. This point is illustrated both in my interviewees' memories and in written accounts of the everyday life and working conditions of the aid workers. The way they perceived Angola and the Angolans was influenced not only by the sociocultural baggage that they brought with them from Cuba but also (and even more so) by the life they led within the defined "Cuban" spaces. An evaluation of the source material demonstrates that the written accounts and oral testimonies have one thing in common: the depiction and memories of daily life in Angola and the memories of interpersonal relationships and encounters refer almost exclusively to life within the closed group. In both written and oral accounts, awareness of Angola and the Angolans played a subordinate role, and Angolans were often reduced to stereotypes. Memories of encounters with Angolans were almost exclusively work-related. In many cases, the workplace (in the context of educational cooperation this mainly meant public educational institutions such as schools, the university, and the Ministry of Education) was the only point of contact the *cooperantes* had with Angolan reality and the sole (legitimate) opportunity they had to meet Angolans.

The first civilians to arrive in Angola in 1976 had enjoyed considerably more "freedom" than those who came later, even though they too had to follow a strict code of conduct. Because they came in small groups mainly comprising politically reliable cadres, they did not need any particular surveillance and were accommodated in hotels or near Angolans.[7] The strict inclusion and exclusion mechanisms designed to segregate Cuban civilians and Angolans were introduced in 1977 following the bilateral agreements on sending large contingents of aid workers to Angola.[8] In the resulting enclaves, the rules and guidelines differed depending on the status of the development workers. Their internal status was defined by their role within the structures of the education cooperation program and the professional fields in which they worked. For example, the underage students who came to Angola from 1978 onward with the DPI were subjected to much stricter internal discipline and regulations governing their right to leave the compounds than were other civil aid workers.[9]

The word my interviewees used to describe these Cuban compounds was the Portuguese *prédio,* meaning "house" or "land." As a rule, only Cubans were permitted to enter these Cuban compounds, though some did have "public" reception areas for non-Cuban visitors. Some of the Luandan *prédios* were an exception to this rule and housed Cuban *cooperantes* in the same blocks as Angolan families.[10] Starting in 1978, Cuban construction brigades began building new compounds, some of which were made of the same "Girón" prefabricated elements as the apartment blocks built in Cuba after the revolution.[11] In Luanda, these Cuban compounds and apartment blocks were spread throughout the whole city.[12] Some were located in the governmental quarter, Futungo de Belas, and some in better-off residential areas. Others were built as sheltered and guarded, gated communities in poorer areas. In the provinces, the Cubans were also housed separately from Angolans. Again their accommodations were often in some of the better residential areas.[13] In Luanda, the Cubans were grouped according to their professions, with the best accommodations reserved for those with political responsibility. In the provinces, however, all civil aid workers co-existed in communal housing blocks. In 1977, the Cuban Civil Administration even opened state-controlled stores selling Western goods to the workforce in an attempt to discourage them from purchasing them on the free or black market.[14]

A welcoming reception introduced the Cuban aid workers to their enclaves. After arriving at the international airport in Luanda, they were officially welcomed by the head of Cuban civil cooperation. The Angolan ministries or their Departments of International Cooperation later hosted a second reception, during which the aid workers were registered and assigned their workplace.[15] In the first weeks of their stay, they received collective temporary housing in Luanda.[16] Between their arrival and transportation to their place of work, the *cooperantes* learned the binding code of conduct and went on excursions in the surrounding area. They also received political instruction, basic military training, and information about common illnesses and the danger of disease in Angola.[17]

In the provinces, accommodations were often close to Cuban military bases. This offered the civil aid workers protection from enemy attacks. The civilians themselves had to take turns at guard duty, which many of my interviewees described as extremely taxing, both physically and mentally, because these duties came on top of their normal work schedules. The reason given for this obligatory duty at all compounds was the precarious political and military situation in Angola. But in reality, guard duty was one of the measures taken to enforce social discipline by maintaining a threat of violence that justified both limitations on the Cubans' movements outside the compounds and surveillance measures within them.[18] Each compound had its own disciplinary panel comprising representatives from the various organizations. This panel was responsible for penalizing those who broke the rules:[19] in the case of serious breaches of conduct, civilians faced "dishonorable discharge" and immediate return to Cuba.[20]

The proximity of civilian accommodations to Cuban garrisons in the provinces had the added advantage of allowing the civilian workforce to benefit from military infrastructure. When the Cuban military first became involved in Angola, the Angolan infrastructure had suffered extensive damage. The resulting difficulties forced the Cubans to build up their own infrastructure to ensure reliable supplies of weapons, ammunition, and food and to guarantee the transport of troops and personnel. So-called *caravanas*—huge convoys with dozens of military transport vehicles and tanks—were responsible for maintaining the military supply chain from the Angolan ports into the country's interior.[21] The *caravanas* were particularly susceptible to UNITA attacks, and the dirt tracks along which they traveled were peppered with land mines. The civilians were therefore often transported by Cuban military plane.[22]

In the 1980s, the fear of enemy attacks on Cuban civilians increased with the escalation of armed conflict in Angola. Transportation services were set up at all civilian locations to ferry the aid workers from their accommodations to their workplaces and back again at the end of the working day. This was to prevent them from becoming easy targets if they were out on their own or in groups. If, as often was the case, transportation did not turn up, the aid workers were forced to remain in their compounds, which in turn led to lessons being cancelled. The minutes of the bilateral meetings record that the transportation problem between compound and workplace proved one of the biggest obstacles to cooperation on the ground.[23]

Although the safekeeping of aid workers was certainly a major reason for establishing enclaves, their primary purpose was to keep an internal check on the Cuban civilians. As in Cuba itself, the authorities enforced strict regulations within the Cuban community and used the potential for outside dangers as an instrument of power to maintain discipline and promote solidarity. Any Cuban engagement in foreign countries carried the risk that Cuban citizens would use their stay abroad to escape into exile. The Cuban government was well aware of this. Although Angola was not considered the most attractive country to settle in permanently, civilians could use it as a passage to a third country. To preempt this danger (whether real or imagined), the Cuban government strictly limited their mobility and prohibited almost all external contacts.[24] Another way of preventing civilians from escaping was to confiscate their passports. These were kept in the Cuban embassy in Luanda until the civilians were due to return to Cuba on leave or permanently.[25]

The controls exerted on Cuban civilians were so extensive that these workers were unable to leave their *prédios* without first receiving permission from their supervisors. If they did receive permission, they were not allowed to go out alone but had to stay in larger groups. There was also a strict curfew at nighttime. Individual contact with Angolans was considered undesirable, and the Cubans were forbidden to consort with other foreigners. The rigidity of these restrictions on contact and movement, however, also varied depending on the political and military situation at the given point in time. At the beginning of cooperation, for example, there was still a considerable amount of leeway.[26] Dr. Rodolfo Puente Ferro, a military doctor and former Cuban ambassador in Angola, was involved in setting up the pilot project of military and civil cooperation in Cabinda from 1976 onward. While confirming that there was a code of conduct, he admitted that at the start of cooperation Cubans were not generally forbidden to associate with Angolans, though they were not allowed to meet up with Portuguese and other foreigners.[27] His statement was backed by my interviewees who went to Angola before 1980 and by some who worked in Luanda during periods where the immediate threat was considered less serious.[28] When the political and military situation came to a head in the 1980s, and in the wake of UNITA attacks on Cuban civilians in the spring of 1984, the restrictions on movement were tightened, above all in the regions where UNITA militia were particularly active. In addition to the restrictions on movement in the enclaves, a nighttime curfew was imposed for the whole population, including in Luanda in the 1980s.[29]

The inclusion and exclusion mechanisms in the Cuban enclaves were interpreted differently depending on the political conviction of the "other." Whereas contact between Cubans and Angolans was not explicitly forbidden, but rather monitored through restrictions on movement, contact with other foreign civilians was explicitly prohibited, except during work. As Puente Ferro put it, the intention was to prevent "the enemies of the MPLA government from receiving too much information."[30] There was a general mistrust of people who, from the Cuban point of view, were politically suspect or came from Western countries. Cuban civilians did indeed have to be safeguarded from attacks by government opponents, but they also had to be protected from politically "wrong" ideologies. On the other hand, it was possible and even desirable to associate with Angolans who belonged to the MPLA or affiliated organizations.

Organized and monitored encounters between Angolans and Cubans generally took the form of political events, celebrations, and anniversaries marking such occasions as national Cuban or Angolan holidays or international holidays like 1 May, 26 July, or 4 February. Angolans were only allowed to attend if they were deemed trustworthy by the Cuban authorities because of their membership in the MPLA or affiliated organizations.[31]

Contact restrictions also applied to visitors who did not live in the Cuban compounds. There seem to have been few opportunities, for example, for Angolan pupils to visit their Cuban teachers, as non-Cubans were generally prohibited from entering the Cuban *prédios*.[32] Likewise, the Cubans were not allowed to visit private Angolan homes. Many of my interviewees recalled having been invited to a celebration or meal by their pupils or their pupils' families. Although they were always glad of such invitations and would have been happy to accept, they were often refused permission from their supervisors on the grounds that there would be a security risk. The only occasion on which Cuban teachers could visit their pupils' homes was in a professional capacity, for example when they inspected the sociocultural environment in which the children lived, or when they tried to include parents in the learning process to promote acceptance of educational measures. Such school "inspections" of the family home were commonplace in Cuba and considered integral to the education process.[33]

Although romantic relationships with Angolans were not explicitly forbidden, the Cubans were emphatically warned against sexual contact with Angolans. In Cuba, there was an overriding fear of unknown diseases from Africa, in particular sexually transmitted infections. The Cuban health authorities were determined to keep foreign diseases out of their country.[34] The preparatory semester that the student teachers underwent before going to Angola placed much emphasis on hygiene, sexuality, and health education.[35] The existing contact restrictions and control mechanisms already kept sexual relationships with Angolans in check, but the emphatic warnings against sexually transmitted disease acted as a further deterrent. Sexual relations between Cubans within their own ranks, however, were not subject to restrictions.[36] Nevertheless, time and again Cubans crossed the boundaries and entered into "unauthorized" friendships and relationships with Angolans. This topic will be covered in greater detail further below.

The principles of social order in the enclaves were comparable to those of the rural boarding schools. Alongside work and guard duty, life was rigidly organized around collective activities. All Cuban civilians were obliged to take part in such collective activities, although the members of the student-teacher brigades were expected to be particularly active. Again, this was a measure to maintain internal discipline, its primary purpose being to distract the aid workers from everyday difficulties, work, and the threat of attack. These activities were arranged by the leaders of the professional groups and the political associations. As in Cuba, the neighborhood committees, the Committee for the Defense of the Revolution (CDR), the Communist Party (PCC), the Young Communist League (UJC), and the civil-defense association (ODP) played an active role in the enclaves at a national, regional and local level. The *prédios* were the smallest organizational unit. Regular party meetings took place at all levels to discuss the organizational, social, and political matters affecting the life and work of the collective. Together with the Civil Administration, the political associations played a crucial role in arranging leisure activities, monitoring performance at work, and structuring everyday life.[37]

The neighborhood committees were charged with drawing up a collective cleaning roster and organizing volunteers to help maintain the compounds. The Party was responsible for calling political meetings and for arranging ceremonies to mark Cuban holidays and anniversaries. The leisure activities included dances, birthday parties, musical and theater performances, group excursions, and regular competitive sporting events.[38] In addition, there were regular visits to the Cuban military cemetery to honor the Cuban soldiers who had fallen in Angola. Attendance at the funerals of soldiers was obligatory. There were also regular gatherings to inform the civil aid workers about important political and social developments in Cuba. In some places, special weekly or monthly information bulletins reported on events in Cuba and provided local news about the activities of the civilians working in Angola.[39] Some of the *prédios* could even receive TV and radio programs from Cuba.[40] Particular importance was attached to maintaining continuous contact with family in Cuba. A military postal service had already been set up at the end of 1975, and it could now be used by the *cooperantes* and their families. Twice a week, private correspondence was sent by air service between Cuba and Angola and distributed by special delivery services. This ensured that the aid workers kept written in contact with their families once a week.[41]

In an attempt to promote work discipline and morale, the political associations organized national performance-related competitions within the various professional groups. The purpose and importance of these competitions are well documented, particularly with reference to the student brigades.[42] According to records, groups were rewarded for the number of hours they worked, group discipline, military exercises, and voluntary work. Further credits were given for the social and political commitment of individuals within the collective. The results of these competitions determined whether groups or individuals would receive extra recognition in the form of a medal or certificate after they had completed their stint in Angola.[43]

The purpose of these political, social, and cultural activities was to kindle the civilians' links with Cuba and remind them of the ideals of the revolution through routine festivities, ceremonies, and rituals. It was hoped that a sense of community would stave off feelings of alienation and prevent the *cooperantes* from doubting the objectives of the cooperation, particularly when confronted with the deaths of soldiers. The government hoped to foster both a fighting spirit and feelings of solidarity between soldiers and civilians, who were all a part of Cuban society despite the thousands of miles between them and their homeland. Moreover, it was important to fill every minute of the aid workers' day with tasks in order to distract them from their difficult circumstances. The majority of my interviewees recalled being homesick and suffering from family separation; many had great difficulty in coping with the war in Angola.

Despite the strict, closely monitored life in the Cuban enclaves, many of my interviewees intimated (often only after the microphone had been switched off) that they had flouted the regulations and controls so as to satisfy their curiosity and explore their Angolan surroundings on their own whenever they could. Apart from friendships and romantic liaisons with Angolans, the main reason for their overstepping limits was the *candonga*, the black market. Some seem only to have stood on the sidelines and watched the hustle and bustle; others seem to have initiated small business transactions to improve their meager allowance or to buy food and other consumer goods.

According to the memories of my interviewees, the *candongas* proffered a stark contrast to their orderly and disciplined lives in the compounds. Those who admitted going to the *candongas* gave the impression that they were both fascinated and repelled by what they saw.[44] The unembellished experience of Angolan reality was a culture shock to some and seems to have had an educative effect, causing them to distance themselves from what they experienced. After all, the black market was the expression of brutal, unbridled, unregulated capitalism—the absolute opposite of everything Cuban society stood for: "I found these *candongas* absolutely horrific. . . . The prices were very high, even though the people who went there were not particularly cultivated. . . . You saw lots of people with very low standards there. . . . People got murdered and killed there; I saw terrible fights. . . . It was all about making money—it's where all the people went who neither worked nor studied."[45]

And so the Cuban enclaves fulfilled (at least in part) the purpose of promoting identity and maintaining the status quo, just as the planners and organizers had intended. The isolated lives the civilians led in the compounds and workplace heightened the contrast between what they perceived as controlled, ordered, and "good"—their own enclaves and society—and what they perceived as uncontrolled and threatening—Angolan reality. Any deeper understanding of Angolan reality, which would have been a prerequisite for a deeper understanding of Angola, was thus largely avoided.

War

The conflict in Angola impacted heavily on the daily life and work of the Cuban civilians. War was part and parcel of everyday life in Angola, and the threat it posed was ever present at the workplace and in the compounds. The intensity with which the war made itself felt, however, differed according to time and region. Open, armed conflict was not the norm everywhere, particularly not in the capital and the surrounding region. Here open conflict was the exception, and the war was expressed through acts of sabotage or targeted, intermittent attacks. Nevertheless, the threat of war was more than just an "external" factor to the Cubans; it was acutely felt insofar as the organization and the aims of the civil cooperation were by and large very closely linked to Cuban military operations. Cuba's military support for the MPLA made all Cubans in Angola legitimate targets for government opponents and their international allies.

Even beyond the pilot phase of cooperation, when the content and structure of the civil cooperative program was much more intertwined with military cooperation, the Cuban civilians were integral to the political and military strategy agreed upon between the Cuban and MPLA governments, and as such they helped stabilize the MPLA's authority through their development aid. Their strategic importance alone was enough to turn them into potential targets for the opposing camp. Evidence shows that the Cuban government was not only consciously willing to accept this risk; it in part actively incorporated civilians into war operations. My interviewees were well aware of the strategic role they played. The life-threatening situations they experienced were reflected in their oral accounts and in the written accounts of Cuban officials. The memories, feelings, and perceptions of the eyewitnesses are therefore central to this chapter. Only they can express the daily threats and real dangers to which the civilians were exposed and the extent of the trauma that these experiences left behind.

When the Cuban government was recruiting volunteers for Angola, it did not hide the fact that civil aid workers would be deployed in a region of military conflict. But all mention of the conflict was implicit rather than explicit. The Cuban population was kept largely in the dark about the actual development of the war in Angola. Reporting on Angola served exclusively propagandistic purposes, covering only what the government considered necessary to illustrate the success of military operations there and the imminent victory of the Angolan FAPLA. From the government's perspective, the successful outcome of this war was a foregone conclusion, and the need for new military and civilian volunteers for the engagement was constant. The media depicted the war exclusively as a great military success and concealed the reasons behind the conflict, the setbacks for the FAPLA, the destruction to Angola's infrastructure, and the number of victims.[46]

The Cuban government engaged in Angola under the banner of political internationalism in the revolutionary tradition of Che Guevara. This kind of involvement—defined as a fight against imperialism, neocolonialism, and apartheid—implied offensive action.[47] From this perspective, internationalist engagement was inseparable from armed struggle, even if the action was explicitly civilian in nature. Civilians who volunteered to go to Angola therefore had to be aware that in an emergency they might have to take up arms to defend their lives. These aims became obvious during recruitment for the student brigades of the DPI in September 1977. Castro personally appealed to the students to follow the ideal of the heroic *guerrillero* and form an elite educational force. The students met the recognition bestowed upon them with great enthusiasm and requested uniforms topped off with emblematic "Che" berets.[48] As they explained it, "We identified with Che to such an extent that we not only wanted to imitate his behavior, we wanted to look like him too. . . . We were now revolutionary commanders . . . and we were going to visit other nations."[49]

Basic military training formed an obligatory part of the student brigades' preparation, when they were taught that during their work in Angola they might be forced to swap their "pencils for a gun."[50] The same principle applied to all other civil aid workers; all of them had to undergo basic military training either before or during their stay in Angola. Depending on the political and military situation at their place of deployment, they were at times obliged to be armed day and night. In regions and provinces where there was imminent danger of armed attack, the Cuban teachers even carried their weapons in the classroom to protect themselves and their pupils. Internal reports written by officials in charge of the *cooperantes* indicate that military committees were organized in the *prédios* as an integral part of the overall civilian structure.[51] In the eyes of the Angolan government, military training was an "extra qualification" for working in Angola, as the civilians could be deployed even under the most difficult military circumstances. Their military skills and readiness to bear arms meant that Cuban civilians could be sent to regions that were in the throes of conflict, unlike other specialists, for example from the Eastern bloc, who could only be deployed in "safe" areas.

Just how dangerous the situation was did not become clear to many aid workers—and indeed to many organizers—until they were actually on Angolan soil. One of my interviewees, a former Cuban deputy minister of teacher training (1970–1990), was responsible for preparing the student brigades for their stay in Angola. During an interview she described how in 1977 she and the minister of education had inspected the places to which the students were to be sent in Angola and realized to their horror that most of them were mined.[52] Despite this realization, the preparations went ahead, and in March 1978, a total of 732 young brigadiers arrived in Angola. Was the Cuban government aware from the outset of the dangers that military activity posed to civilians? Did it simply accept (even tacitly) the risk?

In view of the obvious connection between civil development aid and military cooperation, the question arises as to what extent Cuban civilians fulfilled the dual function of the "civic soldier," in other words soldiers in civilian "guise," as has been asserted by critics of the Cuban government.[53] The fact that all civilians serving in Angola possessed some degree of military training, however, is not enough to prove that they performed this double role. Their training was purely defensive and was intended to protect them if they were under threat. They were not trained to attack. Furthermore, the entire Cuban population was increasingly militarized during the 1980s. Starting in 1981, all adults were obliged to undergo a short military training program. Worried about the implications of the Reagan administration's new foreign policy, the Cuban government was anxious to involve the whole population in its national defense strategy. All those who subsequently went to Angola therefore already had military training. After 1984, the majority of aid workers were obliged to carry a weapon at all times so that they could defend themselves. This measure, however, resulted in Angolans automatically thinking that the Cuban civilians were soldiers. One of my Angolan eyewitnesses told me during an interview that all his school friends had presumed that their Cuban teachers were "really soldiers."[54]

My research found that at least on one occasion civilians were called upon to participate in military activity. Although I do not have any written records to corroborate this,[55] three of my eyewitnesses claimed completely independently of each other that they had been ordered to participate in the same military operation. In July 1983, UNITA besieged the town of Cangamba in the eastern province of Moxico. According to my eyewitnesses, the Cuban civilians working in Luanda were called upon to help the Cuban and Angolan armies guard bridges and arterial roads around Luanda. During the siege of Cangamba, the female civilians in Luanda were put on red alert and the males were detailed to stand guard outside Luanda.[56] It remains unclear how many such operations took place or whether this was an exceptional case. This example does, however, demonstrate that civilians with military training were indeed used for military purposes and thereby did in some cases perform a dual military and civilian function.

Nevertheless, it would be wrong to generalize that all *cooperantes* were "civic soldiers." At most, they were players in an overall political and military strategy. According to this strategy, the authorities used social and humanitarian aid to open up territories for the MPLA and to help consolidate state institutions and the new social order. The main task of the civilians working in education was to "conquer" minds by helping disseminate the MPLA government's new agenda in the classroom. The civilian nature of their role, however, did not discourage government opponents from regarding them as part of military cooperation and consequently as legitimate targets. The threat of attack hung constantly over them.

Events in spring 1984 showed the reality of the military threat to Cuban civilians and illustrated how crucial their small amount of military training was. When on 25 March UNITA's militia attacked the coastal town of Sumbe in the province of Kwanza Sul, they targeted Cuban civilians. Their aim was to take hostages and thus put pressure on the governing MPLA. As Sumbe had been considered completely safe until then, it was not garrisoned, and at the time of attack there was no security beyond a few police patrols in the town. Three days previously, an FAPLA unit had come across the advancing UNITA troops but for some reason had failed to sound the alarm.[57] The civilians who were working in Sumbe, including Cubans and several Portuguese, Italians, Soviets, and Bulgarians, were therefore forced to defend themselves. Some fifty Cuban civilians stood in the front line. They were civil engineers, doctors, teachers, and student teachers of the DPI. In the end, they were saved only by the arrival of a Cuban-Angolan air force unit. A total of twenty Cuban and Angolan civilians were wounded during the attack; three Cubans died, among them one young teacher.[58]

One of my interviewees was a member of the student-teacher brigades and had witnessed the dramatic events in Sumbe. It was only during the preparatory term in Cuba that she and her fellow students had realized that their task in Angola would not be an easy one. And yet they had still been unable to imagine any danger: "We had no idea that we could be attacked! We were more worried about language problems and living in a foreign culture." There had been no Cuban troops stationed at their location just outside the town, she continued, which is why they had not noticed UNITA troops positioning themselves in the surrounding hills. "We were just civilians—construction workers, doctors, teachers, and students, fifty-odd Cubans and other foreigners, and we hardly had any weapons. . . . On Sunday morning at about four o'clock, I was woken up by loud noises. At first I thought it was a storm with thunder and rain. . . . Then there was a knock on the door and someone shouted, 'Everyone out! Attack!' . . . When we came out of the building, the town was already under fire."[59] A truck with Cuban construction workers took them out of town. The men among them carried weapons and the women were taken to the beach to hide. But there they came under fire. "In the afternoon low-flying military planes arrived. At first we didn't know whether they were friends or enemies, . . . but it was the Cubans."[60] The next day they had been taken by helicopter to Benguela, the capital of the province of Benguela to the south of Kwanza Sul. It was only then that they had learned of the magnitude of the attack and the casualties among their group.[61]

One month later, on 20 April 1984, a bomb exploded in the city of Huambo in the southern central highlands. Again Cuban civilians were targeted. The bomb blew up a Cuban housing block, killing over twenty people, seven Angolans and fourteen Cuban construction workers and craftsmen. Over thirty people were injured, some of them seriously. Among the injured were Cuban teachers, technicians, and doctors.[62] This attack left no doubt that UNITA had changed tactics and was aiming at Cuban civilians in an orchestrated fight against the presence of all Cubans on Angolan territory.[63] It is possible that the success of the attacks was a sign that the Angolans themselves increasingly resented the Cuban presence, a feeling that was fomented by UNITA propaganda. To date, however, the extent to which the civilian attacks are indicative of growing resentment remains unclear, as there have been no studies on this matter.

The Cuban government reacted on several different levels to the obvious danger now facing civilians. At first, it tried to stifle or downplay reports about the attacks in the media. The attack on Sumbe initially received little publicity. In Huambo, however, the high number of Cuban casualties meant that the government could no longer remain silent. It therefore opted for an aggressive propaganda strategy using the 1984 May Day celebrations to channel public outcry into a mass political rally against the US government, imperialism, reactionism, and racism.[64] Castro rallied his audience with phrases such as "No one and nothing will ever intimidate us,"[65] to which the demonstrators replied by waving banners with the words "Fidel, we are prepared to do anything, wherever and whenever,"[66] as can be seen from media coverage and photos. The rally was a demonstration to the national and international community that nothing—not even attacks on civilians—could stop the Cubans' determination to remain in Angola.

Despite insisting vociferously that Cuba should continue its engagement in Angola, the Cuban government went on to reduce the number of civil aid workers in Angola after 1984, without issuing any further official statements. The civilians who were already in Angola were quickly withdrawn from the provinces of Cabinda, Bié, Namibe, Uige, Kwanza Norte, Malanje, and Lunda Sul and redeployed in areas where the political and military situation was deemed safe. Statistics from the Angolan Ministry of Education show that already by November 1984, the number of teachers working in Angola was half that of two years earlier.[67] On the other hand, right up until the final withdrawal of Cuban troops in summer 1991, civilians continued to be redeployed in areas where there had been previous military attacks on civilians. Particularly in Huambo and Sumbe, the presence of a civilian workforce remained strong. It is unclear who decided what locations were "safe." Nor is it possible to say whether the overall political and military strategy was again using the aid workers as civilian outposts whose task was to "occupy" the areas that the MPLA had "recaptured."

The personal memories many civilians have of their stay in Angola contradict Cuban government propaganda. They not only reflect a completely different reality of wartime, they also express the sense of threat that the Cubans were exposed to no matter where and when they were involved. For most of my interviewees, it was not just because this was their first experience of war. The war itself and its consequences left a deeper mark on them than any other experience during their entire stay. This overall impression is countered by only a handful of memories in which eyewitnesses depicted their experience of war as an adventure bringing them closer to the ideal of the heroic guerrilla. For those few people, the experience of war turned their stay in Angola into the stuff of personal heroic biographies. This applied to some of my male interviewees who had been involved as reservists in the military engagement until 1975/76 before moving into the civilian sector. Moreover, those who described the war as an "adventure" were without exception deployed in the civilian or military cooperation program prior to 1979.[68] But for the majority of my interviewees—both male and female—the experience of war was shocking and traumatic.

In early autumn 1981, the South African army and UNITA launched major offensives. As the military situation worsened, nighttime curfews were extended to Luanda. Apart from acts of sabotage there was little direct combat between government troops and UNITA in Luanda. Nevertheless, the war was palpable and visible in the capital. Starting in the 1970s, soldiers and military vehicles had been part of normal city life, and in the 1980s war-injured began arriving along with refugees from all over the country.[69] The everyday lives of the Cuban civilians working in the capital were also increasingly militarized. In the compounds they were in a constant state of alert with the obligatory loaded rifle beside the bed. Nighttime guard duty took its toll on the physical and mental well-being of the civilians.

My civilian interviewees recalled feelings of tension and stress, which seem to have been intensified by the permanent warnings of attack issued by the Cubans. The requirement that all civilians join in regular military training exercises in uniform contributed to their feelings of unease and brought home the real possibility of facing danger. The possibility cannot be excluded that those responsible for cooperation consciously exploited such threatening scenarios as a means of keeping the large number of *cooperantes* under control and maintaining discipline. In Cuba itself, the government's insistence upon a permanent threat hanging over the country—for example the supposed imminence of US attacks—was also an instrument of power. Nevertheless, several of my interviewees claimed unanimously that the impact of war on their daily lives was never openly discussed, even though everyone was latently aware of it.[70]

"We turned into soldiers . . . and had rifles and uniforms at the ready day and night,"[71] recalled one of my interviewees, who worked for the Cuban embassy in Luanda between 1982 and 1984. She recollected taking part in military exercises once a week because the embassy staff members had to be able to defend themselves in case of attack. At night there had been a curfew and in the daytime they were only allowed to move around in sizable groups. Though she had only a short distance to work, she had still been driven there and back.[72] The memories of the embassy employee outline the indirect experience of war that similarly affected other interviewees working at the same time in Luanda. A teacher who worked at a Luandan primary school between 1983 and 1985 recalled, "We [were] not used to shooting, but we heard shots every night there; it was . . . well, we had to get used to the situation—separated from our families and loved ones, the constant shooting, a country at war; we had to get used to the curfew. . . . But we had to discipline ourselves and do our duty."[73]

A colleague of hers who worked at the same school between 1983 and 1985 as a mathematics teacher had already served as a civilian in Nicaragua between 1979 and 1981. She insisted that what she experienced in Angola had been very much more difficult to cope with and described the following dramatic event:

> There are no words to describe what we went through there. . . . Often you couldn't tell who was friend or foe. At daytime, the Angolan teachers worked together with you, and then at night they transformed into UNITA supporters . . . , even the school principal. . . . We had a colleague at another school—the Party school of the MPLA . . . a math teacher. . . . He was killed by a bomb. . . . The bomb fuse was attached to the school bell, [and] when the bell rang the whole school exploded; the bomb was for the teacher, but the whole school went up. . . . You can't forget pain

> like that . . . all those sleepless nights because you were frightened they were going to kill you. . . . There are no words to describe it. And the worst thing is all the dead that we buried there, and that we then brought home with us. But we were doing something useful; we brought them education, health, everything. . . . When I got back to Cuba, it was a long time before I could go out in the street, because I was afraid, because in Angola anything could have happened to you in the street; they could have shot you, crushed your skull. . . . It took me a long time to get used to being back home. We were in Angola during a very difficult phase.[74]

In her description, this interviewee touches on a threatening phenomenon that was mentioned time and again by other eyewitnesses and that caused great insecurity: the Angolan population's hostility toward the Cubans, which was both encouraged and exploited by UNITA. "*Cuachas*" was the name Cubans gave to Angolans who worked with them in a duplicitous role.[75] According to my interviewees, the *cuachas* had worked perfectly normally with the Cubans or attended their classes during the day; at night, however, they transformed into the enemy, who used the trust they had gained from Cubans (and other Angolans) to perpetrate acts of sabotage against schools and MPLA establishments and even to attack Cubans themselves.[76]

Another example of such activity was described by a primary-school teacher who worked in Luanda from 1984 to 1986. Apparently, a starving child had been used as "bait" to gain access to the Cuban compounds. My interviewee told of how she had picked up a little, half-starved girl from the street, who seemed to have lost her mother. She took pity on the girl and broke the internal rules by taking her into the building so that the child could sleep in the common room. The next morning the girl had disappeared, and with her all the furnishings. The child had obviously opened the door to her family during the night and they had plundered the building. My interviewee received a caution from the Civil Administration for having exposed everyone to the danger of attack.[77]

The memories of such phenomena are indicative of the deep-felt insecurity that issued from the polarized political situation dividing the whole of Angola into MPLA supporters and MPLA opponents. Moreover, it is probable that not all MPLA supporters approved of the Cuban presence and that they too expressed their dislike by such activities. Even if the above case of the little girl was nothing more than common criminality, the tense situation led to the Cuban civilians increasingly distrusting and rejecting the Angolans, particularly those with whom they worked. None of my interviews allowed me to ascertain how widespread the problem of the *cuachas* was and how dangerous they were. But what is certain is that the fear of the *cuachas* and their attacks, whether real or imagined, was omnipresent and put even more psychological stress on the *cooperantes*.

The memories just cited refer to the situation in Luanda in the mid-1980s. Other interviewees inferred that they had felt very threatened too, as early as the late 1970s, by the atmosphere of war and violence in other parts of Angola. University professors who went to Huambo in the late 1970s to help rebuild the university remember a war-torn city, much of which already lay in ruins. The supposed birthplace of Jonas Savimbi had been violently contested by UNITA, and following independence, acts of violence, attacks, and military insurgency were rife. Land mines had been laid on all arterial roads around the city of Huambo and roads through the Huambo province. The Cuban Civil Administration was aware of this. Internal reports from this period indicate that the situation there was very tense, and the civilians felt highly insecure as a result. One such report describes how young student teachers suffered panic attacks and psychological problems and were terrified of keeping night watch.[78]

An agricultural scientist who worked at the university in Huambo from 1978 to 1979 remembered his stay as follows: "We couldn't, how can I put it, have any proper sort of social life, because we were very constricted; there were lots of problems with what you would call terrorism today—a lot of violence throughout the city. . . . We tried to compensate for a lot of things by working . . . so that we didn't have to think about it. We were worried we might not survive. . . ."[79] During the conversation, my interviewee portrayed threatening scenes:

> We couldn't move around much because of the attacks. You never knew where they were going to take place. They bombed markets—eighty people died in one bomb attack where thousands of people went shopping. And that's where they triggered a bomb. . . . You had to watch out in that climate; as a civilian, I had to avoid places like that in the city—places where people gathered, buses. . . . We had weapons, but we could only use them in self-defense. . . . There were land mines all around Huambo; it was extremely unsafe; nowhere was safe, because nothing is safe when there are mines about. . . . Outside the city, we only traveled in convoys [*caravanas*] and military vehicles. . . . It was always a gamble.[80]

A veterinary surgeon who likewise taught from 1978 at the university in Huambo confirmed that the civilians had suffered from fear and psychological stress.

> There were lots of attacks, lots of mines. We weren't allowed to go to farms, even though we specialized in agriculture and cattle breeding. The agricultural faculty was outside the city, and the animal clinic I worked in

> was even further away. The roads there were unsurfaced, and so there was the constant danger that they had been mined overnight. . . . Almost everything was forbidden because of the mines. . . . Sometimes we went to the farms without permission, because, after all, it was our job to treat sick animals. . . . Once a generator just 150 meters from my office was blown up. . . . The danger of being killed in an attack was a real one.[81]

The central province of Bié was another area that was fiercely contested by UNITA. The recollections of a teacher who worked in its capital, Kuito, some years later (from 1984 to 1986) illustrate that civilians continued to be sent to war zones even after the attacks of 1984 and despite the increased threat they faced. She recalled regular armed fighting and bomb explosions right next to the Cuban compounds. She always had a military escort to her classes and was always armed during lessons. "We couldn't move around freely, because everything was mined. Mines were being found all over the place, and we frequently heard that here or there yet another mine had gone up. . . . We lived under constant tension, and lots of people who were there with me came back mentally ill because of everything they had been through." She told me that when she returned to Cuba, for a while she had not been able to walk on unsurfaced roads for fear of treading on a mine.[82] Her depiction of the danger, however, ended with the affirmation, "But we fulfilled our mission and we did it well."[83]

I also interviewed a primary-school teacher who was sent to Sumbe one year after the attack on the town. Her account illustrates that Cuban government propaganda to recruit new civilian volunteers obviously met with success even in 1984. "After arriving in the country . . . I was completely obsessed with fulfilling my mission and repaying my debt to humanity, as our *Comandante* [Fidel Castro] put it."[84] As soon as she arrived, however, she was confronted with the reality of war in Angola. "My first impression was a truckload of injured Cubans who had been brought to Luanda. I felt all strange, but then I said, 'come on, get a grip.'"[85] She also remembered the tense atmosphere at school. She too reported that some of her pupils were suspected of being, or actually were, *cuachas*.

> I had a lot of pupils who had already been involved in armed combat, and some of them were from the opposition. . . . I got on well with everyone, but I always had my AK with me in lessons. . . . Luckily I never had to use my gun in class. . . . I also had a problem with one of my legs and couldn't walk properly for half a year, . . . but I still picked up my machine gun every day and went to class. . . . I always slept with my machine gun; . . . that sort of thing changes you. . . . I was very homesick, back then—I mean that feeling that you carry round inside you.[86]

This interviewee witnessed how a Cuban colleague had been so desperate that she committed suicide: "I had a very sad time there. . . . Where I lived, there was a nurse called Rosita in the next room. Her nerves went to pieces. . . . I was in my room and suddenly heard a machine gun firing. That wasn't really anything new for me, because that sort of thing happened every day. So I ducked for cover and grabbed my rifle, crept quietly out and opened my neighbor's door. She had shot herself in the head with her machine gun. . . ."[87]

This interviewee also told me how her younger sister had been killed in Angola. The latter had wanted to copy her big sister and signed up as a volunteer, but on her way to join her older sister, she was killed in a plane crash between Luanda and Sumbe. My interviewee remembered weighing only forty kilos when she returned to Cuba, and her nerves were in tatters: "I kept talking really loudly and was paranoid that UNITA was after me."[88]

A doctor who just after completing her studies in pediatric medicine was sent to a hospital in Sumbe from 1987 to 1990 gave a different expression of how the presence of war affected Cuban civilians, particularly toward the end of engagement. She remembered the increased numbers of victims among the Cuban soldiers:

> Perhaps you can imagine what it was like—a country at war. . . . There were bombings; we were hit by one. . . . But we also watched many Cubans die. Comrades. We saw all these coffins covered with the Cuban flag, and that really shocked me. I can't get this image out of my head. . . . They were so young, so young. They had their lives ahead of them. . . . I came back bald; I lost all my hair; I had all these bald patches on my head from pure stress. . . . There was so much I simply couldn't understand. They don't speak your language; they are not your people. . . . All this really shook me; my hair fell out by the handful.[89]

Another two interviewees also described the traumatic experience of being confronted with the coffins of fallen Cuban soldiers. A pediatrician from Santiago de Cuba who worked in a hospital in Luanda from 1987 to 1989 told me of how deeply upset she had been at the sight of the coffins. Even today, she breaks into tears whenever she sees the Cuban national flag or hears the national anthem, she said. We had to break off the interview several times, because the very memory made her weep:[90] "Sometimes I start to analyze whether the problem I have with the flag and national anthem started when we buried the pilot who often came to visit us. He died during an air exercise. They buried him in the Cuban military cemetery [in Viana, a town to the south of Luanda], where we all had to go whenever someone died. We all had to go; we were taken there by bus. And all that was with the anthem and flag—and I think that's where I got it from."[91]

The former employee of the Cuban embassy in Luanda also described the same phenomenon of breaking into tears at the sight of the national flag, even today. She had to deal with personnel matters for the military and civilians working in Angola and was therefore informed of every death. As a member of the embassy staff, she had attended all the funerals of Cuban soldiers in the military cemetery in Viana. "We mourned every single victim as if they had been a close family relative."[92]

Work

This section deals with the main reason why Cuban civilians went to Angola: their work. The general isolation of Cuban civilians from the Angolan population meant that their place of work was one of the few locations where they could meet and exchange with Angolans directly. I focus here on the example of Cuban teachers working at Angolan primary and secondary schools. These schools represented "interspaces," or "interfaces," where encounters between Cubans and Angolans were at their most intensive, and where Cuban aid workers were confronted with Angolan reality. The classroom exemplifies the levels of meaning that were central to the Cuban-Angolan encounter. One level was the interaction between pupils and teachers during the process of teaching and learning; a second level was the collaboration between Cubans and Angolans as colleagues. The new education content and the way it was taught met with both acceptance and rejection, and it is particularly interesting to depict and analyze this dichotomy from different viewpoints. The analysis will take note of Cuban teachers' perception of themselves as "others," the attitudes of the Angolan teachers and superiors, and the perceptions and evaluations of the pupils. During their work at Angolan schools, Cuban teachers were performing their "internationalist duty." They also saw themselves as educational missionaries, as representatives of a superior social system whose task was not only to transfer revolutionary ideology but also to teach new civilizing, cultural values and codes of conduct.

The teachers were responsible for disseminating the new political and patriotic agenda, and to this end they introduced ceremonies such as flag-raising and the singing of the national anthem.[93] They were also charged with introducing extensive educational and teaching innovations. Behind education reform was the desire to raise "new men," and the Cuban teachers were to help carry out this task in Angola's public education institutions. Pupils and colleagues alike saw the Cubans as both representatives of the new authority, as they were working for the MPLA government, and as representatives of a foreign power.

The organization and structures of cooperation thereby determined the sociocultural parameters of the encounters between Cubans and Angolans. These encounters could not be considered voluntary and unprejudiced; the two sides met in hierarchical, asymmetric capacities, as teachers and pupils. Although Cubans and Angolans also met as colleagues, the Cubans again took the role of instructor. They were acting on the government's behalf to introduce education reform into the daily workings of the schools, and they had to explain changes in content and structure to their Angolan colleagues and convince them. Within the schools, the Cuban teachers had the status of an educational and political avant-garde comprising "the new type of teacher"; they were considered the pioneers of socialist modernization in education. They also exercised ideological authority and control, for example when it came to "cleansing" school libraries of literature and teaching material that came from the colonial period or that contradicted the new political dogmas. History and geography teachers were also responsible for conveying the Marxist-Leninist materialist conception of the world and history, which was anchored in the new curricula.[94]

The educational and political tasks of the Cuban teachers included organizational and civilizatory components because it was their job to see that the school ran in a structured manner. They had to ensure that lessons took place regularly and were taught consistently in Portuguese. Moreover, they introduced a new, socialist work ethic: both they and their Angolan colleagues were to set an example to their pupils with regard to working morale, punctuality, discipline, and responsibility; they were even under obligation to keep to the statutory forty-four-hour working week.[95] Precisely at this point the ambivalences and contradictions of cooperation become apparent. Not only the challenges of everyday schooling, but also the problems arising from the internal organization of Cuban cooperation structures reveal the gaping rifts between ideal and reality.

The information upon which this section is based comes partly from documents of the Angolan MED that record the role of Cuban teachers in education, and partly from the memories and appraisals of Angolans involved in organizing education reform. In addition, I was able to draw on several internal reports in which those responsible assessed the work that had been carried out and in so doing revealed their own view of the situation. Further sources include reports and statistics on the work of the student-brigade members of the DPI. These reports were written by members of the local UJC and served as the basis for judging the "socialist competitions" between the various groups.[96]

A valuable insight into school life is also offered by the so-called collective diaries that each local group of student teachers was obliged to keep, and which likewise formed part of the internal performance-monitoring system.[97] Both the diaries and the competition reports, however, provide almost exclusively quantitative, measurable facts, for example the number of teaching hours or exam success rates. As already mentioned, such sources offer greater insight into the internal workings of the Cuban enclaves than reflections on the impact that the new teaching methods had on learner success. This makes the examples of self-awareness contained in the diaries all the more striking. Another salient feature of the collective diaries and competition reports is that they contain virtually no mention of Angolan pupils and colleagues. The only time they do refer to their Angolan counterparts is when they have failed to meet Cuban expectations or when they underline the performance of the Cuban teachers.

These written sources are complemented by the personal memories of the teachers I interviewed and by written, personal memoirs. Unlike the internal reports, these do talk about the daily encounters with Angolan pupils, but again in these memories the teachers concentrate above all on their own roles. A contrast to this Cuban perspective is offered by the memories of former Angolan pupils, who during interviews spoke about how they perceived and judged their Cuban teachers. This multifaceted approach intertwines oral and written accounts from Angolan and Cuban perspectives to present a clearer picture of how Angolan school life and teaching operated and what kind of encounters took place between Cubans and Angolans.

Implementing the New Education Policy

Cuban teachers at all school levels mainly taught natural sciences (mathematics, physics, chemistry, and biology), and their work focused on methodology and its classroom application. It also extended beyond the classroom to include extracurricular and leisure activities. The teachers worked according to the political and educational principle that education was not just about imparting knowledge but was an essential component of integration into the new social order. In order to pass on the education objectives as efficiently and interestingly as possible, they insisted on interactive teaching methods based on the educational concepts that had been developed in Cuba.[98]

With this approach, the Cuban teachers were at the forefront of a true cultural revolution in Angolan schools. They introduced completely new education standards, taught new learning methods, and broke away from the fusty teaching methods of the colonial era that had involved lecture-style teaching and learning by rote.[99] Under the new supervision, homework groups, interest groups, and a monitor system were established. These were all methods of motivating students to participate actively in the learning process while simultaneously accepting responsibility for the entire group. The teachers also worked in the area of cognitive science, researching the influence society had on pupils' mental processes and actions, with the aim of establishing within

Cuban teacher in an Angolan classroom, ca. early 1980s (from the private archive of the author)

Angolan teaching an awareness that it was possible to consciously influence behavior.[100]

After lessons, the Cuban teachers arranged sport and leisure activities. They also organized volunteers to keep schools, communal areas, and leisure facilities in good repair. They introduced consultation hours and parent meetings, and they visited parental homes in an attempt to include parents actively in the educational and political process.[101] They also collaborated with organizations affiliated with the MPLA, above all the JMPLA and the women's organization. With the support of these groups, the Cuban teachers were able to recruit and train Angolan assistant teachers. This was another strategy to establish continuous contact with those living within the school environment and to involve the inhabitants actively in the education process.

The monitor system, which likewise was integral to Cuban socialist pedagogy, involved the specific promotion of gifted pupils. The "monitors" were recruited from the best pupils in the class or the best in a particular subject. Working at their teacher's side, they were given special responsibility in the classroom: for example, they were allowed to carry out their own experiments in chemistry.[102] In return, they had to help their weaker classmates. The educational purpose behind this was to nurture leadership qualities from an early age. Again it was an instrument transferred from Cuba specifically designed to nurture the children. By encouraging interests and abilities as early as possible, the teachers aimed to guide children into making specific career choices and to educate them for the working environment. The members of the interest groups took part in extracurricular visits to production sites where they became familiar with industrial processes.[103]

Alongside all the political and ideological objectives in education, the Cuban teachers were also determined to teach their subjects effectively. With their new teaching methods they explained their lessons clearly and as often as necessary for all pupils to understand.[104] They placed particular importance on preparing the pupils for the regular exams, consistently revising exam material in an attempt to minimize the number of pupils who failed.[105] These endeavors were not without a degree of self-interest: the number of students who passed exams and moved into a higher grade was one of the main criteria of the internal performance-monitoring system according to which the Cuban teachers were assessed.[106] The Cubans were therefore at pains to prepare lessons carefully and adapt their teaching methods and lesson content to suit their pupils' level of knowledge.[107]

Methodology and lesson planning were an integral component of the student teachers' studies during their stay in Angola. The group leaders and accompanying lecturers from Cuban teacher-training colleges were responsible for teaching these skills, and they were supported by so-called methodologists. These methodologists were part of the structure of the cooperation program in education. Located in Luanda, they regularly visited all the student brigades throughout Angola to check on their progress in their specializations and in pedagogy.[108] Methodology and lesson planning were also included in internal teaching workshops, the "Jornadas Pedagógicas," which were organized as part of the education program for all Cuban teachers working in Angola. These workshops gave them the opportunity to discuss teaching and education problems and to coordinate how best to proceed. All evidence to date suggests that although the conclusions drawn at these meetings subsequently found their way into Angolan schools, Angolan teachers and education specialists were not automatically invited to participate.[109]

Personal memories and memoirs indicate that the Cuban teachers also imposed their own understanding of what was "civilizatory": "We made a big contribution to their education. For example we got them out of the habit of walking in and out of classes . . . and we taught them to wear proper clothes at school."[110] Several of my interviewees reported that they also taught the basics of health and hygiene after they became aware of the alarming conditions in which their pupils lived. They taught them daily personal hygiene (such as how to use toilets) and explained bodily functions.[111] One former participant explained that she had told menstruating school girls to participate in physical education lessons, as this was regarded in Cuba as healthy.[112]

Problems in the Day-to-Day Running of Schools

Cubans teaching at Angolan schools were confronted with a difficult environment, especially in rural regions. In Luanda and the provincial capitals such as Huambo, Benguela, and Lubango school life seems to have been relatively "normal," with regular teaching times, acceptable class sizes, and intact buildings. In rural areas, however, the prerequisites for proper schooling were often absent. The problems usually began with the infrastructure. Schools often first had to be repaired or even rebuilt before lessons could begin. If school buildings did exist, they lacked all sorts of furnishings and equipment, from desks, benches, and blackboards to stationery and teaching materials. In some cases, the teachers themselves had to provide their pupils with pens and paper.[113] Particularly at the beginning of cooperation, there was a lack of school books, which meant that the teachers sometimes had to produce their own teaching materials so that lessons could take place at all. At times, they even resorted to using Cuban school books.[114] Moreover, lessons were often interrupted by power outages, particularly in the evenings, when adults were supposed to have the opportunity to attend school.[115]

Owing to the acute lack of teachers, Cubans frequently had to teach subjects they were not trained in. They were also expected to go into lower primary-school classes, even though it had been agreed that their language competence was insufficient to teach anything below the fifth and sixth grades, and the student teachers were not supposed to teach anything lower than the seventh and eighth grades.[116] Although the Angolan MED was responsible for informing its Cuban counterpart about the exact requirements in teacher numbers, coordination problems often arose at this interface. At times, the Angolan education authorities proved unable to assess their needs properly, and at times the cooperating Cuban authorities were unable to provide the required specialists.

Further problems emerged from the internal organization and logistics of cooperation. Some problems had cultural origins, with language as a case in point. The Cuban teachers had the task of ensuring that Portuguese was used as the language of instruction throughout the schools. They themselves, however, were seldom able to speak correct Portuguese. The Angolan Ministry of Education regarded their insufficient knowledge of Portuguese as a perennial problem in the classroom, and they blamed the indifference toward Portuguese on the part of the Cubans responsible for cooperation. The failure of Cubans to learn Portuguese remained a bone of contention during bilateral negotiations right up until the end of cooperation.[117] Indeed, the fully qualified teachers who were sent to Angola received no instruction in Portuguese beforehand, as confirmed by my interviewees. The members of the student brigades did receive lessons in Portuguese during their preparatory course, but this was not sufficient to allow them to use it fluently in class.

Many of my interviewees admitted resorting to *portuñol* in class, particularly at the start of their stay. Over time, they then learned Portuguese—to some extent—usually from teaching Angolan pupils, as they had little contact with Angolans outside the classroom.[118] The negligent Cuban attitude toward learning Portuguese was partly due to the close similarities between Portuguese and Spanish. Because of its phonetics, however, it is much easier for Portuguese speakers to understand Spanish speakers than the other way around. Cuban teachers were therefore able to presume that their pupils could more or less understand them, but they often had difficulty understanding their pupils' responses. The Angolans tried to circumvent the problem by deploying Cuban teachers only from the fifth grade onward, mainly in natural sciences, and by calling upon teachers from Portugal to teach Portuguese in all grades. As mentioned above, however, the situation was often very different in practice. Moreover, some of the pupils did not speak Portuguese as their mother tongue, but one of the many Bantu or Khoisan languages. The extent to which this increased the language barrier was not discussed by the Angolan authorities.[119]

Another two obstacles to the smooth running of schools emerged from the way cooperation was organized: the transportation of teachers to their workplace and the annual leave of Cuban civil aid workers. As already mentioned, the Angolan Ministry of Education undertook in the bilateral cooperation agreements to provide transportation to ferry the Cuban teachers to and from their compounds and schools. Because of the military conflict or organizational and logistical shortcomings, the Angolans often failed to meet this obligation. As a result, up to a third of all lessons were cancelled.[120]

The holiday regulations that applied to Cuban teachers also paralyzed the schools on a regular basis. All aid workers had the right to one month's annual leave in Cuba at the end of May. Although the Angolan academic year had been arranged in accordance with this holiday entitlement, the academic term did not actually finish until the end of June, when the final exams took place. The dates of the exams therefore coincided with the Cuban holidays, which meant that at many schools exams could not take place because there were not enough exam supervisors or people to correct the papers.[121] In the files of the GICI/GII, a pile of letters of complaint from schools and the Provincial Directorates of the Ministry of Education registered their protest over this Cuban practice.[122] The quality of lessons suffered from the internal system for monitoring the performance of Cuban teachers and student teachers. This system took the form of a "socialist competition" in which the only thing of relevance was the success of Cuban teachers in measurable, quantitative terms: work discipline (i.e., the number of hours they worked), the number of exams passed, the proportion of pupils graduating to a higher class, and the teachers' social commitment within their own group.[123] The teachers' pedagogical skills and the effectiveness of their lessons were of subordinate importance. Moreover, the competition was a solely internal Cuban arrangement, and the judgment criteria were set out by the supervisors of the student brigades and the Party. Angolan teachers and school principals were excluded. They had no say in the design of the competitions, nor were they allowed to sit on the juries. None of the competition reports ("Informes de emulación") mentioned that the opinion of Angolan teachers, never mind the opinion of pupils, counted in the evaluation of Cuban teachers.

If Cuban teachers did not meet expectations, their shortcomings had to be explained internally. Poor success rates were automatically blamed on the Angolans. The criticism leveled at the Cuban reports and competition reports extended only to the structural deficits of the Angolan school system and the poor performance of "unruly and lazy" Angolan pupils.[124] The importance of performing well in these competitions is illustrated in their frequent mention in the collective diaries of the student brigades. These entries indicate that the ranking within these competitions was far more important than the progress of Angolan pupils. Success in these competitions decided personal careers: those who ranked highly during their work in Angola had a foot on the career ladder when they completed their studies. Success was rewarded with the honor of "National Vanguard" or with a gift.[125] The accountability reports written for the superiors in the Cuban Civil Administration or the Cuban Ministry of Education also show that, despite all the efforts to motivate the aid workers, there were many problems with work and social discipline.[126] The reports mention that classes frequently had to be cancelled because teachers simply failed to turn up at school or because they had to be sent back to Cuba for disciplinary reasons. Documents from the Angolan Ministry of Education back this.[127]

The relationship between Cuban teachers and their Angolan colleagues and school principals seems to have been one of distance and rejection, which is described in the internal Cuban reports as "problems with authority."[128] The problems of understanding and rejection that the Cubans faced at work were in part cultural and structural. By comparing various sources, however, I discovered that there were also definite power politics at play.[129] Mutual relations seem also to have been strained by the large disparity in education and knowledge. Angolan teachers were usually much less qualified than Cuban teachers, as were the school principals. Even the student teachers of the DPI brigades often possessed a more solid foundation in educational science and better knowledge of their subjects. The presence of Cuban teachers at Angolan schools therefore led to a hierarchy of the "learned" and the "ignorant," and it was not uncommon for Angolan school principals to take part in lessons taught by Cubans.[130]

The Angolan principals and teachers had obvious problems accepting instruction on pedagogy, didactics, methodology, and new curricula.[131] The Cuban teachers, for their part, saw themselves as the educational and political vanguard, and they were not prepared to follow the instructions of the Angolan principals, to whom they were formally subordinate.[132] The gap between them and their Angolan colleagues further increased thanks to the responsibility the Cubans bore not only for introducing the new content and structures of educational reform but also for overseeing the correct implementation of these innovations. This led to mutual distrust. It also encouraged arrogance among the Cubans and inferiority complexes among their Angolan colleagues.[133] Internal Cuban memoranda and reports, along with the memories of Cuban and Angolan eyewitnesses, speak of the paternalism and arrogance that the Cubans displayed toward their Angolan colleagues and pupils.[134] The collective diaries of the student teachers show that the Angolan school principals expressed their disapproval of the Cuban teachers through delaying tactics: when a new contingent of teachers arrived, the principals would try to keep them out of the classrooms for as long as possible. This hostility, however, often applied to the initial phase of their stay following a turnover of Cuban teaching staff.[135] The sources I had at my disposal did not reveal whether and to what degree the situation improved once the teachers had settled in.

The presence of Cuban teachers also represented competition for the Angolan teachers. According to the memories of former pupils, their new teaching methods and friendly classroom manner made Cuban teachers much more popular.[136] Many of the pupils had also been affected by the chaos of war and found themselves in a state of social and psychological instability, which required intensive attention that went way beyond the task of imparting knowledge. In such circumstances, the Cubans were much better than their Angolan colleagues at meeting their pupils' needs because personal attention, social commitment, and care beyond the classroom were integral to their pedagogical and didactic methods.

Another obstacle to fruitful Cuban-Angolan collaboration was the closed internal organization of the Cuban cooperation program in education. Convinced of the superiority of their own education system, the Cubans consulted each other and decided what methods they would use to establish education reform based on their own criteria. In comparison with colonial education methods, the Cuban pedagogical and didactic methods were indeed modern and innovative. However, in order to introduce them, the Cubans had first to overcome Angolan resistance.[137] It seems that there was little attempt at the school level to involve the Angolans in deliberations on how best to introduce and apply the new teaching and learning methods. On the contrary, internal documents and eyewitness reports indicate that the Cuban authorities did not consider it desirable for Cuban teachers to enter into exchanges with their Angolan colleagues that might be of a personal or political nature.

This hierarchy was reinforced by the close political alliance between the Cubans and the MPLA. Although this afforded the Cubans a special degree of authority within the schools, it also led to distrust and conflicts. According to the statements of a former staff member in the Ministry of Education in Luanda, the Cuban teachers were not particularly popular among their Angolan colleagues partly because the Cubans were under obligation to report any deviant political conduct. My interviewee did not wish to conjecture as to whether the Cubans were involved in the Angolan state security, DISA. But she did say that their experience of the much-feared Portuguese secret police, PIDE, had made Angolans extremely wary of anything that "smacked" of political control and state security. Nevertheless, the presence of Cubans in schools was seldom openly questioned because the Angolan colleagues feared reprisals.[138]

The relationship between Angolan pupils and their Cuban teachers was also not always smooth. Again Cuban sources mention "problems of authority," but with a different emphasis. The Angolan pupils were often the same age as or even older than their teachers, particularly the student teachers.[139] One of the problems was that older Angolan male pupils were expected to accept the authority of young women, which contradicted the traditional gender-specific reality of Angolan society in the 1970s and 1980s. Moreover, the classes were often very large and included children, adolescents, and young adults who were of mixed age and ability. This made it very difficult for young, inexperienced teachers to assert their authority.

Memories of School Life in Angola: Perceptions of Self and Other

The Cuban teachers tackled their political and educational duties with a sense of calling and the conviction that they were carrying out a revolutionary mission. "Our work as the educators of this brother nation will be victorious. With our work, we are contributing to the education of the new generation of Angolans and are thereby proving ourselves to be true representatives of Marxism-Leninism."[140] This quote originates from a collective diary of the student brigades. It illustrates how firmly the task of education was anchored in ideological schemata. The quote is undeniably rather extreme in its ideologically loaded terminology. But the internal reports and even the personal memoirs and oral accounts of my interviewees tend to adhere to this notion of cultural superiority informed by ideology, missionary zeal, and a sense of calling. All oral and written sources share another feature: there is little description of the normal workings of a school day, with the exception of lists of activities, and there is virtually no mention of Angolan pupils, who were, after all, absolutely central to teaching and education. When pupils are mentioned, it is usually in a negative context. Memories and written memoirs again emphasize the distance, the alienation, and even the distrust that Cubans seem to have felt toward their Angolan pupils. There are only very few descriptions of episodes indicating that a process of understanding did take place and that there were relationships based on trust between pupils and teachers.

A good example of the detached, paternalistic Cuban attitude is contained in a report written by two student-teacher supervisors. It is one of the accountability reports that had to be submitted to the next level of authority in the Cuban Civil Administration. In these reports groups had to account for their actions. This particular report depicts the local school situation and the enormous structural and organizational problems with which the young teachers were confronted. The report says little about the pupils' circumstances, and when it does, its tone is one of arrogance and paternalism: the Angolan pupils had first to be taught what discipline and work ethic meant, it claimed; they had no interest in learning, were frequently absent, and seldom did their homework—all of which explained the extremely high failure rate.[141]

The oral memories of school life in Angola also concentrate on negative episodes. A common topic was the distrust that Cubans had of pupils and teachers because they suspected that some of them were *cuachas*, as we have already seen in the case of the teachers' accounts. Moreover, most Cuban teachers were unable to cope with the chain of problems confronting them at Angolan schools. Many interviewees experienced school life as an encounter with a completely alien reality and were unable to comprehend the extreme poverty of many pupils or the stark social contrast between rich and poor. Many suffered from culture shock. During one of my interviews, a primary-school teacher who worked for two years in Luanda starting in 1983 suddenly interrupted herself to tell me that she had witnessed a child die in class from a parasite infestation. "The parasites had eaten him from the inside."[142] From then on, she repeatedly spoke of the children's living conditions, telling how they came to school hungry and how they had to go to work after lessons to help their families make ends meet. "It was alarming to see children who were so enthusiastic about going to school, but who couldn't even afford a pencil or exercise book. And then there were some who had everything; they were well fed and were brought to school by car."[143]

The reasons for poverty and social contrasts were generally attributed to Portuguese colonialism. My interviewees did try to put their experiences into a wider social and cultural context, but again their memories demonstrated the great distance they had in perceiving Angola and the Angolans. Their descriptions were generally linked to stereotypical images such as dirt, poverty, and backwardness. They felt sorry for their pupils and tried to help them, but again their accounts demonstrate that they saw themselves as the agents of a culturally superior civilization and superior social system. They were only able to interpret everything they experienced at school as a sign of social "backwardness." The basic tenor of many interviews was that the participants believed that they had "taught something" to the Angolans.[144]

According to my interviewees, the only thing that they could learn in return from Angolan pupils and parents and from their colleagues was Portuguese, and perhaps a few words of an African language. They had not, however, learned a new language out of any profound cultural interest, but rather to create the illusion that they belonged, so that they could then pass on their own message more effectively. "I even learned a few words of local dialect, Kioko, which made it easier for me to get to know their customs and to win over their hearts."[145] And with that there was little difference between the Cuban teachers and the Christian missionaries of centuries gone by, who, convinced of the superiority of their faith and their god, approached those they wished to missionize in friendship and helped them out of pity, always with the intention of passing on their own religion, their own weltanschauung, and their own morals and values.

The aforementioned accountability report on the local schools also indicates that the controls exerted on all teachers, but particularly the student teachers, hindered an unprejudiced encounter between pupils and teachers and encouraged instead misunderstanding and distance. It was assumed that Angolan schools harbored unknown "dangers" for young Cubans because the Angolan pupils confronted their teachers with "ideologically awkward" questions during class. The Angolan pupils—the same pupils who were described as "unruly and lazy" just a few paragraphs earlier—were, according to the report, "extremely curious" and never tired of quizzing their Cuban teachers. They asked about daily life in Cuba, about Cuban laws, the economy, and so forth. Questions about religion in Cuba seemed to come up with particular frequency. The authors of the report were only able (or only wanted) to interpret such questions as an expression of "diversionist tendencies" to spread "imperialism."[146] Without realizing it, they were actually describing what seems to be a perfectly normal classroom encounter. It is obvious that the children and adolescents were curious. The world that Cuban teachers inhabited was completely unfamiliar to them, and they were anxious to find out about it, learn from it, and compare it to the reality of their own lives. As one of the student teachers put it in her own written memoirs,

> I was very excited about meeting my Angolan pupils for the first time. The lack of education during colonial times meant that they were aged between ten and sixteen. They all showed a lot of interest, and they were even inquisitive about having teachers of a different nationality; they were hungry to learn something new. . . . All of them . . . wanted to hear the Cuban teachers speaking Portuguese with their mispronunciation . . . and everybody laughed at the obvious confusion that this caused. . . . Despite these initial misunderstandings . . . we grew accustomed to one another and over time we became a close collective and had encouraging results.[147]

In the eyes of the administration, such normal classroom situations conjured up a major threat to political consciousness, and that threat had to be eliminated. The administration reacted to fraternization between Cubans and Angolans by imposing even greater controls. The authors of the report insisted that much more intensive political and ideological work had to be done with the student teachers in order to prepare them to respond appropriately in such situations.[148] Unfortunately, there is no record of how the Cuban student teachers answered their pupils' questions about everyday life and religion in Cuba.

This is a good juncture for presenting some of the memories former Angolan pupils and students recalled about their Cuban teachers. In general, all the former pupils whom I interviewed had positive memories of their Cuban teachers and their new teaching methods. They were, however, well aware in retrospect that lessons also served to educate and influence them ideologically. In class, the Cuban teachers had apparently been much more interesting and flexible than the Angolan teachers, and they had been less strict. The Angolan pupils appreciated the great commitment of the Cuban teachers and the way that they had sympathized with their pupils and taken much more care of their well-being than the Angolan teachers. All my interviewees came to the similar conclusion that the Cuban teachers had treated their pupils in a friendly manner and had even allowed them to contribute their own suggestions on how lessons should be conducted.[149] "The Cubans did at least educate a generation of Angolans," said one interviewee.[150] Another took a very pragmatic approach. According to him, the Angolan pupils had no choice. In principle, they were all happy to have any chance of an education. It had been a choice between accepting the Cuban teachers or not going to school at all.[151]

My interviewees who were taught by Cubans in the upper grades of secondary school or at the university also recalled controversial political discussions and political misunderstandings they had with Cubans. In pre-university secondary school and higher education, the Angolan pupils and students considered their Cuban teachers and lecturers to be very politically "narrow minded." They claimed that during the transition period between colonialism and independence, they had become accustomed to much more open debate, and they were always amazed at the force with which the Cubans insisted on their worldview.[152]

The new educational concepts such as the monitor system, the interest groups, and the extracurricular activities seemed to have been very popular among primary-school children.[153] They particularly appreciated the teaching methods. In mathematics, for example, the Cuban teachers were more interested in their pupils finding the correct answer and did not insist that there was only one correct way to derive the result, as had been the case in colonial times.[154] A physics teacher and Catholic priest from the southeastern province of Kuando Kubango explained to me that he had started school during the colonial period and had always been very poor at natural science because his teachers had not been able to teach lessons properly. If it had not been for his Cuban teachers, he would never have understood physics, and he was still thankful that they had come in those days to his remote community to teach.[155]

The majority of former pupils did not consider the language difference between Spanish and Portuguese to have been particularly serious. On the contrary, it had led to comic situations in class and, if anything, had only caused the teachers embarrassment. Nevertheless, the Cubans' lack of language skills did on occasion trigger protests, particularly among secondary-school pupils in the capital. Other interviewees relativized the situation and noted that the communication problems they had with Cubans were nothing in comparison with the problems they had with Vietnamese or Bulgarian teachers.[156]

One former pupil recalled that the entire class had presumed Cuba to be a huge country because they had heard on the radio that it was in a position to fight against a superpower like the United States and still send troops, doctors, and so many teachers to Angola. When their geography teacher drew a map of Cuba on the board, they had at first refused to believe that it was just a small island.[157] Two other pupils recalled wondering about the poor living standards of their Cuban teachers. They had not been well dressed nor had they lived in nice houses. The pupils therefore felt sorry for them and would take small gifts to them, which they always accepted gratefully.[158] The pupils noticed that the Cubans were "crazy" about jeans. And so they "often gave them a pair of jeans as a present," which pleased the Cuban teachers more than anything else. But in his particular school, added one of my interviewees with a wink, there had not been any "jeans corruption" as such, where pupils had been able to "buy" their grades with a pair of denims.[159]

The Angolan education institutions, the MED and its Provincial Directorates, were also generally pleased with the work of the Cuban teachers—partly because they were well aware that they depended on the Cuban teachers' help to reform education.[160] Without them many schools would not have been able to offer classes at all. Nevertheless, education specialists, education policy makers, and officials repeatedly pointed out the failings of the cooperation program. They claimed that the Cuban teachers' work was anything but consistent, and by no means did all teachers have the necessary training and experience to provide high-quality instruction. The internal competition system came in for particular criticism. The Angolan education institutions complained that the Cuban teachers gave their pupils inflated grades for the sole purpose of meeting the criteria of the competition. This was, they maintained, very detrimental to teaching quality and the learning achievements of pupils.[161]

It proved very difficult, however, for the Angolan ministry to make a proper assessment of the quality of the Cuban teachers' work, because the education institutions did not keep a full record of the situation at schools and universities. In the mid-1980s, there was vociferous criticism within the ministry that the Angolans had depended too much on the control system of the Cubans.[162] As previously mentioned, the deployment of the student-teacher brigades met with great criticism and was regarded by the Angolans simply as an "emergency stopgap."[163]

To summarize, the strict regulation of their own internal organization, to which the Cuban teachers had to adhere, informed encounters at school between Cubans and Angolans and prevented the Cubans from penetrating deeper into the reality of Angolan school life. Encounters and exchanges were further hampered by the ideology behind cooperation, the missionary calling to disseminate revolutionary ideals, and the teachers' image of themselves as belonging to a superior culture. In general, pupils and teachers remained foreign to each other. The distance that the Cubans felt toward the Angolans is documented in official reports and in the student teachers' collective diaries, which deal almost exclusively with internal matters. The teachers concentrated their efforts on doing their duty; those responsible for the cooperation program in education focused on controlling the conduct of their own aid workers. Observations about school life concentrated on Cuban concerns and lacked any form of self-reflection on Cuban activity. The authors of the reports never once considered that the poor performance of Angolan pupils could be due to communication problems preventing them from following lessons, or to war trauma and social problems. Nor did they consider that many pupils had to work so that their families could make ends meet, or that they were ill and suffering from malnutrition.

Was Cuban engagement therefore more about Cubans raising their own profile, in the sense that their endeavors and work appeared all the more worthy if they depicted the working environment as difficult and demanding? Were the negative depictions of Angolan pupils and Angolan reality nothing more than a surface onto which the Cubans could project their own efforts in an even more positive light? If this assumption is correct, it is little wonder that there was scarcely any opportunity for intercultural understanding and for overcoming feelings of alienation. From a Cuban perspective, the Angolans were mere recipients of the values that they themselves regarded as positive. Within this context, the Cubans were limited in their attempts to understand "the other." Any critical reflection upon their own actions would have necessarily led to a change in their own behavior—which was neither intended nor desired.

Such a conclusion, however, is contradicted by the stark contrast between the perceptions of teachers and pupils. This contrast owes itself to the obvious success that the Cuban teachers had in imparting knowledge to their Angolan pupils using modern teaching methods that were far more effective than any colonial instruction. There was, however, another reason why the presence of Cuban teachers was regarded so positively. Against a social background that was marked by war, poverty, and insecurity, their—comparatively—committed and motivating lessons provided a glimmer of hope for the future. For the school children, the ideology behind the teachers' dedication was of no importance. What they cared about was education, knowledge, and social improvement.

All my Angolan interviewees did indeed manage to better their social situation thanks to the new education system, and not least thanks to the instruction given by Cubans. They became teachers themselves or even university lecturers, businessmen, professionals, artists, or priests. This leads to the conclusion that, at least in some cases, education reform and cooperation were successful as an inclusive and integrative means of creating a new social identity. Seen in this light, education reform and cooperation also appear to have contributed to the establishment of a new social order and to the political restructuring of Angola—even if the originally propounded aim of creating a socialist society had already disappeared from the political agenda by the mid-1980s.

This microanalysis has shown that the processes of education and instruction that were set in motion after independence could not be entirely determined and monitored by the central authorities (of either Cuba or Angola). At the school level, although these processes were directed by the officials, there was also space for individual interests to take hold. The education mission may well have been dominated by ideology and a sense of calling, and Cuban teachers may well have been teaching at the behest of the MPLA government. But it was nevertheless an open-ended process that also generated ambivalent results because the individuals involved used the chance of education to their own ends. The example of Cuban-Angolan cooperation in education is no exception. Not even the Cuban "success story" of revolutionary education was a linear process that automatically created "new men." It too was marked by inconsistencies, failures, and setbacks, and it too was appropriated by individuals. Similar ambivalent conclusions have been drawn in other studies of comparable education missions that took place in different cultural contexts and ages, during which peoples were to be integrated into a (new) social order through the agency of new values and patterns of conduct. These studies likewise highlight the processes of appropriation in gaining an education, and the interaction of acceptance and resistance that are inherent in such missions.[164]

Love

Many of those who engaged in Angola, both civilians and soldiers, found themselves in emotional and psychological turmoil during their stay. This was not only due to the fears and tensions of war. The majority had to leave their families and partners behind in Cuba and face one to two years of separation. The everyday life of civilians in Angola was organized to ensure that community life in the Cuban enclaves offered a type of surrogate family, a piece of "home," and an emotional and psychological haven. The postal service set up especially for the Cuban military and civilians delivered their letters to and from Angola within several days, giving everyone the opportunity to keep in touch with their families and partners at least in writing. They were also granted annual leave, which helped to shorten the period of separation. However, these provisions were not enough to bridge the gap emotionally. Very few could cope with the fact that, in addition to being so far away physically and culturally, they were also isolated emotionally. These feelings of alienation and homesickness were exacerbated by the constant tension and fear of attack. Many Cubans therefore tried to compensate for their emotional imbalance by having love affairs during their stay in Angola, above all within their own ranks. During my research in Cuba, the United States, and Angola, the eyewitnesses I interviewed frequently mentioned and hinted at sexual affairs, romantic liaisons, and long-term relationships during their stay in Angola between Cubans, and between Cubans and Angolans. I was left with the impression that this was a highly emotive issue that deserved to be treated in its own section. I admit that I cannot provide any concrete facts, but I can illustrate obvious tendencies and outline how people perceived each other.

The need for sexual satisfaction was another reason why civilians and soldiers, who were generally very young, sought and found partners in Angola. The topic of love, sexuality, and partnership within the context of Cuban engagement in Angola is still off limits today. Nevertheless, many of my interviewees indicated that affairs and romantic liaisons were part of the everyday agenda. Many spoke at least to some extent about this topic, though most of them very coyly, dropping hints or mentioning it in passing. Most interviewees only spoke of their affairs after I had turned the recorder off; some showed me photos that demonstrated clearly without the need for words that partnerships and sexual relationships existed in Angola. According to the recollections of my interviewees, affairs among Cubans were commonplace, but they also existed between Cubans and Angolans, even though Cuban-Angolan liaisons were generally discouraged if not directly forbidden. A few of the men I interviewed were more open about their relationships and sexual experiences with Angolan women.[165] The women I interviewed only spoke about relationships they had with Cubans, though they did speak of other Cuban women involved with Angolan men.[166]

As already indicated, the Cuban Civil Administration introduced regulations aimed at restricting relationships and sexual contact, both among Cubans and with Angolans or other foreigners. Although I was unable to access the explicit written regulations on this subject, statements by my interviewees and a few passages found in written documents clearly show the existence of such restrictions and prohibitions.[167] Strict rules regarding visitors and the right to leave the compounds, along with extensive social controls within them, were used to monitor and check such “outside relationships” among the aid workers.

The Cuban government was well aware that restrictions on taking spouses to Angola meant that a solution needed to be found for the emotional and sexual needs of civilians and soldiers, particularly in view of the imbalance between the number of men and women involved in Angola. Restrictions on relationships both in the military and civil sphere were primarily intended to prevent sexual contact between Cubans and Angolans.

By preventing such sexual contact, the government also hoped to stop diseases, particularly sexually transmittable ones, that might spread to Cuba from Africa. At the beginning of cooperation with Angola, AIDS was still unknown, but there were plenty of other (known and unknown) sexually transmitted diseases.[168] Anyone leaving for Angola or returning to Cuba from Angola received a strict medical examination. After the discovery of HIV and its transmission at the beginning of the 1980s, the health checks became even more stringent, particularly because HIV was thought to have come from Africa. From 1983 onward, civilians and soldiers were already being tested for HIV in Luanda in a medical laboratory set up especially for this purpose before being allowed to return to Cuba.[169] The students from the student-teacher brigades, most of whom were minors, received intensive education about the dangers of sexually transmitted diseases before setting out for Angola. Again, they were not directly forbidden from having relationships with Angolans, but it was hoped that their awareness of sexually transmitted diseases would act as a preventative measure.[170] Partly because of this, the students were also under much stricter regulations regarding visitors and the right to leave the compounds than other civilians.[171]

Another reason for restrictions was that Cuban aid workers were supposed to be moral role models for the Angolans. They were to represent the Cuban Revolution not only in ideology and politics but even more so in a cultural and civilizing sense. Revolutionary morality implied exemplary social behavior incorporating discipline, responsibility, and abstinence. The "new men" of the Cuban Revolution, and more particularly those "chosen" for the engagement in Angola, had to live up to being in the political and moral vanguard, and this included sexual matters. Those working in education were particularly affected. It was necessary to avoid "immoral" sexual behavior (i.e., frequent sexual contact with Angolans and the possible consequences, such as pregnancy and sexually transmitted disease). It was also essential to prevent any sexual abuse of Angolan women at all costs. The male *cooperantes* were instructed to "respect Angolan woman," which implied that the Cuban Civil Administration would investigate and punish any sexual assaults on Angolan women.[172] After all, the prestige of the entire Cuban cooperation was at stake.[173]

Considerations of its reputation aside, the Cuban government really was anxious to prevent the sexual abuse of Angolan women. During my research I was unable to ascertain how frequently sexual violence by Cuban military personnel or civilians against Angolan women occurred. I only found one case in the files of the Angolan Ministry of Education, which dealt with a complaint made to the school's governing board by female Angolan pupils against their young Cuban teacher. According to the girls, they had failed a biology exam and the teacher had offered to allow them to pass if they agreed to sleep with him. The records do not, however, say whether the teacher was disciplined for his behavior.[174] On the basis of another account given by a former soldier, I was able to deduce that there were cases in which Angolan women living near Cuban bases prostituted themselves in return for a small sum of money or food.[175] Neither of these cases indicates that such events were commonplace. Some of the Angolans I interviewed also commented on the sexual behavior of the Cubans and implied that particularly among Angolan women, Cuban men had a reputation for "making babies and then disappearing."[176] Such fleeting sexual encounters definitely took place, and the Cuban men did disappear at the end of their stint, generally never to return again. But it remains unclear how many children were born as a result of such affairs. None of my Angolan interviewees could give me exact details, and I was unable to find any evidence that it was a common phenomenon.

Restrictions on sexual relations applied not only to Angolans but also to other foreigners working in Angola, particularly from nonsocialist countries. The fear was that Cubans involved intimately with foreigners might divulge political and organizational details about the Cuban cooperation program.[177] Both military and civil cooperation in Angola were treated as top secret because of their political sensitivity at the time of the Cold War.[178] Again the restrictions were particularly stringent for the student teachers, as the organizers considered their revolutionary consciousness unstable and distrusted the strength of their ideological commitment.[179] Such restrictions, however, were not limited to Angola: in the 1970s and 1980s, out of fear of enemy spies, the Cuban government forbade Cubans to form intimate relationships or even friendships with foreigners from nonsocialist countries.

Intimate relations and sexual contact among Cubans, however, were permitted. It was only in the student brigades that the organizers made sure that the young men and women were housed separately in rooms or flats. This formal segregation according to gender revealed a real concern. Many of these students were still minors and their parents had handed responsibility for them to the Cuban government. Such responsibility included ensuring the sexual propriety of the many young women, even though there is no specific mention of this in any document.

The topic of sexuality and particularly female sexuality was also tabooed in Cuban society in the 1970s and 1980s. The traditional expectations regarding gender roles had changed little since the revolution. In contrast to the men, females were expected to show sexual restraint, and women who became pregnant outside marriage were socially stigmatized. The active equality policies that the government developed in cooperation with the federation of Cuban women (FMC) concentrated mainly on the promotion of women's productivity and had little effect on the many social inequalities Cuban women faced in their daily lives.[180] Many mothers probably sent their daughters to Angola with the same words of warning they had heard from their own mothers when they joined the literacy campaign at the beginning of the 1960s: "One goes; two return."[181] The rules concerning pregnancy were clear: any woman who became pregnant in Angola had to break off her stay and return to Cuba.[182]

It would seem that many of the underage and generally unattached members of the student brigades had their first sexual encounters during their stay in Angola. The majority of them had left home for the first time, and their stay in Angola with a large number of their peers offered a lot of space for experimentation. This applied particularly to the female members. Many of them regarded their stint in Angola as a decisive test of their maturity, including sexual maturity. Many of them fell in love for the first time and had their first sexual experience with members of their group or with other Cubans. In the memoirs of the brigade members, feelings and emotions occupied an important place. These memoirs revolve around the fears the students had to overcome, the "adventures" they experienced, their romances, their tests of courage, and the problems that existed within their groups. The memoirs are also full of longing for parents, family, and friends, and the considerable fear caused by the permanent threat of war and alienation—feelings for which many sought to compensate through affairs and relationships.[183]

The recollections of other civilians also show that affairs and sexual contact among Cubans were commonplace in Angola. My Cuban-exile interviewee Alcibíades Hidalgo went as far as to speak of a mass phenomenon. In Cuba, he said, there had even been a special expression to describe such relations: the "Angolan marriage."[184] According to Hidalgo's description and to accounts from other interviewees, these were often just short-term affairs between Cubans, which they entered into during their stay in Angola, regardless of whether they were married or not.[185] The psychological and emotional burden felt by those working in Angola was so heavy that many of them—perhaps even the majority—sought a temporary partner.[186] According to two interviewees who had worked in the Cuban embassy in Luanda, "many" also married in Angola.[187]

There seems to have been a parallel phenomenon of "mass" infidelity among the partners left behind in Cuba. Many of those who were left behind—primarily the wives of soldiers—entered temporary relationships while their partners were absent. Involvement in Angola therefore had an obvious impact on the institution of marriage and on Cuban family structures. A great many marriages failed and many families were torn apart because of the long absence of family members.[188] The rise in divorce rates in Cuba from the mid-1970s may well be linked to Cuba's involvement in Angola, though there are no studies to corroborate this.[189] Several of my interviewees brought to my attention that these marital crises were exacerbated by the Communist Party's meddling in the private affairs of families affected by involvement in Angola. Apparently, the Party monitored the private lives of their members both in Cuba and Angola. If they found that anyone was being unfaithful, they would report the affair to the spouse and demand that they separate from their partner or leave the Party. I was told that this policy had led to considerable protest and above all to mass exodus from the Party by couples who when faced with this ultimatum opted to remain together. The general consensus seemed to be that the Party had no business meddling in private affairs. Involvement in Angola was problematic enough, my interviewees said, without the Party making things worse by divulging infidelity.[190] The Party apparently responded to this sentiment and abandoned the practice at the end of the 1970s.[191]

Within the military, special strategies were developed in order to prevent sexual crises among the soldiers. A journalist writing for the *Verde Olivo* magazine visited Cuban military camps between 1988 and 1991 while investigating the Angolan war. According to her reports, porn movies were shown on a regular basis to prevent sexual frustration among the soldiers.[192] One of my male interviewees, who was involved in civil cooperation, indicated to me that the sexual frustration of Cuban men in Angola was relieved by the arrival of the many young, female Cuban teachers from 1978 onward.[193] Female interviewees who belonged to the student brigades or who went to Angola as young women confirmed that many of them had liaisons with Cuban soldiers (and civilians).[194] Is it possible that the female aid workers who came to work as teachers and nurses had a dual role to play as sexual partners for the Cuban soldiers and for their male colleagues? There is good reason to presume that this "side effect" was indeed intentional on the part of the cooperation organizers. It allowed the troops to satisfy their sexual needs within the Cuban community and prevented sexual contact with Angolan women. The extent to which female soldiers (who constituted 5 percent of the Cuban force in Angola) were affected remains unclear.

The alienation felt by Cubans confronted with nakedness and polygamy in Angola was a further topic that both my male and female interviewees frequently addressed. They generally described the phenomena in stereotypic terms and considered them examples of cultural and social backwardness. Especially my male interviewees described again and again how the Angolan woman had thought nothing of parading around with naked breasts, particularly in rural areas.[195] Some described how they felt alienated and confused by such nakedness, and how they thought such behavior improper. The detailed recollections of what these men perceived as scantily clad female bodies seem to indicate that the Cuban men must have been sexually aroused by them, even though obviously no one explicitly said so. In Cuba there had been no gender training or any type of cultural awareness instruction to prepare participants for the peculiarities and customs of Angolan culture.

Many of the Cubans interviewed also discussed in detail the common practice of polygamy in Angola, using the occasion to dismiss what they perceived as a completely "backward" form of relationship. Only one linguist and anthropologist who had been part of a Cuban-Angolan scientific research project was able to explain to me the cultural and historical origins of polygamy in Southern Central Africa. When my male interviewees expressed their views on polygamy and explicitly distanced themselves from the patriarchal behavior of Angolan men, double standards became evident.[196] Indeed, the many sexual relationships male Cubans appear to have had during their stay in Angola certainly contradict the tendency to condemn polygamy and dominant male behavior in Angola and suggest that the revolution had fallen short of eradicating patriarchal behavior in Cuban culture, despite the fact that this topic was never really discussed publicly.[197]

Despite all the Cuban prohibitions and restrictions on contact between Cubans and Angolans, and despite the Cubans' negative reactions to and rejection of the gender roles in Angolan society, Cuban-Angolan cooperation did lead to friendships, love affairs between Cubans and Angolans, and even Cuban-Angolan marriages. Cubans working in Angola used the few opportunities they had to make personal contact with Angolans and to pursue their own aims in life. Marriage to a foreigner was (and still is) one of the few legal ways of settling outside Cuba without having to flee and without the risk of losing citizenship. An employee of the Cuban embassy in Luanda who was responsible for all consular and registrar activity regarding civilians and soldiers working in Angola maintained that while she was working there (1982–1984) there were "frequent" marriages between Cubans and Angolans. According to her statement, the marriages were mainly between Cuban women and Angolan men. Another interviewee, who worked between 1987 and 1989 as a secretary in the Cuban embassy, confirmed the existence of Cuban-Angolan marriages.[198] But they could give neither exact numbers nor more exact details regarding gender. It therefore remains unclear how many of these marriages were between Cubans and how many of them were mixed Cuban-Angolan marriages. Two of my male interviewees, one an Angolan and the other a Cuban, are married to Cuban and Angolan partners, respectively. Both of them confirmed that Cuban-Angolan marriages were "more common" than might be expected but not "massive" in number.[199]

These two Cuban-Angolan marriages provide the basis for this section's concluding remarks because they illustrate that close relationships did grow out of cooperation and that both parties used the situation in the other country to attain individual goals. Both marriages are unusual cases in that they represent personal "success stories" and involve people who were and are in privileged positions. But they are also "typical" in that both couples used the privilege of a binational marriage to settle in Angola. My interviewees were an Angolan man who has been married for over thirty years to a Cuban, and a Cuban man who has been married for almost the same length of time to an Angolan. Both were in privileged positions when they met their respective wives (i.e., they were not subjected to the usual restrictions regarding whom they could meet and when they could go out). This obviously made it easier for them to get to know and love their partners. The Angolan interviewee was one of the first forty students who from 1976 were able to study education science at the Instituto Superior Pedagógico "Enrique José Varona" in Havana. He met his future Cuban wife during his studies there. His situation was different from the thousands of Angolan pupils and students who attended the boarding schools and colleges on the Isle of Youth, where the young Angolans remained for the most part among themselves far from the Cuban population. With the exception of 1980 to 1986, when my interviewee worked on the Isle of Youth as a coordinating teacher responsible for Angolan pupils, the couple has lived mainly in Angola, where my interviewee is now a professor in a private university in Luanda. One of his three children completed studies in Cuba ("because education there is so good and cheap"), and the family still maintains contact with relatives living in Cuba.[200]

The Cuban interviewee married to an Angolan was one of twelve education specialists sent to Cabinda in 1976 as part of a military-civilian pilot project to promote literacy and establish the cooperative education program. During his first stay, he met his Angolan wife, whom he married in Luanda in 1978. The then head of the Civil Administration acted as their witness, which suggests that at this level at least Cuban-Angolan marriages were officially tolerated. Since their marriage, they have lived mainly in Angola because they were and still are in a better financial position there than in Cuba. My interviewee still works for the Ministry of Education in the department of education research, where he is responsible for the geography curriculum and school books. He told me that he had not been to Cuba for twenty-five years and now felt Angolan. When we were in the company of Angolans he spoke to me exclusively in Portuguese, apparently not wishing to be identified as Cuban in public; when we were on our own, he switched to Spanish. According to what he said, he no longer had any official ties with the Cuban embassy in Angola. I understood this to mean that he wished to distance himself from the Cuban government because, as he clearly indicated to me, he would very much like to travel to Cuba, "but not under the current climate."[201]

Trauma

When I evaluated the interviews I conducted with the "ordinary" participants of the cooperation, I was struck by the preponderance of negative memories that they had of their stints in Angola. In all interview situations, the negative feelings and perceptions of their time in Angola considerably outweighed any positive recollections. Having been socialized in revolutionary Cuba and exposed to information propagated by the state, many of my interviewees were able to provide a rational, materialist analysis of the sociopolitical and military situation in Angola. On an abstract level, they could name the causes of violence, conflict, and poverty. They often provided detached situational analyses during the interviews and repeatedly asserted that they had fulfilled their "internationalist duty." Nevertheless, they remembered their stay in Angola as a traumatic and shocking experience. As they recalled their feelings, their fear, and the traumatic situations with which they were confronted, many found that words failed them: they fell silent, changed the subject, or began to cry.

The overall accumulation of negative feelings and memories stems primarily from the aforementioned omnipresence of war and the resulting direct and indirect violence that my interviewees faced. These experiences were often linked to situations in which the participants could sense the latent hostility from parts of the Angolan population. Such feelings were manifest during these interviews in the frequent mention of the *cuacha* phenomenon, and the insecurity my interviewees had felt not knowing whether the person they were dealing with was "friend" or "foe." The aid workers' negative perceptions, however, were not limited to life-threatening scenarios. Their disturbing depictions of normal daily life and work gave an even more vivid impression of the discomfort that they felt when remembering Angola, as did their observations of Angolan life and their encounters with an environment they found full of unfathomable, alien symbols and cultural practices. Many of them suffered from culture shock, which, rather than abating with time, was exacerbated by the constantly looming threat of violence and conflict. The feelings of culture shock and rejection in this extreme social environment of violence and poverty culminated in personal crises in the form of homesickness, illness, psychological stress, anxiety, and feelings of helplessness. Just by listing the individual memories in which my interviewees talked of trauma, cultural shock, and the resulting personal crises, I was able to see that almost all my interviewees at some point during their stay in Angola suffered from some form of psychological or psychosomatic illness.

Written accounts from the internal working and accountability reports of the Cuban Civil Administration also confirm that Cuban civilians suffered from depression and anxiety as a result of the violence they experienced during their work in Angola and the exceptional circumstances in which they found themselves.[202] Several of my interviewees spoke of post-traumatic disorders, such as anxiety attacks and delusions, with which they struggled on their return to Cuba.[203] The clearest example of such a long-term, post-traumatic disorder is the aforementioned "national flag trauma," from which three of my female interviewees suffered. All three spoke of being incapable even today of controlling their emotions when faced with the Cuban national flag or national anthem because they always brought to mind the coffins of the Cubans who had fallen in Angola.[204]

In the following paragraphs, further examples of memories that were recounted during the interviews illustrate how experiences of violence, insecurity, and culture shock had a cumulative effect. These examples only refer to the war indirectly and reflect either daily observations or experiences made during encounters with Angolans.

Many of my interviewees recalled having been particularly shocked by the sight of the many neglected, sick, and begging children, whom they often portrayed in stereotypical terms. Time and again they called up memories of scores of children rummaging through the rubbish, particularly outside the Cuban compounds because they knew that they would always be able to find something to eat there.[205] A mathematics teacher who worked in Angola between 1983 and 1985 and who had left her small son behind in Cuba said that one of her most lasting impressions of Angola was "the hungry children searching for food in the trashcans."[206]

A professor of agricultural science who worked between 1978 and 1980 at the university in Huambo remembered the following situation: "The poverty was so extreme that I was shocked; . . . we weren't used to that in Cuba. . . . At every mealtime dozens of children would come to our canteen . . . and beg; . . . it was a terrible scene; the children peered through the windows begging and starving and we sat inside eating. . . . Everybody gave them something to eat, but we couldn't give them everything. . . . We ended up eating in our own rooms."[207]

Such experiences of hunger and child poverty not only stood in stark contrast to Cuba; they also put to the test the most fundamental values and highest ideals of revolutionary Cuban society, according to which children and youths were to be cared for and respected as an investment in the future. During their work in Angola, the Cuban teachers and doctors were expected to disseminate and defend this primary civilizatory and cultural tenet.

In addition to starvation, the Cubans also witnessed the outbreak of epidemics, for example cholera, which were preventable and which led to massive loss of life. They also saw the spread of other common illnesses that could have been treated prophylactically.[208] Such accounts underline how helpless the interviewees felt in the face of prevailing circumstances in Angola.

Linked to the above was the alienation and even disgust that Cubans felt when confronted with the Angolan attitudes toward death. Several of my interviewees recalled death being celebrated "as if it were a happy event." The interviewees' accounts seem to be based on their observations of traditional, public and expressive death rituals, which originated from local religions and traditions and offered an extreme counterpoint to the way death was treated in Cuban culture. Despite the official atheism and secularization of Cuban society introduced by the revolutionary state, the death and funeral rites practiced in Cuba during the 1970s and 1980s were strongly influenced by Catholicism and Occidental, Christian ideas. They included a period of quiet, private mourning at the loss of a family member.[209] Some of the observations on death in Angola were made by doctors who were shocked by the alien and unfamiliar treatment of death even though they claimed that by dint of their profession they were accustomed to treating death in a rational and "technical" manner.[210] According to the recollections of my interviewees, their feelings of alienation grew with their realization that far less importance seemed to be attached to the death of a child than to the death of an adult or old person.

According to one doctor who had worked at a hospital in Luanda from 1987 to 1989,

> When a child died, rites were performed in the hospital that I as a pediatrician found shocking, because this was after all a child whose life we had tried to save, and then they treated it like that. . . . It was beyond our comprehension, because we go about it completely differently, and the way they dealt with their dead children always shocked us. . . . They had a strange way of expressing joy at the sight of death. . . . I'll never forget those things. Not a single tear was shed [but rather] they danced, jumped about, others shouted or sang, and they stood around the dead body

> applauding. . . . They did everything except cry. One of the Angolan nurses explained to us that the ceremony depended on the villages they came from. . . . We knew nothing about it.[211]

A professor of engineering who worked at the university in Luanda between 1981 and 1982 recalled the impression that funeral rites had left on him: "I was once invited to the funeral of the young daughter of one of my students. . . . We celebrated, drank coffee and spirits while the dead child was lying in bed upstairs. . . . Then we went to the cemetery to bury her; I was quite shocked by it. It wasn't the death that shocked me, but the indifference toward death."[212]

A pediatrician who worked at a hospital in the coastal town of Sumbe between 1987 and 1990 had similar traumatic experiences with the deaths of children. She too interpreted Angolan behavior as "indifference" toward children and their death:

> It was always hard when a child died and you couldn't do anything about it . . . because when a child dies here in Cuba, it means something. . . . But it meant nothing there. Sometimes we lost thirteen, fourteen children in one night. There were lots of illnesses there that don't exist in Cuba, . . . measles, tetanus, cholera. . . . The death of a child was something normal . . . but when they died there was no big family celebration to mourn them, but there was for old people. . . . When a child died, the family bought themselves food; a death was a happy event for a family, because there was lots to eat. . . . For a Cuban, on the other hand, there is nothing worse than the death of a child.[213]

My interviewees conveyed feelings of helplessness when they spoke of what they perceived as senseless death and the cultural rites that showed "indifference" toward the loss of life. Their feelings have to be interpreted in the light of their experiences with the fallen Cuban soldiers. The Angolan ceremonies, which to their minds expressed "indifference" or even "joy" in the face of death, sharply contrasted with their own way of dealing with death. Their formative cultural background had taught Cubans to treat human life and the life of a child with respect, and their humanism also required them to save life at the risk of their own. Seen in this light, not only did the Angolans fail to share their sentiments, but their alien ceremonies were even an affront to the piety of the observers.

Faced with such "indifference" toward death, the Cubans must have seen the sacrifices that they made for the Angolans and in Angola as absurd. The aforementioned pediatrician concluded her depiction of death in Angola with the following words: "We Cubans believe in solidarity . . . but for us solidarity doesn't mean death, but helping to bring about a change for the better."[214] She was referring particularly to the deaths of children and Cuban soldiers. Her statement is significant on two levels. First, she more or less openly criticized the outcome of Cuba's engagement in Angola, which stood in no relation to the number of casualties it claimed. Second, she expressed something that many other interviewees expressed too: a retrospective self-affirmation and confirmation that all the personal sacrifice they made was not in vain, but that their engagement had served a just cause. Such affirmations represent the only possibility of remembrance that the official Cuban politics of memory allow. It became obvious during my interviews that my interviewees tended to fall back on these affirmations whenever they needed to relativize negative, personal experiences and hide their own feelings of helplessness. After all, those who were "chosen" to go to Angola had been charged with a task of national importance and were committed to success. Moreover, these affirmations seem to function as verbal lifelines that prevent the participants from drowning in their personal trauma and allow them retrospectively to embed their sacrifices within a meaningful biographical and "authorized" social context.

For the majority of my interviewees, our conversation was their first opportunity to talk to someone other than family and friends about their perceptions and feelings during their engagement in Angola. Even today, engagement in Angola remains a tabooed subject in the Cuban public sphere. There is no tolerance of any narrative that might contradict the government's official interpretation of engagement as a success story. The official politics of memory define the permitted "collective memory," which up to the present day (almost) exclusively recalls the military operation and the heroes and martyrs it produced. The casualties of the engagement are shrouded at best in questionable symbolism and myths. Such myth-making is manifest, for example, in statements such as Castro's claim on the thirtieth anniversary of the beginning of Cuban involvement in Angola that "Cuban and Angolan blood" had mixed together on Angolan soil.[215]

The official narrative leaves no space for personal fates and traumatic memories. This makes the results of my interviews all the more surprising. When I evaluated the memories expressed in my presence, I found that the cumulative result was far more disturbing than I had expected considering the tabooed nature of the topic. The negative and traumatic recollections of the eyewitnesses are clearly inconsistent with the official version of events. For the first time, they provide an angle from which Cuba's engagement in Angola could be interpreted as a failure. Although the interviews contain the memories and experiences of individuals, taken together they combine to form a "memory community." When I evaluated the interviews, I therefore realized that the memories could indeed be regarded as representative for what had lodged itself in the communicative memory of the former participants. Many of them had been unable to cope with the challenges they faced in Angola. This and the sacrifices that were made in Angola even led several interviewees to doubt whether the entire venture made sense.[216]

It is true that not all my interviewees were traumatized to the same extent. Some had perhaps managed to repress their negative feelings and experiences or were unable during the interview to express what they had encountered. This attitude was reinforced by their status as "chosen ones," which made it all the more difficult for them to reflect on the trauma they had experienced. To admit having been afraid would come close to admitting personal failure and to being "nothing special." Nevertheless, during most of my conversations there was a clear indication of the participants' fear, helplessness, and inability to cope in the face of the overwhelming objective problems that existed.

The difficulty some of my interviewees had in finding the right words, and their inability to articulate trauma, feelings of alienation, and impotence, are particularly evident in the narrative pattern of many of the interviews. But through this my interviewees communicated to me for the first time what had previously been "unthinkable," unsaid, and unheard. This narrative pattern also revealed that there was a layer of meaning below the level of language—and perhaps even below the level of consciousness. In the aforementioned interview extracts dealing with experiences of war, violence, and alienation, I have tried to depict examples of the narrative structure of the memories. One feature of these memories is that they were never told in a linear fashion. The interviewees constantly interrupted their narration by reaffirming that they had felt "good" or by restating that through their personal engagement they had been fulfilling an important humanitarian and revolutionary duty in the name of solidarity. Their constant insistence on their dedication to the aims of the engagement jars alongside their traumatic memories of war and the threatening and alienating environment in which they found themselves. The historian Lutz Niethammer refers to such dissonant narrative elements as "scenic" or "anecdotal." According to him, these "narrative molecules of memory" are common when people talk about experiencing something new or of emotional significance. These "scenes" serve as "junctions," or "branches" on the path of memory, which have to be retold time and again, particularly when the experience was a traumatic one.[217]

Niethammer's observation is backed by recent cognitive research on biographical memories of traumatic events and experiences involving violence. According to the research's findings, traumatic experience cannot generally be recalled in a coherent fashion, but is interspersed as "memory fragments" in the narrative. These results also show that in many cases trauma can be remembered consistently, reliably, and in detail.[218] Both findings are confirmed in the interviews I conducted. The interview extracts illustrate that the traumatic experiences proved so powerful that those involved could still relate them to me in detail twenty to twenty-five years later.

As part of an interdisciplinary project, the psychologist Werner Bohleber undertook a study of eyewitness interviews involving soldiers of World War II, survivors of the Holocaust, refugees, and bomb victims. The complex interrelationship between individual and collective memories of traumatic experience led him to a conclusion that can also be applied to the narrative pattern used by those who engaged in Angola when they related their memories. According to Bohleber, such "man-made disasters" as war, the Holocaust, or political persecution aim with their forms of dehumanization to annihilate the historical and social existence of the individual. It is therefore not only crucial that traumatic events be remembered, but also that experiences be publicly debated on a social platform and that events be made transparent through scientific and historical investigation. If a society goes on the defensive or imposes silence, the traumatized victims are left alone with their experience and are unable to restore their shaken confidence in themselves and the world.[219] Bohleber's conclusions therefore indicate that the trauma I witnessed among my interviewees might have resulted not only from their negative experiences during their time in Angola but also from their government's failure to recognize the sacrifices they made.

According to my interviewees, when *cooperantes* had fulfilled their "mission" and had proven themselves reliable and disciplined, they were rewarded on their return to Cuba with a certificate or medal for their commitment. This award marked the official end of their "mission," following which their civil engagement disappeared from public discourse in Cuba. The only official commemoration is reserved for those who took part in military engagement and those who lost their lives in Angola. Monuments and commemorative plaques honor the dead in many of the island's cemeteries, and on 7 December, the official "Day of the Martyrs of the Revolution," all fallen heroes of Cuban history are remembered at cenotaphs in cemeteries throughout the island. The Asociación de Combatientes de la Revolución Cubana (the Association of the Combatants of the Cuban Revolution) is partly responsible for organizing these ceremonies. This association was founded in 1993 and claims to represent the interests of the Cubans who committed themselves to defending the revolution on "revolutionary fronts throughout the world."[220] Although it officially represents the civilians of the worldwide "internationalist missions" too, the commemorative celebrations on 7 December continue to focus on military "heroes."[221]

Bohleber contests that the absence of a general platform of social debate often leaves traumatized victims convinced that they themselves are somehow to blame for events. This does not seem to be true of the civilians traumatized by Angola. Instead, they expressed the conviction that they had acted correctly. Their affirmations and examples of self-confirmation replaced self-blame, particularly because the trauma experienced by civilians in Angola was not directly linked to active participation in the conflict.

Through their self-affirming statements, my interviewees were emphasizing their awareness of serving as special representatives of a historical reality, regardless of whether they performed "heroic deeds" or endured "suffering."[222] Nevertheless, there is no doubt that despite the imposition of silence and taboos, memories of trauma, failure, and impotence during engagement in Angola are still very much alive. Indeed, my interviewees demonstrated that (subversive) discursive strategies have developed in the communicative memory of the Cuban population. While adopting the official interpretation and incorporating it into their personal biographies and accounts of Angola, the participants simultaneously call the official version of events into question. The Cuban songwriter Frank Delgado subtly hints at the neglect and silence that accompanies the official success story of engagement in Angola in his song "Veterano" (Veteran). Of particular interest are the last three lines, which make direct reference to the participants: "But what my people gave in battle, please excuse the adjective, cannot fit on a tin medal."[223]

9

Between Encounter, Dissociation, and Re-Identification

In the previous chapters, the numerous examples of experiences and encounters in Angola revealed phenomena of perception that led to dissociation on both sides. In this chapter, I turn to another phenomenon that became apparent during the analysis of my eyewitness interviews. According to my findings, the experience of Angola and the way Cubans dealt with what was regarded as a different culture led them to reflect on themselves and re-identify themselves with Cuba, superelevating their own culture and society. For the Cuban civil aid workers, spatial separation, culture shock, and the trauma of war and violence turned their engagement in Angola into a confrontation with a culture that they perceived as foreign and threatening. This in turn provoked strongly defensive reactions on their part. Their construction of a new, idealized self-image was based on them distancing themselves from what they perceived, often stereotypically, as "Angola," and included all their negative, positive, and ambivalent experiences. The reaction of Angolans to the Cuban presence demonstrates that the Angolans likewise perceived the Cubans as "alien" and distanced themselves from them. Nevertheless, the Angolans had to come to terms with the Cuban presence and came to the conclusion that, despite everything, they had no choice but to accept the Cubans because they relied on their help and could profit from their know-how.

Based on my findings up to this point, I will analyze self-perceptions and perceptions of "the other" that have not been mentioned before. These new examples demonstrate further divergences, but they also include positive encounters and contact. I analyze the junctures at which Cubans and Angolans dissociated themselves from what they saw as Angolan or Cuban reality (in terms of culture, society, and mentality). I also consider the situations in which they came to appreciate their encounter with the other reality as a positive challenge and managed to turn dissociation into understanding. Sometimes the way the Cubans and Angolans perceived and dealt with each other did not result in a definite positive or negative opinion of the other, but shifted between fascination and alienation.

The positive encounters, which the Cuban interviewees recalled with admiration and even enthusiasm, were exceptions. Although the way Cubans perceived Angolans was influenced by asymmetry, paternalism, and distance, the positive memories demonstrate that there were indeed situations in which they had to accept that Angolans possessed valuable and desirable qualities and abilities that they did not have or with which they were completely unfamiliar. The instances illustrating these phenomena have been selected according to the frequency with which they arose during interview.

"Cousins" or "Good Colonizers"?

As I mentioned at the beginning of this book, I conducted far fewer eyewitness interviews with Angolans than with Cubans. Nonetheless, combined with the written records and documents provided by the Angolan Ministry of Education, the interviews I did record provide an overall impression and show tendencies from the Angolan viewpoint that allow me to make certain assumptions. The strange appearance of the Cuban *cooperantes*, their attitudes, clothing, conduct, and gestures—in short, their habitus—made them appear to the Angolans as a closed, homogenous group of "foreigners." The Angolans therefore frequently referred to them as "the Cubans."[1] Nevertheless, the Angolans did differentiate among the Cuban *cooperantes* in accordance with their specific roles as teachers, colleagues, or advisors, and they accepted or rejected them accordingly.

In their memories and accounts, the Angolans were generally more apt than my Cuban interviewees to emphasize the positive aspects of cooperation. They played down asymmetries and underlined that the Cubans and Angolans were equal. They never, however, expressed effusive gratitude. All the statements demonstrated a very high degree of self-confidence, and both the interviews and written documents frequently refer self-critically to their own deficiencies. The files of the Ministry of Education's Department of International Cooperation often mention the problems with its own internal communication, coordination, organization, and logistics. They also concede just as frequently that Cuban support was positive and above all necessary at many schools to compensate for their own lack of teachers. Although the commitment of the Cubans was generally recognized and respected, the Angolans criticized their attitude, particularly when, from the Angolan perspective, the Cubans failed to keep agreements or took "unilateral" action that was perceived as an infringement of Angolan sovereignty.[2]

The way Cubans were perceived in Angola also had a temporal dimension: over the years their presence seems to have been increasingly called into question. The growing rejection of the Cubans owed itself to political and military developments in Angola and probably also to UNITA nationalist propaganda that labeled the Cubans as "conquerors." At the beginning of cooperation, the Cubans were welcomed by the Angolan population as *primos*, meaning "cousins." Toward the end of cooperation the term *bons colonizadores* ("good colonizers") gained currency.[3] The extent to which spatial or sociocultural aspects supported this change in terminology could not, however, be clarified. The blood ties accorded to the Cubans during the first years of cooperation imply both proximity and distance. Cousins belong to the family, but that does not mean that they are automatically friends. In comparison with the word "cousins," the term "good colonizers" illustrates the increasing distance between the Cubans and the Angolans. Angola had only recently emerged from Portuguese colonialism, and such a label bore negative connotations of colonial supremacy and power. The qualifying "good" does not alter the social status of the "colonizers," though it does indicate that this time colonial practice seems to have been regarded as comparatively positive. According to the statements of several interviewees, the use of this term placed the Cubans close to the "colonial masters." But the Angolans had nevertheless regarded the Cubans as "good" because rather than try to claim power or treat people badly, they had shown the Angolans respect and support. The term "good colonizers" also conceals a mixture of admiration and incomprehension. The Angolans admired the Cubans' courage, their hard work, and their willingness to make sacrifices. On the other hand, they pitied them and were unable to understand that these "good" (in the sense of "good-natured") Cubans had been sent by their own government to a faraway, completely foreign land and had committed themselves to supporting strangers without receiving any material recompense.[4]

Several of my Angolan interviewees agreed that in some respects the Cubans had been better organized than they and in many areas possessed knowledge and experience that was lacking throughout Angola. According to my interviewees, the Cubans introduced a completely new sense of dynamism wherever they worked. Whereas a "living-from-day-to-day" mentality dominated Angolan culture during the transitional period between colonialism and independence, the Cubans had shifted the cultural parameters to include planning, structure, and organization.[5] They had never tried to dominate; they had voiced, backed up, and defended their point of view but never enforced it against the will of the Angolans.[6]

One of my Angolan interviewees, who is now a very successful publisher of Angolan literature, studied journalism at a Cuban university in the 1980s. He did not live separated from Cuban society on the Isle of Youth, but had become familiar with the sociocultural contexts of Cuba. He told me that at that time he had regarded Cuba's socialist model of society as exemplary for the construction of independent Angola. His family had been very poor and he had benefited in every respect from his education in Cuba. He admitted, however, that his education in a communist system had sharpened his critical faculties, and as a result he is able today to distance himself from "extremism." This, he said, was partly due to the prevalence of racism in Cuba. There he had witnessed that Afro-Cubans always had less qualified jobs and the worst housing in comparison with white Cubans. Despite this inequality, there had never been any open debate about racism, which is why my interviewee had regarded the relationship between black and white Cubans as an "artificial union."[7]

Another of my interviewees also emphasized that his position as a lecturer at a private university in Luanda was thanks to the education he had received in Cuba, where he had studied pedagogy on the Isle of Youth. But he too remembered being confronted time and again with racism in Cuba and at times having been called a "nigger" in public. To illustrate the mixture of paternalism and racism to which the African pupils and students were subjected, he described an episode that took place in the school canteen. If ever they had complained about the food—and the food in Cuba had been notoriously bad, he claimed—the Cuban canteen staff had retorted, "Stop making such a fuss; you'd have died of starvation in Africa by now!"[8]

The aforementioned Angolan professor of the same university who had married a Cuban after coming to Cuba in 1976 to study teaching also recalls having received a solid and broad education. He himself was a white Angolan and had never personally experienced racism. He had been welcomed wherever he went. According to him the Cubans had done "good work." From his viewpoint as an education specialist, the Cubans had made a crucial contribution to the development of pedagogy in Angola. In his experience, his work with them had been generally free of hierarchy, and he emphasized that he found Cubans and Angolans similar in mentality and character. He praised the self-sacrifices that the Cuban *cooperantes* had been willing to make, which was something that set them apart from aid workers from other countries (East-bloc and Western). According to him, many Angolans had been grateful for Cuban aid, particularly in medicine.[9]

Pepetela explained that during his term as deputy minister of foreign education he had remained on good terms with his Cuban colleagues, despite all the criticism leveled at Cuban advisors in his ministry. He pointed out that the problems implementing Cuban-Angolan cooperation, particularly in its initial phase, were owing to the Angolans' lack of experience in many areas and their resulting dependency on Cuban know-how. This had gone against their spirit of independence. He nevertheless maintained that they had been thankful for Cuban support. To illustrate this general acceptance he recalled that when the first Cuban troops and civilians withdrew from Angola in 1989, an enormous crowd gathered in Luanda spontaneously and without any government organization to thank the Cubans and bid them farewell.[10]

Encounters and Dissociations

From the Cuban perspective, perceptions of the self and "the other" with respect to Angola and the Angolans were likewise determined by the Cubans' own range of experience, their own values, and their own morality. Negative perceptions and dissociations were again the results of a comparison of both societies, mentalities, and cultures. The positive perceptions and memories that my interviewees recalled, however, seldom involved people or interactions, but focused instead on the beauty of nature; the diverse, expansive landscape of Angola; and the modernity of its cities. For many, Angola represented their first encounter with Western modernity: for the first time, they had a chance to see a Mercedes Benz, to drink "real" whisky, or to enjoy Western fashion and clothing—everything that was forbidden or disapproved of in Cuba as a sign of capitalist decadence.[11] However, the Cubans also felt a mixture of fascination and disgust with the accompanying stark social and cultural contrast between the poverty in which the majority of Angolans lived and the wealth of the few. My interviewees remembered their dismay when they saw the huge disparity in development among the various population groups in Angola. They recalled the modern, capitalist cities that stood in sharp contrast to the adjacent slums, and they remembered the lifestyle of the rural population, which they perceived as "backward" and "underdeveloped."

A chemistry professor and her husband went to Alto Catumbela (Huambo province) to help reconstruct a paper mill. While recalling the social contrasts of capitalist society, she also remembered that in Cuba there had been a general lack of consumer goods that were taken for granted in well-off Angolan households: "We met lots of people from the Angolan bourgeoisie whose standard of living was much higher than ours. They didn't cook with gas; they had bathrooms, carpets, hairdryers. . . . We had a few heated discussions with them, because I believed that they had no idea of what it was like to live in a *kimbo* [name for an African village] in inhumane conditions. We experienced for ourselves the huge differences that exist in capitalism."[12]

A neurosurgeon who worked between 1980 and 1981 at the university in Huambo recalled the pronounced social and cultural differences that he witnessed not only between urban and rural areas but also within the towns and cities themselves:

> There are people there who live like two thousand years ago in these *kimbos* with mud huts . . . and in tribes. . . . That shocked me, particularly in such a big, modern city like Luanda. . . . Because of all the refugees, there were lots of these *kimbos* in the middle of the city. But we also went to houses that wouldn't have been out of place in any European city, and this contrast . . . was something that really struck us; I mean, there are people in Cuba who are poor, etc., but [because] the contrast isn't as big, in general they have a more conformed behavior.[13]

A mathematics teacher who did his military service in Luanda between 1986 and 1988 summed up the contrasts within Angolan society, which he observed with some degree of fascination: "Angola is so backward, but you can get everything there: the most expensive cars, every make of car, the newest models . . . always the newest, for clothes as well. . . . But the indigenous people run around almost naked. . . . Those who have money spend it on the most up-to-date cars, and that's the most important thing for them, even if they . . . run around barefoot. But that is the only good thing they have."[14]

The admiration shown for Angolan women was an exception among the otherwise negative perceptions. The Cubans regarded and described them as being especially strong. The poverty in which they lived, the many children they had, and the oppression they suffered from their husbands made them all the more admirable. My Cuban interviewees generally expressed their image of Angolan women, particularly from rural areas and from the poorer classes, in stereotypical and often hyperbolic terms. Some memories seemed to attribute omnipotent, almost superhuman qualities to the women of Angola.

Both male and female interviewees frequently recalled Angolan women who were able to transport several crates of beer and even a fridge on their heads over a long distance, all the while carrying their babies on their backs. These memories were exceeded in several interviews by recollections of seemingly mythological "superwomen" working the fields, carrying their children on their backs, feeding them with one breast thrown over their shoulder while balancing on their heads a small charcoal stove on which they cooked.[15] Although these descriptions seem exaggerated, they do show the great respect Cubans had for the energy and resourcefulness of Angolan women. Such expressions of respect are often linked with the equally frequent criticism and dislike of discrimination against women, which I deal with in greater detail below. Beyond these memories, the Cubans generally limited their positive recollections of people and human encounters to depictions and descriptions of Angolans as "polite," "respectful," "reserved," and "well mannered," despite considering them socially and culturally backward.

The only thing that met with the Cubans' universal enthusiasm was Angolan music and the Angolans' ability to express themselves in dance. This coincided with the Cubans' own love of music and dance. Although many of them expressed feelings of alienation when faced with Angolans dancing and playing music at burials, the Cuban interviewees happily recalled Angolan music and the various dances and dance steps, which they often learned themselves. Cubans were able to experience music and dance primarily on "cross-border" occasions, which were none too frequent in the daily life of the *cooperantes*. These occasions were usually joint Cuban-Angolan celebrations for national holidays or anniversaries, or invitations to private parties, which were often gratefully accepted despite the restrictions. Other interviewees had heard the drum rhythms and singing that frequently accompanied religious ceremonies in the streets and neighborhoods. All of my interviewees could identify with the music and dances, and they drew parallels to Cuban music and dancing, finding striking similarities. Most of them realized here at the latest that part of what they defined as their own culture was rooted in Africa and demonstrated a "link to their ancestors."[16] "You could hear drums all over the place at night . . . ; and yes, we recognized the rhythm, a Cuban rhythm, a Bembé rhythm . . . ta, tacatá, tacatá, tacatá, and singing and shouting," recalled one interviewee as he enthusiastically remembered the music and celebrations that he recognized from Cuba.[17]

As another interviewee concluded,

> The religious celebrations there are like the . . . Afro-Cuban religions here. . . . It was the drum rhythm that I noticed first. . . . They play the drum in the same rhythm as they play here for the gods . . . and like here, they sing to it. . . . They sing in local dialect. . . . There is a lead singer who calls out and a chorus who answers. . . . When I was there I was at one of these religious ceremonies . . . ; they were playing the drums just like, um, this Afro-Cuban culture . . . ; well, okay, it all comes from there, doesn't it; this whole culture comes from Africa.[18]

Another of my interviewees was so taken with Angolan music that he "imported" *kizomba*, a popular Angolan style of music and dance, to Cuba. His efforts to transfer and spread *kizomba* on his return to Cuba resulted in his meeting up with Angolan students who were studying medicine in the town where he lived.

> I learned to dance there [in Angola]; I liked the way they danced; I listened to lots of Angolan music on the radio; great; . . . and I learned to dance *kizomba*; in fact I only danced *kizomba*. . . . Here in Cuba, I improved my skills with a couple of Angolan medical students who were studying at the medical university. . . . Strangely enough, I met them through the "Soundbus" where I was working as a DJ. The "Soundbus" is a mobile disco; I kept on playing *kizomba*, and one day the Angolans heard it and were really happy to hear their music. . . . They talked to me . . . and then we did lots of things together and met up to dance *kizomba*.[19]

It is only possible to speculate whether this example of direct cultural transfer was an exception or whether Cuban culture (e.g., music styles, art, religious manifestations) was altered by the sixteen-year presence of several hundred thousand Cubans in Angola and the presence of Angolans in Cuba. To date there have been no substantial social-scientific or anthropological studies on this subject, only theses and assumptions (mentioned earlier in this work) that were put forward by Cuban researchers living in exile.[20] The impressions I received during my research do indicate that there were indeed elements of Angolan culture that the participants of the Cuban-Angolan cooperation program adopted and transferred to Cuba. Part of the difficulty I had in assessing these influences and transformations lay in the unwillingness of most of my interviewees to express themselves openly as soon as I asked them about cultural transfer, particularly because the subject touched on areas such as religion or manifestations of cultural difference. Although the Cuban government has softened its stance toward religion since the 1990s, and the popularity of Afro-Cuban religions in particular has spread enormously, it still remains difficult to talk about it openly.

One of my interviewees, a journalist, frequently visited military bases and places where the *cooperantes* lived and worked in Angola between 1988 and 1991 for the military journal *Verde Olivo*. She voiced the opinion that at the end of cooperation, Afro-Cuban religions had enjoyed a revival, partly because people had been attracted to religion through their experience of war and danger. She also noticed that particularly those who had been to Angola had been drawn to Afro-Cuban religions, since they had already become familiar with the religions practiced in Angola during their stay there—if only because these religions helped them deal with their difficult circumstances during their stay in Angola.[21]

The "Bearers of Civilization": Auto-Representations and New Constructions of Identity

Such friendly meetings and encounters were indeed a component of cooperation. But the positive memories they left behind were continually outweighed by negative impressions. During the interviews it became clear that my Cuban interviewees often used their negative impressions of Angola and the Angolans to highlight their own merits. The more they described the country and people of Angola as underdeveloped and backward, the more they were able to point to the advantages of Cuban culture, mentality, and civilization. Many of my interviewees revealed a paternalist attitude. Many of them, for example, reiterated how "generous" Cuban cooperation with Angola had been, and how desperately the Angolans had needed Cuban support. They also emphasized the importance of their role in procuring a new consciousness and new moral values. The large majority of my interviewees were convinced that they had brought civilizatory achievements and culture to the Angolans and had imparted to them a work ethic and discipline.[22]

My interviewees frequently mentioned that the gender relationships in Angola demonstrated "backwardness." They observed women's oppression and condemned the attitude of many Angolan men toward their women as patriarchal and "macho." Almost all female interviewees and many of my male interviewees distanced themselves from this attitude while emphasizing that the comparatively emancipated role of women in Cuban society was a particularly positive and modern development. The position and status of women in society was for many interviewees the benchmark for cultural and civilizatory progress. Criticism frequently went hand-in-hand with the condemnation of the apparently widespread practice of polygamy, a practice that they regarded as particularly uncivilized. Often my interviewees' perception of discrimination against women was based on what they had observed in the streets. But they had also witnessed and criticized the unequal gender relationship among sectors of society that they otherwise considered politically "progressive" and "cultivated." Whenever Cubans found themselves in direct contact with Angolans, they felt obliged to explain the advantages of the women's emancipation that had been realized in Cuba, and to motivate the Angolans to change their attitude.

A teacher who worked in Luanda between 1983 and 1985 remembered her culture shock when she observed how Angolan men treated their women:

> It was a huge shock . . . to see these women, how they worked carrying their children on their backs and went out to the fields; it was awful. And

> then . . . the men with three or four wives [working for them]. It was above all the women who struggled there, and it was hard to look on . . . because, well, I was born here in the revolution and I had never seen, never experienced anything like that here . . . and I said to myself, that can't be right that a woman works to keep her husband.[23]

A veterinary surgeon who worked at the university in Huambo from 1978 to 1980 was similarly appalled: "The . . . discrimination against women is shocking; to watch a man walking in front with a machete in his hand and five women walking behind him with their heads full of bundles, pots, firewood . . . ; we found that really shocking. . . . That's their culture, . . . but it is going to have to change one day."[24]

A former soldier who did his military service from 1987 to 1989 in the southeast of Angola felt he had a duty to make Angolan men aware of their attitude in an attempt to change it.

> I couldn't bear watching the women work while the men just sat there . . . particularly in the countryside in Angola . . . you see that a lot there . . . ; the women have their child on their backs or at their breasts and work the fields, and the man, normally, sits there, sometimes with a cigarette in his mouth. . . . When we arrived and saw that, we said to them, "Listen cousin. You have to work too! . . ." We tried to explain that to them. . . . The work should be shared . . . and the man has to do the heavy work.[25]

A gynecologist who worked at a maternity hospital in Luanda from 1978 to 1989 tried to make her female colleagues aware of their situation:

> I got on well with all the nurses. . . . We talked a lot because I wanted to know something about their life, their attitude to life, and I tried . . . to work a bit against this mentality that a woman is her husband's slave. . . . The head nurse [was] a woman who had studied in Europe, someone who had traveled a lot, but who still had this African mentality regarding her husband. . . . So we chatted about my relationship with my husband and I told her that we shared the household chores, that he looked after the children and I took care of other things. At any rate, one day she came and said that she had argued with her husband because she had told him that he could no longer be so macho, and he had replied that he would have to have a word with me, because I was a bad influence on his wife.[26]

Other reasons that gave the Cubans cause to dissociate themselves from the Angolans and Angolan society and to highlight their own cultural achievements were the apparently catastrophic hygiene standards, the dirt, the stench, and the chaos on the streets and in public spaces. The lack of discipline and work ethic was also regarded as appalling. Again the Cubans frequently undertook to civilize the Angolans.

A school principal who worked as a teacher at a primary school in Luanda from 1984 to 1985 thought that "the city was filthy; everyone peed everywhere . . . , all the walls had urine stains on them; the men peed in the middle of the street."[27] Another school principal who had worked at a primary school in Cabinda between 1979 and 1981 recalled the following observations with disgust: "One thing that we really noticed was the lice. . . . For us it's a sign of poor hygiene, and for them it was so normal that they picked the lice off themselves and ate them; the person who looked for lice, ate them. I was absolutely appalled, but for them it was normal. . . . And they always sat on the ground, even if they had the loveliest furniture; they did everything on the ground; they just weren't used to sitting on chairs and chatting like we were."[28]

The aforementioned former soldier recalled the following scenes: "When you caught a bus in Luanda, it wasn't orderly like here, but total chaos; and there were goats and pigs on the bus; the heat and the stench . . . , everything stank terribly of sweat."[29]

A former construction worker reported that his brigade had been assigned to build a high-rise building in Luanda and they had to be finished by a certain deadline. The construction brigade had comprised Cubans and Angolans. There were some very good craftsmen among the Angolans. But their work ethic had been a catastrophe, he said. It had been the Cubans' task "to persuade them to work. . . . We introduced our competitive system; . . . and we suggested it to the construction ministry, . . . and with time it worked . . . and we awarded the first prizes, a weekend in a hotel. . . . We got on well with them; we just knew how to win them round, because . . . that is simply our strength: we know how we have to deal with people."[30]

Many of my interviewees also criticized what they perceived as a lack of national consciousness and the persistence of ethno-cultural regionalism. They regarded these as particularly backward in comparison with their own experience. One Cuban woman observed that the Angolans had "no idea of what it meant at that time to have a united country, the way I thought of Cuba. . . . When they spoke of their homeland they weren't referring to Angola; they meant the province of Zaire or Uige."[31] In contrast, the Cubans regarded their own national identity and the national unity of Cuba as major social progress. As one doctor expressed it, "They lacked the concept of nationality that we have. They didn't even have a clue as to what a province was. . . . We started to develop as a nation as early as Cespedes [initiator of the Cuban struggle for independence in 1868], if not earlier. We started developing a nationality with our indigenous peoples. . . . We were very shocked by this division. . . . And by

Neto versus Savimbi. . . . Savimbi was very strong in the south; . . . they hadn't even heard of Neto there."[32]

When I evaluated and analyzed my interviews with ordinary Cuban *cooperantes* concerning their self-perception and their perception of "the other," one of my major findings was that on their return to Cuba most of them identified more strongly than ever with Cuba and its social achievements. This finding is largely congruent with the findings of other historical, sociological, anthropological, and cultural studies concerned with transcultural encounters in other contexts.[33] It is often only when confronted with "the other" that people begin to describe and portray their own selves and reflect on what they have unquestionably taken for granted and regarded as "familiar." In the case of the Cuban *cooperantes*, this reflection led to a greater appreciation of what was perceived as their "own" culture, nation, and society.

This development is unsurprising for two reasons. First, the experience of violence, the many traumas, and the exigencies of daily life must have made the revolutionary social achievements in Cuba seem all the more positive. Against the backdrop of their experiences in Angola, the *cooperantes* had good reason for developing an even greater appreciation of the positive aspects of Cuban society—women's emancipation, social justice, high education standards, and universal healthcare. In view of the situation in Angola, *cooperantes* saw patriotism and national unity as desirable guarantors of peace and progress. Another factor was the constant and unremitting separation of Cubans and Angolans, which left very little room for better understanding. During the one and a half decades of transatlantic cooperation, both parties remained largely foreign to each other. This experience of foreignness led many of my interviewees to reassert the sense of identity with which they had arrived in Angola. Their encounters led them to reject what they perceived as representative of Angola and Angolans and to double down on their own constructions of themselves as Cubans who identified strongly with the revolution. "When I arrived in Cuba, I saw them there in their country as Angolans and Africans, but I myself felt much more Cuban, even more fulfilled by my revolution, and I was much happier to be here, . . . to reach my potential here, because that's just something about us: we love our country."[34] This response is very typical of almost all my interviewees' answers to the question of whether on their return to Cuba their experience in Angola had led them to identify themselves more with their country or with the continent of Africa.

The "blood ties" that the official propaganda had constantly evoked did not materialize. Nor had Cuban-Angolan cooperation led to the emergence of a new collective, transatlantic, "Afro-Latin American" identity. The "Afro-Latin American nation" that Castro had conjured up in 1975 was nothing but political propaganda that served the ambitions of the Cuban government on the foreign political stage. This conclusion leads in turn to the suspicion that the Cuban government had little intention of fostering a stronger sense of identification with Angola among the Cuban *cooperantes*; rather, the government was actually hoping for an "educational" (side) effect by confronting Cubans with immense social and cultural contrasts in order to attain greater acceptance for the Cuban political system. This raises the question of whether the historian de la Fuente and the social scientist Taylor were right to claim that the foreign policy image of Cuba as an "Afro-Latin American nation" enhanced through cooperation with Angola was nothing more than an example of a symbolic "export identity" to demonstrate the Cuban government's identification with the liberation struggles of nonwhite peoples across the globe.[35]

Whatever the answer, Cuba's engagement in Angola has left deep marks on Cuban society. For an informed debate there needs to be further social-scientific and anthropological research into identity and the phenomena of perception and belonging in contemporary Cuba. I have only been able to speculate about possible cultural transformations resulting from contact with Angolan culture. But what has become clear is that the authorities' handling of the aftermath of engagement in Angola and the culture of silence on trauma, loss, sacrifice, and defeat—even now, more than twenty years after withdrawal from Angola—are potentially explosive. Even if the "ordinary" participants reaffirmed to me their identification with the state and the revolution—and thus demonstrated their familiarity with the lessons taught by official policy—they did not remain quiescent and articulated with extraordinary clarity their criticism of Cuba's engagement in Angola and the silence that surrounds the official politics of memory.

Conclusion

The conclusions to be drawn from my research on this extraordinary South-South cooperation between Cuba and Angola are not unequivocal. Neither military nor civil cooperation was able to solve the conflict between the internal rivals in Angola or overcome the deep rifts within Angolan society. Civil cooperation laid the foundations for political structures in postcolonial Angola. This cooperation, together with the military deployment of Cuban troops, proved instrumental in the long-term consolidation of the MPLA's position of power. Cuba's military engagement was able to secure the territorial integrity of Angola under the leadership of the MPLA; civil cooperation allowed the transfer of power strategies from which the MPLA would profit in the long term. The establishment of a national education system was decisive in spreading the MPLA's political influence throughout the country, consolidating its political power, and building a united nation-state. But within the context of the Cold War the obvious ideological objectives of the cooperation program deepened the already bitter rivalry between the local enemies, thereby catching the civilian population in the crossfire between the MPLA government and UNITA rebels. By the mid-1980s the warring parties had systematically annihilated the modest achievements of civil development aid (in infrastructure, administration, and health and education programs) during the first few years of independence.

After many years of laborious negotiations, the New York Accords were finally ratified by South Africa, Cuba, and Angola.[1] This agreement stipulated the withdrawal from Angola of Cuban troops and civilians as well as the South

African army. It also determined the independence of Namibia, which until then had been a South African protectorate. When all Cubans and South Africans finally left Angola in the summer of 1991, the internal power struggle was far from over. The violence continued to spiral, and the battle between MPLA forces and UNITA rebels resulted in scenes of devastation that eclipsed the preceding decades of colonial and postcolonial conflict. Despite many attempts to bring the armed conflict to an end through negotiations and the intervention of the United Nations, the war continued to rage unabated until Jonas Savimbi, the leader of UNITA, was killed in February 2002. The war claimed the lives of many hundreds of thousands, both directly and indirectly—through landmines and starvation; millions of Angolans were forced to flee and lost their livelihoods.[2] The beneficiary of the war was the MPLA government because the conflict allowed it to extend the centralized and undemocratic political structures of the socialist era, which had been established with the help of Cuban development aid. As a result, corruption within the state apparatus became even more rife since the MPLA was able to hold on to state monopolies in the finance and petroleum sectors and ensure its exclusive control over them.[3] The MPLA was thus able to generate state revenue and finance the war. In 2002, the MPLA emerged from the bloody conflict as the victor under the leadership of President José Eduardo dos Santos, and the party consolidated its position in the parliamentary and presidential elections of September 2008 and August 2012.

It is impossible, however, to limit the conclusions of this analysis to the immediate results of a historical process. My research has brought to light a whole range of new and hitherto unknown phenomena that offer in-depth insight into the dynamics and characteristics of such cooperative relations in the Global South. In this book, I chose a South-South perspective and focused on the civil cooperation program, its implementation at ground level, its social and cultural aspects, and its agents. This approach relativized the significance of the role played by the Cold War powers in Angola's independence and gave priority to the direct political interaction between the Cuban and Angolan governments. The study has thus demonstrated that contrary to all opinion to date on the postcolonial development of Angola, both the Cuban and Angolan governments were able to use their relationship and take advantage of the slipstream of the Soviet Union to pursue their own political ambitions and power interests. Using the example of cooperation in education, I have been able to decode the patterns of interaction between the two governments. My focus on the cooperation, the formal agreements, and the binational negotiation process illustrates that, unlike North-South relations, the relationship between the governments was based on equal partnership. Contrary to all claims to date that Cuba "intervened" in Angola, this study clearly shows that the dynamics of this relationship emanated primarily from the Angolan side. The mechanism of "demand and supply" by which Cuba consistently met Angolan requirements provides clear evidence of this pattern, as exemplified by the financing of civil engagement, which has been dealt with in this study for the first time. By paying for Cuban aid, the MPLA government increased its bargaining power and was able to make demands on the Cubans. This financial aspect of the relationship underlines that Cuban cooperation with Angola was by no means motivated solely by the constantly propagated solidarity and altruism: Cuba also profited financially from its focused support for the MPLA.

Originally the Cuban government had no interest in long-term engagement in Angola and regarded the large-scale deployment of civilians with skepticism. Civil cooperation therefore initially followed the development concept of "help for self-help." Nevertheless, the MPLA managed to secure Cuba's agreement to continue its engagement and provide a huge workforce for a period of one and a half decades. Thus the MPLA was able to draw on Cuba's foreign strategy of "internationalist solidarity" and its ambitions to spread its revolutionary purpose. The political aim of building a socialist nation-state in Angola, which was initially pursued both by the Cuban government and the MPLA, took a back seat in the mid-1980s due to the power ambitions of the MPLA. The MPLA realized an entirely different sociopolitical and economic agenda and finally opted to follow the path of capitalism, which it was paradoxically able to implement thanks to the transfer of power strategies from Cuba. A particularly crucial role in this process was played by the cooperation program in education, which allowed the tried-and-tested basic strategies for consolidating power to be transferred and modified to fit the Angolan context.

Although the impetus for cooperation came from Angola, the actual environment surrounding the cooperation put Angola in an unfavorable position in other respects. The conditions for fast improvements to infrastructure across the country and the consolidation of a nation-state were much more fragile in Angola than they had been in revolutionary Cuba. Cooperation therefore also gave rise to asymmetries and dissonances, mainly because of the disparate development within the two countries. Such asymmetries were particularly evident at the structural, organizational, and implementational levels. Angola's weak administrative structures and its huge lack of qualified workers stood alongside Cuba's deployment of a large, skilled workforce, in a well-orchestrated, structured, and hierarchical (but nevertheless flexible) undertaking. Moreover, the Cubans were well aware of how to take advantage of their military infrastructure to set up an administrative body for managing civil cooperation independently of the Angolan authorities. I have used the cooperation program in education to illustrate how all these specific mechanisms of interaction informed Cuban-Angolan cooperation. Since it can be presumed that both civil and military operations followed very similar patterns, it is possible that this reveals a new basic paradigm to describe relationships of South-South cooperation. Linked to the search for a more polycentric, globally oriented approach to historiography, these findings could offer significant suggestions for research into other, similar relations within the Global South.

The study has also provided differentiated insights into the concrete, everyday implementation of this ambitious cooperation project. It became clear that cooperation could only work with the Cuban population's support and readiness to provide practical support for rebuilding Angola. Particularly in the initial years, the Cuban government was able to secure the support of the majority of the population through a propaganda campaign that was simultaneously ostentatious and subtle. A comparison between official propaganda and individual motivations, however, reveals that, although the Cuban population followed the cooperation policy of their government, they circumvented the political aims of the government and its monopoly on interpretation by combining their engagement with a wide range of personal motives and interests. The insights provided into the motives of individuals also shed light on the subtleties of government propaganda. Contrary to the government's claims that revolutionary conviction alone motivated personal engagement, it has become clear that indirectly very different incentives, for example career opportunities, were offered.

On the basis of eyewitness interviews and using a microhistorical approach, I was able to outline the social and cultural elements of this cooperation and illustrate how it worked on a day-to-day basis beyond binational agreements and political propaganda. The lack of qualified workers in Angola gave the Cuban teachers, education specialists, and advisors a leading role in effecting political, social, and cultural change in Angola, and they came to represent the aims and symbols of the MPLA government. As its representatives, they supported administration and control of the territories to which it laid claim. The downside of this massive commitment of Cuban aid workers, however, was that it hindered the self-dependent development of education in Angola. The availability of Cuban teachers obviated the need to train Angolan teachers. The resulting lack of Angolan teachers was a source of criticism on the part of the Angolan Ministry of Education.

The analysis of this concrete process of education and teaching has shed light on this historic development at a transnational level and showed the various layers of its subjective appropriation. It revealed that as in many education campaigns in other regions and historical contexts, it proved very difficult to implement the cooperation's educational agenda on the ground. The process of introducing the new education system was far from straightforward: it was subject to setbacks and resistance. Moreover, those benefiting from education took the opportunity to advance themselves, thereby moving away to some extent from the educative aims of the government. Furthermore, the organizational and administrative logistics needed to enforce the education program were disproportionate to the results. A large proportion of Cuban planning and organization served to monitor the Cuban workforce: time and effort were spent enforcing stringent political controls, preventing the Cuban civilians from escaping, and maintaining a collective "Cuban" identity. As a result, the Cuban *cooperantes* found themselves separated from the Angolan population outside of work and isolated in clearly defined "Cuban" sociocultural spaces. This in turn encouraged intercultural misunderstandings between Cubans and Angolans and impeded any reciprocal process of learning.

At schools, lessons were affected by the strict regimentation imposed on the Cuban teachers by their own internal organization. Although the Cuban teachers launched a cultural revolution by introducing innovative teaching methods to overcome the colonial legacy in education, their success was considerably hampered by internal regulations. The Cuban teachers were expected to meet targets of a quantitative rather than qualitative nature. Successful exam rates to meet these targets became more important than the enduring education of the Angolan pupils. The Cuban teachers' sense of mission regarding disseminating socialist educational ideals also prevented educational and intercultural exchange, as did the Cubans' conception of themselves as representatives of a superior culture. Nevertheless, the temporary deployment of Cuban teachers and the educational opportunities available at the Angolan boarding schools on the Cuban Isle of Youth did at least promote the education of a small elite group of Angolans, some of whom hold prominent positions in Angolan society (and in politics and administration) today.

The internal war, the destabilizing tactics of UNITA, and the intervention of South African forces also obstructed the cooperation program's success. The war determined the everyday life of the civilians, whose safety was constantly at risk from enemy attack. It is here that the strong links between civil cooperation and the overall military and political strategy become apparent. Not only was the Cuban government prepared to accept the risks posed to Cuban civilians; it was even at times prepared to involve them in military activity. This ambivalent dual function of the civil aid workers highlights the contradictions inherent in combined civilian and military engagement abroad: it hindered the acceptance of civil reconstruction measures among the population, and it deepened the rift between supporters and opponents of the MPLA government. As representatives of both a foreign power and the MPLA, the Cuban civilians thus became the target of oppositional violence.

The biographical interviews with former civilian participants provided a differentiated insight into the emotional dimension of the cooperation. It became obvious that the Cuban civilians suffered enormous psychological pressure from working and living in a war zone. They were neither prepared for the conditions they faced nor familiar with the cultural, ethnic, and linguistic peculiarities of Angola. Many therefore returned traumatized from Angola. Most of my interviews revealed that the culture shock and trauma these civil aid workers suffered were never openly discussed in Cuba, let alone critically analyzed. This is one of the main reasons why many of them still have not come to terms with their disturbing experiences, which in turn have gradually taken shape as a collective trauma within Cuban society that individuals can only express verbally and off the record. Since 1991, engagement in Angola has only been discussed in Cuba within the confines of the government's official politics of memory. Cuba's engagement in Angola is part of the success story of the revolution, where negative associations with Angola and individual or collective trauma have no place.

Through my multifaceted approach to and multilayered analysis of Cuban-Angolan cooperation, I have provided a comprehensive understanding of it on the levels of bilateral governmental relations, institutional organization and planning, and the individual perspectives of its participants. Nevertheless, many questions have had to remain unanswered. The three main desiderata are the links between civilian and military cooperation, a comparison of cooperation in education versus other civil sectors, and research into the traces that cooperation left behind in both societies. These are questions that remain open for several reasons, including the fact that this study is the first to investigate and concentrate on civilian cooperation between Cuba and Angola. With the exception of a few pieces of Cuban propaganda, few publications deal with this topic (and for that reason my study is based mainly on primary sources). As I explained in the introduction, archival research in Angola and Cuba was difficult, and this fact alone limited my research to one of the main cooperative sectors. The relatively contemporary nature of my research topic added further obstacles to accessing archival material, particularly in Cuba, and constrained my ability to detail the links between civil and military cooperation.

The question of reciprocal influences and what traces were left behind is a difficult one. The short period of time in which these contacts took place means that many influences did not become firmly established. In addition, the destructive force of the civil war that followed razed many of the foundation stones that had been laid during cooperation. Furthermore, the withdrawal of Cuban troops and civilians marked the end of Cuban-Angolan relations for almost two decades—for reasons that I will explain below. It nevertheless seems that engagement in Angola probably left much deeper marks on Cuban than Angolan society—by dint of the sheer numbers of Cubans involved in Angola. To find evidence of this, however, it would be necessary to carry out a far more extensive, interdisciplinary research project within both Cuba and Angola, incorporating methodologies from fields such as sociology, cultural anthropology, linguistics, and religious studies. Conventional historical methods are insufficient to pinpoint changes in identities and mentalities. For this reason I adopt research methods from cultural studies and cultural anthropology and include the recollections of eyewitnesses to document the subjective dimension of the encounter between Cubans and Angolans.

Cooperation between Cuba and Angola raises another overriding question that is still relevant today. What purpose does external support in civil wars or postcolonial conflicts serve? Even without the ideological premises of this cooperation, it is questionable whether Cuba's support could ever have mitigated the dynamics of the conflict in Angola. Various recent studies on international involvement to help solve civil and postcolonial conflicts or to stabilize post-Cold War societies have found that external support contributed little to reconciliation. Studies on foreign intervention in Afghanistan, Iraq, Bosnia, Rwanda, and Haiti, for example, have shown that, regardless of the causes of the conflicts and their specific constellations, outside intervention failed, partly because military strategy always took precedence over civil aid. Efforts failed particularly when individual states intervened unilaterally, motivated primarily by their own (security) interests, as was the case, for example, with US intervention in Iraq. The studies concluded that the biggest failing was the lack of coordinated, well-planned strategies adjusted to the specific situations.[4]

Unlike these studies, which mainly focus on political science, the historical and microhistorical approach chosen here does not concentrate solely on intergovernmental interaction and institutions. But it does clearly illustrate that, with regard to technical and administrative procedure, the engagement of Cuban aid workers in Angola did indeed fulfill some of the aims claimed in these studies. The deployment of civilians was well planned and coordinated, and it concentrated on strengthening state administration, helping to modernize infrastructure and promoting social programs. Moreover, it was founded on the enormous personal commitment of a specialized workforce, and it was well coordinated in close cooperation with the Angolan government. The reason why this support was also incapable of stabilizing Angola in the long term, however, may be the following. Despite the extensive civilian program, Cuban engagement concentrated primarily on a political and military strategy to support the MPLA's position of power. All civil development aid was subordinate to this objective. Another difficulty was that civil cooperation did not aim at a reconciliation of enemy factions. It therefore did not primarily serve to improve the life of the civilian population, but above all served the interests of the MPLA. The ideology behind the engagement and the power interests of the MPLA combined with overriding military priorities to deepen the rivalry between local factions. The result was that, after 1991, the ensuing civil war destroyed the efforts of civil reconstruction.

The Cuban government nevertheless continues to insist that Cuban engagement in Angola was a success. But the official story mentions only the political and military triumphs, including the 1988 battle of Cuito Cuanavale in the south of Angola, during which the concerted forces of the FAPLA and the Cuban army repelled the South African army.[5] The Cuban government thereby claims to have made an essential contribution to the demise of the apartheid regime and the independence of Namibia.[6] But the official discourse remains silent about the people of Angola who suffered most from the long and drawn-out war—and about the trauma suffered by the Cuban soldiers and civilians involved.

Outlook

After 1991, relations between the Cuban and Angolan governments deteriorated dramatically, and there was little to no contact between them for many years to come. The political common ground on which Cuban-Angolan cooperation rested had given way. As early as the mid-1980s, the MPLA government had changed political camps and veered from its socialist path by introducing market economic reforms. In keeping with this new direction, the MPLA embarked on negotiations with the United States without informing the Cuban government. It nevertheless continued to take advantage of Cuba's military and civil support.[1] Understandably, Cuba was deeply upset. To make matters worse, the MPLA government refused to support the Cubans in any way after 1991, even though, following withdrawal from Angola, Cuba's economy collapsed and the island plunged into the worst economic crisis in its history when it lost Soviet subsidies.[2] And yet it was Cuba's involvement in Angola that had actually hindered the economic and structural development of Cuba, as the national economy had lost thousands of young qualified workers to the cooperation initiative. Supplies of petroleum from Angola could have helped Cuba stabilize its economy. Indeed, from 1975 to 1991 Cuban troops had actually secured Angolan petroleum production while US companies such as Gulf Oil received concessions from the Angolan government to exploit oil, thus guaranteeing state revenues and enabling the MPLA to finance the war. This sealed the end of relations between Cuba and Angola.[3]

But in the end, Cuba managed to overcome the economic crisis of the 1990s without the assistance of Angola, thanks in large part to economic and political pragmatism. It did not give up its foreign-policy strategy of "internationalist solidarity" without drawing lessons from the past. It was precisely in this period of crisis that its experience in Angola and its first large-scale civil engagement abroad, with all the connected structures and institutions, proved invaluable. In the 1990s, Cuba increasingly professionalized civil engagement, limiting its support to humanitarian, technical, and administrative sectors and stripping it of its ideological agenda. The government increased its deployment of aid workers abroad, and the income from providing specialists became an official source of state revenue and one of the major sources of foreign currency for the Cuban state. If a country could not pay in hard currency for Cuban doctors, teachers, and advisors, the Cuban government accepted raw materials in return. Venezuela, for example, has been compensating Cuba with generous consignments of petroleum since the beginning of this century. Unlike during engagement in Angola, the Cuban aid workers now received about 10 percent of the salaries paid by the beneficiary country, which allowed many Cuban families to survive during the crisis.[4] In the Global South, Cuba's civil engagement emerged as a new symbol of its foreign policy, which was able to build on the "help-through-solidarity" ethos of the 1970s. The professionalization of Cuban development aid and the incentives offered considerably improved the efficiency of Cuban engagement. Cuba's decision to abandon its attempts at exporting revolution and transferring its system to other countries gave this trend further impetus, as did Cuba's new focus on providing efficient support adapted to the specific situation.

On this ideology-free, pragmatic basis, Cuban-Angolan relations also experienced an astonishing revival. At the end of July 2009, the Cuban President, Raúl Castro, made a state visit to Luanda to meet the Angolan President, José Eduardo dos Santos, and finalize an agreement on continued civil and economic cooperation.[5] During the visit, the Cuban daily newspaper *Granma* reported that since 2007 the number of Cuban aid workers in Angola had been rising steadily, and that there were now once again more than two thousand Cuban teachers, professors, doctors, and technicians helping Angola to build its health and education system and improve its infrastructure—with a pronounced upward trend.[6] According to my latest inquiries, there were an estimated eight to ten thousand Cuban specialists working in Angola in summer 2013.[7]

It is worth noting that the constellation of the Cuban and Angolan heads of state who met in Luanda in the summer of 2009 bore a striking resemblance to that of thirty years earlier: Raúl Castro, commander in chief of the Armed Forces, who took over government leadership from his ailing brother Fidel in

February 2008, and José Eduardo dos Santos, who has been president of Angola since Neto's death in 1979. Both these political "dinosaurs" and the power apparatus behind them in the form of the Communist Party of Cuba and the MPLA have survived the deepest crises and wars in their respective countries. The political continuity of both governments and an awareness of the significance of their common past give reason today for rekindling the relations of the 1970s and 1980s. And so in the long term, it does seem as if the Angolan engagement is a Cuban success story after all. Cuba's 1975 aspirations to build political and economic relations with a prosperous partner rich in raw materials and resources seem much more promising today in times of peace.

The Cuban education concepts that were transferred to Angola between 1976 and 1991 also finally seem to be bearing fruit. The ideology disseminated through educational cooperation had no lasting impact and did not lead to the establishment of a socialist society in Angola. But cooperation did enable the education of a small elite who went on to hold important positions in politics, economics, education, and even the Catholic church. And they, directly and indirectly, eventually helped stabilize the rule of the MPLA. If only for that reason, Cuba's education concepts are once again being applied in Angola today, stripped of their ideological baggage but maintaining the principles of modern, interactive teaching methods. And the Angolans and Cubans have been able to take advantage of their former experiences and contacts. The new literacy program developed in Cuba is being implemented with much success by some old acquaintances, the OMA and the JMPLA.[8] Among those working in Angola today are a sizable number of Cubans who were there in the 1970s and 1980s. In contemporary Cuba, Angola is no longer associated with the horrors of its war-torn past, and its dynamic economic growth has turned it into a popular location for Cuban aid workers.

The renewed relations between Cuba and Angola and the new political and economic pragmatism of the Cuban government have, however, had little impact on the official memory politics of engagement in Angola. The government closed this chapter in 1991, and the only remembrances allowed in the public sphere must adhere to the official interpretation of events. The recollections of my interviewees, however, highlight that the Cuban people have by no means overcome the trauma that military and civil engagement inflicted on them. On the contrary, the narratives contained within the framework of this study gave social agents a voice with which they could describe for the first time their experiences during their engagement in Angola. Within the official Cuban politics of memory there is no such opportunity for self-representation. The subjective memories of the eyewitnesses contradicted the official success story, broke taboos, and lifted the veil of silence. They illustrate that the Cuban population does seem to interpret Cuba's engagement in Angola as a failure. These subjective memories can be understood as an indirect challenge to the Cuban government to break the silence and allow an open reappraisal of the past. The great desire for public debate could be seen in the years 2000 and 2002, when the Angolan embassy in Cuba announced a competition under the motto "Angola en la memoria" (Memories of Angola).[9] Several hundred Cubans entered the competition and submitted their personal memories of civil and military engagement in the form of personal memoirs, literary works, and artworks (paintings, photos, and sculptures). However, the conformist contributions of former soldiers were the only entries to be awarded prizes or made public.[10]

The Cuban government's sole attempt to help the population come to terms with the social trauma caused by engagement in Angola was the public glorification of Cuban military success, along with a celebration of political achievements—the independence of Namibia and the demise of the apartheid regime. The documentary series *La epopeya de Angola* (The Angolan epic), first broadcast on Cuban television in 2007, contains little more than the old images of Angolan battles.[11] It features Angolan veterans, high-ranking generals describing military victories, who alone are given the opportunity to comment on events. The series restates that the official number of Cubans who lost their lives in the Angolan engagement was 2,016.[12] There are still doubts as to whether this number tallies with the true number of fatalities, but there has been no way of verifying it to date.[13] What is important is that the memory of huge personal sacrifice and an unbelievably high number of lost lives has lodged itself in the collective memory of the Cuban population. It therefore seems either cynical or foresighted that the credits at the end of each episode of *La epopeya de Angola* cite the words with which Raúl Castro welcomed those returning from Angola in May 1991: "In the new and unexpected challenges, we will always be able to evoke the Angolan epic with gratitude, because without Angola, we would not be as strong as we are today."[14]

Notes

Introduction

1. Cf. US Government Publications 1976, Y4.In 8/16: An 4/2, Hearing before the Committee on International Relations, House of Representatives, Ninety-Fourth Congress, Second Session, 26 January 1976, United States Policy on Angola, 1976, p. 42.

2. Greiner, Müller, Walter, 2006, pp. 7–11; McMahon, 2006, pp. 16–18. In the northern hemisphere, the era of the Cold War may not have been without tensions; it was, however, a relatively peaceful period. On the Cold War in the Northern Hemisphere, see Loth, 2000 (to 1955); and Dülffer, 2004 (to 1990).

3. Cf. George, 2005, p. 324n1. The author is referring to a public speech given by Raúl Castro to mark the final return of soldiers and civilians from Angola on 27 May 1991, in which he quoted that 377,033 soldiers and approximately 50,000 civilians had been involved.

4. Cf. Hippler, 2003, who provided a critical definition of nation building, a previously vague term that had been applied internationally to extremely diverse political contexts. The use of the term in this context is justified by Hippler's reference to the various dimensions and instruments of nation-building processes that include both internal and external agents striving for the creation or strengthening of a sociopolitical system or model of governance based on the nation-state that serves their interests, increases their power or weakens their opponents.

5. The term "internationalist solidarity" is particularly ideologically loaded in the Cuban context, which is why it appears in this study in quotation marks and serves as a historical description of a foreign-policy phenomenon.

6. Appadurai, 1996, p. 10.

7. Reference is only made to the most significant contributions, e.g., Spikes, 1993; Hodges, 2000 and 2001; Wright, 1997; O'Neill, Munslow, 1995; Legum, 1987a and 1987b; Kitchen, 1987.

8. Klinghoffer, 1980; Lazitch, 1989; Bark, 1988.

9. Cf. Mesa-Lago's and Belkin's 1982 anthology, which contains very solid political analyses of the aims of Cuban foreign policy and a wide range of opinions, above all of

Cuban American academics; see also Blasier, Mesa-Lago, 1979; Leogrande, 1980 and 1982; Domínguez, 1982; Erisman, 1985.

10. Díaz-Briquets, 1989; Eckstein, 1980, 1985, pp. 372–389; 1994, pp. 171–203.

11. Westad, 2002; Westad, 2005; Leffler, Westad, 2010a–c (vols. 1–3); Greiner, Müller, Walter, 2006.

12. See Westad's portrayal of the Angolan conflict, which makes very little reference to Cuban or Angolan sources: Westad, 2005, pp. 158–161, 207–209. In the monumental, three-volume *Cambridge History of the Cold War*, published by Leffler and Westad, 2010a–c, the essay on southern Africa by Christopher Saunders and Sue Onslow similarly lacks local and regional sources; see Saunders, Onslow, 2006, pp. 222–225.

13. Gleijeses, 2002, 2004, 2006a, 2006b; Gleijeses's research is possible because he is the only foreign historian with access to the archives of the Cuban government and the military. In contrast to Gleijeses, the British historian and journalist Edward George, 2005, who also focused on Cuban-Angolan cooperation at the military level, deviates from the regime's official version.

14. Gleijeses, 2013.

15. Pélissier, 1978, analyzed from a historic viewpoint Portuguese colonial rule, the background of the colonial war, and the emergence of the anti-colonial movements, as did the historian Basil Davidson, 1972 and 1978. See Marcum, 1969 and 1978, for a very sound and detailed analysis of the origins of the anti-colonial movement. Chilcote, 1972b, published original documents of anti-colonial movements; the British historian David Birmingham also published numerous studies (1978, 1992, 1993, 1999) on Portuguese colonial rule, the colonial war, and postcolonial conflict. Heimer, 1979, analyzed the independence conflict from a sociological perspective, as did Messiant, who presented many detailed sociological studies of the origins of the anti-colonial movements, the independence conflict, the MPLA, and postcolonial society (1993, 1998, 2006, 2007, and 2008). For the postcolonial conflict, see MacQueen, 1997 and 2000; Andresen Guimarães, 2001; Meyns, 1992.

16. Malaquias, 2007a, 2007b; see also Messiant, 2006, 2007, and 2008; Chabal, 2002 and 2007.

17. Carvalho et al., 2000; *Angola rumo à independência: O governo de transição*, n.d. [1975]. Sections of the archives of one of the most important MPLA politicians, Lúcio Lara, have recently been published (Lara, 1999); the Congolese historian Mabeko Tali published in 2001 a critical analysis of the history of the MPLA; a critical, polemic reappraisal of the history of the MPLA was also presented by Pacheco, 1997.

18. The following publications exemplify this perspective: Rey Cabrera, 1989; Ricardo Luis, 1989; Gómez Chacón, 1989; Rius, 1982; Comas Paret, 1983; Valdés Vivo, 1976; Fernández Marrero, Garciga Blanco, 2005. The official memory of Angolan involvement is characterized by hierarchy, as it at best reflects the point of view of military leaders. The exception to this is the 2006 publication *Cangamba*, which contains the comments of sixty Cuban and Angolan soldiers who fought in the conflict on the side of Angolan government troops (Martín Blandino, 2006). The film bearing the same title that was shown to the Cuban public in 2008, however, meets all the clichés of the military operation in Angola and glorifies the role of the Cuban military in this conflict. Concepción, 1987, and Fresnillo, 1983, are an exception as they explicitly deal with civil engagement abroad, but they still remain within the framework of official interpretation. Although Jiménez, 2008, adheres to the official government tenor, she did

break taboos by dealing with the significance of female participation in foreign involvement and in so doing managed to break with the Cuban military's monopoly on interpretation.

19. Castro, 2005, p. 1.

20. Ibid.

21. Ibid.; see also Gleijeses et al., 2007. Additionally, there are numerous films and documentaries that glorify the Cuban engagement in Angola, along with the TV series *La epopeya de Angola* (The Angolan epic), which was first broadcast in 2007.

22. Westad, 2000, pp. 1–25; Westad, 2005, pp. 1–19; Leffler, 2000, pp. 43–47.

23. Cf. Chakrabarty, 2008, and the introductions of the following anthologies, which deal with the new global-historic perspectives: Conrad, Eckert, Freitag, 2007; Osterhammel, Petersson, 2003; Conrad, Randeria, 2002.

24. The Africa historian Frederick Cooper warned in his essay published in 2001 against relativizing global power structures and hierarchies through the "globalization paradigm," which also influences recent historic debate. See Cooper, 2001.

25. Latham, 2010, particularly pp. 268–269.

26. Among others, the historians Godechot (1947) and Verlinden (1966) interpreted the Atlantic in the 1940s and 1950s as a type of "inland sea of Western civilization." This questionable approach, which was later frequently criticized, was also taken up by historians such as Huguette and Pierre Chaunu (1955–1959), who attempted to produce a comprehensive history of the ocean in their monumental, eight-volume work, *Séville et l'Atlantique*.

27. Gilroy, 1993.

28. Schmieder, Nolte, 2010, deal specifically with the South Atlantic; see also Cañizares-Esguerra, Seeman, 2007; Mann, 2001; Mohan, Zack-Williams, 2002; Tiyambe, 2005; Mayer, 2005; Chambers, 2008.

29. Freitag, von Oppen, 2009.

30. See among others Sonderegger, 2010, pp. 172–189; Geiss, 1969; Du Bois, 1963; Senghor, 1970; Sewell, 1990.

31. Castro, 1979, p. 149.

32. Hobsbawm, Ranger, (1983) 2009, pp. 1–14.

33. Cf. Hatzky, 2013; Hatzky, Stites Mor, 2014.

34. Cf. Greiner, Müller, Walter, 2009; Aschmann, 2005; Frevert, 2009, pp. 183–208.

35. Interview Angola 2006, Luanda, 22 March 2006 (António Burity da Silva). At the time of interview, Burity da Silva was the Angolan Minister of Education. In the 1970s and 1980s he was responsible within the MPLA for selecting Angolan pupils and students for a Cuban scholarship. In the 1990s he was the Angolan ambassador in Cuba.

36. This has to do with essential aspects of reflexivity characterizing intercultural communication processes. These aspects have been corroborated by various cultural encounters from other eras and cultural contexts. Cf. Lüsebrink, 2008, and the two anthologies published by Baberowski (Baberowski, Feest, Lehmann, 2008; Baberowski, Kaelble, Schriewer, 2008) in which representations of the self and other are analyzed using historical, socioscientific methods, and methods of cultural comparison on the basis of various examples from different contexts and eras.

37. The unclassified documents used in this study are identified by letterhead, date, reference, and content and signature (if available). A list of the documents can be found in the bibliography. All documents can be viewed in digital form in my private archive.

38. This claim was made, for example, by the former Minister of Education, José Ramón Fernandez, who when in office between 1970 and 1990 was to a large degree responsible for the organization and coordination of cooperation in education. Interview Cuba 2006, Havana, 21 September 2006 (José Ramón Fernández).

39. One of my interview partners, Limbania "Nancy" Jiménez Rodríguez, who was responsible for setting up cooperation in education between 1976 and 1977, held over two hundred biographical and quantitative interviews over a period of ten years with Cuban women who had been involved in the civil and military foreign engagements, with the aim of publishing a historical and social-scientific study. Not only did Nancy Jiménez allow me access to some of the interviews she had conducted, she also provided me with material from her private archive; see also Jiménez Rodríguez 2008a and 2008b. I thank her sincerely for her generous support.

40. Between the years of 1978 and 1986 over 2,000 Cuban youths between the ages of seventeen and twenty were sent with these student brigades to serve for two years in Angola. There is no special chapter dedicated to the brigades, but they are mentioned throughout the study.

41. These texts are to be found in the archives of the Casa de Angola (Angolan House), a cultural center in Havana supported by the Angolan embassy. They include written texts, memoirs, extracts from diaries, poetry and prose, and also visual arts, photos, paintings, and sculptures.

42. The bibliography includes a list of my interviewees. In a few cases, my interviews were conducted with eyewitnesses who were engaged as aid workers in African countries other than Angola (São Tomé and Príncipe, Mozambique, Benin, Nigeria, Equatorial-Guinea, Zimbabwe).

43. In 1966 Jorge Risquet Valdés was a member of the Bataillon Patrice Lumumba, which supported Ernesto "Che" Guevara during his Congo expedition. Valdés then went on to hold several ministerial posts and was in charge of civil cooperation with Angola from 1976 to 1991. Puente Ferro was also a member of the Bataillon Patrice Lumumba. In 1975, he accompanied Cuban troops to Angola as a military doctor and was responsible, among other things, for organizing civil aid. He served as Cuban ambassador in Angola from 1983 to 1986.

44. In this function Benitez de Mendoza was instrumental in all binational negotiations between the Cuban and Angolan governments.

45. Franco was partly responsible for organizing the student brigades of the Destacamento Pedagógico Internacionalista "Che Guevara."

46. Fuentes, after going into exile in 1989, set down his Angolan experiences and his criticism of the entire operation in two autobiographical novels (*El último santuario: Una novela de campaña* [1992] and *Dulces guerreros cubanos* [2002]). Hidalgo, in addition to his advisory role, served as Deputy Foreign Minister. He had been editor in chief of the Cuban newspaper *Trabajadores*. As Cuba's ambassador to the United Nations (1992–1994), he replaced Ricardo Alarcón. Hidalgo escaped to the United States in 2002.

47. Between 1993 and 1996, Burity da Silva also served as the Angolan ambassador in Cuba. Pinda Simão was responsible for planning and personnel in the Angolan Ministry of Education (1981–1984) before taking charge of the Department of International Cooperation (GICI/GII). Manuel Teodoro Quarta set up the Department of International Cooperation in the Ministry of Education in 1977 and was in charge of it until 1983.

48. For example, Thompson, 1988, Vansina, 1973, 1985; Niethammer, 1983a, 1983b, 1988; Plato, 1985, 1998a, 1998b, 2000. An overview of the lively debate surrounding the methodology of oral history and its practical implementation is contained in *Bios*, the journal for biographic research and oral history that has been published since 1987.

49. See Plato, 2000; Welzer, 2000.

50. Plato, 2000, p. 8; 1998a.

51. Halbwachs, 1967, 1985.

52. For example, J. Assmann, (1992) 2007; A. Assmann, Friese, 1988; A. Assmann, 2006, here in particular, pp. 131–133; Niethammer, 1985; 2000, here in particular, pp. 323–325.

53. These institutions and associations included the Institute of Cuban History (Instituto de Historia de Cuba), the National Association of Veterans and Patriots (Asociación Nacional de Veteranos y Patriotas), the Ministries of Education (MINED and MES), the Ministry of Public Health (MINSAP), and the National Union of Writers and Artists of Cuba (UNEAC).

54. After my seventh interview, an acquaintance "communicated" to me—probably on behalf of the state security services—that I would only be able to continue with my research project if I was prepared to be chaperoned by a Cuban colleague. My many years of research in Cuba meant that I had already built up a large network of Cuban colleagues, acquaintances, and friends who supported my research project. I was therefore able to solve the problem by appointing as my chaperone a retired historian whom I had met during previous research trips several years earlier and who as a member of the Communist Party Provincial Committee had the required political credentials. In the end, only a total of fifteen interviews in Santa Clara and Santiago de Cuba were chaperoned, and within just a few weeks the condition was nothing more than a formality.

55. Above all these were scientists from the Cuban Research Institute of Florida International University (FIU) and the Institute for Cuban and Cuban-American Studies of the University of Miami.

56. Centro de Estudos Africanos (CEA) of the Instituto Superior de Ciências do Trabalho e da Empresa (ISCTE) of Lisbon University. Here I wish to extend my thanks above all to Franz-Wilhelm Heimer, the then head of the ISCTE, who supported me in my project.

57. The name can be traced back to the Cuban anthropologist Fernando Ortiz (1881–1969), who from the beginning of the twentieth century dedicated himself to researching (trans)cultural phenomena among the former slave population of Cuba and who published numerous works on this subject; see, for example, Ortiz, 1984, 1993, (1906) 2001.

Chapter 1. Angola's Path toward Independence

1. See Miller, 1988, for a detailed analysis of the mechanisms, structures, and extent of the transatlantic slave trade between Angola and the Portuguese and Spanish colonies of the "New World."

2. Heintze, 2007, 2002; Birmingham, 2010; Zeuske, 2010.

3. Newitt, 2007, p. 19.

4. Miller, 1983, p. 147; Heintze, 2007.

5. Messiant, 2006, pp. 22–23.

6. All details regarding the ethnographical classification of the Angolan population and its distribution throughout Angolan territory should be treated with caution. This classification of the population was first undertaken by the colonizers, and it provides a very inaccurate picture of the ethnographic reality. Moreover, demographic changes in the wake of independence led to further shifts. Nevertheless, scholars continue today to work on the basis of the "nine main groups" described by the Portuguese ethnographer José Redinha, though this classification clearly refers to linguistic borders. See Fleisch, 1994, pp. 85–87; Götz, 2002, pp. 40–43; and Schubert, 1997, pp. 22–24.

7. Messiant, 1998, p. 135.

8. Newitt, 2007, pp. 50–53.

9. Heywood, 2000, pp. 85–86.

10. Messiant, 2006, pp. 90–94.

11. Bender, 1978, p. 97.

12. Ibid., pp. 141–143.

13. Andresen Guimarães, 2001, p. 10.

14. Quoted in Oliveira de Márques, 2001, p. 609.

15. See Messiant, 2006, p. 61.

16. Andresen Guimarães, 2001, pp. 16–18.

17. For more information on Portuguese settlement policy, see Bender, 1978, pp. 95–131.

18. Ibid., pp. 129–130.

19. Group 1: Portuguese born in Portugal. Group 2: Portuguese born in Angola. Group 3: *Mestiços* (politically equal to 1st and 2nd). Group 4: *Assimilados* (culturally assimilated and "civilized" Africans could apply for this status; they had limited political rights). Group 5: *Indígenas* (Africans without political rights). See Birmingham, 2006, p. 77.

20. See Messiant, 2006, pp. 104–106, 313–315.

21. Birmingham, 1992, pp. 15–16.

22. Messiant, 1998, p. 133.

23. Birmingham, 2006, pp. 83–84.

24. MacQueen, 2002, pp. 24–25.

25. Birmingham, 1992, pp. 20–21.

26. Newitt, 2007, p. 78; Birmingham, 1992, p. 33.

27. Messiant, 2006, pp. 149–152.

28. Cf. Heimer, 1979, p. 10; MacQueen, 1997, pp. 17–20.

29. Birmingham, 1992, pp. 42–43.

30. Cf. Messiant, 1998 and 2006.

31. The Portuguese António de Oliveira de Cadornega (approx. 1610–1690) went as an ordinary soldier to Luanda in 1639 and pursued a military career there, culminating in a position within local government. He wrote one of the most enlightening historical works about early colonialism in Angola, the three-volume *História Geral das Guerras Angolanas*. According to Cadornega, the *mestiço* population of Luanda was the result of a lack of Portuguese women, which led to the soldiers, sailors, and other Portuguese civilians entering relationships with African women and resulted in a high number of mixed African and Portuguese offspring. Birmingham, 2006, p. 8, refers to Cadornega in his

depiction of "racial mingling" between Portuguese and Africans as follows: "Many military men married into the local society and joined the ranks of the Creole bourgeoisie. Black genes soon overwhelmed white ones, and by 1681 Cadornega, an old soldier from Portugal, bemoaned the fact that in his beloved Angola sons were swarthy, grandsons were dusky, and all else was blackness." For references to Afro-Portuguese, see also Newitt, 2007, pp. 24–26, 33–36. For references to the biography and works of Cadornega, see Heintze, 1996, pp. 48–58.

32. Schubert, 1997, p. 190; Birmingham, 1998, pp. 267–270; 2008.

33. See Pélissier, 1978, pp. 260–262; Messiant, 2006, pp. 351–353.

34. Messiant, 2006, pp. 357–360.

35. Marcum, 1969 (vol. 1) and 1978 (vol. 2).

36. Chilcote, 1972a.

37. Heimer, 1979; Messiant, 1998 and 2006.

38. Birmingham, 1978, 1992, 1993, 2002, 2003b.

39. Mabeko Tali, 2001a, 2001b.

40. Pacheco, 1997.

41. Lara, 1997, 1999, 2008a, 2008b; Associação Tchiweka de Documentação (ATD), 2009. In 2008, Paulo and Wanda Lara founded the Associação Tchiweka de Documentação in Luanda in order to give public access to their father's private archives; see http://sites.google.com/site/tchiweka/Home (accessed 10 August 2013). As a result of this initiative, the collection of documents was also published.

42. Bridgland, 1986.

43. Heywood, 2000.

44. See Pacheco, 1997, who provides evidence that the MPLA was not founded in Angola in 1956, but that its agenda and objectives were drawn up in Tunis, and the organization was born in Conakry in 1960. Pacheco bases his argument on interviews with the founding members of the MPLA and numerous early MPLA documents. Messiant, 1998, p. 138, also cites 1960 as the year in which the MPLA was founded; see also Messiant, 2008b, pp. 105–107. Mabeko Tali, 2001a, pp. 47–62, also discusses the controversy surrounding the formation of the MPLA, and he too concludes that it was in 1960.

45. Reprinted in Lara, 1999, pp. 54–63.

46. Cf. MacQueen 1997, pp. 18–19; Burchett, 1978, p. 3.

47. For the precursors of the MPLA, see Lara, 1999, pp. 25–28, 64–68. Burness, 1995, refers to the literary, cultural, and political affinities between Caribbean (Cuban) and African (Angolan) authors and poets.

48. Lara, 1999, pp. 25–27; Marcum, 1969 (vol. 1), pp. 38–39; Sonderegger, 2010, pp. 172–175.

49. See also McMahon, 2006, p. 21. The author refers here to the Soviet Union's early interest in the anti-colonial movement and the influence it exerted, partly through the communist parties that had been established in the (former) colonial cities. On relations with the Soviet leadership, see Westad, 2005, pp. 210–213.

50. Chabal, 2002, p. 26.

51. Messiant, 1998, p. 138.

52. For the MPLA's agenda in the 1960s, see Chilcote, 1972b, pp. 228–235.

53. Cf. Heimer, 1979, p. 99.

54. For a revealing account of the political, ideological, and organizational problems of the MPLA up to the mid-1970s, see Heimer, 1979, pp. 98–108.

55. Birmingham, 1992, p. 37. Similar arguments are presented by Keese, 2007, pp. 111–115.

56. Cf. MacQueen, 1997, p. 56.

57. For an in-depth study of the dissolution of the Kingdom of Ndongo, see Heintze, 1996b, pp. 111–168.

58. Marcum, 1969 (vol. 1), pp. 13–15; Heintze, 1996b, pp. 111–168.

59. For more information on relations between the Portuguese conquerors and the Kingdom of Ndongo, and on the history of the Kingdom of Njina, see Heintze, 1996b.

60. See Birmingham, 1992, p. 37. Similar arguments are given by Keese, 2007, pp. 111–113.

61. Neto, 1976.

62. Birmingham, 1992, pp. 40–41.

63. Brinkmann, 2003, pp. 303–325; Newitt, 2007, p. 83.

64. See interview between Kapiassa Husseini and Neto from the year 1971, contained in the archive of the Basler Afrika Bibliographien (BAB): AA5, Archive medic' angola/kämpfendes afrika 1971–1988, Gruppe I: medic' angola 1970–73, I.3. Varia, 1971–72; see also Gleijeses, 2002, pp. 242–244.

65. Gleijeses, 2002, p. 82.

66. For an in-depth study of history, traditions, and identities in northwest Angola, see Marcum, 1969, pp. 49–110; Pélissier, 1978, pp. 259–269; and Messiant, 2006, pp. 352–356; for early FNLA documents, see Chilcote, 1972a, pp. 62–72.

67. Messiant, 1998, p. 138. Following independence, the former colony of Belgian Congo was renamed the Republic of the Congo with the addition of "Léopoldville" in order to distinguish it from the neighboring, formerly French, Republic of the Congo (Brazzaville). In 1964, the country was renamed the Democratic Republic of the Congo, and then from 1971 to 1997 Zaire, as part of the "Africanization" policy of its autocratic head of state Mobouto Sese Soko.

68. Birmingham, 1992, p. 41.

69. Messiant, 1998, pp. 139, 146.

70. Ibid., p. 138.

71. For more detail, see Marcum, 1978, pp. 197–210.

72. Heimer, 1978, pp. 92–93; for the letter regarding Savimbi's resignation from the GRAE, see Chilcote, 1972a, pp. 154–155.

73. Heimer, 1978, pp. 96–100; Messiant, 1998, pp. 145–146.

74. Marcum, 1978, pp. 245–247.

75. Ibid., pp. 166–167.

76. Cf. Birmingham, 1993, p. 10.

77. For details of Ovimbundu under Portuguese colonial rule, see Heywood, 2000.

78. MacQueen, 1997, p. 36.

79. Birmingham, 1992, pp. 47–48.

80. Marcum, 1969, pp. 19–20; Malaquias, 2007b, p. 67.

81. Messiant, 1998, p. 146.

82. Heywood, 2000, pp. 183–184.

83. Heimer also offers a good overview of the various models for postcolonial Angola that were conceived, drawn up, debated, and rejected. Heimer, 1979, pp. 117–119.

84. For a transcription of the Alvor Agreement, see Correia, 1996, pp. 271–274.

85. Andresen Guimarães, 2001, p. 92.

86. Birmingham, 2002, p. 145.

87. For details on the "Eastern Revolt," see Mabeko Tali, 2001b, pp. 119–123.

88. For details on the "Active Revolt," see ibid., pp. 184–195; and Messiant, 1998, p. 148.

89. For more details, see MacQueen, 2002, pp. 28–35.

90. Birmingham, 2002, p. 146.

91. Kapuscinski, 1994.

92. Gleijeses, 2002, pp. 247–249.

93. Ibid., pp. 259–262.

94. Westad, 2005, p. 233.

95. Ibid., pp. 215–217.

96. Gleijeses, 2002, pp. 366–369.

97. *Verde Olivo* 17, no. 18, 4 May 1975, pp. 10–11; *Verde Olivo* 17, no. 21, 25 May 1975, pp. 12–15.

98. *Bohemia*, no. 31, 1975, pp. 42–44.

99. García Márquez, 1977, p. 125. García Márquez's article "Operación Carlota," which justified the Cuban military presence in Angola to the (left-wing) international community, indicated that there had been an agreement between Saraiva de Carvalho and the Cuban government to send Cuban soldiers to Angola.

100. Bia Abudu, 1976, pp. 200–205. The author names (among others) the governments of Algeria, Benin, Burundi, Chad, Equatorial Guinea, Ghana, Guinea-Bissau, Guinea-Conacry, Libya, Mali, Madagascar, Niger, and Nigeria as states within the OAU that supported the MPLA in early 1976 and sanctioned Cuban military intervention.

101. According to the Cuban government's interpretation, the namesake of the Cuban military intervention in Angola, Carlota, was a slave with African roots who worked on the Cuban Triunvirato sugar plantation in the province of Matanzas. She is said to have led the 1843 slave uprising that took place there. The use of her name symbolized the link between resistance by African slaves in Cuba and the Cuban support for Angolan independence.

102. Gleijeses, 2002 (see particularly pp. 266–320); George, Edward, 2005, pp. 60–94.

103. Rey Cabrera, 1989.

104. *Bohemia*, no. 37, 1975, pp. 66–69. The Cuban journalist Hugo Rius, who interviewed Jorge Teixeira, was for many years responsible for reporting on Angola and Africa in the political and cultural weekly magazine *Bohemia*. His reports and articles about Angola (including the interview with Paulo Jorge Teixeira) were published in 1982 under the title *Angola: Crónicas de esperanza y la victoria*. For the interview with Paulo Jorge, see Rius, 1982, pp. 23–33.

Chapter 2. Cuba, 1959–1975

1. For the fundamental ethos and objectives of the universal Christian mission, see Hausberger, 2004, pp. 9–20. In the official and day-to-day language of Cuba, military and civil operations abroad are still referred to as *misiones* (missions) today.

2. Domínguez, 1989, p. 7. The Cuban exile and historian Domínguez is one of the most knowledgeable scholars of Cuban foreign policy after 1959. See also Leogrande, 1980, p. 52. Gleijeses's (2010, pp. 327–329) own research led him to compare Cuban

foreign policy on a global scale with that of the United States, owing to Cuba's military activity.

3. Woodford Bray, Bray, 1985, p. 352.
4. Pérez Jr., 1988, p. 375.
5. Zeuske, 2004, p. 207.
6. LeoGrande, 1980, pp. 4–5.
7. Ibid., p. 6; Guevara, 2003, pp. 146–148.
8. Thomas, 1998, pp. 1194–1195.
9. Zeuske, 2004, pp. 207–208, 216.
10. Within the context of Ibero-American colonial history, the term "Creole" initially only applied to the descendants of white Spanish settlers. It was not until the late eighteenth century that the name began also to refer to Africans (freemen and slaves). In colonial Cuba, the Creole upper class comprised, with very few exceptions, whites of Spanish origin.
11. Zeuske, 2004, pp. 12–15.
12. Initially it was the Partido Socialista Popular (PSP, Popular Socialist Party), and from 1965 it was named Partido Comunista de Cuba (PCC, Communist Party of Cuba).
13. Pérez-Stable, 1994, pp. 100–101.
14. Zeuske, 2002, pp. 192–193.
15. Gleijeses, 2004, pp. 60–63.
16. Guevara, 2003a, p. 218.
17. Valdés, 1979, p. 89.
18. Zeuske, 2004, p. 207.
19. McMahon, 2006, pp. 17–18.
20. Nazario, Benemelis, 1989, p. 13.
21. Guevara, 2003a, p. 193.
22. Skierka, 2002, pp. 238–240.
23. Pérez Jr., 1988, pp. 344–345, 349.
24. Pérez-Stable, 1994, p. 120.
25. Pérez Jr., 1988, pp. 355–358.
26. Valdés, 1979, p. 89.
27. Ibid., p. 90.
28. Pérez-Stable, 1994, pp. 130–131.
29. Ibid., pp. 124–126.
30. The five gray years were heralded by the arrest of the author Heberto Padilla, who had the poetry prize awarded to him by the Cuban Writers' Union for his book of poetry *Fuera del juego* (Out of the game). The prize was withdrawn after government intervention on the grounds that his ideology was "outside the revolution." Prominent European and Latin American writers from the left, who until then had supported the revolution (Jean-Paul Sartre, Mario Vargas Llosa, Julio Cortázar, Hans Magnus Enzensberger, et al.), publicly protested against the withdrawal of the prize and Padilla's subsequent arrest. Padilla was not allowed to leave Cuba until 1981, and he died in the United States in 2000. See Hoffmann, 2009, pp. 166–167.
31. Zeuske, 2004, pp. 222–223.
32. George, 2005, p. 143. George refers to information given by the Chief of the Armed Forces, Raúl Castro, on 27 May 1991.
33. Castro, 2005.

34. Gleijeses, 2006b, p. 138. According to Gleijeses's information, this figure came from the FAR archive.

35. See Roca, 1982, pp. 175–176. For more information on payment made by the Angolan government to the Cuban government in return for civil aid, see chapter 6, pp. 181–188.

36. The parallels between the Cuban and Chinese revolutions have yet to be studied in detail; Patrick Manning and Yinhong Cheng (2003) have compared some of the developments and experiments in the education sector.

37. Valdés, 1979, p. 88.

38. Zeuske, 2004, p. 208.

39. Hatzky, 2004, pp. 257–258.

40. Guevara, 2003a, p. 152.

41. Ibid., p. 225.

42. Ibid., p. 228.

43. Goldenberg, 1963, pp. 442–443.

44. Guevara, 2003a, p. 121.

45. Ibid., pp. 126–127.

46. Guevara, 1968, p. 23.

47. Gleijeses, 2002, p. 30.

48. Ibid., p. 40.

49. Pérez Jr., 1988, pp. 342–345.

50. Castañeda, 1998, pp. 333–334; Anderson, 1997, pp. 544–546.

51. For more details on the controversies surrounding Guevara, see the biographies written by Castañeda, 1998; and Anderson, 1997; and the Castro biography by Skierka, 2002, p. 223.

52. Risquet Valdés, 2000, pp. 20–21.

53. Ibid., p. 24; Gleijeses, 2002, pp. 82–83.

54. Gleijeses, 2002, pp. 82–83. According to Gleijeses, the details of the Brazzaville meeting between the MPLA leaders and Guevara came partly from an interview with Lúcio Lara and his wife, Ruth.

55. See Risquet Valdés, 2000, who recounts from his own personal perspective his experiences and duties within the Bataillon Patrice Lumumba. See the interview with Rolando Kindelán Bles, the military leader of the troop, in Baez, 1996, pp. 57–62, here pp. 61–62. Following Angolan independence, he was responsible for organizing and training the Angolan Presidential Guards.

56. Kindelán Bles confirmed in an interview published in 1996 that support was given to the MPLA; see Baez, 1996, p. 62.

57. Risquet Valdés, 2000, pp. 184–185.

58. Mabeko Tali, 2001b, p. 130.

59. Ibid., pp. 130–132; Gleijeses, 2002, pp. 82–83; for the relationship between Cuba and the MPLA between 1965 and 1967, see Gleijeses, 2002, pp. 244–245.

60. Guevara, 1968, p. 150.

Chapter 3. The "Afro-Latin American Nation"

1. Westad, 2005, p. 239.
2. See Chilcote, 1972b, pp. 228–229.
3. Mabeko Tali, 2001b, p. 131.

4. Guevara, 1968, pp. 143–158.

5. Mabeko Tali, 2001b, pp. 131–132.

6. For more details, see Gleijeses, 2004, pp. vii–lv (preface by Jorge Risquet Valdés), 513–540; George, 2005, pp. 105–115, 116–124.

7. Heimer, 1979, p. 219.

8. Gleijeses, 2004, pp. xviii–xix (preface by Jorge Risquet Valdés).

9. Interview Angola 2006, Luanda, 9 March, 11 March, and 21 March 2006 (Lopo do Nascimento).

10. Ibid.

11. Heimer, 1979, p. 223.

12. Ibid.

13. Interview Angola 2006, Luanda, 9 March, 11 March, and 21 March 2006 (Lopo do Nascimento).

14. Reporting on Cuba was particularly extensive during Agostinho Neto's first state visit to Cuba (see, for example, *Jornal de Angola*, 23 July, 27 July, 28 July, 30 July, and 31 July 1976) and during Fidel Castro's first state visit to Angola in March 1977.

15. As part of the bilateral cooperative agreement, the Cubans and Angolans also signed a cultural agreement in 1976.

16. Guevara, 2003a, p. 222.

17. Mabeko Tali, 2001b, p. 130.

18. Chabal et al., 2002, p. 18.

19. Gleijeses, 2002, p. 227; Gleijeses, 2010, pp. 332–233.

20. LeoGrande, 1980, p. 1.

21. The main contributions to this discussion are LeoGrande, 1980; Blasier and Mesa-Lago, 1979; Mesa-Lago and Belkin, 1982; Erisman, 1985; Díaz-Briquets, 1989.

22. Pascoe, 1988, p. 94.

23. Ibid., p. 89.

24. Eckstein, 1985, pp. 376–377.

25. Gleijeses, 2006b, p. 126; see also Gleijeses, 2010, p. 344.

26. Gleijeses, 2006b, p. 111.

27. Pascoe, 1988, pp. 91–92; Eckstein, 1994, pp.183–184.

28. Gleijeses, 2006b, p. 110.

29. Ibid., p. 103.

30. Gleijeses alludes frequently to Castro's apparently altruistic and idealistic political objectives; see Gleijeses, 2010, pp. 342–345.

31. Valdés, 1979, p. 110.

32. As evidence he cited Castro, who described his own foreign policy as follows: "If you want to be an accurate observer of reality and not a theoretician passing judgment on the problems to this world from an ivory tower . . . you have to understand politics as a principle, one bound by conditions, by reality." Valdés, 1979, p. 110.

33. Eckstein, 1985, p. 375; Eckstein, 1994, p. 186.

34. Interview United States 2005, Miami, 29 May 2005; Interview United States 2005, Miami, 30 June 2005.

35. See chapter 6, pp. 181–188.

36. Interview Angola 2006, Luanda, 9 March, 11 March, and 21 March 2006 (Lopo do Nascimento); Interview Cuba 2005, Havana, 5 January 2005.

37. The documents from the Department of International Cooperation (GICI/GII) of the Angolan Ministry of Education (MED) not only dealt with contracts and

agreements in the education sector. A large number of documents provided evidence of commercial agreements in other areas of cooperation. In 1982, the Cuban state-controlled company IMEXIN submitted a quotation for collecting basic planning data for the organization of education. RPA, MED, Relatório de viagem a Cuba, Luanda, 21 February 1983, signed (pela delegação) J. M. S., 22 pages, here pp. 7–8 (MED archive).

38. Marcum, 1987, p. 73; Messiant, 1998, pp. 155–157.

39. Castro, 1979, p. 134.

40. Castro, 1979, p. 149 (translation by Christine Hatzky and Mair Edmunds-Harrington).

41. The estimates made by Philip C. Curtin in 1969 regarding the extent of the transatlantic slave trade still serve as a guideline today. See Zeuske, 2002, p. 75.

42. Ferrer, 1999.

43. Helg, 1995.

44. Kapcia, 2000.

45. Barnet, 2003.

46. Zeuske, 2002, pp. 115–116; Pérez Jr., 1988, p. 177.

47. García Márquez, 1977.

48. Martí, 1963, p. 17.

49. De la Fuente, 2001, p. 6.

50. Helg, 1995.

51. De la Fuente, 2001.

52. Ibid., p. 280.

53. Carbonell, 1961.

54. Edmundo Desnoes, quoted in Taylor, 1988, p. 19.

55. Publications and contributions are too numerous to list fully. Many contributions can be found on the website of afrocuba (www.afrocubaweb.com, accessed 7 February 2013).

56. Quoted in Taylor, 1988, p. 24.

57. See De la Fuente, 2001, p. 296; Taylor, 1988.

58. Taylor, 1988, p. 27; see also De la Fuente, 2001, pp. 301–303.

59. Taylor, 1988, p. 35; De la Fuente, 2001, p. 307.

60. Castro, 1979, pp. 228–243, here pp. 236–237 (translation by Hatzky and Edmunds-Harrington). For an English translation of the entire speech, see http://lanic.utexas.edu/project/castro/db/1976/19760726.html (accessed 16 September 2013).

61. Erisman, 1985, pp. 43–44; Smith, 1985, pp. 339–340.

62. Smith, 1985, pp. 340–341.

63. Castro, 1979, pp. 228–243, here pp. 236–237.

64. Castro, 1976 ("Angola—Girón africano" [Angola—The African Bay of Pigs]).

65. Díaz-Briquets, 1989, p. 8.

66. Taylor, 1988, p. 34.

Chapter 4. Recruiting for Engagement in Angola

1. See George, 2005, p. 324n1. George is referring to a speech made by Raúl Castro, who on the occasion of the return of civil and military internationalists from Angola on 27 May 1991 put the number of soldiers at 377,033 and the number of civilians at "approximately 50,000."

2. Pérez Jr., 1988, p. 365. Between 1953 and 1970 Cuba's population grew from 5.8 million to 8.5 million; in 1984 there were an estimated 10 million inhabitants.

3. Jiménez Rodríguez, 2008b.

4. Castro, 1979, p. 241.

5. The historian Yinghong Cheng presented a study in 2009 of the origins of the concept of the "new man" during the French Enlightenment and the way it spread within the context of various socialist revolutions during the twentieth century, with a particular emphasis on China and Cuba.

6. Guevara, 2003b, pp. 14–36.

7. Ibid., p. 32.

8. *Bohemia*, no. 31, 30 July 1976, p. 54; Castro, 1979, p. 241.

9. Castro, 1979, p. 240, English translation at http://lanic.utexas.edu/project/castro/db/1976/19760726.html (accessed 16 September 2013).

10. Ibid., p. 237.

11. Ibid., p. 238.

12. The Cuban weekly magazine dedicated a complete issue full of photos to the state visit; see *Bohemia*, no. 31, 30 July 1976.

13. *Bohemia*, no. 31, 30 July 1976, p. 65.

14. Ibid., p. 67.

15. Among the films Vega Belmonte made on behalf of the Cuban armed forces were *Operación Carlota*, *Recuento*, *Fidelito*, *Huambo*, and *Mayombe*. These films are currently unavailable and are obviously being stored in the film archive of the Cuban armed forces. Even Vega Belmonte was unable to provide me with a copy. Despite repeated requests, I was not allowed to watch the films.

16. Interview Cuba 2005, Havana, 5 January 2005 (Belkis Vega Belmonte). "Girón" is the Cuban name for the successful defeat of the Bay of Pigs invasion in April 1961; "Moncada" refers to the attack on the Moncada barracks in Santiago de Cuba on 26 July 1953, which Castro and his group organized.

17. For more details on the Destacamento Pedagógico "Manuel Ascunce Domenech," see Turner Martí et al., 1996; see also Concurso "Angola en la memoria," Una misión internacionalista en la República Popular de Angola con el nombre "Che Guevara," Autora B.E.T.A., Guantánamo, 2002, DPI I, Lubango, Prov. Huila, 1978–1979, 21 pages, here p. 13 (Archive of the Casa de Angola, Havana).

18. Interview Cuba 2006, Havana, 21 September 2006 (José Ramón Fernández, former Cuban Minister of Education, 1970–1990).

19. Martí, 1975, p. 375, quoted in MINED, UJC, FEU, Destacamento Pedagógico Internacionalista "Che Guevara," Documento de Base, October 1977, 4 pages, here p. 1 (MINED archive).

20. Castro, 1979, p. 149.

21. Betto, 1987, pp. 121–122. Only recently, in the introduction of a work published in 2010 by Fidel Castro on the beginnings of the revolutionary guerrilla struggle in the Sierra Maestra, *La victoria estratégica*, Castro underlined in very positive terms his Jesuit education and the values it taught him, and he expressed his admiration for his teachers. I wish to thank Jorge Domínguez for this information.

22. Ibid., pp. 205–206.

23. Ibid., p. 261.

24. One exception is the 2006 publication *Cangamba*, which describes a UNITA

attack on the Cuban unit in the east-Angolan province of Moxico in 1983. It contains the statements of sixty Cuban and Angolan soldiers who fought on the side of the Angolan government (Martín Blandino, 2006). The film *Cangamba*, shown to the Cuban public in 2008, fulfills all the clichés of military engagement in Angola and glorifies the role of the Cuban military in this battle.

25. This was confirmed by one of my Cuban interviewees, living in exile in Miami. She told me that she had worked in Cuba for a governmental publishing house and was commissioned by the government to write a book about what motivated Cubans to volunteer to serve in Angola. Interview United States 2005, Miami, 2 July 2005.

26. Fresnillo, 1982; Concepción, 1987.

27. Jiménez, 2008a, pp. 13–14.

28. Ibid., p. 13; Interview Cuba 2004, Santiago de Cuba, 26 November 2004.

29. Interview Cuba 2004, Santiago de Cuba, 31 October 2004; Interview Cuba 2004, Santa Clara, 11 December 2004; Interview Cuba 2004, Santa Clara, 13 December 2004.

30. Interview Angola 2006, Luanda, 1 February 2006.

31. See Pino, 1987.

32. Aguila, 1989, p. 140. The author provided no information whatsoever about the background to the talks, his interviewees, or his interviewing methods.

33. Castro, 2005.

34. See Interview Cuba 2004, Santiago de Cuba, 1 November 2004; Interview Cuba 2004, Santiago de Cuba, 4 November 2004; Interview Cuba 2004, Santiago de Cuba, 5 November 2004; Interview Cuba 2004, Santiago de Cuba, 9 November 2004; Interview Cuba 2004, Santiago de Cuba, 11 November 2004; Interview Cuba 2004, Santiago de Cuba, 11 November 2004; Interview Cuba 2004, Santiago de Cuba, 12 November 2004; Interview Cuba 2004, Santiago de Cuba, 12 November 2004; Interview Cuba 2004, Santiago de Cuba, 15 November 2004; Interview Cuba 2004, Santiago de Cuba, 22 November 2004; Interview Cuba 2004, Santa Clara, 15 December 2004; Interview Cuba 2004, Havana, 23 December 2004; Interview Cuba 2004, Havana, 25 December 2004.

35. Interview Cuba 2006, Havana, 25 May and 31 May 2006 (Limbania "Nancy" Jiménez Rodríguez).

36. Interview Cuba 2004, Havana, 18 October 2004; Interview Cuba 2004, Santiago de Cuba, 19 November 2004; Interview Cuba 2005, Santiago de Cuba, 11 January 2005.

37. Interview Cuba 2004, Santa Clara, 16 December 2004; Interview Cuba 2004, Santa Clara, 16 December 2004.

38. Interview Cuba 2004, Santiago de Cuba, 22 November 2004; Interview Cuba 2004, Cienfuegos, 9 December 2004; Interview Cuba 2005, Santiago de Cuba, 10 January 2005; Interview Cuba 2005, Santiago de Cuba, 10 January 2005; Interview Cuba 2004, Santiago de Cuba, 29 October 2004; Interview Cuba 2004, Santiago de Cuba, 11 November 2004; Interview Cuba 2004, Santiago de Cuba, 11 November 2004; Interview Cuba 2004, Santiago de Cuba, 15 November 2004; Interview Cuba 2004, Santa Clara, 11 December 2004; Interview Cuba 2004, Santa Clara, 17 December 2004; Interview Cuba 2004, Santiago de Cuba, 11 November 2004.

39. Interview Cuba 2004, Santiago de Cuba, 9 November 2004; Interview Cuba 2004, Santiago de Cuba, 17 November 2004; Interview Cuba 2004, Santiago de Cuba, 15 November 2004; Interview Cuba 2004, Santa Clara, 11 December 2004; Interview Cuba 2004, Santa Clara, 13 December 2004; Interview Cuba 2004, Santa Clara, 17

December 2004; Interview Cuba 2004, Havana, 23 December 2004; Interview Cuba 2004, Havana, 31 December 2004.

40. Interview Cuba 2004, Santiago de Cuba, 1 November 2004.

41. "Quien no tiene de Congo tiene de Carabalí." See Interview Cuba 2004, Santiago de Cuba, 11 November 2004; Interview Cuba 2004, Santa Clara, 11 December 2004; Interview Cuba 2005, Santiago de Cuba, 10 January 2005. Before and during the Atlantic slave trade in the Caribbean, the slaves from the Portuguese territories in the Congo region (e.g., from today's Angola) were known as "Congos"; since the slaves were named according to their (presumed) place of origin, this term is as vague as "Carabali," which is used to describe a group of slaves who were presumed to come from the coastal region between Benin and Camaroon. See Zeuske, 2002, p. 106; Zeuske, 2006, pp. 200–203.

42. Interview Cuba 2004, Havana, 18 October 2004; Interview Cuba 2004, Santiago de Cuba, 19 November 2004; Interview Cuba 2005, Santiago de Cuba, 11 January 2005.

43. Interview Cuba 2004, Santa Clara, 14 December 2004.

44. Interview Cuba 2004, Santiago de Cuba, 3 November 2004; Interview Cuba 2004, Santiago de Cuba, 22 November 2004; Interview Cuba 2004, Santiago de Cuba, 26 November 2004; Interview Cuba 2004, Cienfuegos, 3 December 2004; Interview Cuba 2004, Santa Clara, 11 December 2004.

45. Interview Cuba 2004, Cienfuegos, 3 December 2004.

46. Ibid.

47. See, for example, Benemelis, 1988, 2002.

48. Interview United States 2005, Miami, 30 June 2005.

49. Interview United States 2005, Miami, 29 June 2005.

50. Interview Cuba 2006, Havana, 19 June 2006. In 1965, Puente Ferro was in Congo-Brazzaville with Guevara and worked subsequently for fourteen months as a military doctor for the "Batallion Patricio Lumumba." Immediately after the independence of Angola in November 1975, he went to Angola as a military doctor and worked with a Cuban unit to organize the defense against the military invasion from neighboring Zaire in the enclave of Cabinda. In 1977, he returned to Cuba, where he was, among other things, responsible for organizing the civil campaign. Between 1983 and 1986, he was the Cuban ambassador in Angola. At the time of the interview in 2006, he was head of the Africa department of the Central Committee of the PCC at the age of eighty.

51. Interview Cuba 2004, Santiago de Cuba, 28 October 2004; Interview Cuba 2004, Santiago de Cuba, 17 November 2004; Interview Cuba 2004, Santiago de Cuba, 22 November 2004; Interview Cuba 2004, Santa Clara, 15 December 2004.

52. Interview Cuba 2004, Santiago de Cuba, 17 November 2004; Interview United States 2005, Miami, 8 July 2005 (Alcibíades Hidalgo).

53. Interview Cuba 2004, Santiago de Cuba, 28 October 2004.

54. Interview Cuba 2004, Cienfuegos, 9 December 2004.

55. Concurso "Angola en la memoria," Recuerdos de una misión, Autora D.G.P., Havana, 2002, DPI II, 1979–1982, Prov. Moçamedes, 32 pages, here p. 3.

56. Turner Martí et al., 1996, p. 30.

57. Interview Cuba 2004, Cienfuegos, 9 December 2004; Interview Cuba 2005, Havana, 5 January 2005.

58. Interview Angola 2006, Luanda, 1 February and 21 March 2006 (Pedro Domingos Peterson); Interview Angola 2006, Luanda, 27 January and 17 March 2006 (Artur Pestana, "Pepetela").

59. Interview Cuba 2004, Santiago de Cuba, 31 October 2004; Interview Cuba 2004, Santiago de Cuba, 12 November 2004; Interview Cuba 2004, Santiago de Cuba, 4 November 2004; Interview Cuba 2004, Santiago de Cuba, 12 November 2004; Interview Cuba 2004, Santiago de Cuba, 9 November 2004.

60. Interview Cuba 2004, Santiago de Cuba, 31 October 2004; Interview Cuba 2004, Santiago de Cuba, 29 October 2004; Interview Cuba 2004, Santiago de Cuba, 3 November 2004; Interview Cuba 2004, Santiago de Cuba, 11 November 2004; Interview Cuba 2004, Santiago de Cuba, 15 November 2004; Interview Cuba 2004, Santiago de Cuba, 17 November 2004; Interview Cuba 2004, Santiago de Cuba, 22 November 2004; Interview Cuba 2004, Santa Clara, 12 December 2004.

61. Interview Cuba 2004, Santiago de Cuba, 31 October 2004.

62. Ibid.

63. Ibid.

64. Interview Cuba 2004, Santiago de Cuba, 17 November 2004; Interview Cuba 2004, Santa Clara, 11 December 2004; Interview Cuba 2004, Santa Clara, 11 December 2004; Interview Cuba 2004, Santa Clara, 13 December 2004; Interview Cuba 2004, Santa Clara, 13 December 2004; Interview Cuba 2004, Santa Clara, 14 December 2004; Interview Cuba 2004, Santa Clara, 15 December 2004; Interview Cuba 2004, Santa Clara, 16 December 2004; Interview Cuba 2004, Santa Clara, 16 December 2004; Interview Cuba 2004, Santa Clara, 17 December 2004.

65. Interview Cuba 2004, Santa Clara, 15 December 2004; Interview Cuba 2004, Santa Clara, 16 December 2004.

66. Interview Cuba 2004, Santiago de Cuba, 9 November 2004; Interview Cuba 2004, Santiago de Cuba, 19 November 2004; Interview Cuba 2004, Santiago de Cuba, 24 November 2004.

67. Interview Cuba 2004, Santiago de Cuba, 17 November 2004.

68. Over the last few decades, historical, anthropological, and sociological research on travel and tourism has developed considerably. One of the main research areas is the motivation of travelers. The results of these studies underlined those of my own research. Urry, 1990; Culler, 1981; Henning, 1997.

69. Interview Cuba 2004, Santiago de Cuba, 6 November 2004; Interview Cuba 2004, Santiago de Cuba, 8 November 2004; Interview Cuba 2004, Santiago de Cuba, 18 November 2004; Interview Cuba 2004, Santiago de Cuba, 19 November 2004; Interview Cuba 2004, Santiago de Cuba, 24 November 2004; Interview Cuba 2004, Cienfuegos, 5 December 2004; Interview Cuba 2004, Cienfuegos, 8 December 2004; Interview Cuba 2004, Santa Clara, 15 December 2004.

70. Interview United States 2005, Miami, 2 July 2005; Interview United States 2005, Miami, 14 June 2005.

71. Interview Cuba 2004, Santiago de Cuba, 8 November 2004.

72. Interview Cuba 2004, Santiago de Cuba, 11 November 2004.

73. Interview US 2005, Miami, 2 July 2005.

74. Interview United States 2005, Miami, 14 June 2005.

75. Aguila, 1989, p. 130.

76. Arnaldo Ochoa Sánchez (1930–1989), the prominent and popular general of the Cuban army in Angola and veteran of the Cuban guerrilla war, was sentenced to death along with three other high-ranking military officials in a show trial. They were executed by firing squad in July 1989. The four accused were charged with building up contacts with the Colombian Medellín Cartel and trafficking in drugs and money. Ochoa and several of his most important advisors and high-ranking officials of the Ministry of the Interior, who were all members of the inner power circle of the Cuban government, were accused not only of trafficking with the Colombian cocaine mafia run by Pablo Escobar but also of organizing illegal trade in Angola.

77. Interview United States 2005, Miami, 8 July 2005; Interview United States 2005, Miami, 2 July 2005; Interview United States 2005, Miami, 14 June 2005; Interview Cuba 2004, Santiago de Cuba, 22 November 2004.

78. Castro, 1979, p. 134.

79. *Verde Olivo*, no. 48, 30 November 1975, pp. 40–43.

80. Interview Angola 2006, Luanda, 1 February 2006.

81. Interview Cuba 2004, Santiago de Cuba, 22 November 2004.

82. Interview Angola 2006, Luanda, 1 February 2006.

83. Interview United States 2005, Miami, 29 June 2005. See also *Verde Olivo*, no. 4, 23 January 1977, p. 60–61, a report on the propaganda documentary *La Guerra de Angola* directed by the Cuban director Miguel Fleitas.

84. Aguila, 1989, p. 136.

85. Interview United States 2005, Miami, 14 June 2005.

86. Interview United States 2005, Miami, 8 July 2005 (Alcibíades Hidalgo).

87. See Pino, 1987.

88. Lievesley, 2004, p. 113–114; Zeuske, 2004, pp. 234–235.

89. Aguila, 1989, pp. 137, 140.

Chapter 5. Education Policy in Cuba and Angola

1. Leiner, 1985, p. 29.

2. Pérez Jr., 1988, p. 358.

3. Leiner, 1985, p. 28.

4. Ministerio de Educación, 1973, p. 21.

5. Ibid., pp. 16–18.

6. Smith, Padula, 1996, p. 83.

7. Martí, 1975, p. 375.

8. Pedagogía '86, 1986, p. 13; Pérez Jr., 1988, pp. 358–359.

9. Lewis, Ridgdon, 1977, p. 66.

10. The Conrado Benitez Brigade was named after a young volunteer in the literacy campaign, Conrado Benitez García, who was murdered on 5 January 1961, probably by anti-revolutionaries. Particularly in the two years immediately following the revolution, Cuba was subjected to acts of sabotage, orchestrated by the US secret services among others in an attempt to turn the people against the revolutionary government. See Pérez Jr., 1988, pp. 347–348. Also see Smith, Padula, 1996, p. 84.

11. Ministerio de Educación, 1973, pp. 22–25.

12. Ibid., pp. 33–34; Pérez Jr., 1988, p. 359.

13. Marischen, 1988, pp. 17–20.

14. There has not yet been a systematic, comparative study on Cuban and Chinese education policies. One of the few scholarly articles to point out some of the obvious parallels, but which otherwise only scratches the surface, is by Cheng and Manning (2003).

15. Quoted from Castro, 1993, p. 64.

16. Interview Cuba 2006, Havana, 15 June and 22 June 2006 (Lidia Turner Martí). At the time of interview, she was chairperson of the Cuban Pedagogical Association. She has written numerous studies on education in Cuba (also regarding teaching literacy).

17. Ibid. Alongside Martí, these were primarily the Catholic priest Félix Varela (1787–1853), the spiritual father of liberal education in Cuba, and the philosopher and educator José de la Luz y Caballero (1800–1862). Both were convinced that all people were equal, and they both opposed slavery. Caballero's pedagogical writings—in which he advocated education in the quest for human perfection—were revolutionary in the nineteenth century. The educational principles of Varela, Caballero, and Martí had already found their way into an education reform program for an independent Cuba while it was under US occupancy (1899–1902), though this program was never realized. It was not until the 1920s that their ideas were taken up again and popularized by the Cuban student movement and its leader Julio A. Mella. By establishing the "José Martí worker's university" in 1923, Mella was following the principle of educating the people in order to break away from the "monopoly of the ruling culture" and of emancipating people through instruction.

18. Smith, Padula, 1996, p. 84.

19. Ministerio de Educación, 1973, pp. 35–36.

20. Interview Cuba 2006, Havana, 15 June and 22 June 2006 (Lidia Turner Martí).

21. In 1976, the secondary phase was reduced to three years.

22. Ministerio de Educación, 1973, p. 69.

23. Ibid., p. 36; Interview Cuba 2006, Havana, 15 June and 22 June 2006.

24. Camilo Cienfuegos (1932–1959), alongside Castro and Guevara, was one of the most prominent political and military leaders of the Movimiento 26 de Julio. He died after his plane crashed into the sea under unexplained circumstances only several months after the revolution. Since then, Cienfuegos has been honored as one of the official heroes of the revolution.

25. Interview Cuba 2006, Havana, 15 June and 22 June 2006.

26. Lang, 2004, p. 14.

27. Ministerio de Educación, 1973, pp. 37–38.

28. Smith, Padula, 1996, p. 85.

29. Ministerio de Educación, 1973, pp. 191–192.

30. Pérez Jr., 1988, p. 360.

31. Ibid., p. 361.

32. Ministerio de Educación, 1973, pp. 78–81; Turner Martí et al., 1996, p. 5.

33. Smith, Padula, 1996, pp. 86–87.

34. For statistics and more exact demographic details for the first years after the victory of the revolution, see Pérez Jr., 1988, pp. 365–374.

35. Turner Martí et al., 1996, p. 8.

36. Ministerio de Educación, 1971.

37. Turner Martí et al., 1996, p. v.

38. The word *destacamento* denotes a detachment (of troops). Manuel Ascunce Domenech (1945–1961) was a young participant of the "Conrado Benitez" literacy brigades in 1961. Along with two of his pupils, he was brutally tortured and murdered in 1961, allegedly in an act of sabotage orchestrated by the CIA to hinder the Cuban literacy program.

39. For more details on the Destacamento Pedagógico "Manuel Ascunce Domenech," see Turner Martí et al., 1996. The MINED journal *Educación* dedicated a complete issue to the Destacamento Pedagógico "Manuel Ascunce Domenech" in 1974; see *Educación* 1974, no. 14.

40. Turner Martí et al., 1996, pp. 8–9.

41. Ibid., p. 25.

42. Ibid., p. 23.

43. Minutes of internal meetings in particular emphasized not only the constant attempts to promote the reform process despite all obstacles but also the constant willingness to scrutinize the process.

44. Silva, 1992–1994, p. 117; MPLA, 1978, pp. 8–9.

45. Messiant, 1998, pp. 142–145.

46. Birmingham, 2002, p. 149; Messiant, 1998, pp. 150–151.

47. Bhagavan, 1986, p. 38.

48. Ibid., p. 61 (table 13).

49. Gunn, 1987, p. 187; Bhagavan, 1986, p. 39.

50. Heimer, 1979, p. 230.

51. Bhagavan, 1986, p. 40.

52. Heimer, 1979, p. 233.

53. Bhagavan, 1986, p. 41; Messiant 2007, pp. 96–97; Malaquias, 2007b, pp. 116–118.

54. Marcum, 1987, p. 72.

55. For details on internal political quarrels and factions within the MPLA before and after the Alves coup d'état, see Mabeko Tali, 2001b, pp. 214–217.

56. Details of the circumstances surrounding the Nito Alves putsch are not within the scope of this study. The circumstances under which the putsch was defeated, leaving traumatic memories among the population of Luanda, continue to be debated and remain the subject of historic appraisal. This ongoing debate is illustrated in an article by Lara Pawson based upon eyewitness accounts and published in 2007. See also Burchett, 1978, pp. 106–111; Birmingham, 1978; Birmingham, 2002, pp. 150–151.

57. Wolfers, Bergerol, 1983, pp. 172–175.

58. Interview Portugal 2005, Lisbon, 16 September and 26 September 2005.

59. Messiant, 2007, pp. 95–96.

60. Somerville, 1986, p. 56; Wolfers, Bergerol, 1983, pp. 184–188; Messiant, 2008, pp. 50–52.

61. Bhagavan, 1986, pp. 36–37.

62. Marcum, 1987, pp. 72–73.

63. MPLA, 1978.

64. Ibid., pp. 16–19.

65. Heimer, 1979, p. 235. In his independence day speech, President Neto promised to fight illiteracy and make education accessible to all; see Ministério da Informação, 1975, p. 15. The new constitution guaranteed every citizen of Angola the right to an education; see ibid., p. 27.

66. Silva, 1992–1994, pp. 103–104.

67. Sebastião José de Carvalho e Mello (1699–1782), 1st Marquis of Pombal, is one of the most prominent Portuguese statesmen of the eighteenth century. As a proponent of enlightened absolutism, he introduced far-reaching economic and political reforms in Portugal and throughout the Portuguese empire.

68. Silva, 1992–1994, p. 111.

69. Ibid., pp. 106–107.

70. Vela Ngaba, 2006, pp. 66–69.

71. Silva, 1992–1994, pp. 112–114.

72. Heintze, 2004/5.

73. Silva, 1992–1994, pp. 117–118, 123–124; Vela Ngaba, 2006, pp. 66–69.

74. Silva, 1992–1994, pp. 124–125.

75. Ibid., p. 117; MPLA, 1978, pp. 8–9. Although the figures given in the second study are different, they roughly tally with those quoted by Silva.

76. MPLA, 1978, p. 8.

77. Silva, 1992–1994, pp. 120–121. This is also confirmed in a Cuban report that takes stock of the schools, school types, and teachers in the enclave of Cabinda in 1976: MINED, Memorias del trabajo de la colaboración Cubana en la República Popular de Angola, 1976–1978, 76 pages, here pp. 42–44 (from the private archive of Limbania "Nancy" Jiménez Rodríguez). I thank her for providing me with me this document.

78. MPLA, 1978, p. 9.

79. Ministério da Informação, 1975, p. 15.

80. Ibid., p. 27.

81. See RPA, Ministère de l'Éducation, Développement de l'Éducation en Republique Populaire d'Angola 1978–1980, Rapport pour la 38ème Session de la Conférence International de L'Éducation Genève (10–19 November 1981), Luanda, August 1981, p. 5 (MED archive).

82. See the history book for the seventh grade, RPA, MED, História, Ensino de base—7a Classe, Luanda 1977; and the accompanying teacher's handbook, RPA, MED, História de Angola, Luanda 1976 (MED archive).

83. MPLA, 1978, pp. 29–30, 32.

84. Vela Ngaba, 2006, pp. 91–94.

85. See Agostinho Neto's speech at the campaign launch: "Na Textang: Camarada presidente participiou na inauguração oficial da campanha nacional de alfabetização," *Jornal de Angola*, 23 November 1976, pp. 1–2.

86. Ramírez Villasana, n.d., p. 9.

87. Ministério da Educação e Cultura, 1976b.

88. The beginning of the anti-colonial war is considered to be 4 February 1961.

89. Ministério da Educação e Cultura, 1976b, pp. 78–79.

90. RPA, MED, Centro Nacional de Alfabetização, Documentos do 3. Seminário nacional pedagógico, Luanda, 4–14 April 1978 (MED archive).

91. See Ministério da Educação e Cultura, 1976a.

92. Ibid.

93. Artur Carlos Maurício Pestana dos Santos was born in 1941 in the Angolan coastal city of Benguela. His father's family was of Portuguese origin, and his mother had Brazilian ancestors. After completing his studies in sociology in Algiers, he returned to Angola and joined the MPLA's anti-colonial cause. Alongside his writings, which he

published under the pseudonym "Pepetela," he taught sociology until the mid-1990s at the Agostinho Neto University. After retiring from his post as deputy minister of education, he withdrew from politics.

94. Interview Angola 2006, Luanda, 27 January and 17 March 2006 (Artur Pestana, "Pepetela"). In 1947 Paulo Freire (1921–1997) led a literacy campaign in Brazil with the aim of empowering the poorest classes of Brazilian society (peasants, poor subsistence farmers, and urban slum-dwellers) to develop consciousness, regain their sense of humanity, and act in their own interests. Freire developed a unique method of teaching literacy that was based on the cultural features of village communities or urban neighborhoods, from which day-to-day vocabulary was drawn to develop new vocabulary. Freire's most influential work in critical pedagogy is *Pedagogy of the Oppressed*, which was first published in 1970 and has been translated into eighteen languages.

95. Interview Angola 2006, Luanda, 27 January and 17 March 2006 (Artur Pestana, "Pepetela").

96. Ibid.; see also Interview Angola 2006, Luanda, 9 March, 11 March, and 21 March 2006 (Lopo do Nascimento, the first prime minister of independent Angola, and later foreign minister).

97. Sánchez Otero, 1978, pp. 2–3; Marischen, 1988, pp. 40–43.

98. Cardenal, 2007, pp. 110–113.

99. For more details on Nicaragua's literacy campaign and education reform, see Hanemann, 2001a, 2001b.

100. Guevara, 2003b, pp. 14–16.

101. Ministério da Educação e Cultura, 1976a, pp. 36–37.

102. Interview Angola 2006, Luanda, 27 January and 17 March 2006 (Artur Pestana, "Pepetela"). See also Ramírez Villasana, n.d., p. 7.

103. "Tarefas do Gabinete de Alfabetização provisório," *Jornal de Angola*, 22 August 1976, p. 2.

104. "A Batalha da alfabetização: Ficar de fora na campanha é fazer o jogo do inimigo," *Jornal de Angola*, 24 November 1976, p. 2.

105. Cf. RPA, MED, Centro Nacional de Alfabetização, Documentos do 3. Seminário nacional pedagógico, Luanda, 4–14 April 1978 (MED archive); "Tarefas do Gabinete de Alfabetização provisório," *Jornal de Angola*, 22 August 1976, p. 2; "Ensinar é um dever revolucionário: Alfabetizar os camponeses é tarefa prioritária," *Jornal de Angola*, 4 December 1976, pp. 1, 2; "No museo de Angola iniciado curso de alfabetização," *Jornal de Angola*, 4 December 1976, p. 2.

106. "Educar a mulher angolana na ideologia marxista-leninista: Uma das resoluções tomadas durante a 1° reunião Nacional da OMA," *Jornal de Angola*, 2 December 1976, p. 2.

107. The MPLA member José Mendes de Carvalhao (nom de guerre: Hoji ya Henda), commander in chief of the FAPLA in east Angola, was killed in April 1986 during an attack on a Portuguese barracks in the east Angolan province of Moxico. Following independence he was given mythical status by the MPLA government. Hoji ya Henda is revered as a national hero and role model for the Angolan youth. Numerous heroic poems have been written about him. See Burness, 1996, pp. 93–95.

108. RPA, MED, Analise da situação da alfabetização e educação de adultos em Angola, Luanda, June 2005, p. 6 (MED archive).

109. Ramírez Villasana, n.d., p. 16.

110. The study of the Angolan Ministry of Education (RPA, MED, "Analise da situação da alfabetização e educação de adultos em Angola," Luanda, June 2005, p. 7) quotes different figures to those of the Cuban educator Ramírez Villasana, but both together confirm the assumption that the first years of the campaign were the most successful.

111. RPA, Ministério da Educação, Direcção de Formação de Quadros de Ensino, Cursos de formação de professores, Organização escolar, Luanda, 1977, 24 pages, here p. 16 (MED archive).

112. Domingos Peterson, 2003, p. 61; Vela Ngaba, 2006, p. 82.

113. RPA, Ministério da Educação, Direcção de Formação de Quadros de Ensino, Cursos de formação de professores, Organização escolar, Luanda, 1977, p. 24 (MED archive).

114. MPLA, 1978, p. 45.

115. Ibid., p. 25.

116. Heintze, 2004/5, pp. 182–184, 194–197.

117. Valdés Marquez, 1983, p. 32.

118. Projecto Integral da Questão Nacional (PIQN).

119. See RPA, MED, Analise da situação da alfabetização e educação de adultos em Angola, June 2005, p. 12; Vela Ngaba, 2006, p. 103. In his comparative study, Vela Ngaba analyzes the Angolan education system during colonialism, during the period after independence between 1975 and 1992 and after the introduction of the new system in 1992. Although he does not give explicit details of multilingual teaching in the various African languages, he does mention its introduction.

120. MPLA, 1978, p. 24.

121. Ibid., pp. 38–39.

122. Ibid., pp. 17–18.

123. "Durante as ferias: Tres mil estudantes vão trabalhar no campo; Mensagem do Ministro da Educação," *Jornal de Angola*, 28 February 1976, pp. 1, 7.

124. MPLA, 1978, pp. 27, 31–32, 37.

125. Ibid., p. 38.

126. Ibid., pp. 39–41.

127. There were two types of schools, the Institutos Médios de Educação and the Institutos Médios Normais. The latter emerged from the teacher-training institutes of the colonial period.

128. MPLA, 1978, pp. 43–44.

129. Ibid., p. 9.

130. Interview Portugal 2005, Lisbon, 16 September and 26 September 2005.

131. Cf. RPA, MED, Estatuto Orgânico do Ministério da Educação, Luanda, March 1980 (MED archive); Republique Populaire d' Angola, Projet pour le developpement de l'education, Requête a la Banque Africaine de Developpement, June 1982 (MED archive).

132. For more details on this department, see chapter 6, pp. 175–178.

133. RPA, MED, Mesa redonda sobre educação para todos, July 1991, 105 pages, here pp. 7–8 (MED archive).

134. None of the ministerial files is classified or indexed.

135. The "Mesa redonda sobre educação para todos" was a round table, an internal discussion in the MED about the status and prospects of "education for everyone."

136. RPA, MED/GII ao Gabinete do Plano de MED ao Centro Nacional de Alfabetização, No.49/GII/IV/A.B/82, Luanda, April 1982, 10 pages (MED archive). This is an MED national survey of the number of pupils starting school in the 1980/81 academic year. See also UNICEF to Domingos Peterson, Director do Instituto Nacional de Investigação e Desenvolvimento da Educação do MED (INIDE), Luanda, 23 December 1987, Assunto: Projecto educação sub-programa "A," Formação em produção e aplicação de material de lingua Portuguesa, p. 1 (MED archive).

137. RPA, MED/GII ao Gabinete do Plano de MED ao Centro Nacional de Alfabetização, No.49/GII/IV/A.B/82, Luanda, April 1982, 10 pages, here p. 5 (MED archive).

138. See Empresa Importadora y Exportadora de Infraestructura, Contrato No. 95-64076: Estudio integral para el desarrollo de la educación, Havana, April 1982, 24 pages (MED archive). The MED had checked this offer several times before finally rejecting it, as I was told by the former Angolan Prime Minister Lopo do Nascimento during my interview; see Interview Angola 2006, Luanda, 9 March, 11 March, and 21 March 2006 (Lopo do Nascimento).

139. MINED, Memorias del trabajo de la colaboración Cubana en la República Popular de Angola, 1976–1978, 76 pages, here pp. 57–58 (from the private archive of Limbania "Nancy" Jiménez Rodríguez).

140. RPA, MED, Relatório sobre a execução do plano do sector da educação de 1982, pp. 4–5 (MED archive).

141. UNICEF to Domingos Peterson, Director do Instituto Nacional de Investigação e Desenvolvimento da Educação do MED (INIDE), Luanda, 23 December 1987, Assunto: Projecto educação sub-programa "A," Formação em produção e aplicação de material de lingua Portuguesa (MED archive); see also RPA, MED, Direcção Nacional do Ensino Médio e Pré-Universitário, Relatório sobre a situação do Ensino Médio na R.P.A.—Período 1978–1982, n.d. (approx. 1983) (MED archive).

142. Of these, 7,026 were primary schools up to fourth grade, 157 were primary schools up to sixth grade, and twenty-one were primary schools up to eighth grade; twenty-five were secondary schools, five were senior high schools up to grade twelve, and seven were (polytechnic) universities; see RPA, MED, Relatório sobre a execução do plano do sector da educação de 1982, p. 3 (MED archive).

143. UNICEF to Domingos Peterson, Director do Instituto Nacional de Investigação e Desenvolvimento da Educação do MED (INIDE), Luanda, 23 December 1987, Assunto: Projecto educação sub-programa "A," Formação em produção e aplicação de material de lingua Portuguesa (MED archive).

144. RPA, MED, Relatório sobre a execução do plano do sector da educação de 1982, p. 8 (MED archive).

145. RPA, MED, Direcção do Ensino Secundário, Relatório sobre o ano lectivo de 1979/80, pp. 1–3 (MED archive).

146. RPA, MED, Resolução sobre as medidas imediatas a tomar no sector do ensino, Luanda, 21 January 1983, O presidente da República José Eduardo dos Santos (MED archive).

147. RPA, MED, Gabinete do Plano do Ministério da Educação, Estudo sobre a diminuição dos efectivos escolares no ensino de base regular, n.d. (approx. 1983), 23 pages, here pp. 2–5 (MED archive).

148. RPA, MED, GICI/GII, Problemática dos Gabinetes de Intercâmbio Internacional, Análise do documento, Luanda, 2 January 1985, p. 3 (MED archive).

149. Cf. RPA, MED, Perspectivas de desenvolvimento no sector da educação e ensino para o quinenio 1985–1990, 1984, 37 pages, here p. 2 (MED archive); RPA, MED, Priorização do sistema de educação e ensino, Luanda, 21 March 1985, 14 pages, here p. 4 (MED archive).

150. RPA, MED, Direcção Nacional do Ensino Médio e Pré-universitário, Relatório sobre a situação do ensino médio na R.P.A. Período 1978–1982, n.d. (approx. 1983), 27 pages, here p. 3 (MED archive).

151. RPA, MED, Relatório sobre a execução do plano do sector da educação de 1982, p. 3 (MED archive).

152. RPA, MED, Mesa redonda sobre educação para todos, July 1991, p. 3; see also RPA, MED, Sistema nacional de avaliação para o ensino de base regular, n.d. (approx. 1991), 20 pages (both: MED archive).

153. RPA, MED, Relatório sobre a execução do plano do sector da educação de 1982, p. 4 (MED archive).

154. RPA, MED, Mesa redonda sobre educação para todos, July 1991, p. 5 (MED archive).

155. RPA, MED, VII Conselho consultivo, realizado 8–12 September 1981, Conclusões finais, Luanda, 1982, 47 pages, here p. 29 (MED archive).

156. RPA, MED, Mesa redonda sobre educação para todos, July 1991, p. 2 (MED archive).

157. Ibid., pp. 1–3.

158. Interview Angola 2006, Luanda, 27 January and 17 March 2006 (Artur Pestana, "Pepetela").

159. See Scott, 1994, pp. 91–93; Laudowicz, 1987, pp. 68–70.

160. RPA, MED, Dept. Nacional das escolas provisórias; Projecto de estudo sobre a problemática das escolas provisórias. Elaborado pelo Depto. Nac. das Escolas Provisorias, Luanda, June 1983, 12 pages (MED archive).

161. MPLA, 1978, p. 48.

Chapter 6. Scope of Action

1. Interview Angola 2006, Luanda, 22 March 2006 (António Burity da Silva). At the time of the interview Burity da Silva was the Angolan minister of education. In the 1970s and 1980s he was responsible within the MPLA for selecting Angolan pupils and students for Cuban scholarships. In the 1990s he was the Angolan ambassador in Cuba.

2. Neto, 1987, p. 265.

3. García Pérez-Castañeda, n.d. This information is also endorsed by documents of the Angolan State Secretariat for Cooperation, according to which the education sector was the largest area of cooperation in 1984 (employing 2,030 of the total of 3,927 aid workers). See RPA, Secretaria de Estado da Cooperação, Acta das conversações entre a delegação angolana da Secretaria de Estado da Cooperação e a delegação cubana do Comité Estatal de Cooperação económica, para a conciliação e assinatura do programa de cooperação científico-técnica para o ano de 1985, 26 pages, here pp. 10–12 (MED archive).

4. See George, 2005, p. 324n1. George refers here to a public speech given by the chief of the armed forces, Raúl Castro, to mark the return of civil and military "internationalists" from Angola on 27 May 1991, in which he cites that 377,033 soldiers and "approximately 50,000" civilians had been involved in the engagement.

5. This statistic, which has been broken down according to years, covers the period from 1963 to 2003. It was given to me in Luanda in February 2006 by the then Cuban ambassador in Angola, Noemí Benitez de Mendoza. Between 1977 and 1984, Benitez de Mendoza was deputy minister of the CECE, responsible for Cuba's civil cooperation with Angola. See Interview Angola 2006, Luanda, 8 February and 17 February 2006 (Noemí Benitez de Mendoza).

6. Instituto de Historia de Cuba. The Cuban Historical Institute has been the main institution of Cuban historiography since the revolution. It houses the party Archive of the Communist Party of Cuba (PCC).

7. The manuscript itself is undated. The title, "El internacionalismo de Cuba en la colaboración económica y Científico-técnica: Esbozo histórico de un cuarto siglo de la Revolución Socialista Cubana 1963–1988," suggests that the information covers the years up to 1988. However, as the author includes statistics from 1990, the study must have been completed after 1990.

8. García Pérez-Castañeda, n.d., p. 232.

9. Ibid., passim.

10. I wish to thank Limbania Nancy Jiménez Rodríguez for this information; see Interview Cuba 2006, Havana, 25 May and 31 May 2006 (Limbania "Nancy" Jiménez Rodríguez); see also Jiménez Rodríguez, 2008b, pp. 96–97.

11. García Pérez-Castañeda, n.d., p. 136.

12. Ibid., p. 232.

13. Ibid.; cf. Jiménez Rodríguez, 2008b, pp. 76–77.

14. García Perez-Castañeda, n.d., p. 242.

15. Jiménez Rodríguez, 2008b, p. 96.

16. Ibid., p. 97.

17. The MED did not record data systematically until summer 1977, after the foundation of the GICI and GII.

18. Ortega et al., 2004, p. 8.

19. Jiménez Rodríguez, 2008b, p. 65.

20. RPA, MED, Gabinete de Intercâmbio e Cooperação Internacional, Relatório sobre o trabalho da comissão do MED para seleção dos 1.200 alunos bolseiros angolanos a seguir os seus estudos em Cuba, n.d. (approx. 1978), 5 pages (MED archive).

21. RPA, Embaixada em Havana-Cuba: Ao Cda. Ambrôsio Lukoki, Ministro de Educação da RPA, Luanda, Havana, 9 February 1981, 2 pages, here p. 2 (MED archive). The letter from the Angolan Embassy in Havana to the Minister of Education shows that at the time that the letter was written, 2,041 Angolan pupils resided on the Isla de la Juventud. According to a report of a visit by a delegation from the Angolan Ministry of Education to the Isla de la Juventud in spring 1987, the number of Angolan pupils was 2,290. See RPA, MED, Visita de trabalho à República de Cuba da delegação chefiada pelo Cda. Vice-ministro da educação para o ensino de base, no período de 15 April–2 May 1987, 32 pages (MED archive).

22. See chapter 7, pp. 206–212.

23. Interview Angola 2006, Luanda, 1 February 2006.

24. This depiction of the beginning of cooperation in education is based mainly on congruent eyewitness reports from pilot-project participants and a few internal written records. See Memorias del trabajo de la colaboración Cubana en la República Popular de Angola, 1976–1978, 76 pages, here pp. 2–3 (from the private archive of Limbania "Nancy" Jiménez Rodríguez); Interview Angola 2006, Luanda, 1 February 2006; Interview Cuba 2006, Havana, 16 June 2006; Interview Cuba 2006, Havana, 10 June 2006; Interview Cuba 2006, Havana, 25 May and 31 May 2006.

25. Interview Cuba 2006, Havana, 10 June 2006.

26. Interview Angola 2006, Luanda, 1 February 2006.

27. Ibid.; Interview Cuba 2006, Havana, 16 June 2006.

28. Gleijeses, 2004, p. xix (Preface by Jorge Risquet Valdés).

29. *Jornal de Angola*, 31 July 1976, p. 2; *Bohemia*, no. 32, 6 August 1976, pp. 55–56.

30. The delegation included Carlos Rocha, minister of economy and planning; General João Jacob Caetano, deputy chief of staff of the armed forces and minister of justice, building, and information; and Neto's mother, Dona María Da Silva; see *Jornal de Angola*, 31 July 1976, pp. 1–2.

31. Playa Girón is the Spanish name for the Bay of Pigs. The medal is one of the highest military honors in Cuba. *Jornal de Angola*, 23 July, 27 July, 31 July 1976, each pp. 1–2; *Bohemia*, no. 31, 30 July 1976, pp. 44–47.

32. "La solidaridad entre Cuba y Angola un instrumento sólido contra el imperialismo" Agostinho Neto, *Bohemia*, no. 31, 30 July 1976, p. 50.

33. *Jornal de Angola*, 31 July 1976, p. 2.

34. *Bohemia*, no. 32, 6 August 1976, p. 56, included an extract from the official Cuban-Angolan declaration.

35. *Jornal de Angola*, 28 July 1976, p. 2.

36. See the headlines in *Jornal de Angola*, 23 July 1976: "Presidente Neto chegou a Cuba. Calorosa recepção no aeroporto José Martí" and "Uma cidade em festa recebe o camarada presidente" ("President Neto arrives in Cuba. Warm reception at José Martí Airport" and "A city in festive spirits welcomes comrade President").

37. *Jornal de Angola*, 31 July 1976, p. 2.

38. Ibid.

39. Interview Angola 2006, Luanda, 09 March, 11 March, and 21 March 2006 (Lopo do Nascimento).

40. Ibid.; Interview Cuba 2005, Santiago de Cuba, 10 January 2005.

41. A detailed report on Castro's destinations during his trip round Africa is given by the Cuban weekly journal *Bohemia*, no. 12, 25 March 1977.

42. *Jornal de Angola*, 29 March 1977, pp. 1–2; for further reports on the state visit, see *Jornal de Angola*, 30 March, 31 March, and 1 April 1977.

43. See Pawson 2007; Mabeko Tali, 2001 (II), pp. 214–217. Burchett, 1978, pp. 106–108; Birmingham, 1978; Birmingham, 2002, pp. 150–151; Interview Cuba 2005, Santiago de Cuba, 10 January 2005; Interview Portugal 2005, Lisbon, 16 September and 26 September 2005; Interview Portugal 2005, Lisbon, 8 November 2005.

44. Castro, 1977, pp. 8–9.

45. RPA, Secretaria de Estado da Cooperação, Protocolo da IV. sessão da Comissão Mista Intergovernamental Angolana-Cubana de cooperação económica e científico-técnica, Havana, 4–5 May 1981, 16 pages, here p. 3 (MED archive).

46. In Kassinga, which lies in the southern Angolan province of Huila, suspected

guerrillas of the Namibian liberation movement SWAPO were bombarded and hundreds killed.

47. For details of the South African attack on Kassinga, see George, 2005, pp. 133–135; Brittain, 1998, p. 12.

48. RPA, Secretaria de Estado da Cooperação, Comissão de Avaliação da Cooperação ao Cda. Ministro da Educação, Luanda, Circular No. 1/CACI/SEC/May 1982, Assunto: Avaliação da cooperação, 2 pages (MED archive).

49. MED, GICI/GII, Evaluação das cinco nacionalidades e categoría com a maior expressão (figure), approx. 1985 (MED archive).

50. *Jornal de Angola*, 19 September 1979. Upon my insistence, Neto's prime minister at that time, Lopo do Nascimento, told me during an interview that the Cubans had indeed resented the fact that Neto no longer trusted his Cuban doctors and had turned to Soviet doctors. His loss of political confidence in the Cuban government also obviously played a role. Lopo do Nascimento was, however, reticent about the exact causes. Interview Angola 2006, Luanda, 9 March, 11 March, and 21 March 2006 (Lopo do Nascimento). Apart from Cuba's obvious delay in writing the letter of condolences, there is still no documentary evidence regarding the background of the rift between the governments.

51. *Jornal de Angola*, 21 September 1979.

52. George, 2005, p. 174.

53. For details of P. W. Botha's "total strategy," see Marx, 2004, p. 323.

54. George, 2005, p. 164.

55. Ibid., pp. 165–166.

56. Ibid., pp. 166–170; for the Cuban perspective on Cangamba, see Martín Blandino, 2006, and the film *Kangamba*, which was produced by Rogelio Paris in 2007 on behalf of FAR.

57. George, 2005, pp. 171–173. For details of the negotiations, see also Gleijeses, 2006a and 2006b. For a US perspective, see the memoirs of the US assistant secretary of state for African affairs under President Ronald Reagan, Chester Crocker (Crocker, 1992).

58. Gleijeses, 2006b, pp. 123–125. Gleijeses cites evidence found in written documents from Cuban archives. Appearing here for the first time, this material reflects the tense situation between Castro and Dos Santos and between both governments before and after the Lusaka Accords. See also George, 2005, p. 174.

59. Bhagavan, 1986, pp. 30–31.

60. Diário da República, Orgão Oficial da República Popular de Angola, No. 213, 14 May 1983; Bhagavan, 1986, pp. 85–87.

61. For more details on student teachers, see chapter 7, pp. 202–203.

62. Malaquias, 2007b, p. 115.

63. Ibid., pp. 117–120; Messiant, 2008a, pp. 55–57.

64. MED, GICI/GII, Evaluação das cinco nacionalidades e categoría com a maior expressão (figure), approx 1985 (MED archive).

65. RPA, MED, Provincia de Benguela, Gabinete do delegado provincial de educação, Confidêncial, Informação No. 1/1983, 21 February 1983, 2 pages (MED archive), which was a memo from the Benguela Provincial Directorate about the withdrawal of eighty-three Cuban primary teachers for security reasons; see also RPA, MED, Gabinete do Ministro da Educação ao Cda. Roberto de Almeida, Secretário do Comité Central do MPLA-PT para a esfera ideológica, 26 June 1983, Envío do

memorando das conversaçãoes entre o chefe do Departamento de Superação e Desenvolvimento de Quadros do MED da RPA e director do Gabinete de Intercâmbio Internacional do MED da RPA, 6 pages, here p. 5 (MED archive). A delegation from the Cuban Ministry of Education who visited Angola from 1 to 15 July to see how cooperation was faring announced to the MED that they would be withdrawing Cuban teachers from fifteen municipalities of the Benguela and Malanje provinces for security reasons.

66. RPA, MED, Memorando sobre a cooperação Cubana ao serviço do Ministério da Educação, Luanda, 2 February 1985, 9 pages, here p. 2 (MED archive).

67. RPA, MED, GICI/GII, Força de trabalho estrangeira, República de Cuba, 25 November 1986, 1 page (MED archive).

68. RPA, MED, Plano de cooperação cubana para o sector da educação, ano lectivo 88/89, January 1988, p. 4 (MED archive).

69. RPA, MED, Gabinete do Ministro, Memorando sobre a participação do PNUD e dos VNU na substituçãodos cubanos no domíno de educação, Luanda, 27 July 1989, 2 pages (MED archive).

70. Memorando sobre a audiência concedida pelo camarada Augusto Lopes Teixeira, Ministro da Educação da RPA, ao general cubano Henrique Lusson, 14 April 1990, 2 pages (MED archive).

71. The actual text of the Framework Agreement was not available. Details of the agreement have been taken from internal documents and the subsequent cooperation agreements drawn up on its basis between the Cuban and Angolan ministries. Parts of the agreement were also published in the Angolan and Cuban press; see *Jornal de Angola*, 31 July 1976, p. 2; *Bohemia*, no. 32, 6 August 1976, pp. 55–56.

72. *Jornal de Angola*, 31 July 1976, p. 2.

73. Prior to 1977, culture and education were the responsibility of one ministry. See "De acordo com o artigo II do convênio de Colaboração econômica e Científico-técnica assinado em Havana em 29 de Julho de 1976," from the Acordo especial de colaboração entre o Ministério da Educação da República Popular de Angola e o Ministério da Educação Superior da República de Cuba, Havana, 5 December 1976, p. 1 (MED archive).

74. Interview Angola 2006, Luanda, 27 January and 17 March 2006 (Artur Pestana, "Pepetela"). A few weeks later, Jacinto was replaced by Ambrôsio Lukoki; Pestana and Lukoki remained in office until 1981.

75. Protocolo da I. sessão da Comissão Mista Intergovernamental Angolana-Cubana de colaboração económica e científico-técnica, Luanda, 5 November 1977, 8 pages, and appendix, here p. 2 (MED archive).

76. Acordo especial de colaboração entre o Ministério da Educação da República Popular de Angola e o Ministério da Educação da República de Cuba, signed in Havana on 5 December 1976 (MED archive).

77. Acordo especial de colaboração entre o Ministério da Educação da República Popular de Angola e o Ministério da Educação Superior da República de Cuba, signed in Havana on 5 December 1976 (MED archive).

78. See Acordo especial sobre as condições gerais para a realização da colaboração económica e científico-técnica entre o governo da República Popular de Angola y a República de Cuba, Luanda, 5 November 1977, 14 pages (MED archive).

79. Acordo especial de colaboração entre o Conselho Nacional da Educação Física e Desportos da República Popular de Angola e o Instituto Nacional de Desportos,

Educação Física e Recreação da República de Cuba, signed in Havana on 7 December 1976 (MED archive).

80. Convenio Cultural entre el Gobierno de la República Popular de Angola y el Gobierno de la República de Cuba, signed in Havana on 5 December 1976 (MED archive).

81. Ibid.

82. See Acordo especial sobre o programa de colaboração para 1978 entre o Ministério de Educação da República de Cuba e o Ministério de Educação da República Popular de Angola, signed in Luanda on 4 October 1977 (MED archive).

83. Protocolo da I. sessão da Comissão Mista Intergovernamental Angolana-Cubana de colaboração económica e científico-técnica, Luanda, 5 November 1977, 8 pages, and appendix (MED archive). See also MINVEC, 2002a, p. 4.

84. Acordo especial sobre as condições gerais para a realização da colaboração económica e científico-técnica entre o governo da República Popular de Angola y a República de Cuba, Luanda, 5 November 1977, 14 pages (MED archive).

85. RPA, Secretaria de Estado da Cooperação, Memorando, Luanda, 2 June 1988, 34 pages, here pp. 2–3 (MED archive).

86. See RPA, Secretaria de Estado da Cooperação, Memorando, Luanda, 2 June 1988, 34 pages (MED archive).

87. Neto, 1987, pp. 265–266.

88. See *Gaceta Oficial de la República de Cuba*, Havana, 1 December 1976, Ley No. 1323, Ley de Organización de la Administración Central del Estado, Art. 57, pp. 79–80.

89. See also Gómez, 1986, pp. 2–3.

90. Ibid.; Interview Angola 2006, Luanda, 8 February, 17 February, and 21 March 2006 (Noemí Benitez de Mendoza, Vice President of the CECE 1979–1988; later Cuban ambassador in Angola).

91. Interview Cuba 2004, Havana, 18 October and 23 October 2004.

92. Interview Angola 2006, Luanda, 31 March 2006 (head of the Gabinete de Intercâmbio Internacional of the MED).

93. RPA, MED, Relatório (1977–1979) Gabinete de Intercâmbio e Cooperação Internacional do Ministério da Educação em Luanda, 21 December 1979, O chefe do Gabinete: M. T. Q., 24 pages, here pp. 1–4 (MED archive).

94. At times coordinating meetings between the Cuban Civil Administration and GICI/GII took place every week: see RPA, MED, GICI/GII, Acta sobre as conversações entre os presidentes da Comissão Mista Intergovernamental Angolana-Cubana de colaboração económica e científico-técnica, Luanda, 10 September 1984, 4 pages, here p. 3 (MED archive); RPA, MED, GICI/GII, Acta: Pelas 10 horas do día 9 March 1984, foi recebida pelo camarada J. M. d. S., Director do Gabinete de Intercâmbio Internacional do MED, a camarada S. R. A., Chefe do continente educacional Cubano na RPA, 6 pages, here p. 5 (MED archive).

95. See RPA, MED, GICI/GII, Regulamento interno dos Gabinetes de Intercâmbio e Cooperação Internacional, Luanda, o Gabinete de Intercâmbio Internacional do Ministério da Educação, 1 January 1985, o Director do Gabinete, J. M. S., 21 pages (MED archive).

96. RPA, MED, Relatório (1977–1979) Gabinete de Intercâmbio e Cooperação Internacional do Ministério da Educação em Luanda, 21 December 1979, O chefe do Gabinete: M. T. Q., 24 pages, here p. 5 (MED archive), a 1982 report from the

Secretaria de Estado da Cooperação. The cooperation listed agreements with Cuba, Bulgaria, Portugal, the GDR, Congo-Brazzaville, Cape Verde, the Soviet Union, and Vietnam. See RPA, Secretaria de Estado da Cooperação, Comissão de Avaliação da Cooperação, Gabinete do Secretário de Estado da Cooperação em Luanda, P. P. J., May 1982, p. 1 (MED archive).

97. RPA, MED, Gabinete de Intercâmbio e Cooperação Internacional, Primeiro encontro nacional do GICI com os representantes das provincias. Conclusões. Luanda, 19 October 1979, 4 pages (MED archive).

98. RPA, MED, Regulamento Interno dos Gabinetes de Intercâmbio e Cooperação Internacional, Luanda, o Gabinete de Intercâmbio Internacional do Ministério da Educação, 1 January 1985, o Director do Gabinete, J. M. S., 21 pages, here pp. 6–8 (MED archive).

99. RPA, MED, Relatório (1977–1979) Gabinete de Intercâmbio e Cooperação Internacional do Ministério da Educação em Luanda, 21 December 1979, O chefe do Gabinete: M. T. Q., 24 pages (MED archive); see also Interview Angola 2006, Luanda, 3 March, 21 March, and 28 March 2006 (M. T. Q.).

100. RPA, MED, Relatório (1977–1979) Gabinete de Intercâmbio e Cooperação Internacional do Ministério da Educação em Luanda, 21 December 1979, O chefe do Gabinete: M. T. Q., 24 pages, here p. 23 (MED archive); RPA, MED, GICI/GII Relatório, 25 March 1982 to 31 August 1985, 1 October 1985, o director cessante, J. M. d. S., 30 pages (MED archive). A record from the Secretaria de Estado da Cooperação from 1982 lists cooperation agreements with Cuba, Bulgaria, Portugal, the GDR, Congo-Brazzaville, Cape Verde, the Soviet Union, and Vietnam; see RPA, Secretaria de Estado da Cooperação, Comissão de Avaliação da Cooperação ao Camarada Ministro da Educação, Luanda, Circular No. 1/CACI/SEC/82, 31 May 1980, signed Secretário de Estado P. P. J., 8 pages (MED archive).

101. RPA, MED, Relatório (1977–1979) Gabinete de Intercâmbio e Cooperação Internacional do Ministério da Educação em Luanda, 21 December 1979, O chefe do Gabinete: M. T. Q., 24 pages, here pp. 8–11 (MED archive).

102. In 1978 the status of *cooperantes* changed. Distinctions were now made between *cooperantes* working in Angola on the basis of bilateral agreements, and individual *cooperantes* (e.g., foreigners with residency in Angola). See ibid., p. 8.

103. Interview Angola 2006, Luanda, 31 March 2006 (head of department; between 1981–1991 technical head of the GICI/GII and still employed there at the point of time of the interview); RPA, Secretaria de Estado da Cooperação, Comissão de Avaliação da Cooperação ao Camarada Ministro da Educação, Luanda, Circular No. 1/CACI/SEC/82, 31 May 1980, signed Secretário de Estado P. P. J., 8 pages (MED archive).

104. The systematic monitoring of the *cooperantes* by creating personnel files was not effective until about 1980; see Interview Angola 2006, Luanda, 31 March 2006.

105. RPA, MED, GICI/GII, Relatório, 25 March 1982 to 31 August 1985, 1 October 1985, o director cessante, J. M. d. S., 30 pages (MED archive); Interview Angola 2006, Luanda, 31 March 2006.

106. RPA, MED, GICI/GII, Memorando: Problemática da retirada da cooperação Cubana da RPA, Luanda, aos 15 August 1990, 5 pages, here p. 1 (MED archive).

107. See, for example, reports on the cooperation and internal memos from the Cuban MINED: Memorias del trabajo de la colaboración Cubana en la República

Popular de Angola, 1976–1978, 76 pages (from the private archive of Limbania "Nancy" Jiménez Rodríguez); Memorias de la colaboración del Destacamento Pedagógico ubicado en la Provincia de Huambo en el curso escolar 1978–1979, March–December 1978, Huambo, 26 December 1978, signed E. L. R., Profesor guía and M. d. J. A. H., Jefe del grupo de Educación, 24 pages (MINED archive); MINED, Informe, Diferencias entre los informes recibidos de Angola, D.P.I "Che Guevara," Havana, 25 September 1979, to: Asela de los Santos, Viceministra, from: Z. F. H., Directora General Formación y Perfeccionamento Personal Pedagógico, 3 pages (MINED archive); MINED, Nota al Ministro, Consideraciones sobre el informe del Trabajo en Angola por los Cros. A. O. y J. M. L., Havana, 17 January 1978, signed by Asela de los Santos, Viceministra, 3 pages (MINED archive).

108. Interview Cuba 2006, Havana, 24 May and 23 June 2006 (Jorge Risquet Valdés); Interview Cuba 2006, Havana, 25 May and 31 May 2006 (Limbania "Nancy" Jiménez Rodríguez, deputy in charge of the education cooperation in Angola between 1976 and 1977); Interview Cuba 2006, Havana, 8 August 2006 (head and deputy in charge of Cuban education cooperation in Angola between 1979 and 1981); Interview Cuba 2006, Havana, 1 June and 12 September 2006 (head of Cuban education cooperation in Angola between 1977 and 1980); Interview Cuba 2006, Havana, 2 June 2006 (head of education cooperation between January 1984 and November 1985); Interview Cuba 2006, Havana, 14 September 2006 (head of financial administration in the Cuban Embassy in Luanda, 1976 to mid-1979); Interview Cuba 2006, Havana, 10 June 2006 (Rodolfo Puente Ferro, military doctor from 1975 in Angola, 1983–1986 Cuban ambassador in Angola); Interview Cuba 2006, Havana, 21 September 2006 (José Ramón Fernández, Cuban Minister of Education 1970–1990); Interview Cuba 2006, Havana, 6 June 2006 (former Cuban Deputy Minister of Education, 1970–1990, head of the Department of Teacher Training in MINED); Interview Angola 2002 and 2006, Luanda, 8 February, 17 February, and 21 March 2006 (Noemí Benitez de Mendoza, at the time of the interview Cuban ambassador in Angola). Also, I found information in a publication written by the frequently mentioned Limbania ("Nancy") Jiménez, which was published in Cuba in 2008. Jiménez, who was then the wife of Risquet, was the head of education cooperation in Angola between 1976 and 1977; it is significant that she was deployed in Angola in 1976 via the Cuban military structures. See Jiménez, 2008b, pp. 58–61.

109. In the 1980s he was a member of the Cuban negotiating committee during the negotiations initiated by the US government between South Africa, Angola, and Cuba, which led to the ratification of the 1988 New York Accords. For more information on the political biography of Risquet, see León Rojas, 2006; Gleijeses, 2006b; Gleijeses, 2004, pp. x–xlviii (Preface by Risquet Valdés); see also Risquet's own publication on the Bataillon Patrice Lumumba (Risquet Valdés, 2000).

110. Interview Cuba 2006, Havana, 24 May and 23 June 2006 (Jorge Risquet Valdés).

111. Interview Angola 2006, Luanda, 8 February, 17 February, and 21 March 2006 (Noemí Benitez de Mendoza, at the time of interview Cuban ambassador in Angola). See also Interview Angola 2006, Luanda, 31 March 2006 (head of department, between 1981 and 1991 technical head of the GICI/GII).

112. Interview Cuba 2006, Havana, 6 June 2006 (Cuban Deputy Minister of Education, head of the Department of Teacher Training between 1970 and 1990).

113. See Memorias de la Colaboración del Destacamento Pedagógico ubicado en la Provincia de Huambo en el curso escolar 1978–1979, March–December 1978, 26 December 1978, signed E. L. R., Profesor guía and M. d. J. A. H., Jefe del grupo de Educación, 24 pages (MINED archive).

114. For information on the composition, function, and responsibilities of the disciplinary panel, see MINED, Nota al Ministro, Consideraciones sobre el informe del trabajo en Angola por los Cros. A. O. y J. M. L., Havana, 17 January 1978, signed by Asela de los Santos, Viceministra, 3 pages, here p. 1 (MINED archive).

115. Interview United States 2005, Miami, 10 June 2005 (Norberto Fuentes); Interview United States 2005, Miami, 30 June 2005 (Juan Benemelis); Interview United States 2005, Miami, 8 July 2005 (Alcibíades Hidalgo). The reasons for Risquet being recalled to Cuba are not clear from the information I had at my disposal, and I am therefore only able to speculate.

116. Castro, 2005.

117. RPA, MED, GICI/GII ao Gabinete do Plano do MED, Confidencial, Oficial Circular No. 013/GII/ 171/I/1983, Cálculo de custos de Força de Trabalho Estrangeira e incremento previsto para 1983/1984, Luanda, 27 March 1983, o Director do Gabinete, J. M. d. S., 10 pages (MED archive).

118. RPA, Secretaria de Estado da Cooperação ao camarada José Eduardo dos Santos, Presidente do MPLA-PT e da República Popular de Angola, Memorando, Assunto: Cooperação com a República Socialista de Cuba, Luanda, March 1980, 3 pages, here p. 2 (MED archive).

119. See Acordo especial sobre as condições gerais para a realização da colaboração económica e científico-técnica entre o governo da República Popular de Angola y a República de Cuba, Luanda, 5 November 1977, 14 pages (MED archive); Interview Angola 2006, Luanda, 31 March 2006; Interview Angola 2006, Luanda, 1 February 2006.

120. Interview Angola 2006, Luanda, 31 March 2006; Interview Angola 2006, Luanda, 1 February 2006.

121. See Acordo especial sobre as condições gerais para a realização da colaboração económica e científico-técnica entre o governo da República Popular de Angola e y a República de Cuba, Luanda, 5 November 1977, 14 pages (MED archive).

122. RPA, MED, GICI/GII ao Gabinete do Plano do MED, Confidencial, Oficial Circular No. 013/ GII/171/I/1983, Cálculo de custos de força de trabalho estrangeira e incremento previsto para 1983/1984, Luanda, 27 March 1983, o Director do Gabinete, J. M. d. S., 10 pages, here p. 2 (MED archive).

123. RPA, MED, GICI/GII, Proposta de tabela salarial, contratação individual e para cooperação com o Brasil, Anexo, n.d. (approx. 1983), 3 pages (MED archive); RPA, MED, GICI/GII, Proposta de tabela salarial para cooperação Portuguesa ao abrigo do acordo, n.d., approx. 1983, 1 page (MED archive).

124. RPA, MED, GICI/GII ao Gabinete do Plano do MED, Confidencial, Oficial Circular No. 013/ GII/171/I/1983, Cálculo de custos de força de trabalho estrangeira e incremento previsto para 1983/1984, Luanda, 27 March 1983, o Director do Gabinete, J. M. d. S., 10 pages, here pp. 3–4 (MED archive).

125. Ibid., pp. 4–5.

126. Ibid., p. 10.

127. Dpto. Económico Cubatécnica a Ministerio de Educación (cc. Sec. Estado para la Cooperación), Luanda, 8 December 1987 (MED archive).

128. Interview United States 2005, Miami, 8 July 2005 (Alcibíades Hidalgo).

129. Interview Cuba 2006, Havana, 21 September 2006 (José Ramón Fernández).

130. Interview Angola 2006, Luanda, 8 February and 17 February 2006 (Noemí Benitez de Mendoza).

131. Interview Angola 2006, Luanda, 22 March 2006 (António Burity da Silva).

132. Interview Angola 2006, Luanda, 1 February 2006.

133. See Gleijeses, 2006b, p. 118.

134. Gleijeses, 2013, pp. 82–84.

135. The propaganda surrounding "mercenary discourse" is exemplified in the 1976 Cuban publication *Angola: Fin del mito de los mercenaries* (*Angola: An End to the Mercenaries' Myth*, Valdés Vivó, 1976).

136. Several of my interviewees informed me of this strategy. Interview Cuba 2006, Havana, 25 May and 31 May 2006 (Limbania "Nancy" Jiménez Rodríguez); Interview Cuba 2006, Havana, 6 June 2006 (Zoila Franco Hidalgo, former deputy minister of education); Interview Cuba 2006, Havana, 15 June and 22 June 2006 (Lidia Turner Martí, chairperson of the Cuban Association of Educators).

137. Interview Angola 2006, Luanda, 1 February 2006 (Pedro Domingos Peterson, former director of the Instituto Nacional de Investigação e Desenvolvimento da Educação [INIDE]).

138. See RPA, Secretaria de Estado da Cooperação, Protocolo da V. sessão Mista Intergovernamental Angolana-Cubana de cooperação económica e científico-técnica, Luanda, 28 October 1983, Luanda, 15 December 1983, o Director Nacional, M. M. D., 7 pages (MED archive); or RPA, MED, GICI/GII, 78/GII/I/83 ao Camarada Ministro da Educação, Luanda, 18 October 1983, o Director do Gabinete, J. M. d. S., 4 pages, a report on the GICI/GII in which the head of the department asserts that the department is unable to fulfill its main task of overseeing the Cuban cooperation.

139. See, for example, Acta sobre as conversações entre os presidentes da Comissão Mista Intergovernamental Angolana-Cubana de colaboração económica e científico-técnica, Luanda, 10 September 1984, 4 pages, here p. 3 (MED archive); Acta: Pelas 10 horas do día 9 March 1984, foi recebida pelo camarada J. M. d. S., Director do Gabinete de Intercâmbio Internacional do MED, a camarada S. R. A., Chefe do contingente educacional cubano na RPA, 6 pages, here p. 5 (MED archive).

140. RPA, MED, GICI/GII, Ponto da situação relativo a cooperação de nacionalidade cubana em serviço do Ministério da Educação, 27 April 1982, 6 pages, here p. 1 (MED archive).

141. Ibid.

142. RPA, MED, GICI/GII, Relatório, 25 March 1982 to 31 August 1985, 1 October 1985, o Director Cessante, J. M. d. S., 30 pages, here p. 2 (MED archive).

143. RPA, MED, Provincia de Benguela MED, Gabinete do Delegado Provincial de Educação, Confidêncial, Informação No. 1/1983, 21 February 1983, 2 pages (MED archive). This is a memo from the Benguela Provincial Directorate of the MED regarding the withdrawal of eighty-three Cuban primary teachers for security reasons; see also RPA, Gabinete do Ministro da Educação ao Cda. Roberto de Almeida, Secretário do Comité Central do MPLA-PT para a esfera ideológica, 26 June 1983, Envío do memorando das conversaçãoes entre o Chefe do Departamento de Superação e

Desenvolvimento de Quadros do MED da RPA e Director do Gabinete de Intercâmbio Internacional do MED da RPA, 6 pages, here p. 5 (MED archive). A delegation from the Cuban Ministry of Education who visited Angola from 1 to 15 July 1983 to assess the progress of cooperation announced to the MED that they would be withdrawing Cuban teachers from fifteen municipalities of the Benguela and Malanje provinces for security reasons.

144. See, for example, RPA, Secretaria de Estado da Cooperação, Protocolo da V. sessão da Comissão Mista Intergovernamental Angolana-Cubana de cooperação económica e científico-técnica, Luanda, 26–28 October 1983, Luanda, 15 December 1983, o Director Nacional, M. M. D., 7 pages; or RPA, MED, GICI/GII, 18 October 1983 ao Camarada Ministro da Educação, o Director do Gabinete, J. M. S., 4 pages (MED archive), a report of the GICI/GII in which the head of department asserts that the department is unable to fulfill its main task of overseeing Cuban cooperation.

145. See, for example, RPA, MED, Secretaria de Estado da Cooperação ao Gabinete de I. Internacional do MED, Protocolo da V. sessão da Comissão Mista Intergovernamental Angolana-Cubana de cooperação económica e científico-técnica, Luanda, 26–28 October 1983, Luanda, 15 December 1983, o Director Nacional, M. M. D., 7 pages, here p. 4 (MED archive); RPA, MED, GICI/GII, Ponto da situação relativo à cooperação de nacionalidade Cubana em serviço do MED, 27 April 1982, 6 pages (MED archive).

146. RPA, MED, GICI/GII ao Camarada Ministro da Educação, 18 October 1983, o Director do Gabinete, J. M. S., 4 pages (MED archive).

147. See Acordo especial sobre as condições gerais para a realização da colaboração económica e científico-técnica entre o governo da República Popular de Angola y a República de Cuba, Luanda, 5 November 1977, 14 pages, here p. 3 (MED archive).

148. See RPA, MED, GICI/GII, Relatório, 25 March 1982 to 31 August 1985, 1 October 1985, o Director Cessante, J. M. d. S., 30 pages, here p. 12 (MED archive). This is an accountability report of the departing head of the GICI/GII.

149. RPA, MED, GICI/GII, 78/GII/I/83 ao Camarada Ministro da Educação, Luanda, 18 October 1983, o Director do Gabinete, J. M. d. S., 4 pages, here p. 1 (MED archive).

150. See here a document from the GICI/GII. Although it discusses all the coordination and communication problems with the Cuban partners mentioned and their "autonomous" activity, it is more concerned with taking a critical look at its own failings; see RPA, MED, GICI/GII, Ponto da situação relativo a cooperação de nacionalidade Cubana em serviço do Ministério da Educação, 27 April 1982, 6 pages (MED archive).

151. MED, Projecto de Estudo sobre mercados alternativos a contratação de técnicos docentes (8/1983, handwritten comment), 6 pages (MED archive).

152. "Caracterização sumária da Universidade de Angola," *Jornal de Angola*, 27 November 1982, p. 4.

153. Embajada de Cuba, Oficina Económica, Av. General Carmona No. 42, Luanda, Angola, Cda. Augusto Lopes Teixeira, Ministro da Educação da R.P.A, Luanda, 4 January 1983 (signature illegible), 2 pages, here p. 2 (MED archive).

154. See RPA, MED, GICI/GII, Memorando (handwritten date 14 April 1984), 11 pages (MED archive).

Chapter 7. *Cooperantes* and Cooperation Programs

1. Acordo especial de eolaboração entre o Ministério da Educação da República Popular de Angola e o Ministério da Educação da República de Cuba, signed in Havana on 5 December 1976 (MED archive).

2. Ibid.

3. Figures according to Turner Martí et al., 1996, p. 30. Of the 2,026 participants, 1,195 were female (58.9 percent) and 831 male.

4. There is no absolutely reliable information about the percentage of women, but the study by Jiménez Rodríguez, 2008b, pp. 65–70, indicates that at least half of the civil aid workers were women. Two of my female interviewees (both of whom had positions of responsibility in the Cuban education system) gave a similar estimate. See Interview Cuba 2006, Havana, 15 June and 22 June 2006 (Lidia Turner Martí, chairperson of the Association of Cuban Educators); Interview Cuba 2006, 6 June 2006 (former Cuban deputy minister of education between 1970 and 1990, head of the Department of Teacher Training in the MINED).

5. Interview Cuba 2006, 25 May and 31 May 2006 (Limbania "Nancy" Jiménez Rodríguez, head of education cooperation in Angola, 1976–1977); Interview Cuba 2006, 25 September 2006 (former advisor in the Angolan Ministry of Education, 1977–1979).

6. Interview Cuba 2006, Havana, 15 June and 22 June 2006 (Lidia Turner Martí, chairperson of the Association of Cuban Educators); Interview Cuba 2006, Havana, 6 June 2006 (former Cuban deputy minister of education, 1970–1990, head of the Department of Teacher Training in the MINED); Interview Cuba 2006, Havana, 13 June 2006 (member of the DPI Brigades in Angola, 1982–84).

7. MINED, UJC, FEU, Destacamento Pedagógico Internacionalista "Che Guevara," Documento de Base, October 1977, 4 pages, here pp. 2–3 (MINED archive).

8. MINED, Reunión sobre el Destacamento Pedagógico Internacionalista "Che Guevara," Havana, 7 October 1977, 3 pages (MINED archive).

9. See Turner Martí et al., 1996, p. 30; *Bohemia*, no. 6, 10 February 1978, p. 32. DPI internal reports on performance and work also always quote the number of politically active participants; this again indicates that obviously more than half of the participants were members of the UJC or the FEU.

10. Interview Angola 2006, Luanda, 1 February 2006; Interview United States 2005, Miami, 2 July 2005; Interview United States 2005, Miami, 14 June 2005.

11. Interview Angola 2006, Luanda, 27 January and 17 March 2006 (Artur Pestana, "Pepetela," Angolan deputy minister of education between 1976 and 1982); Interview Angola 2006, Luanda, 17 March 2006 (economic scientist, university professor in Luanda since 1976); see also Acordo especial de colaboração entre o Ministério da Educação da República Popular de Angola e o Ministério da Educação Superior da República de Cuba, signed in Havana on 5 December 1976 (MED archive), and subsequent agreements.

12. Interview Angola 2006, Luanda, 27 January and 17 March 2006 (Artur Pestana, "Pepetela"); Interview Angola 2006, Luanda, 8 February 2006. Following independence, this economist worked in the Angolan Ministry of Planning (for a time as its deputy minister).

13. MINED, Memorias del trabajo de la colaboración Cubana en la República Popular de Angola, 1976–1978, 76 pages, here pp. 3–5 (from the private archive of Limbania "Nancy" Jiménez Rodríguez).

14. Until 1978, the department was called the Centro de Investigação Pedgagócia (CIP, Center of Pedagogical Research), then Centro de Investigação Pedagógica e Inspecção Escolar (CIPIE, Center of Pedagogical Research and School inspection) and from 1991 Instituto Nacional de Investigação e Desenvolvimento da Educação (INIDE, National Institute for Research and Development of Education).

15. In 1979, the administration of the province of Luanda was divided up. The province of Bengo was founded to administer the area around the capital, and the province of Lunda was split into north and south (Lunda Norte and Lunda Sul), leading to a total of eighteen provinces today. See Acordo especial sobre o programa de colaboração para 1978 entre o Ministério de Educação da República de Cuba e o Ministério de Educação da República Popular de Angola, signed in Luanda on 4 October 1977, Signatories: J. R. Fernández, Ministro de Educação da República de Cuba, Ambrôsio Lukoki, Ministro de Educação da República Popular de Angola, 6 pages.

16. Interview Angola 2006, Luanda, 27 January and 17 March 2006 (Artur Pestana, "Pepetela," Angolan deputy minister of education from 1976 to 1981).

17. Ibid.; Interview Angola 2006, Luanda, 3 March, 21 March, and 28 March 2006 (Manuel Teodoro Quarta, head of GICI/GII of the MED from 1977 to 1984).

18. Interview Angola 2006, Luanda, 9 March, 11 March, and 21 March 2006 (Lopo do Nascimento).

19. See note 14.

20. Interview Angola 2006, Luanda, 27 January and 17 March 2006 (Artur Pestana, "Pepetela").

21. Interview Angola 2006, Luanda, 1 February and 21 March 2006 (Pedro Domingos Peterson).

22. Interview Cuba 2006, Havana, 25 September 2006.

23. MINED, Memorias del trabajo de la colaboración Cubana en la República Popular de Angola, 1976–1978, 76 pages, here pp. 32–34, 38–40 (from the private archive of Limbania "Nancy" Jiménez Rodríguez).

24. MED/MINED, Acordo especial de eolaboração entre o Ministério da Educação da República Popular de Angola e o Ministério da Educação da República de Cuba, Luanda, 30 November 1978 (MED archive).

25. Interview Angola 2006, Luanda, 20 January 2006; Interview Angola 2006, Luanda, 27 January and 17 March 2006 (Artur Pestana, "Pepetela"); Interview Angola 2006, Luanda, 1 February and 21 March 2006 (Pedro Domingos Peterson).

26. Following the death of Agostinho Neto in September 1979, the University of Angola was renamed Universidade Agostinho Neto (UAN).

27. Interview Cuba 2004, Santa Clara, 14 December 2004 (physicist, Luanda, 1978–1980); Interview Cuba 2004, Santa Clara, 15 December 2004 (two veterinary doctors, Huambo, 1977–1978); Interview Cuba 2004, Santa Clara, 16 December 2004 (agricultural scientist, Huambo, 1978–1980); Interview Cuba 2004, Santa Clara, 16 December 2004 (mechanical engineer, Luanda, 1981–1982); Interview Cuba 2004, Santa Clara, 17 December 2004 (veterinary doctor, Huambo, 1978–1980).

28. RPA, Universidade Agostinho Neto ao Gabinete de Intercâmbio Internacional do MED, Luanda, 23 January 1986, 4 pages (MED archive).

29. Interview Cuba 2004, Santa Clara, 15 December 2004 (two veterinary doctors, Huambo, 1977–1978).

30. Interview Angola 2006, Luanda, 17 March 2006 (economist and at time of interview dean of the Law Faculty at UAN).

31. Ibid.

32. Interview Angola 2006, Luanda, 27 January and 17 March 2006 (Artur Pestana, "Pepetela").

33. RPA, MED, Direcção Nacional do Ensino Médio e Pré-universitário, Relatório sobre a situação do Ensino Médio na R.P.A.—Período 1978–1982, n.d., approx. 1983, 12 pages, here p. 3 (MED archive); RPA, Secretaria de Estado da Cooperação, Comissão de Avaliação da Cooperação ao Cda. Ministro da Educação, Luanda, Circular No. 1/CACI/SEC/May 1982, Assunto: Avaliação da cooperação, 2 pages (MED archive).

34. RPA, Secretaria de Estado da Cooperação, Comissão de Avaliação da Cooperação ao Cda. Ministro da Educação, Luanda, Circular No. 1/CACI/SEC/May 1982, Assunto: Avaliação da cooperação, 2 pages, here p. 2 (MED archive).

35. Ibid.

36. Statistics are from RPA, MED, GICI/GII, Existência de trabalhadores estrangeiros, 9 November 1981, p. 1 (MED archive).

37. Ibid.

38. RPA, MED, GICI/GII, Memorando: Problemática da retirada da cooperação Cubana da RPA, Luanda, 15 August 1990, 5 pages, here p. 1 (MED archive).

39. See, for example, Second jornada pedagógica del contingente educacional Cubano en la RPA (Programa), May 1983, 6 pages; Second jornada pedagógica del contingente educacional Cubano en la RPA (Libro de resumen), May 1983, 21 pages (both MED archive); Interview Cuba 2004, Santiago de Cuba, 4 November 2004.

40. Interview Cuba 2004, Santa Clara, 15 December 2004 (former Cuban teacher of MPLA school for cadres); Interview Angola 2006, Luanda, 26 January 2006 (former Angolan teacher of MPLA school for cadres).

41. Castro, 1977.

42. Information on internal meetings of the MINED on the establishment of the DPI comes from nonclassified MINED documents to which I had access between June and September 2006 in the Museo de la Alfabetización in Havana. I wish to extend my thanks to the museum curator who provided me with the material. In addition, I conducted many interviews with organizers and protagonists of the project. For information regarding the preparation of the DPI brigades, see MINED, Reunión sobre el DPI, 7 October 1977; MINED, UJC, FEU, Destacamento Pedagógico Internacionalista "Che Guevara," Documento de Base, October 1977, 4 pages, here pp. 2–3 (both: MINED archive).

43. Figures according to Turner Martí et al., 1996, p. 30. Of the 2,026 participants, 1,195 were female (58.9 percent) and 831 male.

44. Interview Angola 2006, Luanda, 27 January and 17 March 2006 (Artur Pestana, "Pepetela"); Interview Angola 2006, Luanda, 1 February and 21 March 2006 (Pedro Domingos Peterson); Interview Angola 2006, Luanda, 17 January 2006.

45. Direcção Provincial de Educação da Huila ao C. Director do Gabinete de Intercâmbio e Cooperação Internacional do MED, Lubango, 7 November 1978, 8 pages, here p. 2 (MED archive).

46. Ibid.

47. Interview Angola 2006, Luanda, 31 March 2006; Interview Angola 2006, Luanda, 9 March, 11 March, and 21 March 2006 (Lopo do Nascimento).

48. Interview Cuba 2004, Santiago de Cuba, 6 November 2004; Interview Angola 2006, Luanda, 31 March 2006.

49. RPA, MED, Gabinete de estudo para o eiagnóstico, relatório de balanço do trabalho realizado pelo grupo de prognóstico do Ministério da Educação da República Popular de Angola, March–June 1986, 78 pages, here pp. 5–6, 35–36 (MED archive).

50. RPA, MED, GICI/GII, Memoranduo: Problemática da retirada da cooperação Cubana da RPA, Luanda, 15 August 1990, 5 pages, here p. 1 (MED archive).

51. RPA, MED, Direcção Nacional do Ensino Médio e Pré-universitário, Relatório sobre a Situação do Ensino Médio na R.P.A.—Período 1978–1982, n.d., approx. 1983, 12 pages, here pp. 3–4 (MED archive).

52. RPA, MED, Mesa redonda sobre educação para todos, July 1991, pp. 1–2 (MED archive).

53. Programa das Nações Unidas para o Desenvolvimento, Programa dos voluntários das Nações Unidas. Projecto do governo da República Popular de Angola, 1989, p. 3 (MED archive) (translation by Christine Hatzky and Mair Edmunds-Harrington).

54. In 1977, the island was still called "Isla de Pinos." It was not renamed "Isla de la Juventud," (Isle of Youth) until 1978, the year in which Cuba hosted the World Festival of Youth and Students.

55. According to information from a speech given at the Pedagogía 90, which took place on the Isle of Youth in 1990, there were still children and adolescents from the following twenty-three countries at international schools: Nicaragua, Bolivia, Democratic Republic of Yemen, Cambodia, Democratic People's Republic of Korea, Sudan, Angola, Ghana, Ethiopia, Mozambique, Zimbabwe, South Africa, Mali, Benin, Republic of Guinea, Namibia, People's Republic of the Congo (Congo-Brazzaville), Sahrawi Arab Democratic Republic, Equatorial Guinea, Cape Verde, São Tomé and Príncipe, Guinea-Bissau, and Burkina Faso. See Gutiérrez Menéndez, 1990, pp. 6–7.

56. See Jiménez Rodríguez, 2008b; Ortega et al., 2004, pp. 8–11; Dorsch, 2008, p. 231. All figures regarding the number of foreign graduates are inaccurate. They can nevertheless be used as approximate values representing the scope of the education program.

57. Acordo Especial entre o governo da República Popular de Angola e o governo da República de Cuba sobre as escolas angolanas na Ilha da Juventude (Projecto), n.d., approx. December 1976, 4 pages (MED archive); see also Interview Angola 2006, Luanda, 20 January 2006. In 1970 he graduated in education in Havana. Between 1980 and 1986 he taught at the Angolan boarding schools on the Isle of Youth.

58. See Gutiérrez Menéndez, 1990, pp. 2–3, passim.

59. Interview Angola 2006, Luanda, 31 January 2006 (studied education science at the teacher-training university of the Isle of Youth from 1986 to 1991).

60. Informação sobre a situação da escola angolana—Isla de Pinos, Cuba ao Cda. Ministro da Educação, Luanda, RPA, Isla de Pinos, 13 January 1978, 6 pages (partly handwritten, MED archive).

61. For statistics on pupil numbers, see RPA, MED, Relatório, Visita de trabalho à República de Cuba da delegação chefiada pelo camarada vice-ministro da educação do ensino de base, no período de 15 April–2 May 1987, Ano do X. aniversario do Partido e da consolidação do Poder Popular, 35 pages, here pp. 32–34 (MED archive).

62. Interview Angola 2006, Luanda, 6 February 2006; MINED, José Ramón Fernández to Ambrôsio Lukoki, Havana, 16 September 1980 (MED archive), a letter from the Cuban minister of education to his Angolan colleagues, in which he informs them of the qualifications achieved by the first 119 Angolan pupils and the possibility of continuing their education.

63. Interview Angola 2006, Luanda, 3 March and 28 March 2006 (as the first director of the GICI/GII of the MED [1977–1981], my interviewee was one of the main people responsible for awarding scholarships for the Isle of Youth); Interview Angola 2006, Luanda, 22 March 2006. (In the 1970s and 1980s, António Burity da Silva was responsible within the MPLA for awarding scholarships for the Isle of Youth.)

64. Interview Angola 2006, Luanda, 20 January 2006.

65. Interview Angola 2006, Luanda, 31 January 2006; Interview Angola 2006, Luanda, 6 February 2006.

66. Interview Angola 2006, Luanda, 3 March, 21 March, and 28 March 2006; Interview Cuba 2006, Havana, 21 September 2006 (between 1988 and 1995, the director of international schools on the Isle of Youth).

67. Interview Cuba 2006, Havana, 21 September 2006 (between 1988 and 1995, the director of international schools on the Isle of Youth).

68. Ibid.

69. Interview Angola 2006, Luanda, 6 February 2006. From 1986 to 1993, the interviewee studied in Cuba and was, as a member of the JMPLA, responsible for pupils and students staying in Cuba, for example by mediating in problem cases and disciplinary actions. Other interviewees also confirmed that the education on the Isle of Youth gave priority to the formation of a homogenous national identity. Interview Cuba 2006, Havana, 21 September 2006; Interview Cuba 2006, Havana, 15 June and 22 June 2006 (Lidia Turner Martí, chairperson of the Association of Cuban Education Specialists).

70. Interview Cuba 2006, Havana, 21 September 2006.

71. Interview Angola 2006, Luanda, 6 February 2006.

72. Ibid.

73. RPA, MED, Relatório, Visita de trabalho à República de Cuba da delegação chefiada pelo camarada vice-ministro da educação do ensino de base, no período de 15 April–2 May 1987, Ano do X. aniversario do Partido e da consolidação do Poder Popular, 35 pages (MED archive). Disciplinary problems are listed for each school.

74. RPA, MED, Relatório de viagem a Cuba e Portugal de uma delegação do MED, Luanda, 5 April 1983, 17 pages, here pp. 10–13 (MED archive).

75. Interview Cuba 2006, Havana, 21 September 2006.

76. RPA, MED, Relatório da delegação partidário-governamental que se deslocou a Cuba, no período de 19 March–14 April 1988, para indagar e averiguar as causas que determinaram a "greve" de alguns estudiantes e consequentemente restablecer a respectiva situação, 25 pages (MED archive).

77. Interview Angola 2006, Luanda, 3 March, 21 March, and 28 March 2006.

78. The island's climate makes it an ideal location for growing citrus fruits (oranges, tangerines, lemons, limes, and grapefruit).

79. Interview Angola 2006, Luanda, 3 March, 21 March, and 28 March 2006.

80. Interview Angola 2006, Luanda, 27 January and 17 March 2006 (Artur Pestana, "Pepetela," Angolan Deputy Minister of Education between 1976 and 1982).

81. Interview Angola 2006, Luanda, 6 February 2006; Interview Angola 2006, Luanda, 27 January and 17 March 2006 (Artur Pestana, "Pepetela"); Interview Angola 2006, Luanda, 31 January 2006. There are no studies dealing with the correlation between a Cuban education and career prospects in Angola. But my interviewees frequently pointed out that "many" of those who had studied in Cuba now held lucrative positions in government, the military, or private enterprise.

82. Interview Angola 2006, Luanda, 29 March 2006 (since mid-1984, the interviewee has occupied various posts within the Angolan Ministry of Education. She has been deputy education minister since 1996).

Chapter 8. Memories of Everyday Life

1. I use the terms "trauma" and "traumatic" to describe experiences with which the survival strategies of those in question were unable to cope.

2. See Lüsebrink, 2008, who summarizes essential recurring aspects in situations of intercultural communication. See also Baberowski, Feest, Lehmann, 2008 and Baberowski, Kaelble, Schriewer, 2008, in which representations of the self and other are analyzed on the basis of various examples from different contexts and epochs using historic, social-scientific and cultural-comparative methods.

3. Interview Cuba 2004, Santiago de Cuba, 26 November 2004.

4. Bourdieu, 1985.

5. República Popular de Angola, Destacamento Pedagógico Internacionalista "Che Guevara," orientaciones generales, Luanda, March 1978, 11 pages (MED archive).

6. I was able to find information about the norms, control mechanisms, and functions of these Cuban enclaves in the "collective diaries" of the student brigades of the Destacamento Pedagógico Internacionalista "Che Guevara." The diaries to which I had access covered the period of 1978 to 1981 and came from the provinces of Moxico, Benguela, Moçamedes (today: Namibe), Uige, and Huila. Further information was provided in several internal accountability reports dated 1985 to 1986 from Huila, Benguela, and Namibe.

7. Interview Cuba 2006, Havana, 10 June 2006 (Rodolfo Puente Ferro).

8. I only had access to one written example of such an internal control mechanism: Programa a cumplimentar en las visitas a los municipios donde se mantiene abierta la colaboración, N'dalatando, 14 July 1979, signed J. B. B., Agregado económico de la Embajada de Cuba, Provincia Kwanza Norte, 8 pages (MINED archive).

9. República Popular de Angola, Destacamento Pedagógico Internacionalista "Che Guevara," orientaciones generales, Luanda, March 1978, 11 pages (MED archive).

10. Interview Angola 2006, Luanda, 1 February 2006.

11. Interview Angola 2006, Luanda, 31 March 2006; Interview Angola 2006, Luanda, 1 February 2006; Interview Cuba 2004, Santiago de Cuba, 12 November 2004; Concurso "Angola en la memoria," De Cuba a Angola, Memorias de una maestra internacionalista, Autora M. V. C. A., Havana, 2002, 23 pages, here pp. 2–3.

12. Interview Angola 2006, Luanda, 1 February 2006. I accompanied these eyewitnesses on a trip around the city of Luanda, during which they pointed out to me all the former "Cuban" *prédios*.

13. See the collective-diary entries of the members of the student brigades: Diario del DPI II, 1979–80, Provincia de Moxico, here: entry dated 14 March 1979 (MINED archive).

14. Interview Angola 2006, Luanda, 1 February 2006.

15. Interview Angola 2006, Luanda, 3 March, 21 March, and 28 March 2006 (Manuel Teodoro Quarta, former head of the GICI/GII of the Angolan Ministry of Education).

16. Diario del DPI II, 1979–80, Provincia de Moxico, entry dated 14 March 1979.

17. Ibid., entry dated 16 March 1979.

18. Interview Cuba 2004, Santa Clara, 15 December 2004; Interview Cuba 2004, Havana, 18 October 2004; Interview Cuba 2004, Santiago de Cuba, 29 October 2004.

19. For the composition, function, and responsibilities of the disciplinary commission, see MINED, Nota al Ministro, Consideraciones sobre el informe del Trabajo en Angola por los Cros. A. O. y J. M. L., Havana, 17 January 1978 (signed Asela de los Santos, Viceministra), 3 pages, here p. 1.

20. República Popular de Angola, Destacamento Pedagógico Internacionalista "Che Guevara," orientaciones generales, Luanda, March 1978, p. 5 (MED archive).

21. George, 2005, pp. 152–153; Interview Cuba 2004, Santa Clara, 16 December 2004. See also the Cuban propaganda film *Caravana*, directed by Rogelio Paris and released in 1990, information at http://www.socialistfilms.org/2008/01/convoy-cuba-angola-1990.html (accessed 15 August 2009).

22. Interview Cuba 2004, Santiago de Cuba, 6 November 2004; Interview Cuba 2004, Santiago de Cuba, 5 November 2004; Interview Cuba 2005, Havana, 5 January 2005.

23. See, for example, RPA, MED, GICI/GII, Problemática do transporte da cooperação cubana para a RPA, 8 May 1982, 4 pages (MED Archive); RPA, MED, Memorando sobre a cooperação Cubana ao serviço do Ministério da Educação, Luanda, 2 February 1985, 9 pages, here p. 4 (MED archive); RPA, Protocolo da IV. sessão da Comissão Mista Intergovernamental Angolana-Cubana de cooperação económica e científico-técnica, Havana, May 1981, 8 pages, here p. 4 (MED archive).

24. See Programa a cumplimentar en las visitas a los municipios donde se mantiene abierta la colaboración, N'dalatando, 14 July 1979, signed J. B. B., Agregado económico de la Embajada de Cuba, Provincia Kwanza Norte, 8 pages, here pp. 1–3 (MINED archive).

25. Interview Cuba, Santa Clara, 15 December 2004. From 1982 to 1984, the interviewee was responsible in the Cuban embassy for all matters to do with passports and travel formalities of civilian development workers and the military.

26. Programa a cumplimentar en las visitas a los municipios donde se mantiene abierta la colaboración, N'dalatando, 14 July 1979, signed J. B. B., Agregado económico de la Embajada de Cuba, Provincia Kwanza Norte, 8 pages (MINED archive).

27. Interview Cuba 2006, Havana, 10 June 2006 (Rodolfo Puente Ferro).

28. For accounts by those who went to Angola before 1980, see Interview Cuba 2004, Santiago de Cuba, 19 November 2004; Interview Cuba 2004, Santiago de Cuba, 22 November 2004; Interview Cuba 2004, Cienfuegos, 3 December 2004. For accounts of those who worked in Luanda during relatively calm periods, see Interview Cuba 2004, Santiago de Cuba, 15 November 2004; Interview Cuba 2004, Santa Clara, 16 December 2004.

29. Interview Cuba 2004, Santiago de Cuba, 29 November 2004; Interview Cuba 2004, Santiago de Cuba, 31 October 2004; Interview Cuba 2004, Santiago de Cuba, 4 November 2004.

30. Interview Cuba 2006, Havana, 10 June 2006 (Rodolfo Puente Ferro). This was confirmed by other eyewitness statements; see Interview Angola 2006, Luanda, 1 February 2006; Interview Cuba 2004, Santiago de Cuba, 26 November 2004.

31. Interview Cuba 2004, Santiago de Cuba, 1 November 2004.

32. Interview Angola 2006, Luanda, 29 November 2006.

33. Interview Cuba 2004, Santiago de Cuba, 1 November 2004.

34. Interview Cuba 2006, Havana, 25 May 2006; Interview Cuba 2006, Havana, 25 May 2006.

35. MINED, Reunión sobre el Destacamento Pedagógico Internacionalista "Che Guevara," Havana, 7 October 1977, 3 pages, here p. 2.

36. Concurso "Angola en la memoria," Recuerdos de una misión, Autora D. G. P., Havana, 2002, DPI II, 1979–1982, Prov. Moçamedes, 32 pages, here p. 10.

37. The collective diaries of the DPI brigades, of which I had excerpts from 1979–1986 dealing with the deployment of the student teachers in various Angolan provinces, give detailed insights into the strictly regimented daily life of the civilian aid workers.

38. UJC, Destacamento Pedagógico Internacionalista "Che Guevara," Emulación especial, Provincia de Namibe, October–December 1985, 12 pages (MED archive).

39. Interview Cuba 2004, Santiago de Cuba, 1 November 2004. My interviewee showed me cuttings from these bulletins, some of which she had written herself.

40. Interview Cuba 2004, Santiago de Cuba, 3 November 2004.

41. Interview Cuba 2004, Havana, 18 October 2004. This interviewee was responsible for organizing the postal service in Luanda from 1978 to 1982.

42. See UJC, Comité Nacional, Aspectos más significativos del II. contingente del Destacamento Pedagógico Internacionalista "Ernesto Che Guevara" en la RPA—según la información que hemos recibido del comité de la UJC—con fecha de la elaboración 18 April 1979, 5 pages (MINED archive).

43. See UJC, Destacamento Pedagógico Internacionalista "Che Guevara," Informe de emulación, Provincia de Namibe, curso escolar 1985–1986, segundo semestre, 21 pages, here pp. 3–6 (MINED archive).

44. Interview Cuba 2004, Santiago de Cuba, 31 October 2004; Interview Cuba 2004, Cienfuegos, 5 December 2004; Interview Cuba 2004, Santa Clara, 11 December 2004; Interview Cuba 2004, Santa Clara, 13 December 2004; Interview Cuba 2004, Santa Clara, 16 December 2004; Interview Cuba 2004, Santa Clara, 17 December 2004.

45. Interview Cuba 2004, Santiago de Cuba, 4 November 2004.

46. There were continuous reports about Angola both in the weekly journal of the Cuban forces (FAR), *Verde Olivo*, and in the weekly journal *Bohemia*. At the end of the 1970s, numerous propaganda films were made, such as Miguel Fleitas's *Guerra de Angola* (1977), in order to convince the population that Cuban engagement was necessary. Examples of Cuban war reporting from Angola between 1975 and 1979 are contained in the chronicles of the journalist Hugo Rius (1982), published in *Bohemia*. The official Cuban version of the Angolan war is contained in the volume *La Guerra de Angola* (Rey Cabrera, 1989).

47. Castro, 1979, pp. 180–181.

48. UJC, Resultados de la encuesta realizada en el Primer Contingente del DPI "Che Guevara" en la relación a la conveniencia práctica de incluir en su uniforme una boina similar que a la que usó el Guerrillero Heróico, 29 December 1977, 1 page (MINED archive).

49. Concurso "Angola en la memoria," Una misión internacionalista en la República Popular de Angola con el nombre "Che Guevara," Autora B. E. T. A., Guantánamo, 2002, DPI I, Lubango, Prov. Huila, 1978–1979, 21 pages, here p. 13.

50. Ibid., p. 4.

51. MINED, Informe anual sobre la colaboración cubana en la Facultad de Ciencieas Agropecuarias de la República Popular de Angola, Huambo, 26 December

1978, signed J. M. R. D., Resp. del Grupo de Educación Superior, 6 pages, here p. 3 (MINED archive).

52. Interview Cuba 2006, Havana, 6 June 2006.

53. George, 2005, pp. 157–158.

54. Interview Angola 2006, Luanda, 29 November 2006.

55. In a 2006 publication by the Cuban military on the siege of Cangamba, which includes a large number of eyewitness reports from former soldiers who had been involved in the fighting, the contribution of the civilians receives no mention whatsoever. See Martín Blandino, 2006.

56. Interview Cuba 2004, Santiago de Cuba, 12 November 2004; Interview Cuba 2004, Santa Clara, 15 December 2004; Interview Angola 2006, Luanda, 1 February 2006.

57. George, 2005, p. 185.

58. RPA, MED, Gabinete do Ministro, ao Camarado Fernández, Minstro da Educação Cuba, Luanda, 2 April 1984 (MED archive). This is a letter of condolence. See also "Bandidos massacram populações civis," *Jornal de Angola*, 27 March 1984, p. 2; "Sumbe: Material capturado ao inimigo," *Jornal de Angola*, 31 March 1984, p. 1; "Do Camarada Presidente: Louvar à corajosa população de Sumbe," *Jornal de Angola*, 19 April 1984, p. 1. See also Interview Cuba 2006, Havana, 13 June 2006. The civil education workers killed in Sumbe appear also in an undated list from the Cuban Ministry of Education along with the words "muerto en combate" ("died in combat").

59. Interview Cuba 2006, Havana, 13 June 2006.

60. Ibid.

61. See "Na cidade de Huambo: Atantado terrorista ceifa vida a trabalhadores," *Jornal de Angola*, 21 April 1984, p. 1; "Huambo repudia com vigor cobarde atentado criminoso," *Jornal de Angola*, 24 April 1984, p. 1; *Jornal de Angola*, 24 April 1984, p. 2; "Transformar o luto e a dor em armas contra a reacção," *Jornal de Angola*, 26 April 1984, pp. 1, 2 (comment). Numerous other articles followed in the *Jornal de Angola*; see also "Reacción popular ante el brutal acto imperialista y racista contra colaboradores civiles en Angola: Nada y nadie podra jamás intimidarnos," *Bohemia*, no. 18, 4 May 1984, pp. 41–43; "Los catorze cubanos caídos en Angola: Unidos en la sangre derramada y en la lucha por la victoria de los pueblos," *Bohemia*, no. 18, 4 May 1984, pp. 48–50.

62. See "Na cidade de Huambo: Atantado terrorista ceifa vida a trabalhadores," *Jornal de Angola*, 21 April 1984, p. 1; "Huambo repudia com vigor cobarde atentado criminoso," *Jornal de Angola*, 24 April 1984, p. 1; "Transformar o luto e a dor em armas contra a reacção," *Jornal de Angola*, 26 April 1984, pp. 1, 2 (comment). Numerous other articles followed in the *Jornal de Angola*; see also "Reacción popular ante el brutal acto imperialista y racista contra colaboradores civiles en Angola: Nada y nadie podra jamás intimidarnos," *Bohemia*, no. 18, 4 May 1984, pp. 41–44.

63. "Los catorze cubanos caídos en Angola: Unidos en la sangre derramada y en la lucha por la victoria de los pueblos," *Bohemia*, no. 18, 4 May 1984, pp. 48–51.

64. "Nada y nadie podrá jamás intimidarnos," *Bohemia*, no. 18, 4 May 1984, p. 41.

65. Ibid., pp. 41–53, here pp. 51, 53.

66. Ibid.

67. A letter addressed to the GICI/GII of the MED in Luanda from the Provincial Directorate of the MED in Malanje, dated 21 May 1984, shows that the Cuban aid workers were withdrawn from this province earlier than planned. Attached to the letter

are numerous telegrams from other Provincial Directorates to the MED in Luanda, which state that Cuban teachers had already departed, above all from Uige, Kwanza Norte, Bié, Cabinda, and Lunda Sul.

68. Interview Cuba 2004, Santiago de Cuba, 11 November 2004; Interview Cuba 2004, Santiago de Cuba, 17 November 2004; Interview Cuba 2004, Santiago de Cuba, 22 November 2004.

69. Interview Cuba 2004, Santa Clara, 16 December 2004.

70. Interview Cuba 2004, Santiago de Cuba, 29 December 2004; Interview Cuba 2004, Santiago de Cuba, 29 October 2004; Interview Cuba 2004, Santiago de Cuba, 1 November 2004; Interview Cuba 2004, Santiago de Cuba, 4 November 2004; Interview Cuba 2004, Santiago de Cuba, 9 November 2004.

71. Interview Cuba 2004, Santa Clara, 15 December 2004.

72. Ibid.

73. Interview Cuba 2004, Santiago de Cuba, 1 November 2004.

74. Interview Cuba 2004, Santiago de Cuba, 4 November 2004.

75. The pejorative name *cuacha*, which was used to describe the political opponents of the MPLA, derived from the Umbundu word *kwacha*. In Umbundu, *kwacha* means "dawn." The word was used by the Ovimbundu merchant caravans in the central highlands as a command for setting off in the morning. It is therefore used metaphorically to refer to a new start. UNITA adopted the expression as a military command and exhortation to bring about a new political dawn, for example in the slogan "Kwacha UNITA! Kwacha Angola!" that was broadcast by UNITA radio for many years. This catchword ("os kwatchas") was then picked up by the MPLA to describe UNITA supporters, UNITA troops, and their sympathizers. It was then adopted by the Cubans, who changed the spelling. I wish to thank Franz Heimer and Maria da Conceição Neto for this explanation.

76. Interview Cuba 2004, Santiago de Cuba, 29 October 2004; Interview Cuba 2004, Santiago de Cuba, 31 October 2004; Interview Cuba 2004, Santiago de Cuba, 4 November 2004; Interview Cuba 2004, Santiago de Cuba, 5 November 2004; Interview Cuba 2004, Santiago de Cuba, 8 November 2004.

77. Interview Cuba 2004, Santiago de Cuba, 4 November 2004.

78. MINED, Memorias del trabajo realizado por el primer Contingente Pedagógico Internacionalista "Che Guevara" en la Provincia de Huambo, curso escolar 1978–1979, 23 pages, here p. 3 (MINED archive).

79. Interview Cuba 2004, Santa Clara, 16 December 2004.

80. Ibid.

81. Interview Cuba 2004, Santa Clara, 17 December 2004.

82. Interview Cuba 2004, Santiago de Cuba, 22 November 2004.

83. Ibid.

84. Interview Cuba 2004, Santiago de Cuba, 5 November 2004.

85. Ibid.

86. Ibid.

87. Ibid.

88. Ibid.

89. Interview Cuba 2004, Santiago de Cuba, 3 November 2004.

90. Interview Cuba 2004, Santiago de Cuba, 29 October 2004.

91. Ibid.

92. Interview Cuba 2004, Santa Clara, 15 December 2004.

93. Domingos Peterson, 2003, p. 61; Vela Ngaba, 2006, p. 82.

94. Second jornada pedagógica del contingente educacional Cubano en la RPA (Libro de resumen), May 1983, 23 pages, here pp. 10–11 (MED archive).

95. MINED, Informe de la Provincia de Huambo a la reunión nacional de profesores guías que se efectuará en Luanda, 7 June 1978, signed E. L. R., Prof. Guía Prov. Huambo, 8 pages, here p. 8 (MINED archive); Interview Cuba 2004, Santiago de Cuba, 26 November 2004.

96. While doing research for this work I had access to excerpts from the "competition reports" (Spanish: "Informes de emulación") from the years 1985 and 1986 covering the student-teacher brigades' deployment in the provinces of Benguela, Huila, and Namibe.

97. I had access to extracts from the so-called collective diaries of the student brigades from the years 1978 to 1981 in the provinces of Huila, Benguela, Moxico, Namibe, and Uige.

98. Interview Cuba 2004, Santiago de Cuba, 1 November 2004; Interview Cuba 2004, Santiago de Cuba, 4 November 2004; Interview Cuba 2004, Santiago de Cuba, 6 November 2004; Interview Cuba 2004, Santiago de Cuba, 9 November 2004; Interview Cuba 2006, Havana, 6 June 2006 (former Cuban deputy minister of education from 1970 to 1990, head of the Department of Teacher Education in MINED); Interview Cuba 2006, Havana, 8 September 2006 (head of Cuban education cooperation in Angola, 1979 and 1981).

99. Interview Angola 2006, Luanda, 17 January 2006 (former employee in the Angolan Ministry of Education from 1977 to 1980).

100. Second jornada pedagógica del contingente educacional Cubano en la RPA (Libro de resumen), May 1983, 21 pages (MINED archive).

101. Interview Cuba 2006, Havana, 15 June and 22 June 2006; Interview Cuba 2004, Santiago de Cuba, 1 November 2004.

102. Interview Angola 2006, Luanda, 31 March 2006.

103. Second jornada pedagógica del contingente educacional Cubano en la RPA (Libro de resumen), May 1983, 21 pages, here p. 14 (MINED archive).

104. Interview Angola 2006, Luanda, 15 March 2006; Interview Angola 2006, Luanda, 25 February 2006; Interview Angola 2006, Luanda, 29 November 2006.

105. Interview Angola 2006, Luanda, 15 March 2006; Interview Angola 2006, Luanda, 25 February 2006; Interview Angola 2006, Luanda, 29 November 2006.

106. MINED, Plan de medidas a desarollar en el Destacamento Pedagógico para perfeccionar el trabajo docente-educativo en el segundo período, Huambo, 8 August 1978, signed E. L. R., M. d. J. A. H., 6 pages (MINED archive).

107. Interview Cuba, 2004, Santiago de Cuba, 26 November 2004.

108. MINED, Al Co. J. R. Fernández, Ministro de Educación, de Asela de los Santos, Viceministra de Educación, Havana, 5 December 1977, 2 pages (MINED archive).

109. Second jornada pedagógica del contingente educacional Cubano en la RPA (Libro de resumen), May 1983, 21 pages (MINED archive). Documents from the national conference contain no mention of Angolan participation. According to a "competition report" of the student brigades, Angolan teachers did take part in a provincial conference. See Informe de emulación, Benguela, 1 October–15 December 1985, 31 pages, here pp. 5–6 (MINED archive).

110. Interview Cuba 2004, Santiago de Cuba, 26 November 2004.

111. Concurso "Angola en la memoria," Memorias de una misión, Autora C. D. C. O., Havana, 2002, DPI I, 1978–1979, Luena, Prov. Moxico, 20 pages, here p. 8; Interview Cuba 2004, Santiago de Cuba, 9 November 2004; Interview Cuba 2004, Santiago de Cuba, 12 November 2004.

112. Concurso "Angola en la memoria," Memorias de una misión, Autora C. D. C. O., Havana, 2002, DPI I, 1978–1979, Luena, Prov. Moxico, 20 pages, here p. 8; Interview Cuba 2004, Santiago de Cuba, 9 November 2004.

113. MINED, Informe de la Provincia de Huambo a la reunión nacional de profesores guías que se efectuará en Luanda, 7 June 1978, signed E. L. R., Prof. Guía Prov. Huambo, 8 pages, here p. 3 (MINED archive).

114. MINED, Guía de información interna para la visita del Cro. José R. Fernández. Vice Presidente del Consejo de Ministros, Luanda, 20 June 1979, 11 pages, here p. 8 (MINED archive).

115. See UJC, Comité Nacional, Aspectos más significativos del II. contingente del Destacamento Pedagógico Internacionalista "Ernesto Che Guevara" en la RPA—según la información que hemos recibido del comité de la UJC—con fecha de la elaboración 18 April 1979, 5 pages (MINED archive).

116. MINED, Informe de la Provincia de Huambo a la reunión nacional de profesores guías que se efectuará en Luanda, 7 June 1978, signed Eustacio León Rodríguez, Prof. Guía Prov. Huambo, 8 pages, here p. 2 (MINED archive).

117. RPA, MED, GICI/GII, Deslocação a Cuba, April 1982. Delegação chefiada pelo camarada Ministro da Educação, Luanda, 27 April 1982 (MED archive).

118. Interview Cuba 2004, Havana, 31 December 2004 (linguist and anthropologist, member of a joint Cuban-Angolan research project on the state of language in Angola); Interview Cuba 2004, Santiago de Cuba, 31 October 2004; Interview Cuba 2004, Santiago de Cuba, 12 November 2004; Interview Cuba 2004, Santiago de Cuba, 22 November 2004; Interview Cuba 2004, Santiago de Cuba, 22 November 2004; Interview Cuba 2004, Santa Clara, 15 December 2004; Concurso "Angola en la memoria," Autora B. E. T. A., Havana, 2002, DPI I, 1978–1979, Prov. Moçamedes, 21 pages, here p. 2; Concurso "Angola en la memoria," De Cuba a Angola, Memorias de una maestra internacionalista, Autora M. V. C. A., Havana, 2002, 23 pages, here pp. 4–5, 14–15.

119. Interview Angola 2006, Luanda, 27 January and 17 March 2006 (Artur Pestana, "Pepetela").

120. MINED, Informe, Diferencias entre los informes recibidos de Angola, DPI "Che Guevara," Havana, 25 September 1979, to Asela de los Santos, Viceministra, from: Z. F. H., Directora General Formación y Perfeccionamento Personal Pedagógico, 3 pages, here p. 2 (MINED archive).

121. RPA, MED, GICI/GII, Protocolo reunião 10–12 November 1980, Ministério da Educação em Luanda, 17 November 1980, os secretários, J. A. T., J. M. d. S, 10 pages, here pp. 3–4 (MED archive). The problem still existed in 1985. See RPA, MED, GICI/GII, Relatório, 25 March 1982 to 31 August 1985, 1 October 1985, signed o director cessante, J. M. S., 30 pages, here p. 13 (MED archive).

122. In view of the large effort to coordinate the holiday schedules, the GICI/GII set up their own file, which included complaints and responses from the provinces. See RPA, MED, GICI/GII Assunto: Ferias Cooperação Cubana, 1983 (MED archive).

123. Interview Cuba 2006, Havana, 25 May 2006; Interview Cuba 2006, Havana, 25 May 2006.

124. Memorias de la colaboración del Destacamento Pedagógico ubicado en la Provincia de Huambo en el curso escolar 1978–1979, March–December 1978, Huambo, 26 December 1978, signed E. L. R., Profesor guía and M. d. J. A. H., Jefe del grupo de Educación, 24 pages, here p. 8 (MINED archive).

125. Interview Cuba 2006, Havana, 25 May 2006.

126. See Memorias de la colaboración del Destacamento Pedagógico ubicado en la Provincia de Huambo en el curso escolar 1978–1979, March–December 1978, Huambo, 26 December 1978, signed E. L. R., Profesor guía and M. d. J. A. H., Jefe del grupo de Educación, 24 pages, here p. 13 (MINED archive); Plan de medidas a desarrollar en el Destacamento Pedagógico para perfeccionar el trabajo docente-educativo en el segundo período, Huambo, 8 August 1978, signed E. L. R., Profesor guía and M. d. J. A. H., Jefe del grupo de Educación, 6 pages, here p. 1 (MINED archive).

127. RPA, MED, Gabinete do Ministro da Educação, Análise da Cooperação com a República de Cuba, Luanda, 13 March 1980, signed Ministro da Educação, Ambrôsio Lukoki (MED archive).

128. Memorias de la colaboración del Destacamento Pedagógico ubicado en la Provincia de Huambo en el curso escolar 1978–1979, March–December 1978, Huambo, 26 December 1978, signed E. L. R., Profesor guía and M. de J. A. H., Jefe del grupo de Educación, 24 pages, here p. 9 (MINED archive).

129. Centro dos cursos pré-universitários de Luanda ao GICI/GII, 16 June 1985, signed o Director do Centro, 2 pages (MED archive), in which a school principal complains about the behavior of the Cuban teachers at his school, who, he claims, keep neither to his rules nor to mutual agreements.

130. Interview Cuba 2004, Santiago de Cuba, 22 November 2004.

131. MINED, Memorias del trabajo realizado por el primer Contingente Pedagógico Internacionalista "Che Guevara" en la Provincia de Huambo, curso escolar 1978–1979, 23 pages, here pp. 8–9 (MINED archive).

132. Interview Cuba 2004, Santiago de Cuba, 4 November 2004; Interview Angola 2006, Luanda, 17 January 2006.

133. Interview Cuba 2004, Santiago de Cuba, 4 November 2004.

134. Interview Angola 2006, Luanda, 17 January 2006; Interview Angola 2006, Luanda, 1 February and 21 March 2006 (Pedro Domingos Peterson); Interview Cuba 2004, Santiago de Cuba, 26 November 2004.

135. Interview Cuba 2004, Santiago de Cuba, 4 November 2004.

136. MINED, Memorias del trabajo realizado por el primer Contingente Pedagógico Internacionalista "Che Guevara" en la Provincia de Huambo, curso escolar 1978–1979, 23 pages (MINED archive); Interview Cuba 2004, Santiago de Cuba, 1 November 2004; Interview Angola 2006, Luanda, 15 March 2006; Interview Angola 2006, Luanda, 25 February 2006; Interview Angola 2006, Luanda, 29 November 2006.

137. See Diario del Destacamento Pedagógico Internacionalista "Che Guevara" (DPI) II, 1979–1981, Provincia de Huila, entry dated 6 April 1979 (MINED archive); Interview Cuba 2004, Santiago de Cuba, 4 November 2004.

138. Interview Angola 2006, Luanda, 17 January 2006.

139. Memorias de la colaboración del Destacamento Pedagógico ubicado en la Provincia de Huambo en el curso escolar 1978–1979, March–December 1978, Huambo,

26 December 1978, signed E. L. R., Profesor guía and M. de J. A. H., Jefe del grupo de Educación, 24 pages, here p. 8 (MINED archive).

140. Diario del Destacamento Pedagógico Internacionalista "Che Guevara" (DPI) II, 1979–1980, Provincia de Moxico, entry dated 2 May 1979 (MINED archive).

141. Memorias de la colaboración del Destacamento Pedagógico ubicado en la Provincia de Huambo en el curso escolar 1978–1979, March–December 1978, Huambo, 26 December 1978, signed E. L. R., Profesor guía and M. d. J. A. H., Jefe del grupo de Educación, 24 pages, here p. 9 (MINED archive).

142. Interview Cuba 2004, Santiago de Cuba, 1 November 2004.

143. Ibid.; Interview Cuba 2004, Santiago de Cuba, 12 November 2004.

144. This assertion was also made by Cuban civilians working in other sectors. Interview Cuba 2004, Santiago de Cuba, 4 November 2004; Interview Cuba 2004, Santiago de Cuba, 6 November 2004; Interview Cuba 2004, Santiago de Cuba, 9 November 2004; Interview Cuba 2004, Santiago de Cuba, 9 November 2005; Interview Cuba 2004, Santiago de Cuba, 12 November 2004; Interview Cuba 2004, Santiago de Cuba, 12 November 2004; Interview Cuba 2004, Santiago de Cuba, 17 November 2004; Interview Cuba 2004, Santiago de Cuba, 17 November 2004; Interview Cuba 2004, Santiago de Cuba, 18 November 2004; Interview Cuba 2004, Santa Clara, 3 December 2004; Interview Cuba 2004, Santa Clara, 13 December 2004; Interview Cuba 2004, Santa Clara, 13 December 2004; Interview Cuba 2004, Santa Clara, 14 December 2004; Interview Cuba 2004, Santa Clara, 15 December 2004; Interview Cuba 2004, Santa Clara, 15 December 2004; Interview Cuba 2004, Santa Clara, 16 December 2004; Interview Cuba 2004, Havana, 23 December 2004.

145. Concurso "Angola en la memoria," Memorias de una misión, Autora C. D. C. O., Havana, 2002, DPI I, 1978–1979, Luena, Prov. Moxico, 20 pages, here p. 2.

146. Memorias de la colaboración del Destacamento Pedagógico ubicado en la Provincia de Huambo en el curso escolar 1978–1979, March–December 1978, Huambo, 26 December 1978, signed E. L. R., Profesor guía and M. d. J. A. H., Jefe del grupo de Educación, 24 pages, here p. 8 (MINED archive).

147. Concurso "Angola en la memoria," Memorias de una misión, Autora C. D. C. O., Havana, 2002, DPI I, 1978–1979, Luena, Prov. Moxico, 20 pages, here pp. 2–3.

148. Memorias de la colaboración del Destacamento Pedagógico ubicado en la Provincia de Huambo en el curso escolar 1978–1979, March–December 1978, Huambo, 26 December 1978, signed E. L. R., Profesor guía and M. d. J. A. H., Jefe del grupo de Educación, 24 pages, here p. 9 (MINED archive).

149. Interview Angola 2006, Luanda, 15 March 2006; Interview Angola 2006, Luanda, 26 November 2006; Interview Angola 2006, Luanda, 1 April 2006; Interview Angola 2006, Luanda, 25 February 2006; Interview Angola 2006, Luanda, 31 January 2006.

150. Interview Angola 2006, Luanda, 26 November 2006.

151. Interview Angola 2006, Luanda, 31 January 2006.

152. Interview Angola 2006, Luanda, 10 March 2006; Interview Portugal, Lisbon, 26 October 2005.

153. Interview Angola 2006, Luanda, 15 March 2006; Interview Angola 2006, Luanda, 25 February 2006; Interview Angola 2006, Luanda, 29 November 2006; Interview Angola 2006, Luanda, 31 March 2006.

154. Interview Angola 2006, Luanda, 26 November 2006; Interview Angola 2006, Luanda, 31 March 2006.

155. Interview Angola 2006, Luanda, 15 March 2006.

156. Interview Angola 2006, Luanda, 10 March 2006.

157. Interview Angola 2006, Luanda, 1 April 2006.

158. Interview Angola 2006, Luanda, 29 November 2006.

159. Interview Angola 2006, Luanda, 1 April 2006.

160. RPA, MED, Projecto de estudo sobre mercados alternativos a contratação de técnicos docentes (8/1983, handwritten annotations), 6 pages (MED archive).

161. RPA, MED, GICI/GII, Deslocação a Cuba, April 1982, Delegação chefiada pelo camarada Ministro da Educação, Luanda, 27 April 1982 (MED archive); RPA, Delegação Provincial da educação da Lunda-Norte ao GII/MED, Luanda, Nota 598/SPAC/DPE/83, 4 July 1983, Assunto: nota informativa, 2 pages (MED archive). See also the interviews I conducted with two Angolans who now live in Portugal and who had both worked with Cuban development workers: Interview Portugal 2005, Lisbon, 16 September and 26 September 2005; Interview Portugal 2005, Lisbon, 24 September 2005.

162. RPA, MED, Memorando sobre a cooperação Cubana ao serviço do Ministério de Educação, Luanda, 2 February 1985, 9 pages (MED archive).

163. Direcção Provincial de educação da Huila ao C. Director do Gabinete de Intercâmbio e Cooperação Internacional do MED, Lubango, 7 November 1978, 8 pages, here p. 2 (MED archive); see also Interview Angola 2006, Luanda, 27 January and 17 March 2006 (Artur Pestana, "Pepetela"); Interview Angola 2006, Luanda, 17 January 2006.

164. See Martínez Valle, Oelsner, Roldán Vera, 2008, pp. 195–219. This study compares two education missions in Mexico and Argentina that also aimed to integrate parts of the population into a new national and social project. The educational objectives and mechanisms, the self-awareness of the teachers, and the teacher-pupil relationship all resembled my own findings.

165. Interview Cuba 2004, Santiago de Cuba, 28 October 2004; Interview Cuba 2004, Santiago de Cuba, 11 November 2004; Interview Cuba 2004, Cienfuegos, 8 December 2004; Interview Cuba 2004, Santa Clara, 14 December 2004.

166. Interview Cuba 2004, Santiago de Cuba, 29 October 2004; Interview Cuba 2004, Santiago de Cuba, 31 October 2004; Interview Cuba 2004, Santiago de Cuba, 4 November 2004; Interview Cuba 2004, Santiago de Cuba, 6 November 2004; Interview Cuba 2004, Santiago de Cuba, 22 November 2004; Interview Cuba 2004, Santa Clara, 15 December 2004; Interview United States 2005, Miami, 2 July 2005.

167. Interview Cuba 2006, Havana, 10 June 2006 (Rodolfo Puente Ferro); Interview Angola 2006, Luanda, 1 February 2006; Interview United States 2006, Miami, 8 July 2006 (Alcibíades Hidalgo); Interview Cuba 2006, Havana, 25 May 2006; Interview Cuba 2006, Havana, 25 May 2006; MINED, Plan de preparación política para el Destacamento Pedagógico Internacionalista "Che Guevara," approx. October 1977, 3 pages (MINED archive).

168. Interview Cuba 2006, Havana, 25 May 2006; Interview Cuba 2006, Havana, 25 May 2006.

169. Interview Angola 2006, Luanda, 1 February 2006.

170. MINED, Reunión sobre el Destacamento Pedagógico Internacionalista "Che Guevara," Havana, 7 October 1977, 3 pages (MINED archive).

171. MINED, Reunión sobre el Destacamento Pedagógico Internacionalista "Che Guevara," 7 October 1977, 3 pages (MINED archive).

172. Interview Cuba 2006, Havana, 10 June 2006 (Rodolfo Puente Ferro).

173. MINED, Reunión sobre el Destacamento Pedagógico Internacionalista "Che Guevara," 7 October 1977, 3 pages (MINED archive).

174. RPA, MED, GICI/GII, 6 March 1985, ao Camarada Vice-Ministro para o Ensino de Base, Luanda, . . . Informação proveniente da escola do ensino de base do III Nivel "N'Gola Kiluanji" . . . , 8 pages, here pp. 6–8 (MED archive).

175. Interview Cuba 2004, Cienfuegos, 8 December 2004.

176. Interview Angola 2006, Luanda, 25 February 2006; Interview Cuba 2004, Santa Clara, 14 December 2004.

177. Programa a cumplimentar en las visitas a los municipios donde se mantiene abierta la colaboración, N'dalatando, 14 July 1979, signed J. B. B., Agregado económico de la Embajada de Cuba, Provincia Kwanza Norte, 8 pages, here p. 4 (MINED archive).

178. Interview Angola 2006, Luanda, 1 February 2006.

179. See Tareas principales para el mes de julio, DPI "Che Guevara," Huambo, 3 July 1978, signed M. d. A. H., 2 pages, here p. 1 (MINED archive).

180. Lang, 2004, pp. 11–27.

181. Lewis, Lewis, Rigdon, 1977, p 66.

182. Interview Cuba 2006, Havana, 25 May 2006; Interview Cuba 2006, Havana, 25 May 2006.

183. Concurso "Angola en la memoria," Recuerdos de una misión, Autora D. G. P., Havana, 2002, DPI II, 1979–1982, Prov. Moçamedes, 32 pages, here pp. 16–17; Interview Cuba 2004, Santiago de Cuba, 1 November 2004; Interview Cuba 2004, Santiago de Cuba, 4 November 2004; Interview Cuba 2004, Santiago de Cuba, 6 November 2004.

184. Interview United States 2005, Miami, 8 July 2005 (Alcibíades Hidalgo).

185. Interview United States 2005, Miami, 2 July 2005.

186. Interview United States 2005, Miami, 8 July 2005 (Alcibíades Hidalgo); see also Interview Cuba 2004, Santiago de Cuba, 4 November 2004; Interview Cuba 2004, Santiago de Cuba, 6 November 2004; Interview United States 2005, Miami, 2 July 2005.

187. Interview Cuba 2004, Santa Clara, 15 December 2004; Interview Cuba 2004, Santiago de Cuba, 29 October 2004.

188. Lang, 2004, p. 14.

189. On the rise in divorce rates, see Smith, Padula, 1996, pp. 68–71.

190. Interview Cuba 2005, Santiago de Cuba, 10 January 2005.

191. Interview United States 2005, Miami, 8 July 2005 (Alcibíades Hidalgo).

192. Interview Cuba 2004, Havana, 23 December 2004.

193. Interview Cuba 2004, Santa Clara, 14 December 2004.

194. Interview Cuba 2004, Santiago de Cuba, 4 November 2004; Interview Cuba 2004, Santiago de Cuba, 6 November 2004.

195. Interview Cuba 2004, Santiago de Cuba, 28 October 2004; Interview Cuba 2004, Santiago de Cuba, 11 November 2004; Interview Cuba 2004, Santiago de Cuba, 11 November 2004; Interview Cuba 2004, Santiago de Cuba, 11 November 2004; Interview Cuba 2004, Santiago de Cuba, 11 November 2004; Interview Cuba 2004, Santiago de Cuba, 12 November 2004; Interview Cuba 2004, Santiago de Cuba, 22 November

2004; Interview Cuba 2004, Santiago de Cuba, 22 November 2004; Interview Cuba 2004, Santiago de Cuba, 22 November 2004; Interview Cuba 2004, Santiago de Cuba, 24 November 2004; Interview Cuba 2004, Cienfuegos, 8 December 2004; Interview Cuba 2004, Santa Clara, 14 December 2004; Interview Cuba 2004, Santa Clara, 17 December 2004.

196. Interview Cuba 2004, Santa Clara, 17 December 2004; Interview Cuba 2004, Cienfuegos, 8 December 2004.

197. Lievesley, 2004, p. 143; Lang, 2004.

198. Interview Cuba 2004, Santa Clara, 15 December 2004; Interview Cuba 2004, Santiago de Cuba, 29 October 2004.

199. Interview Angola 2006, Luanda, 20 January 2006; Interview Angola, 2006, Luanda, 1 February 2006.

200. Interview Angola 2006, Luanda, 20 January 2006.

201. Interview Angola 2006, Luanda, 1 February 2006.

202. See, for example, MINED, Memorias del trabajo realizado por el primer Contingente Pedagógico Internacionalista "Che Guevara" en la Provincia de Huambo, curso escolar 1978–1979, 23 pages, here p. 3 (MINED archive).

203. Interview Cuba 2004, Santiago de Cuba, 5 November 2004; Interview Cuba 2004, Santiago de Cuba, 22 November 2004; Interview Cuba 2004, Santiago de Cuba, 4 November 2004; Interview Cuba 2004, Santiago de Cuba, 1 November 2004. Others indicated that some "went crazy"—e.g., Interview Cuba 2004, Santa Clara, 13 December 2004.

204. Interview Cuba 2004, Santiago de Cuba, 29 October 2004; Interview Cuba 2004, Santiago de Cuba, 3 November 2004; Interview Cuba 2004, Santa Clara, 15 December 2004.

205. Interview Cuba 2004, Santiago de Cuba, 29 October 2004; Interview Cuba 2004, Santiago de Cuba, 6 November 2004; Interview Cuba 2004, Santa Clara, 16 December 2004; Interview Cuba 2004, Santa Clara, 15 December 2004.

206. Interview Cuba 2004, Santiago de Cuba, 4 November 2004.

207. Interview Cuba 2004, Santa Clara, 16 December 2004.

208. Interview Cuba 2004, Santiago de Cuba, 3 November 2004; Interview Cuba 2004, Santiago de Cuba, 29 October 2004; Interview Cuba 2004, Santiago de Cuba, 31 October 2004; Interview Cuba 2004, Santiago de Cuba, 15 November 2004; Interview Cuba 2004, Santiago de Cuba, 22 November 2004.

209. For further reflections on the way society deals with death from a sociological and comparative perspective, see Hahn, 2002, pp. 55–89.

210. Interview Cuba 2004, Santiago de Cuba, 11 November 2004; Interview Cuba 2004, Santiago de Cuba, 15 November 2004; Interview Cuba 2004, Santiago de Cuba, 22 November 2004; Interview Cuba 2004, Santiago de Cuba, 3 November 2004; Interview Cuba 2004, Santiago de Cuba, 29 October 2004.

211. Interview Cuba 2004, Santiago de Cuba, 29 October 2004.

212. Interview Cuba 2004, Santa Clara, 16 December 2004.

213. Interview Cuba 2004, Santiago de Cuba, 3 November 2004. Other interviewees confirmed similar attitudes; see Interview Cuba 2004, Santiago de Cuba, 31 October 2004; Interview Cuba 2004, Santiago de Cuba, 17 November 2004.

214. Interview Cuba 2004, Santiago de Cuba, 3 November 2004.

215. Castro, 2005.

216. Interview Cuba 2004, Santiago de Cuba, 22 November 2004; Interview Cuba 2004, Santiago de Cuba, 17 November 2004.

217. Niethammer, 1988, p. 33.

218. See Bohleber, 2007, p. 92.

219. Bohleber, 2007, pp. 89–90.

220. Asociación de Combatientes de la Revolución Cubana, http://www.vencere mos.co.cu/pags/varias/hipertextos/A/asociacion_combatientes_3024288.html (accessed 27 August 2013).

221. In 2004, I attended one such memorial ceremony organized by the Party and the Association of Combatants at a cemetery cenotaph in the town of Cienfuegos on the Cuban south coast. In the speeches given by local Party officials and members of the military, the "internationalists" were only mentioned very briefly, particularly in comparison with the national heroes of the War of Independence, such as Antonio Maceo Grajales (1845–1896, second-in-command of the Cuban Army of Independence) and the heroes of the revolution.

222. See Plato, 2000, p. 10.

223. "Pero lo que dio mi gente en esa batalla perdónenme el adjetivo pero no cabe en la calamina de una medalla." The song was released in Havana in 2000 on the album *A guitarra limpia*. For the complete lyrics, see http://www.cancioneros.com/nc.php ?NM=4544 (accessed 27 August 2013). Frank Delgado (b. 1960 in Pinar del Río) is one of the younger representatives of the Cuban Nueva Trova musical movement (derived from folk musicians, the troubadours of the Middle Ages). The Nueva Trova movement emerged in the mid-1960s in Cuba. Its most important exponents are Silvio Rodríguez, Vicente Feliu, Carlos Varela, and Pablo Milanés. Although the movement dissolved in 1986, it still has offshoots. Delgado belongs to Nuevísima Trova. For the history of Nueva Trova, see Broughton, Ellingham, 2000, pp. 408–413.

Chapter 9. Between Encounter, Dissociation, and Re-Identification

1. Interview Angola 2006, Luanda, 1 February 2006; Interview Cuba 2004, Cienfuegos, 5 December 2004; Interview Cuba 2004, Cienfuegos, 8 December 2004; Interview Angola 2006, Luanda, 31 March 2006.

2. See, for example, RPA, MED, Secretaria de Estado da Cooperação ao Gabinete de Intercâmbio Internacional do MED, envío do Protocolo da V. sessão da Comissão Mista Intergovernamental Angolana-Cubana de cooperação económica e científico-técnica, Luanda, 26–28 October 1983, Luanda, 15 December 1983, o Director Nacional, M. M. D., 7 pages, here p. 4 (MED archive); RPA, MED, GICI/GII, Ponto da situação relativo à cooperação de nacionalidade Cubana em serviço do MED, 27 April 1982, 6 pages (MED archive); RPA, MED, GICI/GII, Avaliação da Cooperação, Gabinete de Intercâmbio Internacional do MED, 19 July 1982, 8 pages (MED archive).

3. Interview Cuba 2004, Santiago de Cuba, 1 November 2004; Interview Cuba 2004, Santiago de Cuba, 4 November 2004; Interview Cuba 2004, Santiago de Cuba, 6 November 2004; Interview Cuba 2004, Santiago de Cuba, 31 October 2004; Interview Angola 2006, Luanda, 17 January 2006; Interview Angola 2006, Luanda, 15 March 2006; Interview Angola 2006, Luanda, 25 February 2006; Interview Angola 2006, Luanda, 29 November 2006; Interview Angola 2006, Luanda, 31 March 2006.

4. Interview Cuba 2004, Santa Clara, 11 December 2004; Interview Cuba 2004, Santa Clara, 17 December 2004; Interview Angola 2006, Luanda, 31 March 2006; Interview Angola 2006, Luanda, 1 February 2006.

5. Interview Angola 2006, Luanda, 1 February and 23 March 2006 (Pedro Domingos Peterson); Interview Angola 2006, Luanda, 26 January 2006; Interview Angola 2006, Luanda, 8 February 2006 (former Angolan minister of planning and financial planning).

6. Interview Angola 2006, Luanda, 9 March, 11 March, 21 March 2006 (Lopo do Nascimento, former Angolan prime minister); Interview Angola 2006, Luanda, 30 January 2006 (agricultural economist, former state secretary in the Angolan Ministry of Agriculture).

7. Interview Angola 2006, Luanda, 6 February 2006.

8. Interview Angola 2006, Luanda, 31 January 2006.

9. Interview Angola 2006, Luanda, 20 January 2006.

10. Interview Angola 2006, Luanda, 27 January and 17 March 2006.

11. See Interview Cuba 2004, Santiago de Cuba, 29 October 2004; Interview Cuba 2004, Santiago de Cuba, 31 October 2004; Interview Cuba 2004, Cienfuegos, 5 December 2004; Interview Cuba 2004, Cienfuegos, 8 December 2004.

12. Interview Cuba 2004, Santa Clara, 13 December 2004.

13. Interview Cuba 2004, Santa Clara, 13 December 2004.

14. Interview Cuba 2004, Santiago de Cuba, 8 November 2004.

15. Interview Cuba 2004, Havana, 18 October 2004; Interview Cuba 2004, Santiago de Cuba, 3 November 2004; Interview Cuba 2005, Santiago de Cuba, 10 January 2005.

16. Interview Cuba 2004, Santa Clara, 17 December 2004.

17. Interview Cuba 2004, Cienfuegos, 3 December 2004. A Bembé is an Afro-Cuban nighttime religious ceremony that summons the Orishas with a special drumbeat. The Cuban anthropologist Fernando Ortiz carried out in-depth studies of Afro-Cuban traditions and religions as early as the beginning of the twentieth century. He published many works on the topic, for example, Ortiz, 1984, 1993, (1906) 2001. More recent studies have been conducted by the Cuban anthropologists Lydia Cabrera in the 1950s (Cabrera, [1954] 1993) and Natalia Bolívar Aróstegui in the 1980s (Bolívar Aróstegui, 1990) and Miguel Barnet (Barnet, 2000).

18. Interview Cuba 2004, Cienfuegos, 5 December 2004; Interview Cuba 2004, Santiago de Cuba, 17 November 2004.

19. Interview Cuba 2004, Cienfuegos, 8 December 2004.

20. See De la Fuente, 2001; Taylor, 1988.

21. Interview Cuba 2004, Havana, 23 December 2004.

22. Interview Cuba 2004, Santiago de Cuba, 4 November 2004; Interview Cuba 2004, Santiago de Cuba, 6 November 2004; Interview Cuba 2004, Santiago de Cuba, 9 November 2004; Interview Cuba 2004, Santiago de Cuba, 9 November 2005; Interview Cuba 2004, Santiago de Cuba, 12 November 2004; Interview Cuba 2004, Santiago de Cuba, 12 November 2004; Interview Cuba 2004, Santiago de Cuba, 17 November 2004; Interview Cuba 2004, Santiago de Cuba, 17 November 2004; Interview Cuba 2004, Santiago de Cuba, 18 November 2004; Interview Cuba 2004, Santa Clara 3 December 2004; Interview Cuba 2004, Santa Clara, 13 December 2004; Interview Cuba 2004, Santa Clara, 13 December 2004; Interview Cuba 2004, Santa Clara 14 December 2004; Interview Cuba 2004, Santa Clara, 15 December 2004; Interview Cuba 2004, Santa

Clara, 15 December 2004; Interview Cuba 2004, Santa Clara, 16 December 2004; Interview Cuba 2004, Havana, 23 December 2004.

23. Interview Cuba 2004, Santiago de Cuba, 12 November 2004.

24. Interview Cuba 2004, Santa Clara, 17 December 2004; see also Interview Cuba 2004, Santiago de Cuba, 6 November 2004.

25. Interview Cuba 2004, Cienfuegos, 8 December 2004.

26. Interview Cuba 2004, Santiago de Cuba, 15 November 2004.

27. Interview Cuba 2004, Santiago de Cuba, 9 November 2004.

28. Interview Cuba 2004, Santiago de Cuba, 12 November 2004.

29. Interview Cuba 2004, Cienfuegos, 8 December 2004.

30. Interview Cuba 2004, Cienfuegos, 3 December 2004.

31. Interview Cuba 2004, Santiago de Cuba, 15 November 2004.

32. Interview Cuba 2004, Santiago de Cuba, 22 November 2004.

33. For an overview of the state of research and the various approaches to research in intercultural communication, cultural transfer, and perceptions of "others," see Lüsebrink, 2008; for a historical, non-European perspective, see also Baberowski, Kaelble, Schriewer, 2008.

34. Interview Cuba 2004, Santiago de Cuba, 12 November 2004.

35. See chapter 3, pp. 85–87; De la Fuente, 2001, p. 296; Taylor, 1988.

Conclusion

1. For background information and details of the negotiations, see George, 2005, pp. 171–191; Gleijeses, 2006a and 2006b; Hampson, 1996, pp. 84–88; O'Neill, Munslow, 1995.

2. For details on developments up to 1991, see Meyns, 1992, pp. 61–96; for developments until 1997, see Brittain, 1998; for developments up to 2000 and for socio-economic aspects, see Hodges, 2004; on developments until 2002, see Malaquias, 2007b.

3. The phenomenon of state corruption is explained by Malaquias, 2007b, pp. 115–136; and Messiant, 2008a, pp. 55–60.

4. See, for example, Rathmell, 2005, pp. 1014–2019; Dobbins et al., 2003; Berger, 2006, p. 9.

5. For details on the battle of Cuito Cuanavale, see George, 2005, pp. 209–235; for details on fact versus governmental myth, see pp. 223–225.

6. Castro, 2005. In resolution 435, the UN Security Council demanded on 29 September 1978 that the South African government withdraw from Namibia, allow free elections, and recognize SWAPO as the sole legitimate representative of the Namibian people.

Outlook

1. Gleijeses, 2006b, p. 123.

2. Interview United States 2005, Miami, 8 July 2005 (Alcibíades Hidalgo). For the drastic effects of this crisis, see Burchardt, 1999; Zeuske, 2004, pp. 245–289.

3. Marcum, 1987, p. 73; Messiant, 1998, pp. 155–160.

4. Interview Cuba 2004, Santiago de Cuba, 20 November 2004 (this interviewee worked as a doctor in Nigeria from 1992 to 1996); Interview Cuba 2004, Santiago de

Cuba, 10 November 2004 (this interviewee worked as a doctor from 2000 to 2002 in Equatorial Guinea).

5. A resumption of relations was signaled by Dos Santos's state visit to Cuba in July 2007, during which the first cooperation agreements were signed; see http://www.topnews.in/raul-castro-angola-second-visit-six-months-2191525 and http://www.topnews.in/more-cuban-doctors-en-route-angola-after-castros-second-visit-2192036 (accessed 11 July 2014).

6. *Granma*, 22 July 2009.

7. There are no available official figures. I have based my assumption on estimates provided by Cubans currently working in Angola.

8. *Granma*, 24 July 2009. The new literacy campaign is called "Yes, I can" in translation. It was launched across the country in February 2009. See the homepage of the Angolan news agency, Angop, Agência Angola Press, http://www.portalangop.co.ao/angola/pt_pt/ noticias/educacao/2009/7/34/Generalizacao-projecto-Sim-posso-vai-atingir-240-mil-alunos,81f12ec8-d6bb-4f78-99dd-c5c84ba5d833.html (accessed 29 August 2013).

9. The contributions to which I was given access have been archived in the "Casa de Angola," a cultural center in Havana subsidized by the Angolan embassy.

10. Interview Cuba 2004, Havana, 23 December 2004; Interview Cuba 2006, Havana, 25 May and 31 May 2006 (Limbania "Nancy" Jiménez Rodríguez).

11. Several episodes of *La epopeya de Angola* are now available on YouTube, starting with the introduction: https://www.youtube.com/watch?v=8E2bkF5y5Ho (accessed 27 August 2014).

12. Gleijeses, 2006b, p. 138, cites 2,077 war victims, a number that he found in the FAR archive. Raúl Castro also quotes this number in his speech, http://lanic.utexas.edu/project/castro/db/1991/19910527.html (accessed 27 October 2013).

13. George, 2005, p. 268, casts doubt on the official figures but is unable to provide any other reliable figures for the number of fatalities.

14. A translation of the complete speech is available at http://lanic.utexas.edu/project/castro/db/1991/19910527.html (accessed 27 October 2013).

Bibliography

Archival Sources

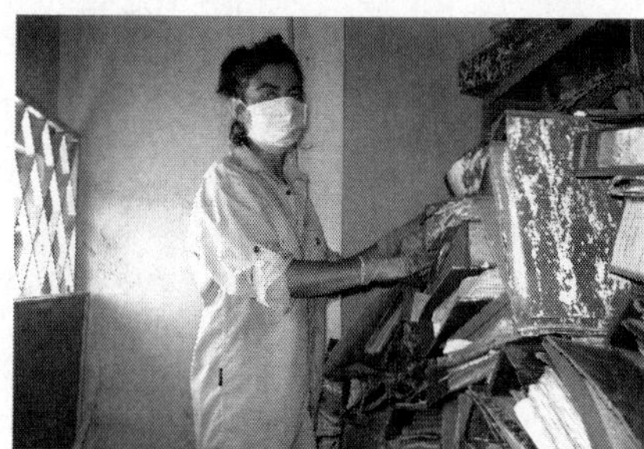

The author in the "archive" of the Ministry of Education in Luanda, February 2006 (photo by Christine Hatzky)

*Documents from the Angolan Ministry of Education, Ministério da Educação (MED)**

1976

Acordo especial de colaboração entre o Ministério da Educação da República Popular de Angola e o Ministério da Educação da República de Cuba, signed in Havana on 5 December 1976.

Acordo especial de colaboração entre o Ministério da Educação da República Popular de Angola e o Ministério da Educação Superior da República de Cuba, signed in Havana on 5 December 1976.

Acordo especial de colaboração entre o Conselho Nacional da Educação Física e Desportos da República Popular de Angola e o Instituto Nacional de Desportos,

* All MED documents are available in digitalized form in my private archive.

Educação Física e Recreação da República de Cuba, signed in Havana on 7 December 1976.

Convenio cultural entre el gobierno de la República Popular de Angola y el Gobierno de la República de Cuba, signed in Havana on 5 December 1976.

Acordo especial entre o governo da República Popular de Angola e o governo da República de Cuba sobre as escolas angolanas na Ilha da Juventude (Projecto), n.d., approx. December 1976, 4 pages.

RPA, MED, História de Angola, Luanda, 1976.

1977

Acordo especial sobre o programa de colaboração para 1978 entre o Ministério de Educação da República de Cuba e o Ministério de Educação da República Popular de Angola, signed in Luanda on 4 October 1977, J. R. Fernández, Ministro de Educação da República de Cuba, Amrósio Lukoki, Ministro de Educação da República Popular de Angola, 6 pages.

Acordo especial sobre as condições gerais para a realização da colaboração económica e científico-técnica entre o governo da República Popular de Angola y a República de Cuba, Luanda, 5 November 1977, 14 pages.

Protocolo da I. sessão da Comissão Mista Intergovernamental Angolana-Cubana de colaboração económica e científico-técnica, Luanda, 5 November 1977, 8 pages and appendix.

RPA, MED, História, Ensino de base—7a Classe, Luanda, 1977.

RPA, Ministério da Educação, Direcção de Formação de Quadros de Ensino, Cursos de formação de professores, Organização escolar, Luanda, 1977.

1978

Informação sobre a situação da escola angolana—Isla de Pinos, Cuba ao Cda. Ministro da Educação, Luanda, RPA, Isla de Pinos, 13 January 1978, 6 pages (partly handwritten).

República Popular de Angola, Destacamento Pedagógico Internacionalista "Che Guevara," orientaciones generales, Luanda, March 1978, 11 pages.

RPA, MED, Centro Nacional de Alfabetização, Documentos do 3. Seminário nacional pedagógico, Luanda, 4–14 April 1978.

Direcção provincial de educação da Huila ao C. Director do Gabinete de Intercâmbio e Cooperação Internacional do MED, Lubango, 7 November 1978, 8 pages.

MED/MINED, Acordo especial de cooperação entre o Ministério da Educação da República Popular de Angola e o Ministério da Educação da República de Cuba, Luanda, 30 November 1978.

RPA, MED, Gabinete de Intercâmbio e Cooperação Internacional, Relatório sobre o trabalho da comissão do MED para seleção dos 1.200 alunos bolseiros angolanos a seguir os seus estudos em Cuba, n.d., approx. 1978, 5 pages.

1979

RPA, MED, Gabinete de Intercâmbio e Cooperação Internacional, Primeiro Encontro nacional do GICI com os representantes das provincias, Conclusões, Luanda, 19 October 1979, 4 pages.

RPA, MED, Relatório (1977–79), Gabinete de Intercâmbio e Cooperação Internacional do Ministério da Educação em Luanda, 21 December 1979, O chefe do Gabinete: M. T. Q., 24 pages.

1980

RPA, MED, Gabinete do Ministro da Educação, Análise da cooperação com a República de Cuba, Luanda, 13 March 1980, signed Ministro da Educação, Ambrôsio Lukoki.

RPA, MED, Estatuto Orgânico do Ministério da Educação, Luanda, March 1980.

RPA, Secretaria de Estado da Cooperação ao camarada José Eduardo dos Santos, Presidente do MPLA-PT e da República Popular de Angola, Memorando, Assunto: Cooperação com a República Socialista de Cuba, Luanda, March, 3 pages.

RPA, Secretaria de Estado da Cooperação, Comissão de Avaliação da Cooperação ao Camarada Ministro da Educação, Circular No. 1/CACI/SEC/82, Luanda, 31 May 1980, signed Secretário de Estado P. P. J., 8 pages.

MINED, José Ramón Fernández a Ambrôsio Lukoki, Havana, 16 September 1980.

RPA, MED, GICI/GII, Protocolo reunião 10–12 November 1980, Ministério da Educação em Luanda, 17 November 1980, os secretários, J. A. T., J. M. d. S., 10 pages.

RPA, MED, Direcção do Ensino Secundário, Relatório sobre o ano lectivo de 1979/80.

1981

RPA, Embaixada em Havana-Cuba: Ao Cda. Ambrôsio Lukoki, Ministro de Educação da RPA, Luanda, Havana, 9 February 1981, 2 pages.

RPA, Secretaria de Estado da Cooperação, Protocolo da IV. sessão da Comissão Mista Intergovernamental Angolana-Cubana de cooperação económica e científico-técnica, Havana, 4–5 May 1981, 16 pages.

RPA, Protocolo da IV. sessão da Comissão Mista Intergovernamental Angolana-Cubana de cooperação económica e científico-tecnica, Havana, May 1981, 8 pages.

RPA, Ministère de L'Éducation, Développement de l' Éducation en Republique Populaire d'Angola 1978–1980, Rapport pour la 38ème Session de la Conférence International de L'Éducation Genève (10–19 November 1981), Luanda, August 1981, p. 5.

RPA, MED, GICI/GII, Existência de Trabalhadores Estrangeiros, 9 November 1981, p. 1.

1982

RPA, MED, GICI/GII, Deslocação a Cuba, April 1982, Delegação chefiada pelo camarada Ministro da Educação, Luanda, 27 April 1982.

RPA, MED, GICI/GII, Ponto da situação relativo a cooperação de nacionalidade Cubana em serviço do MED, 27 April 1982, 6 pages.

Empresa Importadora y Exportadora de Infraestructura, Contrato No. 95–64076: Estudio integral para el desarrollo de la educación, Havana, April 1982, 24 pages.

RPA, MED, GICI/GII ao Gabinete do Plano do MED ao Centro Nacional de Alfabetização, No.49/GII/IV/A.B/82, Luanda, April 1982, 10 pages.

RPA, MED, GICI/GII, Problemática do transporte da cooperação cubana para a RPA, 8 May 1982, 4 pages.

RPA, Secretaria de Estado da Cooperação, Comissão de Avaliação da Cooperação, Gabinete do Secretário de Estado da Cooperação em Luanda, P. P. J., May 1982.

RPA, Secretaria de Estado da Cooperação, Comissão de Avaliação da Cooperação ao Cda. Ministro da Educação, Luanda, Circular No. 1/CACI/SEC/May 1982, Assunto: Avaliação da cooperação, 2 pages.

Republique Populaire d'Angola, Projet pour le developpement de l'education, Requête a la Banque Africaine de Developpement, June 1982.

RPA, MED, GICI/GII, Avaliação da Cooperação, Gabinete de Intercâmbio Internacional do MED, 19 July 1982, 8 pages.

RPA, MED, Relatório sobre a execução do plano do sector da educação de 1982.

RPA, MED, VII Conselho consultivo, realizado 8–12 September 1981, Conclusões finais, Luanda, 1982, 47 pages.

1983

Embajada de Cuba, Oficina Económica, Av. General Carmona No. 42, Luanda, Angola, Cda. Augusto Lopes Teixeira, Ministro da Educação da R.P.A, Luanda, 4 January 1983 (signature illegible), 2 pages.

RPA, MED, Resolução sobre as medidas imediatas a tomar no sector do ensino, Luanda, 21 January 1983, O presidente da República José Eduardo dos Santos.

RPA, MED, Relatório de viagem a Cuba, Luanda, 21 February 1983, signed (pela delegação) J. M. S., 22 pages.

RPA, MED, Provincia de Benguela, Gabinete do Delegado provincial de educação, Confidêncial, Informação No. 1/1983, 21 February 1983, 2 pages.

RPA, MED, GICI/GII ao Gabinete do Plano do MED, Confidencial, Oficial Circular No. 013/GII/171/I/1983, Cálculo de custos de Força de Trabalho Estrangeira e incremento previsto para 1983/1984, Luanda, 27 March 1983, o Director do Gabinete, J. M. d. S., 10 pages.

RPA, MED, Relatório de viagem a Cuba e Portugal de uma delegação do MED, Luanda, 5 April 1983, 17 pages.

Second jornada pedagógica del contingente educacional Cubano en la RPA (Libro de resumen), May 1983, 21 pages.

Second jornada pedagógica del contingente educacional Cubano en la RPA (Programa), May 1983, 6 pages.

RPA, MED, Gabinete do Ministro da Educação ao Cda. Roberto de Almeida, Secretário do Comité Central do MPLA-PT para a esfera ideológica, 26 June 1983, Envío do memorando das conversaçãoes entre o chefe do Departamento de Superação e Desenvolvimento de Quadros do MED da RPA e director do Gabinete de Intercâmbio Internacional do MED da RPA, 6 pages.

RPA, MED, Dept. Nacional das escolas provisórias; Projecto de estudo sobre a problemática das escolas provisórias. Elaborado pelo Depto. Nac. das Escolas Provisorias, Luanda, June 1983, 12 pages.

RPA, Delegação Provincial da educação da Lunda-Norte ao GII/MED, Luanda, Nota 598/SPAC/DPE/83, 4 July 1983, Assunto: Nota Informativa, 2 pages.

RPA, MED, Projecto de estudo sobre mercados alternativos a contratação de técnicos docentes (8/1983, handwritten annotations), 6 pages.

RPA, MED, GICI/GII, 78/GII/I/83 ao Camarada Ministro da Educação, Luanda, 18 October 1983, o Director do Gabinete, J. M. d. S., 4 pages.

RPA, MED, Secretaria de Estado da Cooperação ao Gabinete de Intercâmbio Internacional do MED, Protocolo da V. sessão da Comissão Mista Intergovernamental Angolana-Cubana de cooperação económica e científico-técnica, Luanda, 26–28 October 1983, Luanda, 15 December 1983, o Director Nacional, M. M. D., 7 pages.

RPA, MED, GICI/GII, Assunto: Ferias Cooperação Cubana, 1983 (dossier).

RPA, MED, Direcção Nacional do Ensino Médio e Pré-universitário, Relatório sobre a situação do Ensino Médio na R.P.A. Período 1978–1982, n.d., approx. 1983, 12 pages.

RPA, MED, GICI/GII, Proposta de tabela salarial, contratação individual e para cooperação com o Brasil, Anexo, n.d., approx. 1983, 3 pages.

RPA, MED, GICI/GII, Proposta de tabela salarial para cooperação Portuguesa ao abrigo do acordo, n.d., approx. 1983, 1 page.

RPA, MED, Gabinete do Plano do Ministério da Educação. Estudo sobre a diminuição dos efectivos escolares no ensino de base regular, n.d., approx. 1983, 23 pages.

1984

RPA, MED, GICI/GII, Acta: Pelas 10 horas do día 9 March 1984, foi recebida pelo camarada J. M. d. S., Director do Gabinete de Intercâmbio Internacional do MED, a camarada S. R. A., Chefe do contingente educacional Cubano na RPA . . . , 6 pages.

RPA, MED, Gabinete do Ministro, ao Camarado Fernández, Minstro da Educação Cuba, Luanda, 2 April 1984.

RPA, MED, GICI/GII, Memorando (handwritten date 14 April 1984), 11 pages.

RPA, MED, Acta sobre as conversações entre os presidentes da Comissão Mista Intergovernamental Angolana-Cubana de colaboração económica e científico-técnica, Luanda, 10 September 1984, 4 pages.

RPA, MED, Perspectivas de desenvolvimento no sector da educação e ensino para o quinenio 1985–1990, 1984, 37 pages.

1985

RPA, MED, Regulamento interno dos Gabinetes de Intercâmbio e Cooperação Internacional, Luanda, o Gabinete de Intercâmbio Internacional do Ministério da Educação, 1 January 1985, o Director do Gabinete, J. M. S., 21 pages.

RPA, MED, GICI/GII, Problemática dos Gabinetes de Intercâmbio Internacional, Análise do documento, Luanda, 2 January 1985.

RPA, MED, Memorando sobre a cooperação Cubana ao serviço do Ministério da Educação, Luanda, 2 February 1985, 9 pages.

RPA, MED, GICI/GII, 6 March 1985, ao Camarada Vice-Ministro para o Ensino de Base, Luanda, . . . Informação proveniente da escola do ensino de base do III Nivel "N'Gola Kiluanji" . . . , 8 pages.

RPA, MED, Priorização do sistema de educação e ensino, Luanda, 21 March 1985, 14 pages.

RPA, MED, Visita e trabalho à República de Cuba da delegação chefiada pelo Cda. Vice-ministro da Educação para o Ensino de base, no período de 15 April–2 May 1987, 32 pages.

Centro dos cursos pré-universitários de Luanda ao GICI/GII, 16 June 1985, signed o Director do Centro, 2 pages.

RPA, MED, GICI/GII Relatório, 25 March 1982 to 31 August 1985, 1 October 1985, o director cessante, J. M. d. S., 30 pages.
RPA, Secretaria de Estado da Cooperação, Acta das conversações entre a delegação angolana da Secretaria de Estado da Cooperação e a delegação cubana do Comité Estatal de Cooperação económica, para a conciliação e assinatura do programa de cooperação científico-técnica para o ano de 1985, 26 pages.
MED, GICI/GII, Evaluação das cinco nacionalidades e categoría com a maior expressão (figure), approx. 1985.

1986

RPA, Universidade Agostinho Neto ao Gabinete de Intercámbio Internacional do MED, Luanda, 23 January 1986, 4 pages.
RPA, MED, Gabinete de estudo para o diagnóstico, relatório de balanço do trabalho realizado pelo grupo de prognóstico do Ministério da Educação da República Popular de Angola, March–June 1986, 78 pages.
RPA, MED, GICI/GII, Força de trabalho estrangeira, República de Cuba, 25 November 1986, 1 page (Statistic).

1987

RPA, MED, Relatório, Visita de trabalho à República de Cuba da delegação chefiada pelo camarada vice-ministro da educação do ensino de base, no período de 15 April–2 May 1987, Ano do X. aniversario do Partido e da consolidação do Poder Popular, 35 pages.
RPA, MED, Visita de trabalho à República de Cuba da delegação chefiada pelo Cda. Vice-ministro da educação para o ensino de base, no período de 15 April–2 May 1987, 32 pages.
Dpto. Económico Cubatécnica a Ministerio de Educación (cc. Sec. Estado para la Cooperación), Luanda, 8 December 1987.
UNICEF to Domingos Peterson, Director do Instituto Nacional de Investigação e Desenvolvimento da Educação do MED (INIDE), Luanda, 23 December 1987, Assunto: Projecto educação sub-programa "A," Formação em produção e aplicação de material de lingua Portuguesa.

1988

RPA, MED, Plano de cooperação Cubana para o sector da educação, ano lectivo 88/89, January 1988.
RPA, MED, Relatório da delegação partidário-governamental que se deslocou a Cuba, no período de 19 March–14 April 1988, para indagar e averiguar as causas que determinaram a "greve" de alguns estudiantes e consequentemente restablecer a respectiva situação, 25 pages.
RPA, Secretaria de Estado da Cooperação, Memorando, Luanda, 2 June 1988, 34 pages.

1989

RPA, MED, Gabinete do Ministro, Memorando sobre a participação do PNUD e dos VNU na substituçãodos cubanos no domíno de educação, Luanda, 27 July 1989, 2 pages.

Programa das Nações Unidas para o Desenvolvimento, Programa dos voluntários das Nações Unidas, Projecto do governo da República Popular de Angola, 1989.

1990

Memorando sobre a audiência concedida pelo camarada Augusto Lopes Teixeira, Ministro da Educação da RPA, ao general cubano Henrique Lusson, 14 April 1990, 2 pages.

RPA, MED, GICI/GII, Memorando: Problemática da retirada da cooperação Cubana da RPA, Luanda, 15 August 1990, 5 pages.

1991

RPA, MED, Mesa redonda sobre educação para todos, July 1991, 105 pages.

RPA, MED, Sistema nacional de avaliação para o ensino de base regular, n.d., approx. 1991, 20 pages.

2005

RPA, MED, Analise da situação da alfabetização e educação de adultos em Angola, Luanda, June 2005.

*Documents from the Cuban Ministries of Education – the Ministerio de Educación (MINED) and Ministerio de Educación Superior (MES)**

1977

MINED, Reunión sobre el Destacamento Pedagógico Internacionalista "Che Guevara," Havana, 7 October 1977, 3 pages.

MINED, UJC, FEU, Destacamento Pedagógico Internacionalista "Che Guevara," Documento de Base, October 1977, 4 pages.

MINED, Plan de preparación política para el Destacamento Pedagógico Internacionalista "Che Guevara," approx. October 1977, 3 pages.

MINED, Al Co. J. R. Fernández, Ministro de Educación, de Asela de los Santos, Viceministra de Educación, Havana, 5 December 1977, 2 pages.

UJC, Resultados de la encuesta realizada en el Primer contingente del DPI "Che Guevara" en la relación a la conveniencia práctica de incluir en su uniforme una boina similar que a la que usó el Guerrillero Heróico, 29 December 1977, 1 page.

1978

MINED, Nota al Ministro, Consideraciones sobre el informe del Trabajo en Angola por los Cros. A. O. y J. M. L., Havana, 17 January 1978 (signed Asela de los Santos, Viceministra), 3 pages.

RPA, Destacamento Pedagógico Internacionalista "Che Guevara," Luanda, March 1978.

* Some of the documents listed from the Cuban Ministry of Education come from private archives (e.g., Limbania "Nancy" Jiménez Rodríguez) or were to be found in the archive of the Museum of Literacy (Museo de la Alfabetización) in Havana. All documents are available in digitalized form in my private archive.

MINED, Informe de la Provincia de Huambo a la reunión nacional de profesores guías que se efectuará en Luanda, 7 June 1978, signed E. L. R., Prof. Guía Prov. Huambo, 8 pages.

Tareas principales para el mes de julio. DPI "Che Guevara," Huambo, 3 July 1978, signed M. d. A. H., 2 pages.

MINED, Plan de medidas a desarollar en el Destacamento Pedagógico para perfeccionar el trabajo docente-educativo en el segundo período, Huambo, 8 August 1978, signed E. L. R., M. d. J. A. H., 6 pages.

Memorias de la colaboración del Destacamento Pedagógico ubicado en la Provincia de Huambo en el curso escolar 1978–1979, March–December 1978, Huambo, 26 December 1978, signed E. L. R., Profesor guía and M. d. J. A. H., Jefe del grupo de Educación, 24 pages.

MINED, Informe anual sobre la colaboración cubana en la Facultad de Ciencieas Agropecuarias de la República Popular de Angola, Huambo, 26 December 1978, signed J. M. R. D., Resp. del Grupo de Educación Superior, 6 pages.

MINED, Memorias del trabajo de la colaboración Cubana en la República Popular de Angola, 1976–1978, 76 pages (from the private archive of Limbania "Nancy" Jiménez Rodríguez).

1979

UJC, Comité Nacional, Aspectos más significativos del II. contingente del Destacamento Pedagógico Internacionalista "Ernesto Che Guevara" en la RPA—según la información que hemos recibido del comité de la UJC—con fecha de la elaboración 18 April 1979, 5 pages.

Programa a cumplimentar en las visitas a los municipios donde se mantiene abierta la colaboración, N'dalatando, 14 July 1979, signed J. B. B., Agregado económico de la Embajada de Cuba, Provincia Kwanza Norte, 8 pages.

MINED, Informe, Diferencias entre los informes recibidos de Angola, DPI "Che Guevara," Havana, 25 September 1979, to Asela de los Santos, Viceministra, from Z. F. H., Directora General Formación y Perfeccionamento Personal Pedagógico, 3 pages.

MINED, Guía de información interna para la visita del Cro. José R. Fernández, Vice Presidente del Consejo de Ministros, Luanda, 20 June 1979, 11 pages.

MINED, Memorias del trabajo realizado por el primer contingente Pedagógico Internacionalista "Che Guevara" en la Provincia de Huambo, curso escolar 1978–1979, 23 pages.

1980

Diario del Destacamento Pedagógico Internacionalista "Che Guevara" (DPI) II, 1979–80, Provincia de Benguela.

Diario del Destacamento Pedagógico Internacionalista "Che Guevara" (DPI) II, 1979–80, Provincia de Moxico.

Diario del Destacamento Pedagógico Internacionalista "Che Guevara" (DPI) II, 1979–80, Provincia de Uige.

1981

Diario del Destacamento Pedagógico Internacionalista "Che Guevara" (DPI) II, 1979–1981, Provincia de Huila.

1985

UJC, Destacamento Pedagógico Internacionalista "Che Guevara," Informe de emulación, Provincia de Benguela, 1 October–15 December 1985, 31 pages.

UJC, Destacamento Pedagógico Internacionalista "Che Guevara," Emulación especial, Provincia de Namibe, October–December 1985, 12 pages.

1986

UJC, Destacamento Pedagógico Internacionalista "Che Guevara," Informe de emulación, Provincia de Huila, January–May 1986, 10 pages.

UJC, Destacamento Pedagógico Internacionalista "Che Guevara," Informe de emulación, Provincia de Namibe, curso escolar 1985–1986, segundo semestre, 21 pages.

*Archive of the Casa de Angola, Havana**

Concurso "Angola en la memoria," De Cuba a Angola, Memorias de una maestra internacionalista, Autora M. V. C. A., Havana, 2002, 23 pages.

Concurso "Angola en la memoria," Memorias de una misión, Autora C. D. C. O., Havana, 2002, DPI I, 1978–1979, Luena, Prov. Moxico, 20 pages.

Concurso "Angola en la memoria," Recuerdos de una misión, Autora D. G. P., Havana, 2002, DPI II, 1979–1982, Prov. Moçamedes, 32 pages.

Concurso "Angola en la memoria," Una misión internacionalista en la República Popular de Angola con el nombre "Che Guevara," Autora B. E. T. A., Guantánamo, 2002, DPI I, 1978–1979, Lubango, Prov. Huila, 21 pages.

Hillman Library, University of Pittsburgh, Pennsylvania

Paterson Papers (US/Cuba)

Foreign Broadcast Information System (FBIS), 1979–1991

US Government Documents

Cuba. A Staff Report, Prepared for the Use of the Committee on Foreign Relations United States Senate, GOP, Washington, 1974.

Cuban Realities: May 1975, A Report by Senator Geroge S. McGovern to the Committee on Foreign Relations United States Senate, GOP, Washington, 1975.

Disaster Assistance in Angola, Hearings before the Subcommittee on International Resources, House of Representatives, 19 November 1975; 26 February 1976; 16 March 1976, GOP, Washington, 1976.

United States Policy on Angola, Hearing before the Committee on International Relations, House of Representatives, 26 January 1976, GOP, Washington, 1976.

U.S. Government Publications 1976, Y4.In 8/16: An 4/2 United States Policy on Angola, 1976, Hearing before the Committee on International Relations, House of Representatives, Ninety-Fourth Congress, Second Session, 26 January 1976, US-Government Printing Office, Washington.

* All Casa de Angola documents are available in digitalized form in my private archive.

United States-Angolan Relations, Hearing before the Subcommittee on International Relations, House of Representatives, 25 May 1978, GOP, Washington, 1978.

Possible Violation of the Clark Amendment, Hearing before the Subcommittee on Africa of the Committee on Foreign Affairs, House of Representatives, 1 July 1987, GOP, Washington, 1987.

Congressional Research Service, Report for Congress, Angola/Namibia Peace Prospects: Background, Current Problems, and Chronology, by Raymond W. Copson, Specialist in International Relations and Foreign Affairs and National Defense Division, 16 August 1988.

Archive of the Basler Afrika Bibliographien (BAB)

AA5, Archive medic' angola/kämpfendes afrika 1971–1988, Gruppe I: medic' angola 1970–73, I.3. Varia, 1971–72, Interview Kapiassa Husseinis with Neto from the year 1971.

Oral Sources: Interviewees

Angola, 2006. Maria da Conceição Neto, Daniel Dias, Padre Candido Herculano Feliciano, Mario Rui Duarte, Fernando Pacheco Santos, Benedicto Pinheiro, Artur Pestana ("Pepetela"), Julian Zerquera, Pedro Domingos Peterson, Carlos Silva, Arlindo Isabel, Emanuel Moreira Carneiro, Noemí Benitez de Mendoza, Carlos Moncada Valdez, Paulo Jorge, Padre Urbano Gaspar, Manuel Teodoro Quarta, Lopo do Nascimento, Paulo Lara, Wanda Lara, Padre Salomão, Fernando Costa, António Burity da Silva, Pinda Simão, Cornélio Macundo Capita, Padre Francisco Javier Pedro, Rui Oliveira, Ondjaki.

Cuba, 2004. Gladys Macola, Marcelino Domínguez, Gilberto Stable, Arismel Mancebo, Marta Ribeaux, Georgina Portuondo, Maria del Carmen Aciego Infante, Daisy Trujillo, Enrique Vázquez, Xiomara Guerra, Irma Lion, Marta Cabrales, Magaly Puente Perpiñan, Xiomara Silva Matamoros, María Montoya Abreu, Rosario Vidal, Eduardo Silegas, Alberto Alvarez, Angela Marín, Jorgelina Barrera Portuondo, Luisa María Díaz Cruz, Rolando Amiot, Lesly Tamayo Torres, Gerónimo Izquierdo Hernández, Gerardo González, Marta Castro Bosch, María Elena González Armas, Idalmis Cómas Maceo, Sonia González, Fernándo Díaz García, Wilkie Delgado, Marta López, Rodolfo González Barreras, Gilberto Rizo, Emma Bastart Ortiz, Hermilio Vidal Anido, Marcos Fuentes Cabo, Juan Alvarez Riva, Inés Galarza Carrión, Gustavo, Alina Mons Montoya, Hiran Quiñones, Ramón Famada Jorrín, Eduardo Ramírez, Jorge Bravo Villarpando, Manuel Panal Cortéz, José Ramón Borges Soto, Jesus Fuentes Guerra, Grisel Gómez Gómez, Juan Carlos García Villavicencia, Emilio Castellaño Cepero, Alberto Marcelino Osorio Cabrera, Agustín García Rodríguez, Pablo Roque Díaz, Margot Benito, Pedro Arco, Israel Molejón González, Francisco Arturo Ruiz Martínez, Luis Alfaro Echavarría, Maira Avilés, Alberto Soriano Brunet, Teresita Ramírez, Lázaro Castro, Mirta Teresita Carranza Baez, Abilio Hurtado Bermúdez, Carlos Pérez Navarro, Roberto Ballesteros, Hiran Cabrera Díaz de Villegas, Miguel Hernández Barreto, Pilar Santana Gallardo, Elsa Blaquier Ascaño, Félix Aguiar Polier, Carmen Almodóvar Muñoz, Olga Montalban, Sergio Valdés Bernal.

Cuba, 2005. Belkis Vega Belmonte, José Carracedo Soto, Jorge Berenguer Cala, Rogelio Meneses Benitez.

Cuba, 2006. Jorge Risquet Valdés, Manuel García González, Sixto Rolando Espinosa Dorta, Limbania "Nancy" Jiménez Rodríguez, Sonia Romero, Zoila Franco Hidalgo, Rodolfo Puente Ferro, Gloria Valdés, Augusto Valdés Gay, Georgina Veloz Massano, Lidia Turner Martí, Sara Legón, Emilio Rodríguez Salomón, Rolando Carballo, Emiliano Manresa, José Ramón Fernández, Oscar Elejalde, Roberto Manzano Guzmán.

Portugal, 2005. Nelson Pestana, Ana Paula Tavares, Simão Cacete, Manuel Ennes Ferreira, Carlos Pacheco.

United States, 2005. Norberto Fuentes, Jorge de la Fuente, Domingo Amuchástegui, Juan Benemelis, Ileana Fuentes, Ena Curnow, Eugenio Yañez, Ofelia Nardo, Alcibíades Hidalgo.

Newspapers and Periodicals

Ahora (Holguin), 1976–1983 (Cuba).
Bohemia, 1975–1991 (Cuba).
Colaboración Internacional, 1983–1986, 1988–1990 (Cuba).
Cuba Internacional, 1975–1991 (Cuba).
Cuba Socialista, 1985–1990 (Cuba).
Cuba Socialista, 1983–1986 (Cuba).
Diário da República, Orgão Oficial da República Popular de Angola (Angola).
Direct from Cuba, 1975–1977 (Cuba).
Educación, 1974, 1976, 1977, 1980, 1981, 1983–1985 (Cuba).
Escambray (Sancti Spiritus), 1976–1979 (Cuba).
Espresso, 1975–1991 (Portugal).
Gaceta Oficial de la República de Cuba, 1975–1991 (Cuba).
Jornal de Angola, 1976–1990 (Angola).
Prisma del Meridiano, 1976–1991 (Cuba).
Revolución y Cultura, 1976–1983 (Cuba).
Sierra Maestra (Santiago de Cuba), 1976–1977 (Cuba).
Tricontinental, 1980–1988 (Cuba).
Verde Olivo, 1975–1991 (Cuba).
Yumurí (Matanzas), 1977–1980 (Cuba).

Films and Documentaries

Caravana, Rogelio Paris, 1990 (Cuba).
El Brigadista, Octavio Cortázar, 1977 (Cuba).
Kangamba, Rogelio Paris, 2008 (Cuba).

Documents and Information from the World Wide Web

Asociación de Combatientes de la Revolución Cubana, the Association of Combatants of the Cuban Revolution. http://www.venceremos.co.cu/pags/varias/hipertextos/A/asociacion_combatientes_3024288.html (accessed 27 August 2013).

Associação Tchiweka de Documentação, Luanda. In 2008, Paulo and Wanda Lara founded this association in order to give public access to their father's private archives. As a result of this initiative, the collection of documents was also published. http://sites.google.com/site/tchiweka/Home (accessed 10 August 2013).

Caravana, Cuban film about Rogelio Paris's involvement in Angola. http://www.socialistfilms.org/2008/01/convoy-cuba-angola-1990.html (accessed 15 August 2013).

Castro speech database of the Latin American Network Information Center of the University of Texas. http://lanic.utexas.edu/project/castro/db/ (accessed 27 October 2013).

La epopeya de Angola, Cuban TV documentary series on the Angolan engagement, which has been broadcast at irregular intervals since autumn 2007. Several episodes are now available on YouTube, beginning with the introduction. https://www.youtube.com/watch?v=8E2bkF5y5Ho (accessed 27 August 2014).

Literacy program developed in Cuba with the title "Yo sí puedo/Eu sim posso" ("Yes, I can"), which was introduced in Angola in February 2009. http://www.portalangop.co.ao/angola/pt_pt/ noticias/educacao/2009/7/34/Generalizacao-projecto-Sim-posso-vai-atingir-240-mil-alunos,81f12ec8-d6bb-4f78-99dd-c5c84ba5d833.html (accessed 29 August 2013).

Lyrics to "Veterano" ("Veterans") by Frank Delgado, which appeared in 2000 on the album *A guitarra limpia*. http://www.cancioneros.com/nc.php?NM=4544 (accessed 27 August 2013).

Raúl Castro's state visit to Angola in July 2009. http://www.topnews.in/raul-castro-angola-second-visit-six-months-2191525 and http://www.topnews.in/more-cuban-doctors-en-route-angola-after-castros-second-visit-2192036 (accessed 11 July 2014).

Secondary Literature

Adick, Christel, Hans-Martin Große-Oetringhaus, and Renate Nestvogel. 1982. *Bildungsprobleme Afrikas zwischen Kolonialismus und Emanzipation*. Hamburg.

Aguila, Juan M. del. 1989. "The Domestic Attitude toward Internationalism: Evidence from Emigre Interviews." In *Cuban Internationalism in Sub-Saharan Africa*, edited by Sergio Díaz-Briquets, 124–143. Pittsburgh.

Alarcón Ramírez, Dariel ("Benigno"). 2003. *Memorias de un soldado cubano: Vida y muerte de la Revolución*. Barcelona.

Amuchástegui Alvarez, Domingo. 1988. *Historia contemporánea de Asia y Africa*. Vol. 4. Havana.

Anderson, Jon Lee. 2004. *Che: Die Biographie*. Munich.

Andrade, Mario de, and Marc Ollivier. 1975. *The War in Angola: A Socio-Economic Study*. Dar-es-Salaam.

Andresen Guimarães, Fernando. 2001. *The Origins of the Angolan Civil War: Foreign Intervention and Domestic Political Conflict*. Houndsmills/London.

Angola after Independence. 1975. *Struggle for Supremacy*. Conflict Studies, no. 64, November.

Angola rumo à independência: O governo de transição. n.d. [1975]. Luanda.

Appadurai, Arjun, 1996. *Modernity at Large: Cultural Dimensions of Globalization*. Minneapolis.

Aschmann, Birgit, ed. 2005. *Gefühl und Kalkül: Der Einfluss von Emotionen auf die Politik des 19. und 20. Jahrhunderts*. Stuttgart.

Associação Tchiweka de Documentação (ATD). 2009. *Lúcio Lara "Tschiweka"—80 anos—Imagems de um precurso*. Luanda.

Assmann, Aleida. 2006. *Erinnerungsräume: Formen und Wandlungen des kulturellen Gedächtnisses*. Munich.

Assmann, Aleida, and Gudrun Friese, eds. 1998. *Identitäten: Erinnerung, Geschichte, Identität 3*. Frankfurt am Main.

Assmann, Jan. (1992) 2007. *Das kulturelle Gedächtnis: Schrift, Erinnerung und politische Identität in frühen Hochkulturen*. 6th ed. Munich.

Assmann, Jan, and Rolf Trauzettel, eds. 2002. *Tod, Jenseits und Identität: Perspektiven einer kulturwissenschaftlichen Thanatologie*. Freiburg/Munich.

Baberowski, Jörg, David Feest, and Maike Lehmann, eds. 2008. *Dem Anderen begegnen: Eigene und fremde Repräsentationen in sozialen Gemeinschaften*. Frankfurt am Main.

Baberowski, Jörg, Hartmut Kaelble, and Jürgen Schriewer, eds. 2008. *Selbstbilder und Fremdbilder: Repräsentationen sozialer Ordnungen im Wandel*. Frankfurt am Main.

Baez, Luis. 1996. *Secretos de generales*. Havana.

Bailyn, Bernard. 2005. *Atlantic History: Concept and Contours*. Cambridge.

Baller, Susann, et al. 2008. *Die Ankunft des Anderen: Repräsentationen sozialer und politischer Ordnungen in Empfangszeremonien*. Frankfurt am Main.

Baptista, Cristina. 2000/2001. "O 'Jornal de Angola'—um estudo de Imprensa." *Africa Debate, Revista Internacional Inter-Universitária de Estudos Africanos* 2:38–45.

Bark, Dennis L., ed. 1988. *The Red Orchestra*. Vol. 2, *The Case of Africa*. Stanford.

Barnet, Miguel. 2000. *Afrokubanische Kulte*. Frankfurt am Main.

———, ed. 2003. *Biography of a Runaway Slave*. Willimantic, CT.

Barnett, Don. 1976. *With the Guerillas in Angola*. Richmond.

Barros, Mauricio José. 1977. "Die Entwicklung der nationalen Befreiungsbewegung in Angola: Eine kritische Betrachtung." PhD dissertation, Freie Universität Berlin.

Baumann, Zygmunt. 1992. *Moderne und Ambivalenz: Das Ende der Eindeutigkeit*. Hamburg.

Bender, Gerald. 1978. *Angola under the Portuguese: The Myth and the Reality*. Berkeley/Los Angeles.

Benemelis, Juan. 1988. *Castro, Subversión y terrorismo en Africa*. Madrid.

———. 2002. *Las guerras secretas de Fidel Castro*. Miami.

Berger, Mark T. 2006. "From Nation-Building to State-Building: The Geopolitics of Development, the Nation-state System and the Changing Global Order." *Third World Quarterly* 27 (1): 5–25.

Bernecker, Walter, and Horst Pietschmann. 2000. *Geschichte Portugals*. Munich.

Betto, Frei. 1986. *Nachtgespräche mit Fidel*. Fribourg.

Bhagavan, M. R. 1986. *Angola's Political Economy, 1975–1985*. Uppsala.

Bia Abudu, Paul. 1976. *Cuban Policy toward Africa and the African Responses, 1959–1976*. PhD dissertation, Howard University, Washington, DC.

Bielefeld, Uli, ed. 1991. *Das Eigene und das Fremde*. Hamburg.

Birmingham, David. 1978. "The Twenty Seventh of May: An Historical Note on the Abortive Coup Attempt in Angola." *African Affairs* 77 (3): 37–56.

———. 1992. *Frontline Nationalism in Angola and Mozambique*. Oxford.

———. 1993. "The Historical Background to the War in Angola and the Context of Ethnicity." In *Proceedings of the Seminar on Democratization in Angola, 18.09.1992 in Leiden, organized by EMS, KZA, ASC*, 3–11. Leiden/Amsterdam.

———. 1998. "Asking Historical Questions: Angola and the Church 1491–1990." *Nouvelle Revue de science missionaire* 54 (4): 259–274.
———. 1999. *Portugal and Africa*. New York.
———. 2002. "Angola." In *A History of Postcolonial Lusophone Africa*, edited by Patrick Chabal et al., 137–184. London.
———. 2003a. *A Concise History of Portugal*. Cambridge.
———. 2003b. *The Decolonization of Africa*. London.
———. 2006. *Empire in Africa: Angola and Its Neighbors*. Athens.
———. 2008. "Is 'Nationalism' a Feature of Angola's Identity?" Unpublished manuscript in author's possession.
———. 2010. "Die Sklavenstadt: Luanda aus deutscher Sicht." In *Periplus: Jahrbuch für außereuropäische Geschichte 2010: Sklaverei und Postemanzipations-gesellschaften in Afrika und der Karibik*, edited by Christine Hatzky and Ulrike Schmieder, 37–56. Münster.
Birmingham, David, and Phyllis Martin. 1998. *History of Central Africa: The Contemporary Years since 1960*. London.
Blaquier Ascaño, Elsa. 2002. "Concurso: Angola en la memoria, Por esos ojos tan tristes." Unpublished manuscript in author's possession.
Blasier, Cole, and Carmelo Mesa-Lago, eds. 1979. *Cuba in the World*. Pittsburgh.
Bogle, Lori Lyn, ed. 2001. *The Cold War*. Vol. 3, *Hot Wars of the Cold War*. New York.
Bohleber, Werner. 2007. "Zum Problem der Veridikalität von Erinnerungen." *Bios: Zeitschrift für Biographieforschung, Oral History und Lebensverlaufsanalysen* 20, edited by Almut Leh and Lutz Niethammer, special issue, "Kritische Erfahrungsberichte und grenzüberschreitende Zusammenarbeit: The Networks of Oral History; Festschrift für Alexander von Plato," 89–96.
Bolívar Aróstegui, Natalia. 1990. *Los orishas en Cuba*. Havana.
Bourdieu, Pierre. 1985. *Sozialer Raum und "Klassen": Leçon sur la leçon; 2 Vorlesungen*. Frankfurt am Main.
Bridgland, Fred. 1986. *Jonas Savimbi: A Key to Africa*. New York.
Brinkmann, Inge. 2003. "War, Witches and Traitors: Cases from the MPLA's Eastern Front in Angola (1966–1975)." *Journal of African History* 44: 303–325.
Brittain, Victoria. 1998. *Death of Dignity: Angola's Civil War*. London.
Broughton, Simon, and Mark Ellingham. 2000. *World Music*. Vol. 2, *Latin and North America, Caribbean, India, Asia and Pacific*. London.
Bujard, Otker, and Ulrich Wirper, eds. 2007. *Die Revolution ist ein Buch und ein freier Mensch: Die politischen Plakate des befreiten Nicaragua 1979–1990 und der internationalen Solidaritätsbewegung*. Cologne.
Bunck, Julie Marie. 1994. *Fidel Castro and the Quest for a Revolutionary Culture in Cuba*. University Park.
Burchardt, Hans-Jürgen. 1999. *Im Herbst des Patriarchen*. Stuttgart.
Burchett, Wilfred. 1978. *Southern Africa Stands Up: The Revolutions in Angola, Mozambique, Zimbabwe, Namibia, and South Africa*. New York.
Burness, Donald. 1995. *On the Shoulder of Martí: Cuban Literature of the Angolan War*. Colorado Springs.
Cabrera, Lydia. (1954) 1993. *El monte*. Havana.
Cahen, Michel. 2000. "Nationalism and Ethnicities: Lessons from Mozambique." In *Ethnicity Kills? The Politics of War, Peace and Ethnicity in Sub-Saharan Africa*, edited by Einar Braathen, Morten Boås, and Gjermund Saether, 163–187. London.

———. 2005. "Success in Mozambique?" In *Making States Work*, edited by Simon Chesterman, Michael Ignatieff, and Ramesh Thakur, 213–233. Tokyo/New York.

Campbell, Horace. 1999. "The Search for Peace in Angola: The Crucial Role of Women, II." *Africa Quarterly* 39 (2): 105–140.

Cañizares-Esguerra, Jorge, and Eric S. Seeman, eds. 2007. *The Atlantic in Global History, 1500–2000*. Upper Saddle River, NJ.

Carbonell, Walterio. 1961. *Crítica: Como surgió la cultura nacional*. Havana.

Cardenal, Fernando. 2007. "Die Faust erhoben, das Buch geöffnet." In *Die Revolution ist ein Buch und ein freier Mensch: Die politischen Plakate des befreiten Nicaragua 1979–1990 und der internationalen Solidaritätsbewegung*, edited by Otker Bujard and Ulrich Wirper, 109–148. Cologne.

Carvalho, Adélia de, et al. 2000. *Angola: A festa e o luto; 25 anos de independência*. Luanda.

Castañeda, Jorge G. 1998. *Che Guevara: Biographie*. Frankfurt am Main.

Castiano, José P. 1997. *Das Bildungssystem in Mozambik (1974–1996): Entwicklung, Probleme, Konsequenzen*. Hamburger Beiträge zur Afrika-Kunde 55. Hamburg.

Castro, Fidel. 1969a. "Rede über die Universitäts-Revolution vom 13. März 1969." *Kursbuch* 18 (October): 160–168.

———. 1969b. "Rede über die Zukunft der Universität vom 8. Dezember 1968." *Kursbuch* 18 (October): 155–159.

———. 1969c. "Rede zur Revolutionären Offensive vom 13. März 1968." *Kursbuch* 18 (October): 130–154.

———. 1976. *Angola, Girón africano*. Havana.

———. 1977. "Discurso Pronunciado por Fidel Castro Ruz, Presidente de la República de Cuba, en el acto de inauguración del curso escolar 1977–1978, efectuado en la escuela vocacional 'José Martí,' Holguin, el 10 de septiembre de 1977, Año de la institucionalización." http:www.cuba.cu/gobierno/discursos/1977/esp/f010977e.html (accessed 19 October 2007).

———. 1979. *Discursos*. Vol. 3. Havana.

———. 1983. *Die ökonomische und soziale Krise der Welt: Bericht an die VII. Gipfelkonferenz der Nicht-paktgebundenen*. Dresden.

———. 1990. *Ciencia, Tecnología y Sociedad*. Vol 1, *1959–1989*. Havana.

———. 1993. *La historia me absolverá*. Edited and with notes by Pedro Alvarez Tabío and Guillermo Alonso Fiel. Havana.

———. 2005. "30. Aniversario de la Misión Militar Cubana en Angola: Discurso pronunciado por el Comandante en Jefe Fidel Castro Ruz, Primer Secretário del Comité Central del Partido Comunista de Cuba y Presidente de los Consejos de Estado y de Ministros, en el acto conmemorativo por el aniversario 30 de la Misión Militar cubana en Angola y el aniversario 49 del desembarco del Granma, Día de las FAR, efectuado en el Palacio de las Convenciones, el 2 de diciembre de 2005." *Granma*, 3 December, 1.

———. 2010. *La victoria estratégica*. Havana.

Causa 1/89: Fin de la conexión cubana. 1989. Havana.

Chabal, Patrick, ed. 2002. *A History of Postcolonial Lusophone Africa*. London.

Chabal, Patrick, and Nuno Vidal, eds. 2007. *Angola: The Weight of History*. London.

Chakrabarty, Dipesh. 2008. *Provincializing Europe: Postcolonial Thought and Historical Difference*. Princeton.

Chambers, Douglas B. 2008. "The Black Atlantic: Theory, Method and Practice." In

The Atlantic World, 1450–2000, edited by Toyin Falola and Kevin D. Roberts, 151–174. Bloomington.

Chang, Laurence, and Peter Kornbluh, eds. 1998. *The Cuban Missile Crisis, 1962: A National Security Archive Documents Reader*. New York.

Chaunu, Huguette, and Pierre Chaunu. 1955–1959. *Séville et l'Atlantique, 1504–1650*. 8 vols. Paris.

Cheng, Yinghong. 2009. *Creating the "New Man": From Enlightenment Ideals to Socialist Realities*. Honolulu.

Chesterman, Simon, Michael Ignatieff, and Ramesh Thakur, eds. 2005. *Making States Work*. New York.

Chilcote, Ronald H. 1967. *Portuguese Africa*. Englewood Cliffs, NJ.

———. 1972a. *Emerging Nationalism in Portuguese Africa: Documents*. Stanford, CA.

———, ed. 1972b. *Protest and Resistance in Angola and Brazil: Comparative Studies*. Berkeley.

Choy, Armando, Gustavo Chui, and Moses Sío Wong. 2005. *Our History Is Still Being Written: The Story of Three Chinese-Cuban Generals in the Cuban Revolution*. New York.

Clarence-Smith, W. G. 1979. *Slaves, Peasants, and Capitalists in Southern Angola, 1840–1926*. New York.

Comas Paret, Emilio. 1983. *De Cabinda a Cunene*. Havana.

Comité estatal de estadísticas. 1980. *Cuba en cifras*. Havana.

———. 1982. *Cuba en cifras*. Havana.

———. 1989. *Cuba en cifras*. Havana.

———. 1990. *Anuario demográfico de Cuba*. Havana.

Concepción, Eloy. 1987. *Por que somos internacionalistas*. Havana.

Conrad, Sebastian, Andreas Eckert, and Ulrike Freitag, eds. 2007. *Globalgeschichte: Theorien, Ansätze, Themen*. Frankfurt am Main.

Conrad, Sebastian, and Shalini Randeria, eds. 2002. *Jenseits des Eurozentrismus: Postkoloniale Perspektiven in den Geschichts- und Kulturwissenschaften*. Frankfurt am Main.

Cooper, Frederick. 2001. "What Is the Concept of Globalization Good For? An African Historian's Perspective." *African Affairs* 100: 189–213.

Correia, Pedro de Pezarat. 1996. *Angola: Do Alvor a Lusaka*. Lisbon.

Crocker, Chester. 1992. *High Noon in Southern Africa: Making Peace in a Rough Neighborhood*. New York.

Culler, Jonathan. 1981. "Semiotics of Tourism." *American Journal of Semiotics* 1–2: 127–140.

Davidson, Basil. 1972. *In the Eye of the Storm: Angola's People*. New York.

———. 1984. "Portuguese Speaking Africa." In *The Cambridge History of Africa*, vol. 8, *1940–1975*, edited by Michael Cowder, 755–810. New York.

Decke, Bettina. 1981. *A terra é nossa: Koloniale Gesellschaft und Befreiungsbewegung in Angola*. ISSA—wissenschaftliche Reihe 12. Bonn.

de la Fuente, Alejandro. 2001. *A Nation for All: Race, Inequality, and Politics in Twentieth-Century Cuba*. Chapel Hill.

Deutschmann, David, ed. 1989. *Changing the History of Africa*. Melbourne.

Díaz-Briquets, Sergio, ed. 1989. *Cuban Internationalism in Sub-Saharan Africa*. Pittsburgh.

Dickinson, Margeret, ed. 1972. *When Bullets Begin to Flower: Poems from Resistance from Angola, Mozambique, and Guiné*. Poets of Africa 3. Nairobi.

Dobbins, James, et al. 2003. *America's Role in Nation-Building: From Germany to Iraq*. Santa Monica.

Domingos Peterson, Pedro. 2003. *O professor do ensino básico: Perfil e formação*. Lisbon.

Domínguez, Jorge I. 1978. *Cuba: Order and Revolution.* Cambridge.
———, ed. 1982. *Cuba: Internal and International Affairs.* Beverly Hills.
———. 1989. *To Make a World Safe for Revolution: Cuba's Foreign Policy.* Cambridge.
Dorsch, Hauke. 2000. *Afrikanische Diaspora und Black Atlantic: Einführung in Geschichte und aktuelle Diskussion.* Münster.
———. 2008. "Übergangsritus in Übersee? Zum Aufenthalt mosambikanischer Schüler und Studenten in Kuba." *Afrika Spectrum* 43 (2): 225–244.
Drumond, Jaime, and Hélder Barber. 1999. *Angola: Depoimentos para História Recente.* Vol. 1, *1950–1976.* Luanda.
Du Bois, W. E. B. 1963. *An ABC of Color: Selections from over a Half Century of the Writings.* Berlin.
Dülffer, Jost. 2004. *Europa im Ost-West-Konflikt 1945–1990.* Munich.
Eckstein, Susan Eva. 1980. "The Global Political Economy and Cuba's African Involvement." *Cuban Studies/Estudios Cubanos* 10 (July): 38–59.
———. 1985. "Cuban Internationalism." In *Cuba: Twenty-Five Years of Revolution, 1959–1984,* edited by Sandor Halebsky and John M. Kirk, 372–390. New York.
———. 1994. *Back from the Future: Cuba under Castro.* Princeton.
Erll, Astrid. 2005. *Kollektives Gedächtnis und Erinnerungskulturen.* Stuttgart.
Erisman, Michael H. 1985. *Cuba's International Relations: The Anatomy of a Nationalistic Foreign Policy.* Boulder.
Fagen, Richard. 1969. *The Transformation of Political Culture in Cuba.* Stanford.
Ferrer, Ada. 1999. *Insurgent Cuba: Race, Nation and Revolution, 1868–1898.* Chapel Hill.
Fleisch, Axel. 1994. "Die ethnographische und linguistische Situation in Angola." In *Angola, Naturraum, Wirtschaft, Bevölkerung, Kultur, Zeitgeschichte und Entwicklungsperspektiven,* edited by Manfred Kuder and Wilhelm Möhlig, 85–134. Munich.
Franzbach, Martin, and Hella Ulferts. 1995. *Togo, Kamerun und Angola im euro-afrikanischen Dialog: Dokumentation des 1. Bremer Afro-Romania Kolloquiums vom 26.–28. Oktober 1995.* Bremen.
Freire, Paulo. 1971. *Pädagogik der Unterdrückten.* Stuttgart.
———. 1981. *Der Lehrer ist Politiker und Künstler: Neue Texte zu befreiender Bildungsarbeit.* Reinbek.
Freitag, Ulrike, and Achim von Oppen, eds. 2009. *Translocality: The Study of Globalizing Processes from a Southern Perspective.* Leiden.
Fresnillo, Estrella. 1982. *En otras tierras del mundo.* Havana.
Frevert, Ute. 2009. "Was haben Gefühle in der Geschichte zu suchen?" *Geschichte und Gesellschaft* 35:183–208.
Frey, Marc. 2006. "Die Vereinigten Staaten und die Dritte Welt im Kalten Krieg." In *Studien zum Kalten Krieg,* vol. 1, *Heiße Kriege im Kalten Krieg,* edited by Bernd Greiner, Christian Th. Müller, and Dierk Walter, 35–60. Hamburg.
Fuentes, Norberto. 1992. *El último santuario: Una novela de campaña.* Mexico.
———. 1999. *Dulces guerreros cubanos.* Barcelona.
Fursenko, Aleksandr, and Timothy Naftali. 1997. *One Hell of a Gamble: Krushchev, Castro, and Kennedy, 1958–1964.* New York.
García Márquez, Gabriel. 1977. *Operacion Carlota: Los Cubanos en Angola; El Che Guevara en Africa; La Batalla contra el Reich Sudafricano.* Lima.
García Pérez-Castañeda, Angel R. n.d. "El internacionalismo de Cuba en la colaboración económica y científico-técnica: Esbozo histórico de un cuarto de siglo

de la Revolución Socialista Cubana 1963–1988." Unpublished manuscript, Instituto de Historia de Cuba, Havana.

Geertz, Clifford. 1987. *Dichte Beschreibung: Beiträge zum Verstehen kultureller Systeme*. Frankfurt am Main.

Geiss, Immanuel. 1969. *Panafrikanismus: Zur Geschichte der Dekolonisation*. Frankfurt am Main.

George, Edward. 2005. *The Cuban Intervention in Angola, 1965–1991: From Che Guevara to Cuito Cuanavale*. New York.

Gilroy, Paul. 1993. *The Black Atlantic: Modernity and Double Consciousness*. Cambridge.

Gleijeses, Piero. 2002. *Conflicting Missions: Havana, Washington, and Africa, 1959–1976*. Chapel Hill.

———. 2004. *Misiones en conflicto: La Habana, Washington y África; 1959–1976*. Prologue by Jorge Risquet. Havana.

———. 2006a. "Kuba in Afrika 1975–1991." In *Studien zum Kalten Krieg*, vol. 1, *Heiße Kriege im Kalten Krieg*, edited by Bernd Greiner, Christian Th. Müller, and Dierk Walter, 469–510. Hamburg.

———. 2006b. "Moscow's Proxy? Cuba and Africa 1975–1988." *Journal of Cold War Studies* 8 (4): 98–147.

———. 2010. "Cuba and the Cold War, 1959–1980." In *The Cambridge History of the Cold War*, vol. 2, *Conflicts and Crises, 1962–1975*, edited by Melvyn P. Leffler and Odd Arne Westad, 327–348. New York.

———. 2013. *Visions of Freedom: Havana, Washington, Pretoria, and the Struggle for Southern Africa, 1976–1991*. Chapel Hill.

Gleijeses, Piero, Jorge Risquet, and Fernando Remírez. 2007. *Cuba y África: Historia común de lucha y sangre*. Havana.

Götz, Johanna. 2002. *Ethnische Grenzen und Frontlinien in Angola*. Cologne.

Godechot, Jacques. 1947. *Histoire de l'Atlantique*. Paris.

Goldenberg, Boris. 1963. *Lateinamerika und die kubanische Revolution*. Cologne.

———. 1969. "Die kubanische Revolution und Lateinamerika." In *Was treibt die Revolutionäre? Motive, Aktionen, Ziele*, 17–43. Freiburg.

Gómez, Marlene. 1989. "Con motivo del X del Comité Estatal de Colaboración Económico propusimos realizar: Una entrevista singular." *Colaboración* 28 (June–Sep. 1986): 2–3.

Gómez Chacón, César. 1989. *Cuito Cuanavale: Viaje al centro de los héroes*. Havana.

González López, David. 2002. "Relaciones Cuba-África: Marco para un bojeo bibliográfico." *Estudios Afro-asiáticos* 24:3.http://www.scielo.br/scielo.php?script=sci_arttext&pid=S0101-546X2002000300007#tx01 (accessed 21 January 2009).

Grau, Inge, Christian Mährdel, and Walter Schicho, eds. 2000. *Afrika, Geschichte und Gesellschaft im 19. und. 20. Jahrhundert*. Vienna.

Greiner, Bernd, Christian Th. Müller, and Dierk Walter, eds. 2006. *Studien zum Kalten Krieg*. Vol. 1, *Heiße Kriege im Kalten Krieg*. Hamburg.

———, eds. 2009. *Studien zum Kalten Krieg*. Vol. 3, *Angst im Kalten Krieg*. Hamburg.

Guevara, Ernesto Che. 1968. *Guerilla: Theorie und Methode*. Berlin.

———. 1977. *Escritos y discursos*. Vol. 1, *La guerra de guerrillas: Consejos al combatiente*. Havana.

———. 2000. *Der afrikanische Traum: Das wieder aufgefundene Tagebuch vom revolutionären Kampf im Kongo*. Cologne.

———. 2003a. *Ausgewählte Werke in Einzelausgaben*. Vol. 4, *Schriften zum Internationalismus*, edited by Horst-Eckart Gross. Bonn.

———. 2003b. *Ausgewählte Werke in Einzelausgaben.* Vol 6, *Der neue Mensch—Entwürfe für das Leben in der Zukunft,* edited by Horst-Eckart Gross. Bonn.

Gunn, Gillian. 1987. "The Angolan Economy." In *Afro-Marxist Regimes: Ideology and Public Policy,* edited by Edmond J. Keller and Donald Rothchild, 181–197. Boulder.

Gutiérrez Menéndez, Gabriel Enrique. 1990. "Las escuelas internacionalistas de la Isla de la Juventud, Pedagogía 1990 'Encuentro de educadores para un mundo mejor.'" Unpublished manuscript in author's possession.

Hahn, Alois. 2002. "Tod und Sterben in soziologischer Sicht." In *Tod, Jenseits und Identität: Perspektiven einer kulturwissenschaftlichen Thanatologie,* edited by Jan Assmann and Rolf Trauzettel, 55–89. Freiburg.

Halbwachs, Maurice. 1967. *Das kollektive Gedächtnis.* Stuttgart.

———. 1985. *Das Gedächtnis und seine sozialen Bedinungen.* Frankfurt am Main.

Halebsky, Sandor, and John M. Kirk, eds. 1985. *Cuba: Twenty-Five Years of Revolution, 1959–1984.* New York.

Hampson, Fen Osler. 1996. *Nurturing Peace: Why Peace Settlements Succeed or Fail.* Washington, DC.

Hanemann, Ulrike. 2001a. *Educación Popular im sandinistischen Nicaragua: Erfahrungen mit der Bildungsreform im Grundbildungsbereich von 1979 bis 1990.* Vol. 1. Hamburg.

———. 2001b. *Educación Popular im sandinistischen Nicaragua: Erfahrungen mit der Bildungsreform im Grundbildungsbereich von 1979 bis 1990.* Vol.2. Hamburg.

Hanimäki, Jussi M., and Odd Arne Westad, eds. 2003. *The Cold War: A History in Documents and Eyewitness Accounts.* New York.

Harding, Leonhard. 1999. *Geschichte Afrikas im 19. u. 20. Jahrhundert.* Munich.

Harsch, Ernest, and Tony Thomas. 1976. *Angola: The Hidden History of Washington's War.* New York.

Hatzky, Christine. 2004. *Julio A. Mella (1903–1959): Eine Biographie.* Frankfurt am Main.

———. 2005. "Die Karibik: Diktaturen, Revolutionen und Mythen im 20. Jahrhundert." In *Die Karibik, Geschichte und Gesellschaft 1492–2000,* edited by Bernd Hausberger and Gerhard Pfeisinger, 119–136. Vienna.

———. 2008a. "Bildungspolitik und Transnationalismus im postkolonialen Angola: Dimensionen und Herausforderungen der Kooperation mit Kuba." *Afrika Spectrum* 43 (2): 245–268.

———. 2008b. *Biografía de Julio A. Mella.* Santiago de Cuba.

———. 2008c. "'Os bons colonizadores': Cuba's Educational Mission in Angola 1976–1991." *Safundi: The Journal of South African and American Studies* 9 (1): 53–68.

———. 2011. "Internacionalismo, política exterior y cooperación civil de Cuba en África: El ejemplo de Angola." In *Kuba: 50 Jahre zwischen Revolution, Reform und Stillstand?,* edited by Christina Eßer and Mareike Göttsch et al., 163–181. Berlin.

———. 2013. "Cuba's Concept of 'Internationalist Solidarity': Political Discourse, South-South-Cooperation with Angola, and the Molding of Transnational Identities." In *Human Rights and Transnational Solidarity in Cold War Latin America,* edited by Jessica Stites Mor, 143–174. Madison.

Hatzky, Christine, and Ulrike Schmieder, eds. 2010. "Sklaverei und Postemanzipationsgesellschaften in Afrika und der Karibik." Special issue, *Periplus: Jahrbuch für außereuropäische Geschichte* 20, no. 4: 57–115.

Hatzky, Christine, and Jessica Stites Mor, eds. 2014. "Latin American Transnational

Solidarities: Contexts and Critical Research Paradigms." Special issue, *Journal of Iberian and Latin American Research* 20, no. 2: 127–40.

Hatzky, Christine, and Michael Zeuske, eds. 2008. *Cuba en 1902: Despúes del imperio—una nueva nación*. Münster.

Hausberger, Bernd, ed. 2004. *Im Zeichen des Kreuzes: Mission, Macht und Kulturtransfer seit dem Mittelalter*. Vienna.

Heimer, Franz-Wilhelm. 1976. *Der Entkolonisierungsprozess in Angola: Eine Zwischenbilanz*. Freiburg.

———. 1979. *Der Entkolonisierungskonflikt in Angola*. Munich.

Heintze, Beatrix. 1987. "Written Sources, Oral Traditions and Oral Traditions as Written Sources: The Steep and Thorny Way to Early Angolan History." *Paideuma: Mitteilungen zur Kulturkunde* 33:263–287.

———. 1988. "Das Ende des unabhängigen Staates Ndongo (Angola), Neue Chronologie und Reinterpretation (1617–1630)." *Paideuma: Mitteilungen zur Kulturkunde* 27:197–274.

———. 1996a. "António de Oliveira de Cadornegas Geschichtswerk über Angola: Eine außergewöhnliche Quelle des 17. Jahrhunderts." *Paideuma: Mitteilungen zur Kulturkunde* 42:85–104.

———. 1996b. *Studien zur Geschichte Angolas im 16. und 17. Jahrhundert*. Cologne.

———. 2002. *Afrikanische Pioniere, Trägerkaravanen im westlichen Zentralafrika (ca. 1850–1890)*. Frankfurt am Main.

———. 2003. "Propaganda Concerning 'Man eaters' in West-Central-Africa in the Second Half of the Nineteenth Century." *Paideuma: Mitteilungen zur Kulturkunde* 49:125–135.

———. 2004/5. "A lusofonia no interior da África Central na era pré-colonial: Um contributo para s sua história e compreensão na actualidade." *Cadernos de Estudos Africanos* 7 (8): 181–207.

———. 2007. "Between Two Worlds: The Bezerras, a Luso-African Family in Nineteenth-Century Western Central Africa." In *Creole Societies in the Portuguese Empire*, edited by Philip J. Havik and Malyn Newitt, 127–154. Lusophone Studies 6. Bristol.

Heintze, Beatrix, and Achim von Oppen, eds. 2008. *Angola on the Move/Angola em Movimento: Transport Routes, Communications and History/Vias de Transporte, Comunicação e História*. Frankfurt am Main.

Helg, Aline. 1995. *Our Rightful Share: The Afro-Cuban Struggle for Equality, 1986–1912*. Chapel Hill.

Henning, Christoph. 1997. "Jenseits des Alltags: Theorien des Tourismus." *Voyage: Jahrbuch für Reise und Tourismusforschung*, no. 1, *Schwerpunktthema: Warum reisen?*, edited by Tobias Gohlis et al., 35–53.

Henning, Doris. 1996. *Frauen in der kubanischen Geschichte*. Frankfurt am Main.

Heywood, Linda. 2000. *Contested Power in Angola, 1840s to the Present*. Rochester.

Hippler, Jochen, ed. 2003. *Nation-Building: Ein Schlüsselkonzept für friedliche Konfliktbearbeitung?* Eine Welt-Texte der Stiftung Entwicklung und Frieden. Bonn.

Hobsbawm, Eric, and Terence Ranger, eds. (1983) 2009. *The Invention of Tradition*. Cambridge.

Hodges, Tony. 2001. *Angola: From Afro-Stalinism to Petro-Diamond Capitalism*. Bloomington.

Hoffmann, Bert. 2009. *Kuba*. Munich.

Hofmeier, Rolf, ed. 1992. *Vergessene Kriege in Afrika*. Göttingen.

Hodges, Tony. 2004. *Angola: Anatomy of an Oil State*. Bloomington.

Humbaraci, Arslan, and Nicole Muchnik. 1974. *Portugal's African Wars: Angola, Guinea Bissao, Mozambique.* London.

Iglesias, Alfonso. 1986. "Internacionalismo, ayuda y colaboracion." *Colaboración Internacional* 2:16–18.

Isaacman, Allen, and Barbara Isaacman. 1983. *Mozambique: From Colonialism to Revolution, 1900–1982.* Boulder.

Jiménez Rodríguez, Limbania. 2002. "Un combate diferente." Unpublished manuscript in author's possession.

———. 2008a. "De mujeres y sus memorias." Unpublished manuscript in author's possession.

———. 2008b. *Mujeres sin fronteras.* Published version of "De mujeres y sus memorias." Havana.

Kambwa, Eduardo Augusto, et al. 1999. "Angola." In *Comprehending and Mastering African Conflicts: The Search for Sustainable Peace and Good Governance*, edited by Adebayo Adedeji, 55–79. New York.

Kapcia, Antoni. 1979. "Cuba's African Involvement: A New Perspective." *Survey* 24 (2): 142–159.

———. 2000. *Cuba: Island of Dreams.* New York.

Kapuscinski, Ryszard. 1994. *Wieder ein Tag im Leben: Innenansichten eines Bürgerkriegs.* Frankfurt am Main.

Karol, K. S. 1970. *Les guérilleros au pouvoir: L'itérinaire politique de la révolution cubaine.* Paris.

Keese, Alexander. 2007. *Living with Ambiguity: Integrating an African Elite in French and Portuguese Africa, 1930–61.* Stuttgart.

Keller, Edmond J., and Donald Rothchild, eds. 1987. *Afro-Marxist Regimes: Ideology and Public Policy.* Boulder.

Kitchen, Helen, ed. 1987. *Angola, Mozambique, and the West.* The Washington Papers 130. New York.

Klinghoffer, Arthur Jay. 1980. *The Angolan War: A Study in Soviet Policy in the Third World.* Boulder.

Kuder, Manfred, and Wilhelm J. G. Möhlig, eds. 1994. *Angola: Naturraum, Wirtschaft, Bevölkerung, Kultur, Zeitgeschichte und Entwicklungsperspektiven.* Munich.

Lang, Miriam. 2004. "Staatssozialismus, ökonomische Gleichstellung und Frauenpolitik." In *Salsa Cubana—Tanz der Geschlechter: Emanzipation und Alltag auf Kuba*, edited by Miriam Lang, 11–27. Hamburg.

Lara, Lúcio. 1999. *Documentos e comentários para a história do MPLA: Até Fev. 1961.* Lisbon.

Lara, Lúcio, and Ruth Lara. 1997. *Um amplo movimento.* Vol. 1 *(até fév. 1961), Itinerário do MPLA através de documentos e anotações de Lúcio Lara.* Lisbon.

———. 2008a. *Um amplo movimento.* Vol 2 *(1961–1962), Itinerário do MPLA através de documentos e anotações de Lúcio Lara.* Lisbon.

———. 2008b. *Um amplo movimento.* Vol 3 *(1963–1964), Itinerário do MPLA através de documentos e anotações de Lúcio Lara.* Lisbon.

Latham, Michael. 2010. "The Cold War in the Third World, 1963–1975." In *The Cambridge History of the Cold War*, vol. 2, *Conflicts and Crises, 1962–1975*, edited by Melvin Leffler and Odd Arne Westad, 258–280. New York.

Laudowicz, Edith, ed. 1987. *Befreites Land—befreites Leben? Frauen in Befreiungsbewegungen und Revolutionen.* Cologne.

Lazitch, Branko. 1989. *Angola: Eine Niederlage des Kommunismus.* Stuttgart.

Leffler, Melvin. 2000. "Bringing It Together: The Parts and the Whole." In *Reviewing the Cold War: Approaches, Interpretations, Theory*, edited by Odd Arne Westad, 43–63. London.

Leffler, Melvin, and Odd Arne Westad, eds. 2010a. *The Cambridge History of the Cold War*. Vol. 1, *Origins, 1945–1962*. New York.

———. 2010b. *The Cambridge History of the Cold War*. Vol. 2, *Conflicts and Crises, 1962–1975*. New York.

———. 2010c. *The Cambridge History of the Cold War*. Vol. 3, *Endings, 1975–1991*. New York.

Legum, Colin, and Tony Hodges. 1978a. *After Angola: The War over Southern Africa*. New York.

———. 1978b. *Krieg um Angola*. Cologne.

Leh, Almut, and Lutz Niethammer, eds. 2007. "Kritische Erfahrungsberichte und grenzüberschreitende Zusammenarbeit: The Networks of Oral History; Festschrift für Alexander von Plato." Special issue, *Bios: Zeitschrift für Biographieforschung, Oral History und Lebensverlaufsanalysen* 20.

Leiner, Marvin. 1985. "Cuba's Schools: 25 Years Later." In *Cuba: Twenty-Five Years of Revolution, 1959–1984*, edited by Sandor Halebsky and John M. Kirk. New York.

Lievesley, Geraldine. 2004. *The Cuban Revolution: Past, Present and Future Perspectives*. New York.

LeoGrande, William. 1980. *Cuba's Policy in Africa, 1959–1980*. Berkeley.

———. 1982. "Cuban-Soviet Relations and Cuban Policy in Africa." In *Cuba in Africa*, edited by Carmelo Mesa-Lago and June Belkin, 13–50. Pittsburgh.

León Rojas, Gloria M. 2006. *Jorge Risquet: Del Solar a la Sierra*. Havana.

Lewis, Oscar, Ruth M. Lewis, and Susan M. Rigdon. 1977. *Four Women: Living the Revolution; An Oral History of Contemporary Cuba*. Urbana.

Loth, Wilfried. 2000. *Die Teilung der Welt: Geschichte des Kalten Krieges 1941–1955*. Munich.

Loth, Wilfried, and Jürgen Osterhammel, eds. 2000. *Internationale Geschichte: Themen-Ergebnisse-Aussichten*. Munich.

Lüsebrink, Hans-Jürgen. 2008. *Interkulturelle Kommunikation: Interaktion, Fremdwahrnehmung, Kulturtransfer*. Stuttgart.

Mabeko Tali, Jean-Michel. 2001a. *Dissidências e poder de estado: O MPLA perante si próprio (1962–1977)*. Vol. 1, *1962–1974*. Luanda.

———. 2001b. *Dissidências e poder de estado: O MPLA perante si próprio (1962–1977)*. Vol. 2, *1974–1977*. Luanda.

MacQueen, Norrie. 1997. *The Decolonization of Portuguese Africa*. New York.

———. 2000. "An Ill Wind? Rethinking the Angolan Crisis and the Portuguese Revolution, 1974–1976." *Itinerario: European Journal of Overseas History* 26 (2): 22–44.

McMahon, Robert J. 2006. "Heiße Kriege im Kalten Krieg." In *Studien zum Kalten Krieg*, vol. 1, *Heiße Kriege im Kalten Krieg*, edited by Bernd Greiner, Christian Th. Müller, and Dierk Walter, 16–34. Hamburg.

Maier, Karl. 2007. *Angola: Promises and Lies*. London.

Malaquias, Assis. 2007a. "How to Lose a Guerilla War." In *African Guerillas: Raging against the Machine*, edited by Morten Boas and Kevin Dunn, 199–220. Boulder.

———. 2007b. *Rebels and Robbers: Violence in Post-Colonial Angola*. Uppsala.

Mallin, Jay, Sr. 1987. *Cuba in Angola*. Coral Gables.

Mann, Kristin. 2001. "Shifting Paradigms in the Study of the African Diaspora and of Atlantic History and Culture." In *Rethinking the African Diaspora: The Making of a Black Atlantic World in the Bight of Benin and Brazil*, edited by Kristin Mann and Edna Bay, 3–21. London.

Marcum, John. 1969. *The Angolan Revolution*. Vol. 1, *The Anatomy of an Explosion (1950–1962)*. Cambridge, MA.

———. 1978. *The Angolan Revolution*. Vol. 2, *Exile Politics and Guerilla Warfare (1962–1976)*. Cambridge, MA.

———. 1984. "A Quarter Century of War." In *Angola, Mozambique, and the West*, edited by Helen Kitchen, 17–35. The Washington Papers 130. New York.

———. 1987. "The People's Republic of Angola: A Radical Vision Frustrated." In *Afro-Marxist Regimes: Ideology and Public Policy*, edited by Edmond J. Keller and Donald Rothchild, 67–83. Boulder, CO.

Marischen, Beate. 1988. *Alphabetisierung und Entwicklung: Eine Diskussion der Zusammenhänge von Alphabetisierung und Entwicklung im Allgemeinen und ihrer Konkretisierung am Beispiel Mozambik*. Heidelberger Dritte Welt Studien 25. Heidelberg.

Martí, José. 1963. "Nuestra América." In *Obras Completas*, vol. 6, 15–22. Havana.

———. 1975. *Obras Completas*. Vol. 19. Havana.

Martin, Phyllis M., and Patrick O'Meara, eds. 1995. *Africa*. Bloomington.

Martín Blandino, Jorge. 2006. *Cangamba*. Havana.

Martínez Valle, Carlos, Verena Oelsner, and Eugenia Roldán Vera. 2008. "Bildungsmission als Begegnung: Modernisierung und Herrschaftskonstruktion im postrevolutionären Mexiko und peronistischen Argentinien." In *Dem Anderen begegnen: Eigene und fremde Repräsentationen in sozialen Gemeinschaften*, edited by Jörg Baberowski, David Feest, and Maike Lehmann, 195–219. Frankfurt am Main.

Marx, Christoph. 2004. *Geschichte Afrikas: Von 1800 bis zur Gegenwart*. Paderborn.

Matthies, Volker, ed. 1982. *Süd-Süd-Beziehungen: Zur Kommunikation, Kooperation und Solidarität zwischen Entwicklungsländern*. Munich.

Mayer, Ruth. 2005. *Diaspora: Eine kritische Begriffsbestimmung*. Bielefeld.

Meier, Thomas. 1998. *Die Reagan-Doktrin*. Bern.

Mesa-Lago, Carmelo, and June Belkin, eds. 1982. *Cuba in Africa*. Pittsburgh.

Messiant, Christine. 1993. "Social and Political Background to the 'Democratization' and the Peace Process in Angola." In *Proceedings of the Seminar on Democratization in Angola, 18.09.1992 in Leiden, organized by EMS, KZA, ASC*, 13–41. Leiden/Amsterdam.

———. 1998. "Angola: The Challenge of Statehood." In *History of Central Africa: The Contemporary Years since 1960*, edited by David Birmingham and Phyllis Martin, 131–165. London.

———. 2006. *1961: L'Angola colonial, histoire et sociéte; Les prémisses du mouvement nationaliste*. Basel.

———. 2007. "The Mutation of Hegemonic Domination." In *Angola: The Weight of History*, edited by Patrick Chabal and Nuno Vidal, 93–123. London.

———. 2008a. *L'Angola postcolonial*. Vol. 1, *Guerre et paix sans démocratisation*. Paris.

———. 2008b. *L'Angola postcolonial*. Vol. 2, *Sociologie politique d' une oléocratie*. Paris.

Meyns, Peter. 1990. "Entwicklungen und Fehlentwicklungen des Sozialismus in Afrika und der Dritten Welt." Universität-Gesamthochschule—Duisburg, Veröffentlichungen des Fachbereichs 1: Philosophie-Religionswissenschaft-Gesellschaftswissenschaften, Heft 4. Duisburg.

———. 1992. "Angola: Vom antikolonialen Befreiungskampf zu externer Destabilisierung und internem Bürgerkrieg." In *Vergessene Kriege in Afrika*, edited by Rolf Hofmeier and Volker Matthies, 61–96. Göttingen.

Miller, Joseph C. 1983. "The Paradoxes of Impoverishment in the Atlantic Zone." In

History of Central Africa, edited by David Birmingham and Phyllis M. Martin, vol. 1, 118–159. London.

———. 1988. *Way of Death: Merchant Capitalism and the Angolan Slave Trade, 1730–1830.* Madison.

Miller, Joseph C., and John Thornton. 1987. "The Chronicle as Source, History, and Hagiography: The Catálogo dos Governadores de Angola." *Paideuma: Mitteilungen zur Kulturkunde* 33: 359–390.

Ministério da Educação e Cultura. 1976a. *A vitória é certa: Guia do alfabetisador.* Luanda.

———. 1976b. *A vitória é certa: Manual de alfabetização.* Luanda.

———. 1977. *Eu sei ler: Livro da leitura para o 2. semestre da educação de adultos.* Luanda.

Ministério da Informação. 1975. *Angola, 11 de Novembro de 1975, Documentos da Independência.* Luanda.

Ministerio de Educación. 1971. *Congreso Nacional de Educación y Cultura, Memorias (Abril).* Havana.

———. 1973. *La educación en Cuba.* Havana.

Ministerio para la Inversión Externa y la Colaboración Económica (MINVEC). 2002a. Historia de la Colaboración entre la República de Cuba y la República de Angola. Havana. Unpublished manuscript in author's possession.

———, ed. 2002b. "Ministerio para la Inversión Extranjera y la Colaboración Económica, Colaboración cubana a otros países 1960–2001." Havana. Unpublished manuscript in author's possession.

Mohan, Giles, and Tunde Zack-Williams, eds. 2002. *Review of African Political Economy* 29 (92).

Moreira Carneiro, Emmanuel. 2004. *Especialização Rendeira e Extroversão na África Subsariana: Caracterização e Consequências.* S. João do Estoril.

MPLA. 1978. *Princípios de base para a reformulação do sistema de educaçãoe ensino na R.P.A.* Luanda.

Nazario, Olga, and Juan Benemelis. 1989. "Cuba's Relations with Africa: An Overview." In *Cuban Internationalism in Sub-Saharan Africa*, edited by Sergio Díaz-Briquets, 13–28. Pittsburgh.

Neto, Agostinho. 1976. *Angola: Heilige Hoffnung, Vorwort von Basil Davidson.* Cologne.

———. 1987. *Textos políticos escolhidos.* Luanda.

Newitt, Malyn. 1981. *Portugal in Africa: The Last Hundred Years.* London.

———. 2007. "Angola in Historical Context." In *Angola: The Weight of History*, edited by Patrick Chabal and Nuno Vidal, 19–92. London.

Niethammer, Lutz, ed. 1983a. *"Die Jahre weiß man nicht, wo man sie heute hinsetzen soll": Faschismuserfahrungen im Ruhrgebiet.* Berlin.

———, ed. 1983b. *"Hinterher weiß man, daß es richtig war, daß es schiefgegangen ist": Nachkriegserfahrungen im Ruhrgebiet.* Berlin.

———, ed. 1985. *Lebenserfahrung und kollektives Gedächtnis: Die Praxis der "Oral History."* Frankfurt am Main.

———. 1988. "Annäherung an den Wandel: Auf der Suche nach der volkseigenen Erfahrung in der Industrieprovinz der DDR." *Bios: Zeitschrift für Biographieforschung und Oral History* 1: 19–66.

———. 2000. *Kollektive Identität: Heimliche Quellen einer unheimlichen Konjunktur.* Reinbek.

Niethammer, Lutz, and Alexander von Plato, eds. 1985. *"Wir kriegen jetzt andere Zeiten": Auf der Suche nach der Erfahrung des Volkes in nachfaschistischen Ländern.* Berlin.

Núñez Jiménez, Antonio. 2002. *El pueblo cubano.* Havana.

Nzongola-Ntalaja. 1987. *Revolution and Counter-Revolution in Africa: Essays in Contemporary Politics.* London.

Offermann, Michael. 1988. *Angola zwischen den Fronten: Internationales Umfeld, sozioökonomisches Umfeld, Innenpolitik.* Pfaffenweiler.

"'Ohne Kultur wird die Welt immer gefährlicher': Theo Pischke im Gespräch mit dem angolanischen Schriftsteller Carlos Maurício Pestana dos Santos." 2006. *Frankfurter Rundschau,* 12 October.

Oliveira de Marques, A. H. 2001. *Geschichte Portugals und des portugiesischen Weltreichs.* Stuttgart.

Olivier, B. J. 1984. *The Strategic Significance of Angola.* Pretoria.

Ondjaki. 2003. *Bom dia camaradas.* Lisbon.

———. 2006. *Bom dia camaradas: Ein Roman aus Angola.* Zürich.

O'Neill, Kathryn, and Barry Munslow. 1995. "Angola: Ending the Cold War in Southern Africa." In *Conflict in Africa,* edited by Oliver Furley, 183–198. I. B.Tauris Studies. London.

Oppenheimer, Andrés. 1992. *Castro's Final Hour: The Secret Story behind the Coming Downfall of Communist Cuba.* New York.

Ortega, Vívino, et al. 2004. "Estudiantes extranjeros en la Isla de la Juventud (1977–1996)." MINVEC. Havana. Unpublished manuscript in the author's possession.

Ortiz, Fernando. 1984. *Ensayos etnográficos.* Havana.

———. 1993. *Etnia y sociedad.* Havana.

———. (1906) 2001. *Los negros brujos.* Havana.

Osterhammel, Jürgen. 2000. "Transfer und Migration von Ideen: China und der Westen im 19. und 20. Jahrhundert." In *Das Eigene und das Fremde: Festschrift für Urs Bitterli,* edited by Urs Faes and Béatrice Ziegler, 97–115.

———. 2009. *Sklaverei und die Zivilisation des Westens: Erweiterte Fassung eines Vortrags gehalten in der Carl-Friedrich-von-Siemens-Stiftung am 28. Februar 2000.* Munich.

Osterhammel, Jürgen, and Niels P. Petersson. 2003. *Geschichte der Globalisierung: Dimensionen, Prozesse, Epochen.* Munich.

Ottaway, Marina. 1998. "Angola's Failed Elections." In *Postconflict Elections, Democratization, and International Assistance,* edited by Krishna Kumar, 133–151. Boulder.

Pacheco, Carlos. 1997. *MPLA: Um nascimento polémico.* Lisbon.

Pascoe, William W. 1988. "The Cubans in Africa." In *The Red Orchestra,* vol. 2, *The Case of Africa,* edited by Dennis L. Bark, 84–99. Stanford.

Pawson, Lara. 2007. "The 27th May in Angola: A View from Below." *Revista Relações Internacionais* 14 (June): 1–18.

Pedagogía '86. 1986. *Encuentro de educadores por un mundo mejor: Conferencia "Desarrollo de la educación en Cuba," 27 al 31 de enero de 1986, Palacio de las Convenciones.* Havana.

Pélissier, René. 1978. *La colonie du Minotaure: Nationalismes et révoltes en Angola (1926–1961).* Orgeval.

Pérez, Louis A., Jr. 1988. *Cuba: Between Reform and Revolution.* New York.

———. 1990. "Cuba, c. 1930–1959." In *The Cambridge History of Latin America,* vol. 7, *Latin America since 1930,* edited by Leslie Bethell, 419–455. New York.

Pérez-Stable, Marifeli. 1994. *The Cuban Revolution: Origins, Course, and Legacy.* New York.

Pino, Rafael del. 1987. *General del Pino Speaks: An Insight into Elite Corruption and Military Dissension in Castro's Cuba.* Miami.

Placencia, Azucena. 1975. "Montaña adentro: La batalla del sexto grado." *Bohemia* 67 (7 March): 34–36.

Plato, Alexander von. 1998a. "Erfahrungsgeschichte: Von der Etablierung der Oral History." In *Biographische Methoden in den Humanwissenschaften*, edited by Gerd Jüttemann and Hans Thomae, 57–83. Weinheim.

———. 1998b. "Geschichte und Psychologie: Oral History und Psychoanalyse." *Bios: Zeitschrift für Biographieforschung und Oral History* 11, no. 1: 171–200.

———. 2000. "Zeitzeugen und die historische Zunft: Erinnerung, kommunikative Tradierung und kollektives Gedächtnis in der qualitativen Geschichtswissenschaft—ein Problemaufriss." *Bios: Zeitschrift für Biographieforschung, Oral History und Lebensverlaufsanalysen* 13, no. 1: 5–29.

Platt, Kristin, and Mihran Dabag, eds. 1995. *Generation und Gedächtnis: Erinnerungen und kollektive Identäten.* Opladen.

Pössinger, Hermann. 1968. *Landwirtschaftliche Entwicklung in Angola und Moçambique.* Afrika-Studien 31. Munich.

Pratt, Mary Louise. 1992. *Imperial Eyes: Travel Writing and Transculturation.* New York.

Quirk, Robert E. 1996. *Fidel Castro: Die Biographie.* Berlin.

Ramírez Villasana, Luis. n.d. "Algunas experiencias de la batalla de alfabetización en la República de Angola, Concurso sobre la colaboración internacionalista en la educación 'maestros internacionalistas,' Género: Testimonio." Unpublished manuscript in author's possession.

Rathmell, Andrew. 2005. "Planning Post-conflict Reconstrution in Iraq: What Can We Learn?" *International Affairs* 81 (5): 1013–1038.

Reinhard, Wolfgang, ed. 1988. *Geschichte der europäischen Expansion.* Vol. 3, *Die Alte Welt seit 1818.* Stuttgart.

———. 1990. *Geschichte der europäischen Expansion.* Vol. 4, *Dritte Welt Afrika.* Stuttgart.

———. 1999. *Verstaatlichung der Welt? Europäische Staatsmodelle und außereuropäische Machtprozesse.* Munich.

Reuter, Lutz, with the cooperation of José P. Castiano. 1995. *Das Bildungssystem in Mosambik: Strukturen, Probleme, Perspektiven.* Beiträge aus dem Fachbereich Pädagogik der Universität der Bundeswehr Hamburg 3. Hamburg.

Reuter, Lutz, and Annette Scheunpflug. 2006. *Die Schule der Freundschaft: Eine Fallstudie zur Bildungszusammenarbeit zwischen der DDR und Mosambik.* Münster.

Rey Cabrera, Marina. 1989. *La Guerra de Angola.* Havana.

Ricardo Luis, Roger. 1989. *Prepárense a vivir: Crónicas de Cuito Cuanavale.* Havana.

Risquet Valdés, Jorge. 1989. "Angola and Namibia Accords: Defeating the South Africans Was Decisive for Africa. Interview with Jorge Risquet by David Deutschmann." In *Angola and Namibia: Changing the History of Africa*, edited by David Deutschmann, 1–40. Melbourne.

———. 1999. *40 años de solidaridad de Cuba con Africa.* Havana.

———. 2000. *El segundo frente del Che en el Congo: Historia del Batallón Patricio Lumumba.* Havana.

Rius, Hugo. 1982. *Angola: Crónicas de la esperanza y la victoria.* Havana.

Roberts, Andrew. 1986. "Portuguese Africa." In *The Cambridge History of Africa*, vol. 7, *1905–1940*, edited by Andrew Roberts, 494–536. New York.

Roca, Sergio. 1982. "Economic Aspects of Cuban Involvement in Africa." In *Cuba in Africa*, edited by Carmelo Mesa-Lago and June Belkin, 161–185. Pittsburgh.

Samuels, Michael A. 1972. "A Failure of Hope: Education and Changing Opportunities in Angola under the Portuguese Republic." In *Protest and Resistance in Angola and Brazil: Comparative Studies*, edited by Ronald H. Chilcote, 53–65. Berkeley.

Sánchez Otero, José. 1978. "Interview mit Paulo Freire, Duisburger Materialien zur Sozialen Arbeit und Erziehung." Edited by D. Dankwerts. Universität Duisburg.

Saunders, Chris, and Sue Onslow. 2010. "The Cold War and Southern Africa, 1976–1990." In *The Cambridge History of the Cold War*, Vol. 3, *Endings, 1975–1991*, edited by Melvyn Leffler and Odd Arne Westad, 222–243. New York.

Schmieder, Ulrike, and Hans-Heinrich Nolte, eds. 2010. *Atlantik: Sozial- und Kulturgeschichte der Neuzeit.* Vienna.

Schubert, Benedict. 1997. *Der Krieg und die Kirchen.* Lucerne.

Scott, Catherine. 1994. "'Men in Our Country Behave Like Chiefs': Woman and the Angolan Revolution." In *Women and Revolution in Africa, Asia, and the New World*, edited by Mary Ann Tétreault, 89–110. Columbia.

Senghor, Léopold Sédar. 1970. "Négritude: A Humanismo of the Twentieth Century." In *The Africa Reader: Independent Africa*, edited by Wilfred Cartey and Martin Kilson, 179–192. New York.

Serviat, Pedro. 1986. *El problema negro en Cuba y su solución definitiva.* Havana.

Sewell, Tony. 1990. *Garvey's Children: The Legacy of Marcus Garvey.* London.

Shubin, Vladimir. 2009. *The Hot "Cold War": The USSR in Southern Africa.* London/Scottsville, SA.

Silva, Elisete Márques. 1992–1994. "O papel societal do sistema de ensino na Angola colonial (1926–1974)." *Revista Internacional de Estudos Africanos* 16–17:103–130.

Silver, Harold, ed. 1969. *Robert Owen on Education.* London.

Skierka, Volker. 2002. *Fidel Castro: Eine Biographie.* Reinbek.

Smith, Lois M., and Alfred Padula. 1996. *Sex and Revolution: Women in Socialist Cuba.* New York.

Smith, Wayne. 1985. "U.S.-Cuba Relations: Twenty-Five Years of Hostility." In *Cuba: Twenty-Five Years of Revolution, 1959–1984*, edited by Sandor Halebsky and John M. Kirk, 333–351. New York.

Somerville, Keith. 1986. *Angola: Politics, Economics, and Society.* Boulder.

Sonderegger, Arno. 2010. "Atlantische Wellen—Afrikanische Positionen: Zur panafrikanischen Idee bis 1945." In *Atlantik: Sozial- und Kulturgeschichte der Neuzeit*, edited by Ulrike Schmieder and Hans-Heinrich Nolte, 172–192. Vienna.

Spikes, Daniel. 1993. *Angola and the Politics of Intervention: From Local Bush War to Chronic Crisis in Southern Africa.* Jefferson, NC.

Steffen, Marco. n.d. *Paulo Freire und Julius Nyerere: Ihre Bedeutung für die heutige Zeit.* Aspekte der Freire-Pädagogik 35. Oldenburg.

Stites Mor, Jessica, ed. 2013. *Human Rights and Transnational Solidarity in Cold War Latin America.* Madison.

Taibo II, Paco Ignacio, Froilan Escobar, and Felix Guerra. 1996. *Das Jahr, in dem wir nirgendwo waren: Ernesto Che Guevara und die afrikanische Guerilla.* Berlin.

Taylor, Frank. 1988. "Revolution, Race, and Some Aspects of Foreign Policy in Cuba since 1959." *Cuban Studies* 18:19–41.

Thomas, Hugh. 1977. "Cuba in Africa." *Survey: A Journal of Soviet and East European Studies/International Association for Cultural Freedom* 23 (Autumn): 181–188.

Thompson, Paul. 1988. *The Voice of the Past: Oral History.* New York.

Thornton, John. 1987. "The Correspondence of the Kongo Kings, 1614–35." *Paideuma: Mitteilungen zur Kulturkunde* 33:407–421.

———. 1988. "The Art of War in Angola, 1575–1680." *Comparative Studies in History and Society* 30 (2): 360–378.

———. 1992. *Africa and Africans in the Making of the Atlantic World, 1400–1680*. New York.

Tiyambe, Zeleza (Paul). 2005. "Rewriting the African Diaspora: Beyond the Black Atlantic." *African Affairs* 104 (414): 35–68.

Torriente Brau, Pablo de la. 1965. *Pluma en ristre*. Havana.

Turner Martí, Lidia, et al. 1996. *Breve historia de un destacamento*. Havana.

Turner Martí, Lidia, Domingo Amuchástegui, and Justo Chávez, et al. 1983. "Evaluación del desarrollo de los estudiantes africanos durante el proceso docente-educativo en las escuelas secundarias en el campo de la Isla de la Juventud." *Ciencias Pedagógicas* 4, no. 6 (January–June): 3–30.

União Nacional para a Independência Total de Angola (UNITA). 1988. *Der Weg zum nationalen Wiederaufbau Angolas: Definition von Prinzipien und Zielen*. Bammenthal.

———. n.d. "Union für die vollständige Unabhängigkeit Angolas, 1990: Die Führung der UNITA." Jamba/Angola.

Urry, John. 1990. *The Tourist Gaze: Leisure and Travel in Contemporary Societies*. London.

Valdés, Nelson P. 1979. "Revolutionary Solidarity in Angola." In *Cuba in the World*, edited by Cole Blasier and Carmelo Mesa-Lago, 87–117. Pittsburgh.

Valdés Marquez, Félix Manuel. 1983. "Problemática lingüistica y colaboración educacional cubana en Angola." Havana. Unpublished study of the Facultad de Ciencias Sociales of the University of Havana, the Instituto Superior de Ciencias Sociales, and the Instituto Superior Pedagógico "Enrique José Varona."

Valdés Vivó, Raúl. 1976. *Angola: Fin del mito de los mercenarios*. Havana.

Vansina, Jan. 1966. *Kingdoms of the Savanna*. Madison.

———, ed. 1973. *Oral Tradition: A Study in Historical Methodology*. Harmondsworth.

———. 1985. *Oral Tradition as History*. London.

———. 1987. "The Ethnographic Account as a Genre in Central Africa." *Paideuma: Mitteilungen zur Kulturkunde* 33:433–444.

———. 1990. *Paths in the Rainforests*. London.

Vasco Rodrigues, Adriano. 1989. "Contribução para a história do Ensino em Angola." *Africana* 5:249–296.

Vela Ngaba, André. 2006. "Transnacionalismo e políticas educativas: O caso angolano (1975–2005)." Master's thesis, Universidade Católica Portuguesa, Lisbon.

Verlinden, Charles. 1966. *Les origines de la civilisation atlantique: De la Renaissance à l'Age des Lumières*. Neuchâtel/Paris.

Villegas, Harry. 1997. *Junto a Che Guevara: Entrevistas a Harry Villegas (Pombo)*. New York.

Welzer, Harald. 2000. "Das Interview als Artefakt: Zur Kritik der Zeitzeugenforschung." *Bios: Zeitschrift für Biographieforschung, Oral History und Lebensverlaufsanalysen* 13, no. 1: 51–63.

Westad, Odd Arne, ed. 2000. *Reviewing the Cold War: Approaches, Interpretations, Theory*. London.

———. 2005. *The Global Cold War*. New York.

Wheeler, Douglas L. 1972. "Origins of African Nationalism in Angola: Assimilado Protest Writings, 1859–1929." In *Protest and Resistance in Angola and Brazil: Comparative Studies*, edited by Ronald H. Chilcote, 67–87. Berkeley.

Wilson, Zoë J. 2005. "State Making, Peace Making, and the Inscription of Gendered Politics into Peace: Lessons from Angola." In *Gender, Conflict, and Peacekeeping*, edited by Dyan Mazurana, Angela Raven-Roberts, and Jane Parpart, 338–369. Lanham, MD.

Windeler, Elmar. 2008. *Angolas blutiger Weg in die Moderne: Portugiesischer Ultrakolonialismus und angolanischer Dekolonisationsprozess*. Berlin.

Wolfers, Michael, and Jane Bergerol. 1983. *Angola in the Frontline*. London.

Woodford Bray, Marjoric, and Donald Bray. 1985. "Cuba, the Soviet Union and Third World Struggle." In *Cuba: Twenty-Five Years of Revolution, 1959–1984*, edited by Sandor Halebsky and John M. Kirk, 352–371. New York.

Wright, George. 1997. *The Destruction of a Nation: United States' Policy Toward Angola since 1945*. London.

———. 2000. *A destruição de um país: A política dos Estados Unidos para Angola desde 1945*. Lisbon.

Zeuske, Michael. 2002. *Kleine Geschichte Kubas*. Munich.

———. 2004. *Insel der Extreme: Kuba im 20. Jahrhundert*. Zürich.

———. 2006. *Sklaven und Sklaverei in den Welten des Atlantiks 1400–1940: Umrisse, Anfänge, Akteure, Vergleichsfelder und Bibliographien*. Münster.

———. 2010. "Mongos und Negreros: Atlantische Sklavenhändler im 19. Jh. und der iberische Sklavenhandel 1808/1820–1873." *Periplus: Jahrbuch für außereuropäische Geschichte* 20, no. 4, edited by Christine Hatzky and Ulrike Schmieder, special issue, "Sklaverei und Postemanzipationsgesellschaften in Afrika und der Karibik," 57–115.

———. 2012. *Kuba im 21. Jahrhundert: Revolution und Reform auf der Insel der Extreme*. Zürich.

Index

Page numbers in italics indicate illustrations.

Africa and the Diaspora
History, Politics, Culture

Series Editors

Spirit, Structure, and Flesh:
Gendered Experiences in African Instituted Churches among the Yoruba of Nigeria
Deidre Helen Crumbley

A Hill among a Thousand:
Transformations and Ruptures in Rural Rwanda
Danielle de Lame

Defeat Is the Only Bad News:
Rwanda under Musinga, 1896–1931
Alison Liebhafsky Des Forges; edited by David Newbury

Power in Colonial Africa:
Conflict and Discourse in Lesotho, 1870–1960
Elizabeth A. Eldredge

Nachituti's Gift:
Economy, Society, and Environment in Central Africa
David M. Gordon

Cubans in Angola:
South-South Cooperation and Transfer of Knowledge, 1976–1991
Christine Hatzky

Intermediaries, Interpreters, and Clerks:
African Employees in the Making of Colonial Africa
Edited by Benjamin N. Lawrance, Emily Lynn Osborn, and
Richard L. Roberts

Naming Colonialism:
History and Collective Memory in the Congo, 1870–1960
Osumaka Likaka

Mau Mau's Children:
The Making of Kenya's Postcolonial Elite
David P. Sandgren

Whispering Truth to Power:
Everyday Resistance to Reconciliation in Postgenocide Rwanda
Susan Thomson

Antecedents to Modern Rwanda:
The Nyiginya Kingdom
Jan Vansina

Being Colonized:
The Kuba Experience in Rural Congo, 1880–1960
Jan Vansina

The Postcolonial State in Africa:
Fifty Years of Independence, 1960–2010
Crawford Young